STREET WARS

Also by Tom Hayden

Irish on the Inside

The Zapatista Reader

Rebel: A Memoir

The Lost Gospel of the Earth

STREET WARS

Gangs and the Future of Violence

TOM HAYDEN

THE NEW PRESS

NEW YORK
LONDON

Requests for permission to reproduce selections from this book should be mailed to:
Permissions Department, The New Press, 38 Greene Street, New York, NY 10013

Published in the United States by The New Press, New York, 2005
Distributed by W. W. Norton & Company, Inc., New York

LIBRARY OF CONGRESS CATALOGING-IN-PUBLICATION DATA

Hayden, Tom.
    Street wars : gangs and the future of violence / Tom Hayden.
        p. cm.
    Includes bibliographical references and index.
    ISBN 1-56584-876-4 (hc.) ISBN 1-59558-030-1 (pbk.)
    1. Gangs—United States. 2. Urban violence—United States. 3. Urban policy—United
States. I. Title.

HV6439.U5H39 2004
364.1'06'60973—dc22   2003066114

The New Press was established in 1990 as a not-for-profit alternative to the large, commercial
publishing houses currently dominating the book publishing industry. The New Press
operates in the public interest rather than for private gain, and is committed to
publishing, in innovative ways, works of educational, cultural, and
community value that are often deemed insufficiently profitable.

www.thenewpress.com

Composition by Westchester Book Composition

Printed in the United States of America

2   4   6   8   10   9   7   5   3   1

The gang is a distemper of the slums; a friend come to tell us something is amiss in our social life.

—Jacob Riis, 1890, from Frederic Thrasher,
The Gang: A Study of 1,313 Gangs in Chicago,
University of Chicago, 1927, 1963, p. 342

Contents

Preface to the Paperback Edition

"I think it'd be interesting if we could find some real experts on attacking gangs and send them to Iraq to work on this operation."
—*Paul Wolfowitz, former U.S. undersecretary of defense, now president of the World Bank, November 19, 2004*[1]

"In the end, every child with a tattoo and street child is stigmatized as a criminal who is creating an unfriendly climate for investment or tourism in the country."
—*United Nations investigator's report on Honduras, 2001*[2]

"What is clear is that the contemporary mega-slum poses unique problems of imperial order and social control that conventional geopolitics has barely begun to register. If the aim of the 'war on terrorism' is to pursue the erstwhile enemy into his sociological and cultural labyrinth, then the poor peripheries of developing cities will be the permanent battlefields of the twenty-first century." —*Mike Davis,* Planet of Slums

The good news is that the peacemakers chronicled in *Street Wars*—Alex, Silvia, Luis, Manny, Dewayne, Father Greg, Aqeela, Blinky, Hector—are still alive, still peacemaking despite their meager resources. The new mayor of Los Angeles, Antonio Villaraigosa, was elected in 2005 against an incumbent who called him "soft on gangs" and proposed a gang injunction across the entire city of Los Angeles. Villaraigosa promises to fund a revival of the community-based street worker programs highlighted in *Street Wars* and banished two decades ago due to law enforcement hostility. In addition, in accordance with court orders, Governor Arnold Schwarzenegger has restored rehabilitation as the primary policy goal of California's youth authority and penal colony.

We shall see. The police and prison lobbies remain powerful and permanent, while teenage gangbangers count for nothing in American politics.

While dedicated peacemakers can save some lives, they cannot overcome the conditions that demand a serious commitment by society to rehabilitation, inner-city jobs, and police and prison reform. In the city of Los Angeles alone, there are 93,000 sixteen- to twenty-four-year-olds classified as "out of school, out of work"—that is, *one of every five* in this age range. (There are 638,000 in California, 4.6 million nationally.)[3]

Los Angeles's General Fund budgets $53 million for police suppression (the former CRASH program), $12.8 million for "prevention," and *only $2.2 million* for "gang intervention" (working to reduce violence and promote meaningful alternatives). That's a minuscule, marginal, and meaningless investment in a city budget of more than $6 billion, including an LAPD budget of nearly $2 billion. By comparison, city taxpayers spent $70 million to secretly settle some 200 police misconduct cases arising from the Rampart scandals—thirty-five times more money to compensate complaints of criminality by the police than for intervention programs aimed at avoiding gang crimes.

Outside Los Angeles, those currently in power seem more interested in demonizing gang members as domestic terrorists than promoting initiatives to stem the violence. As of this writing, more repressive legislation is rolling through the U.S. Congress. One, by Representative Randy Forbes (R-Virginia) allows federal prosecutors to send sixteen-year-olds to adult courts without judicial review, and imposes mandatory minimum sentences of ten years. Under this policy, the new purpose of the juvenile justice system seems to be hardening teenagers for the road to adult prison. (It is opposed by the ACLU, the National Council of La Raza, and the NAACP.)

Worse, the phenomenon first described in *Street Wars* as the "globalization of gangs" is rapidly expanding as part of the administration's global war on terrorism. The current issue of *Foreign Affairs*, a main organ of the U.S. national security establishment, proclaims in a headline that L.A.–related street gangs have "taken Central America," which would certainly come as a surprise to the homeboys in Central America's overcrowded penal system.[4] Since the gang phenomenon is assumed to be satanic, there apparently is little reason to search for any causes beyond the metaphysic of evil (some cannot be saved). Evil must be exorcised by force and faith.

There is no mention in *Foreign Affairs* of the fact that there were no Central American gangs of any significance before the U.S. military interventions of the seventies. Nor is it emphasized that the Central American gang members are the migratory children of war refugees. Nor that places like Honduras, a virtual Pentagon colony in the contra wars, lacks any services for homeless youth. Nor is there any focus on the humiliating sweeps, detentions, police executions, and fires in prisons that perpetuate the cycles of hate.

Perhaps most important, there is little if any linkage of the security and economic issues on either side of the borders. The administration's proposed Central American Free Trade Agreement, endorsed by the *New York Times*, will make the region one gigantic maquiladora. In essence, the purpose of what police budgets describe as "suppression" seems to be to make the world's barrios and ghettos safe for low-wage and sweatshop havens.

What is needed for the inner cities across the world is a focused Marshall Plan, not an open-ended, secretive war on gangs, drugs, and terror.

Instead, the *Foreign Affairs* analysis subtly suggests that the gangs are becoming a channel for al-Qaeda, using evidence even thinner than that which alleges Saddam's Iraq was the sanctuary for Osama bin Laden. *Foreign Affairs* states that unknown Hondurans have "reported sighting" an al-Qaeda operative. (Who reported? Is the report available for review?) Next, the article states, "rumors circulated." (By whom?) Actual meetings were denied; nevertheless, "the danger of such a link remains real" since, "*if* they can smuggle people looking for a job . . . they can smuggle people interested in terror." This is what C. Wright Mills, speaking of nuclear weapons strategists long ago, called "crackpot realism." Based on "sightings" and "rumors" but no evidence of meetings, we are to believe that the terrorists are tunneling into the United States. Why not start with a more logical concern: that someone already here is assembling a suitcase bomb or has infiltrated an unguarded American port? These are not hypothetical threats, but they don't support greater funding for the repression and imprisonment of gang members. As *Street Wars* argues, the war on gangs is terrible policy but wonderful politics.

In 2004, I traveled to Honduras to investigate a May 17 prison fire in which 105 MS (Mara Salvatrucha) members lost their lives. My contacts in Los Angeles were receiving frantic phone calls from gang members in Tegucigalpa who were worried that the authorities had unleashed a massacre. They were not paranoid. One year before, on April 5, 2003, sixty-eight 18th Street inmates perished in a suspicious fire, but an official examination showed that fifty-one were killed by bullets to the head. No charges were filed against any officers.[5]

It was an unusual visit, arranged by an ex–MS member in Los Angeles through inmates inside the prisons with street names no one recognized. I joined my son Troy, Silvia Beltran of Homies Unidos (see chapter 7), a sixteen-year-old Los Angeles girl being mentored by Silvia, and several Salvadoran Homies Unidos members with 18th Street backgrounds. Another traveler, a deportee from a Hollywood gang called Los Amigos who was nicknamed Trusty, was rolled up in the open trunk of our station wagon. He was most comfortable there, he said, because he had just been released from prison in El Salvador, where he had enjoyed the "privilege" of sleeping under a metal cot in his cell— for safety reasons. He had an easy disposition and sense of humor as he focused himself on our security needs.

During our week's stay I was able to meet with U.S. embassy political and security officers, and our group visited juvenile facilities, human rights groups, MS inmates, and even self-described MS leaders, armed and in disguise, on the second floor of a McDonald's.

Honduras is a disaster zone with a population of 6.7 million. Eighty percent of its people are officially classified as poor, I was told by an embassy analyst, with 40 percent earning less than one U.S. dollar per day. It is unsurprising that drugs and corruption are mainstays of the economy, along with a sweatshop (maquiladora) zone near the isolated and lovely tourist beaches on its north shore. According to the Ministry of Labor, some 400,000 children under fourteen years of age work illegally.[6]

Over the previous five years, more than 700 Honduran kids—most of them homeless—have turned up dead on the streets or in dumpsters.[7] Adjusting for population, that would be the equivalent of 40,000 American youngsters. According to credible estimates, as many as 20 percent were killed by death squads or off-duty security officers.[8] Social workers told us the country lacked any capacity to shelter or provide essential services to a homeless population of 20,000 youths under the age of eighteen on the streets of Tegucigalpa.

Honduras's official solution to this crisis came directly from the "zero tolerance" playbook of former New York Mayor Rudolph Giuliani.[9] The Honduran president, Ricardo Maduro, had visited New York and was favorably impressed with the sweeps of tens of thousands of youth by Giuliani's cops in the nineties (see chapter 5). Later the private-sector Giuliani Group would visit Honduras briefly as advisers, as would representatives of the Los Angeles Sheriffs Department. Maduro, whose son was kidnapped and killed in a non-gang-related incident, became so enamored of Giuliani's methods that he strapped on body armor and personally led early-morning street sweeps. He succeeded in passing a *mano dura* (strong fist) law criminalizing anyone with a tattoo. Since many former gang members (and even non-gang members) were unable to afford the removal of their tattoos, it was inevitable that most of the country's street children were being incarcerated. Under Maduro, half the Honduran army joins local police in patrolling the streets. Maduro has been candid about his circumvention of due process for gang members, saying that most of them were going free "because there wasn't enough evidence to hold them . . . so instead of taking the long route of accumulating proof of types of crimes committed, we opted to make it illegal to belong to gangs."[10] One critic, a former Honduran supreme court justice, notes that Maduro's policy means "youth being punished for who they are," not what they do.[11] In 2001, a UN human rights investigator called on the Honduran government to prevent what she called "the extra-judicial killings."[12] Despite the fact that U.S. immigration law forbids the deportation of anyone likely to be tortured or killed in their country of origin, the de facto policy toward gangs appears to be: we sweep out the trash and let others burn it.

The U.S. embassy officers briefing me described the rule of law as "a work in progress" in Honduras. The abusive penal system lacks sufficient funds for an overflow population. Almost 90 percent of all inmates are being held on pretrial detention.[13] The Honduran Human Rights Commission says the prison police have used electric shocks and water immersions on inmates.[14] A human rights lawyer who originally accepted the "zero tolerance" approach now says the law "creates a climate of incitement" for the country's security forces.

If these facts seem relentless, firsthand observations are personally wrenching. One day we visited a prison-like facility for juveniles outside of Tegucigalpa. Armed guards silently opened the gates into a world of boys as young as eleven and no older than seventeen. They hung out in an outdoor courtyard the size of two basketball courts, eyeing us curiously until Panza Loca ("Crazy Belly," in chapter 7), a veteran Homie from El Salvador, began asking them in a friendly way, "Where you from?" Forced to use a walker by diabetes, the thirty-eight-year-old Panza Loca elicited a lively group conversation among teenagers who looked starved for adult mentors. They were serving indeterminate terms, without trial dates or attorneys. Whatever ugly deeds they may have committed, these clearly were young lost boys. We asked to see where they lived, and were taken to a cell perhaps twenty by thirty feet wide where thirty crowded themselves together. Their urinal was a Coke bottle. Most of them were barefoot. Exposed electrical wires dangled across the blankets on their double bunks; I kept imagining them going up in flames. Yet they were orderly and engaged, listening carefully to Panza Loca and telling him their stories. It was a classic instance of "gang intervention" at work, but it could last only fifteen minutes.

We visited a church-sponsored rural facility for juveniles that was spectacular in comparison with the lockup. Here the boys lived in cottages, took remedial classes, worked at growing their own food, and struggled to overcome drugs, alcohol abuse, and lives smothered by violence. We saw 18th Street members mingling with MS members but were told a crushing fact: boys who could be integrated behind the fence could not be integrated back into Honduran society. There was nowhere for them but the street.

Who were these boys? The only study I have seen was a survey commissioned by Casa Alianza, a Central American agency working with homeless youth. When more than 500 youthful respondents were asked their reason for joining gangs, 33 percent said *la diversion* ("something to do"); 29 percent said *la amistad* ("camaraderie"); and 17.4 percent said *la baile* ("learning to disco").[15] The survey showed once again a central fact about "gang members": though capable of frightful acts, they are malleable boys and young men, not hardened criminals gripped by evil from birth. If life conditions have hardened them, different life conditions might change them, including interventions by peers they can relate to.

But the prison we visited suggested that, beyond a certain point, MS members find it almost impossible to safely leave their old lives. Imagine, if you can, a facility composed of dead gray cell blocks housing hundreds of men in their twenties and thirties. With bald heads, wearing tank tops or else bare-chested, they are covered with tattoos ranging from huge gothic letters to wavy inscriptions to names of mothers, girlfriends, homeboys, neighborhoods. It is a visiting day, and some of them stroll hand-in-hand with their infants while others pursue a few intimate minutes with homegirls or wives. Circulating among them are preachers waving Bibles. Surrounding them are young guards with automatic weapons at the ready. These are the transferred survivors of the May 17 fire, and with silent precision they escort the men through a maze of corridors. Inmates stand staring blankly along the walls. Blankets are hung over open cell doors for privacy. A compact disc player throbs softly. We suddenly pass through a blanketed entrance into a small cell with a double bunk where victims of the fire have agreed to see us. I pull a small digital camera from inside my coat and begin taking pictures of their burns while Silvia translates. They will heal, but the burns cover whole chests, backs, legs, feet. They are amazingly calm while stationing lookouts for any guards who might detect the camera.

There is no doubt in their minds that the May 17 fire, only two weeks before, was implemented by the guards. It is a prisoners' logic, to be sure, but it is not illogical—unless an incarcerated gang member's word is to be discounted automatically. First, of fifteen possible cell blocks, the fire only occurred in the one inhabited by MS inmates. Second, several inmates recalled smelling gas just before the flames exploded, as if someone had thrown a flammable container into the corridors. Third, the guards and police took up positions outside a gate that enclosed an open yard, and panicking inmates were crushed against an inside gate while trying to reach the safety of that yard. Not only were they blocked from reaching safety, they heard volleys of epithets and gunshots from the guards. Outside witnesses reported that the nearby fire department took forty-five minutes to reach the scene, long after most of the inmates were burned alive. Several investigations were under way; according to one human rights lawyer we interviewed, "if it wasn't an execution by plan, it was an execution by negligence."

Many people have asked me, How could you talk to these people? Aren't they dangerous, unreliable, murderous, unpredictable? Maybe I have been lucky—more likely the stereotypes are exaggerated—but the truth is that gang members are human beings who have their good moments. They may be lethal but they are not unintelligent. They have stories to tell that no one wishes to hear, and so their desire to talk—to anyone—builds up. Not having the right to speech for most of their lives, according to James Gilligan (chapter 3), is one of the reasons they explode.

I felt no fear in the prison, but became nervous when Troy, Silvia, and I were sent to wait in a crowded shopping mall to interview some outside representatives of the MS inmates. It was a very hot afternoon, and I spotted our first contact at once. He wore a blue turtleneck shirt pulled down to conceal the tattoos that covered his neck and hands. This wasn't a disguise, I thought, but a dead giveaway. We approached him carefully, and he asked if we were "the writers." Satisfied by our nods, we started casually walking through tables of young people caught up in conversation and coffee. In a moment, our other contact arrived, the acknowledged leader, looking like a happy Central American tourist in khaki pants and a golf shirt. We soon learned that he had taken care never to be tattooed on the face, neck, arms, or hands.

Leaving the mall, we jumped in their small car and drove a short distance to a two-story McDonald's. We grabbed fries and Cokes while our contacts took nothing from the counter, then walked us upstairs to a second floor with a children's play center and wide windows looking down on the street. They converted our McDonald's table into a combination hideaway and observation post in the center of San Pedro Sula.

I do not know their real names and cannot divulge their street names, except to note that they were absurdly funny. I learned that our friend in the turtleneck spent nearly all his time in a safe house. The McDonald's excursion was a delight for him, his first time outdoors in days. His older brother, he said, was imprisoned in the States and then deported back to Honduras, where he formed the first MS group. He confirmed that most youth who joined the gang wanted mainly "to hang out" and be protected from police and rivals. They were engaged in a deadly street war with 18th Street, a war that began in Los Angeles (see chapter 7) so many years ago that the causes were almost forgotten.

Now the other MS homeboy took charge of the conversation. Clearly he had only the slightest information about us, but we had been vouched for as people who would "tell the truth." Like most gang members, he professed to have no idea why the media chose to sensationalize and demonize them. It wasn't a time to give him any advice. To show (and flaunt) his seriousness, he drew a gleaming silver nine-millimeter pistol from below his belt. I looked around the restaurant, wondering where to duck if undercover police or 18th Street showed up. I imagined the headline: "Mystery Deaths at McDonald's!"

But the conversation continued rationally. He claimed that the severe repression was because "MS don't pay no rent, no dues" to the corrupt police force. 18th Street, unlike MS, was cutting the police in on their street profits. "If the police want to arrest us when we break the law, that's all right, but they shouldn't be arresting every homie on the street with a tattoo. They are trying to exterminate us."

It was extreme and self-serving, of course, but there was a basic logic. For one thing, it was the universal story of all the ethnic gangs that had preceded the Central Americans (see chapter 8). Serious rehabilitation and economic development could channel most of their base into legal jobs that paid a living. Second, he

hardly fit the law enforcement stereotype. Our contact grew up in Miami, not
Central America, was more or less middle-class, and, when I asked what he was
doing in San Pedro Sula, he reddened, laughed, and answered, "My wife divorced
me and I had to leave." He was part of a transnational network, to be sure, but it
was fragmented, chaotic, improvised, and not the hierarchal "John Gotti" mafia
that Paul Wolfowitz and most prosecutors imagined.

He in part was an idealist, in the sense that a belief in ultimate fairness motivated his encounter with us. Somehow, the same media that demonized him
could be made to listen to his story and print it. Couldn't the outside world, with
all its racism and indifference, understand that the tattooed homies had no options but the underground economy for income and the gulag for a home?

I promised we would try to represent his views fairly in every public forum
and media venue available.

I contacted a *New York Times* reporter, Ginger Thompson, who was probing
the prison deaths in San Pedro Sula at the same time. She never called back but
instead appeared at my office in Culver City several weeks later, seeking background information. She seemed to be a very thorough, earnest reporter, and I
talked to her for two hours. I was fulfilling a promise to the MS contact but also
following a game plan. I guessed that the *Los Angeles Times* would investigate the
fires if the *New York Times* went first.

I was both right and wrong. After an interminable wait, the *New York Times*
printed Thompson's lengthy piece, which the *Los Angeles Times* indeed followed
up with its own article a few weeks later. The heavily edited Thompson piece,
while quoting human rights observers and myself in its later paragraphs, laid emphasis on the scary threat to America's borders. Five obligatory photos of tattooed homies accompanied the piece.[16]

The later *Los Angeles Times* piece took up the same sensational themes, adding
a recent bus massacre that President Maduro attributed to Honduran gang members waging war against the state. As usual, no evidence was provided to buttress
the case, except from unnamed sources who suggested without evidence that an
MS deportee from Los Angeles was "an accused mastermind." If it was the launching of a war, there has been no follow-up thus far. If it was a vendetta between ri-

vals, the work of a drug-crazed handful of individuals or former guerrillas, we may never know. The *Times* published four vivid photos along with its article.[17]

What I do know is that several weeks after our McDonald's interview, the MS contact wearing casual clothes was gunned down by unknown assassins. So was Trusty, who had traveled in the trunk of our car to encourage peace meetings.

Who knows whether some in MS would respond if the media covered their views, if the employers offered them treatment and jobs, if the cops and guards concentrated on crimes instead of tattoos? Tiring of their lives, would some homeboys respond to offers of respect and, ultimately, education and jobs? And if they did, would the doors open to greater numbers until only the most hopeless were reduced to a minor threat to urban peace? And if *elements* of those gangs were beyond the reach of respect or unconditional love—an assumption rarely, if ever, tested—what about the broad base of their desperate membership destined to live and die on the streets? Would they not respond to a global New Deal? That is precisely what occurred with the white ethnic gangs of America between the 1840s and 1930s.

Until new policies are tried on a grand scale, it appears that the globalization of gang violence will continue to confound us, merging with the larger "war on terrorism." The comparison made by Paul Wolfowitz above suggests that the Iraq war planner seems oblivious to the fact that Iraq-bound U.S. soldiers have already been learning from the anti-gang units of the Los Angeles police department.[18] One soldier in Iraq with experience in Chicago police gang units says the work is no different. He investigates family backgrounds, relies on "snitches" among captured insurgents, knocks down doors, and incarcerates his suspects. "It's straightforward police work," he says, without offering a definition of success.[19] The bizarre possibility exists that U.S. military recruiters are channeling gang members to fight in Iraq; at the least, the recruiters are ignoring police records and accepting high-school dropouts.[20] As Evan Wright reports in *Generation Kill*, "there's no shortage of guys who came in to escape life in street gangs, sometimes with a little nudge from a local prosecutor."[21]

The folly of believing in military solutions to social, racial, and economic problems makes the present war on gangs reminiscent of the Roman Empire in its long battles against the "barbarians."

The voices of the peacemakers still await a hearing. For now, their message is written on subway stalls and tenement halls.

Los Angeles
June 20, 2005

Foreword: *Adelante*

This is the story of a decade among homeboys and homegirls (labeled everything from "at-risk" youths to "super-predators"), young people trying to survive on the streets of such cities as Los Angeles, San Salvador, Chicago, New York, and Boston. The personal stories on which I focus are the tales of transformation: those moving from gangbanging to peacemaking, against all odds.

I estimate that more than 25,000 young people—nearly all of them African American and Latino—have been slain in street wars during the past two decades. This book revolves around survivors who, like traumatized war veterans, have a message to deliver that is difficult to articulate and that many wish not to hear. It's hard to tell your story when you're a nobody in the street, crying out in a sound-proofed room.

The message is that gang violence is preventable, not inevitable. Street-wise peacemakers need to be recognized, not shunned. They need a vast, self-managed rehabilitation effort to turn their lives around, not perpetual disrespect and punishment. They need a New Deal targeted at the inner cities of the world, not more corporate disinvestments.

After three decades of thundering law-and-order rhetoric from politicians, police and prison officials, it is time to recognize that the war on gangs has become a bloody quagmire with no end in sight.

Even the moderate U.S. Supreme Court justice Anthony Kennedy has concluded that the "harsh justice" of American courtrooms and prisons is intended "to degrade and demean the prisoner," and is "intoxicated with treating an entire class of people as inferior."[1]

We are tougher on crime than any comparable nation in the world, measured by arrests, incarcerations, and police and prison expenditures. And yet the crisis deepens. Professor James Alan Fox, who once warned of a super-predator bloodbath, then retracted his claim when he was proven wrong, is warning once again of a rising wave of gang violence in 2004.[2] His solution stresses more of the same: bolster police antigang units further. Simultaneously, U.S. senators Dianne Feinstein and Orrin Hatch are proposing $650 million in federal funds to expand the war on gangs, and more severe sentences for young offenders than ever before. Father Gregory Boyle, who has worked the streets of East Los Angeles for two decades, responds that "we already have enough gang- and gun-related sentencing 'enhancements' to send a 17 year old who has never been in trouble with the law to prison for 35 years to life. And that's without his ever touching a gun or ever being an actual member of a gang."[3]

When it comes to the inner city, our country thrives politically on scapegoating rather than finding solutions. What isn't even considered is that the bloody madness won't end without the participation of those who started it, the former gang members themselves. That is what this decade of research has taught me.

I am grateful to my son Troy, now thirty, for introducing me to his world of hip-hop, graffiti, and homeboys when he was in high school. Through the eyes of his generation, I learned how the civil rights movements of my generation had failed to end the culture of hopelessness in our inner cities. It appears that my little son Liam will have to carry on the fight for a better world as well. So be it—*adelante*.

I want to thank Occidental College in Los Angeles for allowing me to research and teach this subject during a semester in 2002, and Harvard University's Kennedy School of Government, Institute of Politics, for inviting me to lead a study group that addressed the globalization of gangs in 2003.

Thanks go as well to my former state Senate staff who plunged into gang peace work: Rocky Rushing, Silvia Beltran, Manny Lares, Celina Martin, Dewayne Holmes, John Heyman, Connie Brown, Mary Burbidge, Thad Koussen, Stephanie Rubin, Lisa Hoyos, Anna Blackshan, Ann Holler, and Sandy Brown. Thanks also to my allies and (friendly) critics, Greg Boyle, Connie Rice, and Luis Rodriguez.

And above all, *saludos* to the homies on the hazardous front lines of peace, especially Alex Sanchez and Aqeela Sherrells, and those many others who make up the soul of this story.

Thanks finally to Amy Scholder, my editor, and Colin Robinson, my publisher, who patiently waited through a period of long delays due to health problems. I seem to have left my heart at the office in 2001, but the *animo* returned so that I could finally finish the manuscript. And thanks to my wife, Barbara, whose heart is larger than my own.

—Los Angeles, December 2003

STREET WARS

1

These Dead Don't Count

Back in the day, I was a freedom rider in the Deep South and a community organizer knocking on doors in the slums of Newark. We weren't afraid of walking after dark in the slums, but trying to integrate lunch counters could be scary. There wasn't much gang violence, but plenty of police brutality. Some believed the fight could be over soon. On the New Frontier, officials believed ending poverty would be a mopping-up operation.

Then our world changed. A Kennedy died, then Malcolm X and Medgar Evers. The war in Vietnam exploded. Then King and another Kennedy went down. Riots broke out in Watts, in Newark, in East Los Angeles, in Chicago, in hundreds of cities.

As the promise of the nation's war on poverty was erased by the war in Vietnam, a new politics of law and order was born. Being tough on crime replaced a primary emphasis on social justice as the staple of winning politics. The frightening menace of youthful "super-predators" scared many Americans into funding more prisons and police. Like riders on the storm, violent street gangs grew and expanded in the vacuum left by the civil rights movement and Vietnam.

Three decades later, we are sinking amidst a bloody urban quagmire and overflowing prisons.

This book is about what I call inner-city peacemakers, who show us that alternatives to this deadly cycle are possible. Their collective experience may suggest the policy changes needed for this turn toward peace. The peacemakers come from gang backgrounds, and the vast majority have committed violent crimes. Their own experience eventually taught them the futility and waste of gang culture, and the possibility of another way of life. Instead of fighting each other, they could fight the power—aggressively, but nonviolently. First they had to rid themselves of their inner demons, like traumatized soldiers and war victims anywhere. Then they had to empower themselves and their communities to end the madness they had created. Finally, they struggled to influence the powerful leaders of law enforcement, government, and business.

Through these community peacemakers, I learned street histories of Watts, East Los Angeles, Chicago, and New York that are rarely taught in schools. I came to understand America's historic roots in gang culture, and the rapid globalization of gangs beneath the glitter of the new world economy.

The young peacemakers I met saved many lives in addition to their own. They forged solutions out of their own experience. After ten years, most are still at it. But they are largely invisible and unrecognized. Few in power feel the need to legitimize a former gangbanger. Society still recoils automatically against the tattooed gang member. There are many who refuse to listen to a story that may upset their stereotypes.

My hope is that more Americans than ever are ready to listen, learn, and reinterpret the official version of daily events in our streets. Let us hope the time has come to name, understand, and engage ourselves in ending the quagmire of gang wars. Surely the richest society in the world can meet the challenge. If we don't, the gang crisis will blight our society, further shift our priorities from justice to jails, and bleed across the world in the wake of globalization.

Naming is an important but complicated task in understanding gangs. For the longest time, gangs never called themselves gangs, and many still don't. No one knows where the term came from—perhaps from the nineteenth-century Yiddish word *ganef*, for "thief." To this day, the term lacks a clear definition in law.

One gang member said in an interview that gangs are about "holding your own neighborhood so nobody can come into your neighborhood and try to take the bread out of your mouth."[1] Another said "a gang ain't nothing but people come together to do crime and make money and be a family to each other. That's the original idea." It is difficult to reduce gangs to organizational units alone, since there is a mercurial subculture of posses, cliques, crews, taggers, and other factions, all blending into the larger worlds of gangsta rap and hip-hop. By and large, gangs have semipermeable boundaries, fluid membership, and fluctuating levels of affiliation.[2] In addition, there is an overarching "code of the street" that regulates behavior. This street code, a "cultural adaptation" by those outside the formal system, is a prescriptive set of rules for navigating the inner-city streets and schools whether one is gang-affiliated or not.[3]

Such organizational untidiness poses a problem for prosecutors and police. An example of the elusiveness of organizational definitions is found in the official state police terminology of Illinois:

> Street gang or gang or organized gang means any combination, confederation, alliance, network, conspiracy, understanding . . . conjoining, in law or fact, of three or more persons with an established hierarchy that, through its membership or through the agency of any member, engages in a course or pattern of criminal activity.[4]

Similarly, the National Crime Information Center uses an elastic definition of a gang as "an ongoing organization, association, or group of three or more persons [that] have a common interest and/or activity characterized by the commission of or involvement in a pattern of criminal or delinquent conduct."[5] Under such terms, concepts like family, neighborhood, solidarity, protection, and economic need—all factors in the formation and endurance of gangs—are eliminated, leaving the core definition of the gang as *essentially a criminal enterprise.*

In reality, gangs like Mara Salvatrucha, 18th Street, the Latin Kings, or the Blackstone Rangers are sprawling, fluid operations divided into constantly created, territorially based cliques or factions, with estimated "membership" in the tens of thousands. Under the typical antigang law, the "leaders" of the gang are criminally accountable for the behavior of any single "member," even if that "member" is a rogue individual on a vendetta against other gang members.

Such definitions are designed by officialdom to vilify certain forms of group behavior, a custom frequently employed against outlaws in the past (Apache and Sioux both mean "enemy," for example) and to simplify the business of prosecutors. Officers routinely stop and frisk anyone who "looks" like a gang member on a street corner. Normally such stops are prohibited by the U.S. Constitution unless there is "reasonable suspicion." That legal nicety is finessed by standards that essentially render suspicious anyone who looks like a gangbanger or has been fingered by an informant. If the frisk reveals little evidence, the officer still can mark the suspect down as a "gang associate," despite the fact that there simply is no such membership category in the gang world. The California Street Terrorism Enforcement and Prevention (STEP) Act defines a criminal street gang as a group of three or more persons who individually and informally engage in a pattern of crime. The STEP Act goes further, requiring that a gang member or associate convicted of a felony have their sentence "enhanced" by an additional one to three years.[6] Thus in addition to serving time for a burglary or carjacking, an identified "gang associate" will serve additional time because of their identity, and their data will be permanently listed.

In the alternative universe of the street, gang members commonly call themselves *homies* or *homeboys* and *homegirls,* labels shunned as repugnant by law enforcement and ignored by the media. Speaking of their territory, the homies say they *represent the neighborhood* or simply the *'hood.* These are instructive self-labels. They humanize, rather than demonize the gang member, conveying an aspiration for belonging, family, and home that is otherwise denied. In this book, I frequently will use the term *homies* because that is what my subjects call themselves. I will interchangeably use the term *gang member,* too, where it's the clearest term to employ, even though it is rarely used by gang members. I will refer to police as *police* or *law enforcement,* though those are not always the terms used by gang members.

There is another reason to pay attention to the definitions, symbols, and forms of communication used by gang members. They are signifiers of a parallel realm, a separate nation, that they have created out of nothing more than the alienation they feel from society. Gangs are defined as nations, tribes, cliques, and sets. Their symbols evoke memories of past kingdoms, ancient gods, competing spirits. The language of graffiti and hand signs is purposefully elaborate and inscrutable to outsiders. Street names range from the impish (Clever, Sleepy) to the threatening (Snipe, Monster) and become as important as the names imposed at baptism. Some will see in all of this a design to evade surveillance. But the real motive is to be reborn as *someone,* to carve out a recognition and respect that society denies. In this book, I often will use the gang members' terms of reference where they make sense in context, to emphasize that we are talking here about bridging warring worlds, not simply adjusting wayward behavior to a standard defined by law enforcement.

The terminology of war has crept into repeated speeches by politicians and police against "urban terrorism," and law enforcement defines its mission against gangs as *suppression,* a notion far different from service or protection. The public appearance is that police are deterring violent, criminal outbursts from spiraling further out of control. But there are signs that suppression crosses the line from conventional law enforcement to a low-visibility paramilitary strategy, embodied in specialized, high-tech SWAT teams or antigang units with acronyms like CRASH (Community Resources Against Street Hoodlums). The general public is conditioned to the police perspective by countless films that sympathetically portray heavily armored officers kicking down doors and pointing automatic weapons. There are special laws and loopholes that permit exemptions to constitutional rights for targeted gang members. (For example, under gang injunctions, there is no right to a lawyer for the indigent.) At one time or another, most residents of poor neighborhoods have considered the police an "occupying army." The police shoot, maim, and kill scores, even hundreds, of people every year, many of them allegedly gang members. It is assumed in mainstream discourse that nearly all these deaths are deserved. But beyond police-inflicted violence, there is a larger self-inflicted death toll, depicted as savage backwardness. The victims are blamed, as if they have not risen to the level of civilized society, as if their situation is unrelated to poverty and unemployment. No root causes are emphasized except a moral deficit in the victims. The only solution, in the language of the STEP Act, is "eradication."

If twenty-five thousand white people killed each other in ethnic wars, you can be sure that Americans would pay attention.

If white people were dying, there would be headlines such as: "Death Toll Mounts to 25,000 in Street War!" Politicians would step forward with peace plans. Mediators would be dispatched. Cease-fire talks would be encouraged, along with reforms in policing. Aid packages would be offered for healing and reconstruction.

For a comparison, take the example of the famous one-hundred-year Hatfield-McCoy gang feud, which captured the sympathetic fascination of generations of Americans. The Hatfields and McCoys only killed twelve family members during the twelve-year height of their feud. After a century of trying, a Hatfield-McCoy truce was achieved in 2003 between the sixty remaining family members. Now there are official Hatfield-McCoy Reconciliation Days in both Kentucky and West Virginia. In contrast, few remember or recognize the 1992 truce efforts between Crips and Bloods in South Central Los Angeles. Instead of an official day memorializing the gang truce, L.A. city leaders instead chose a cosmetic makeover, officially changing the name from South Central to South Los Angeles in 2003.

Probably more than 25,000 have died in our gang wars during the past three decades. Yet the body count is little mentioned. Even a book called *Body Count* (1995), meant by neoconservatives to stir fear of violent and menacing super-predators, never tabulates an actual body count of victims. These deaths are treated as lesser deaths, deserved deaths. Only the occasional killings of innocent bystanders really matter, stir outcry and media headlines. Gang-related deaths are what happens in the jungle, a matter for containment rather than concern. Too many people think to themselves, and perhaps confide to friends, it's good riddance.

Before arguing that these are *preventable* deaths, let me first elaborate on why they are such *invisible* ones.

The recognized authorities admit how little they know. "Our best national indicators of crime do not provide information specifically about gang crime," says a spokesman for Attorney General John Ashcroft's Office of Juvenile Justice and Delinquency Prevention.[7] Adds gang research expert Cheryl Maxson, "There is no systematic source of national and truly representative . . . counts of gang homicides, victims of lethal gang violence or gang members killed or anything like that" before 1996, when a national youth gang survey was instituted.[8]

Gang body counts are not included in the mortality data published in *Vital Statistics of the United States*.[9] Neither are they counted in the *Uniform Crime Reports* (UCRs) collected by the FBI from local police departments. UCRs were created by the International Association of Chiefs of Police (IACP) in the 1930s when they felt that newspapers were fabricating crime waves, according to an analyst in the U.S. Department of Justice, who said "I don't know what motivation they have for including or excluding" gang data from the reports.[10]

The FBI does obtain locally generated data in *Supplementary Homicide Reports* (SHRs), which include such categories as "gangland killing" and "youth gang killing." These reports showed a toll of gang homicide victims of 15,102 from 1980 to 2000.[11] The count ranged from 200-plus from 1980 to 1985, a jump from 300-plus to 678 by 1989, peaks between 900 and 1,300 from 1990 to 1995, and a downward trend to 800-plus starting in 1998. Going back further, it is necessary to rely on a federal Justice Department study by Walter Miller, who estimated 3,509 gang killings in the period from 1967 to 1980, a total based on reports from fifty-nine cities, which increased from 181 in 1967 to 633 in 1980 (in the latter year the FBI reported only 221).[12]

Those official FBI numbers were too low, and derived from underreporting. Beginning in 1996, the new National Youth Gang Survey (NYGS) of the Justice Department began tracking the numbers through interviews with a sample of local police agencies. By this technique, they arrived at significantly higher numbers than the FBI's SHRs: for example, 2,221 gang-related fatalities in 1996, 2,236 in 1997, and a reported decline to 1,335 in 132 cities with populations over 100,000 in 2001, compared to the FBI's lesser totals of 1,091 in 1996, 999 in 1997, and 842 in 2000.[13] One reason for the disparity is that the FBI traditionally has collected data on *juvenile* gang killings, a definition that ignores homicides among young adults.[14] According to Maxson, "Periodically, researchers compare FBI homicide Supplemental Report counts of gang homicides with the better data available within a given jurisdiction, and the FBI data always comes up short."[15] The undercount is worsened by differing methods of local data collection that bury the dead in carelessness and confusion.

The body count in Los Angeles County for the same two decades was over 10,000. I first heard this number from a former Grape Street Crip, Aqeela Sherrells, who recited the numbers as he spoke passionately at rallies for peace. L.A. sheriffs' internal data indicate that the official death toll for gang-related violence from 1980 to 2000 was 11,689.[16] At least 2,400 inner-city homicides were unsolved. In interviews, L.A. police and sheriffs give contradictory numbers, so 10,000 is a minimum count.

These L.A. numbers were described on a human scale, however briefly, in a 1995 study for the *Journal of the American Medical Association* (JAMA). For that single year:

- One third of those killed were not associated with a violent gang at all. Their median age was twenty-one.
- The motivation in 62 percent of the cases was "rivalry." Less than 5 percent were related to drug deals.
- The death rate among African American males, ages fifteen to nineteen, tripled, while the rate among same-aged Latinos rose 30 percent.
- Of a total 807 deaths, just 28 were whites killed by blacks or Latinos, and 7 were white-on-white; 390 were Hispanic-on-Hispanic, 170 black-on-black, while only 49 were black-on-Hispanic and 38 Hispanic-on-black; 9 were Asian-on-Asian, 4 were Asian-on-Hispanic, and only 9 were listed as black or Hispanic on Asians; 31 percent of the total were walk-up killings while 22 percent were drive-bys.[17]

An unchecked intra-tribal war was going on. It was neither an assault on the police[18] nor on white, property-owning civilization. It was a mass suicide by a definable segment of young men of color, just as Aqeela feared. The homicide rate was an ultimate measure of lost lives, but only a small measure of the full, unreported carnage in the gang wars. Using the available L.A. police department figures for the period 1993–2003, a picture of wider immolation emerges:

Gang-related attempted homicides:	5,359
Gang-related drive-by shootings (December 1995–December 2002):	6,380
Victims of gang-related drive-bys (same period):	8,508
Gang-related felony assaults:	26,972
TOTAL L.A. violent gang-related incidents (excluding victims' total), December 1993–December 2002:	38,711[19]

If the cumulative Los Angeles gang homicide numbers were correct, it meant that Los Angeles accounted for 80 percent of all gang-related homicides nationally over the two decades. That was simply impossible, despite Los Angeles's deserved image, along with Chicago, as the capital city of modern gang violence.

The numbers still understated the magnitude of the national death toll. They were based on vague definitions and competing methods of counting. For example, Los Angeles uses a definition of gang-*related* homicide, which means a killing where one of the parties is defined by police as a gang member or associate. This is an expansive definition, though it gives a palpable sense of the scales of gang wars. The "gang-related" category can be stretched to include two young tattooed men who kill each other over a girl, or someone with gang tattoos who gets shot robbing a liquor store for poverty-related reasons.

The City of Chicago counts those homicides that are gang-*motivated,* that is, which further a gang interest, like a drive-by shooting or the killing of a drug dealer in a feud over territory. In the case of the two homeboys who kill each other over a homegirl, that doesn't count. This narrower definition establishes a stricter standard of evidence, permitting officials to announce a lower body count than the gang-*related* standard does.

One team of researchers has counted 1,138 gang homicides in Chicago between 1980 and 1993, the year their study concluded.[20] Carolyn and Richard Block arrived at that number by delving into the Chicago police department's murder files. But the Blocks unintentionally may have underestimated the gang-related homicide numbers by creating a category of "non-family expressive homicides," including "confrontational competitions," some of which certainly were gang-related. After months of phone calls and a formal public records request, the Chicago police Strategic Services Division sent me their figures for 1985 through May 2003. The figures revealed 2,533 homicides involving street gangs during that period, ranging from 60 in 1985 to 293 in 1994. In the first quarter of 2003, street gang homicides represented 40 percent of the city's total. These were in all likelihood minimum estimates because they excluded deaths that were listed as narcotics-related, "altercations," or "undetermined." Causing further confusion was an unexplained change in definitions in 1994, when street gangs were blamed for 293 homicides and "organized criminal activity-narcotics" for 127.[21]

Chicago remained the country's overall per capita murder capital in 2002, with 658 deaths, up from 646 the year before,[22] the thirty-fifth consecutive year that the toll exceeded 600. In all respects, it was a case apart, and what part of the violence was gang-related was left unclear. Police experts sometimes alleged in the media that over half the city's death toll was related to drug-dealing street gangs, a body count higher than the percentages revealed in their internal data.

If police data could be assembled for the whole two-decade period from 1980 to 2003, the cumulative total of gang homicides would approximate 3,000 by whatever definition. Given those numbers, the combined body count for Chicago and Los Angeles would nearly equal the FBI's entire estimate for gang homicides in the United States in the same period.[23] Granted that although these two metropolises suffered the greatest toll, there still was something flawed in the national count.

A twenty-year break-out of gang-related homicides is not possible for most other cities. What little data that is reported through the recent NYGS is wildly unreliable.[24] For example, Detroit reported just 4 gang homicides in 2001; Las Vegas identified 11. Memphis counted 5 "motive-based" deaths for the same year. Baltimore totaled 100 "member-based" back in 1998, but only 20 in 2000. Milwaukee reported 95 "member-based" in 1999, but no data was listed for 2000–2001. This

was "pretty cheesy" data, the low-keyed Maxson complained.[25] But, hypotheti-
cally, if 100 cities averaged 3 gang-related deaths annually, that would total approximately 20,000, including L.A. and Chicago.

How to count the dead from gang-related activity is certainly less than scientific, and subject to legitimate question. My intent is not to defend these methods
as producing accurate totals, but to reveal a serious lack of attention to the gang
wars' body count.

For example, in New York City, the dead bodies disappear in a cemetery of
twisted bookkeeping. Police officials regularly promote with pride a claim that
New York City doesn't have a gang problem like Los Angeles's.[26] The official New
York numbers seem to bear this out, but they show a suspiciously tiny handful of
deaths in "youth gang clashes" since 1980, as in the following samples from New
York police data:

1973: 41
1976: 12
1980: 16
1985: 10
1986: 5
1991: 1
1995: 2
1996: 2[27]

Bear in mind, this was New York City, the legendary site of *West Side Story*, *The
Capeman*, *Down These Mean Streets*, and *Manchild in the Promised Land*. Where had
all the bodies gone? Was it all a fantasy? How could there be only one death in
"youth gang clashes" in 1991? The only explanation is that those dead were
dumped into other categories of violence. In the same years when gang homicides
were made officially insignificant, the police regularly recorded 200-plus annual
slayings during robberies, 300–500-plus murders during drug-related incidents,
and 500–900 deaths in "all other" lethal disputes. In 1991, when there was only *one*
officially recorded homicide due to gang clashes, 351 New Yorkers were killed

during robberies, 670 during drug feuds, and 912 in "all other" lethal disputes, creating a remarkable—and incredible—contrast between the apparent success in approaching zero gang murders compared to extraordinary mayhem involving drugs, robberies, and "all other" incidents.[28] New York City was officially gang-free, but in reality it was a case of statistical negligence.

The improbability of these numbers led Dr. Andrew Karmen, an expert at John Jay College of Criminal Justice, to charge "serious statistical undercounting of the true dimensions of gang violence" in New York.[29] There likely were cooked books: one set for public consumption, another for the inner sanctum. An example of the potential for manipulation surfaced in 2002, when it was discovered that over 200 crimes reported in Chelsea and Midtown Manhattan had been improperly reduced to misdemeanors, thus "making that area of Manhattan seem safer on paper than it really was."[30] Another investigation was initiated in the Bronx. Cooked books was an old New York recipe.

Though much research remains to be completed, clearly there is a national pattern that has the *effect* of covering up or manipulating homicide data. "Police departments are under tremendous, almost unprecedented pressure to come up with rosy crime data," concluded Jack Levin, a professor of criminology at Northeastern University in Boston.[31] Philadelphia police officials discovered a pattern in 1997 of undercounting aggravated assaults; when they were reclassified from misdemeanors, the numbers shot up from approximately 6,000 in 1997 to 11,047 by 2000.[32] In Detroit, where the city paid more than $137 million to settle lawsuits against the police in the period 1997–2003, "the city's homicide arrest figures were so seriously inflated that they skewed the FBI's data for the entire nation."[33]

Sometimes no manipulation is needed, only benign neglect. For example, President George Bush's home state of Texas saw a significant explosion of gang-related violence in the nineties, but the actual numbers were shaded from public view.[34] The 100-page 2001 overview from the state attorney general's office gave no data on the number and nature of gang homicides, only their prevalence by jurisdictions. The Texas results therefore represented only the percentage of agencies reporting a gang-related incident, not actual data on body counts. The death toll should have been quite high, since Dallas, Houston, and San Antonio have all ranked among the ten cities with the highest murder rates per capita.[35] According to a University of Texas criminology expert, Dr. Timothy Bray, there is no repository of gang homicides because "they may not be looking for them."[36]

Through the welter of statistics, the question persists: does anyone care how many deaths have occurred in this invisible war on America's streets? The number of gang-related homicides are never announced in national press releases on crime, never noted by the White House or FBI, never mentioned by the people who regularly raise the menace of gang super-predators. Are these killings only a menace when white people or bystanders are threatened? Are the numbers of casualties too insignificant to total and report, like the "enemy dead" in wars like Iraq and Afghanistan? Would a greater national focus on these deaths force the authorities to admit the existence of a hidden war at home, one that is permitted to go on and on?

Why do we have—to borrow a phrase from Karmen—this gang murder mystery? The smell is more than cheesy data. There certainly is a need for uniform reporting on a nationwide level. As long ago as 1995 there had been over 700 academic studies on youth gangs, with none providing long-term systematic data on the homicide rates among gangs.[37] But the problem is not fundamentally one of research. Public and private agencies are overflowing with detailed information on nearly every aspect of the gang violence crisis *except the nature and extent of gang violence.* The officially funded national surveys by John Ashcroft's Department of Justice confidently provide a picture overflowing with details on everything but gang-related deaths:

- There were on average, nationally, over 750,000 gang members during the period 1996–2000, organized into 12,850 gangs in cities with a population of 250,000 or higher.
- Ninety-one cities with a population of over 250,000 reported at least one gang-related homicide from 1999 to 2000.
- In 1999, 47 percent of gang members were Hispanic, 31 percent African American, 13 percent white, 7 percent Asian, and 2 percent "other."[38]

We are told, in a frightening summation, that the number of cities reporting a youth gang problem has mushroomed nearly tenfold, from fewer than 300 in the late seventies to over 2,500 in the late nineties.[39] This makes valuable reading, but fails to notice the most important fact that leaps from between the lines: *that gang-related homicides occur at levels that would be unacceptable in any other conflict on American soil, and that this demographic suggests a virtual death wish among certain at-risk youth. The mother of one nineteen-year-old victim says the violence is akin to "trying to make your race extinct."*[40]

This book is about that death wish. Many homies describe themselves as a species of living dead. They often plan their funerals meticulously. If they die an unrecognized death after an unrecognized life, it is like dying again. By refusing to sympathize with, or even record, their death toll, society sends a message that the homies already understand, that their lives and deaths are unworthy of respect. This is by no means a simple matter, but what is striking is the sheer avoidance of the nature of all these deaths in official studies and public discourse.

One gang research expert, Glen D. Curry, who published several government-funded studies in the nineties, has a blunt explanation: "It is my opinion that gang homicides have not been tracked more carefully because selected presidential administrations don't really care about violent crimes where 99 percent of the victims are minorities."[41]

In policy circles, the master work on gangs covering the three decades 1970 through 1998 is by Walter Miller under the auspices of the Office of Juvenile Justice and Delinquency Prevention.[42] The 100-page report charts the explosive growth of reported gang violence in thousands of municipalities, then turns briefly to an "explanation":[43]

The most common explanation for gangs, favored particularly by law enforcement, is the growth of the drug trade. This is the model that allows prosecutors to attack gangs as syndicates fighting over markets. A closer look might suggest parallels between alcohol Prohibition and the current drug wars. But Miller, like most researchers, finds that the drug model lacks an empirical foundation. There is, he points out, "considerable evidence that the number of gangs directly involved in the drug trade is much smaller than claimed by proponents of this position, that many gangs are involved only minimally with drugs, and that the development of cross-locality alliances and centralized control is much less in evidence than has been claimed," a view in which I concur.[44]

Second is immigration growth, which Miller concedes is a partial explanation for the growth of gangs, while pointing out that the growth among African Americans, American-born Asians and Hispanics "cannot be attributed to immigration." In dismissing a simplistic immigration model, however, this book will try to show how sharp displacements, from such experiences as slavery or war, can have the same impact as the classic immigration experience did on the formation of nineteenth-century white ethnic gangs.

Third is "names and alliances"—i.e. the exporting of the names Crips and Bloods to 115 cities, according to 1994 data. Similarly, he points to the migration of outside gang members to expand their gang reach into new territories. As an explanation, however, this underestimates the nature of street gangs as a grassroots, more-or-less spontaneous phenomenon. As Maxson's 1996 study showed, "cities where migration provides the catalyst for indigenous gang formation are the exception rather than the rule."

Fourth is the view that the gang is a "product of the broken home," a cultural view shared by many, particularly by religious neoconservatives. Miller finds that the data shows a correlation, but that the increase in gang populations is greater than the increase in fatherless families. However, he makes no mention of macroeconomic forces like unemployment and low wages in causing family stress and breakdown.

The failure to connect the economy and disenfranchisement to the growth in gangs is Miller's most serious deficiency, reflecting a larger disconnect in public policy that developed during the most explosive era of gang violence, the Reagan-Bush era of 1980–92. It will be one of the challenges of this book to question Miller's theme, which blames the sixties counter-culture for the later growth of gangs. Miller's case goes like this: the civil rights movements and riots of the sixties fostered a more permissive and even supportive stance toward "many of the customary practices of inner-city communities."[45] Customary practices? Miller cloaks any racial meaning by referring to "language patterns," "family arrangements," "child-rearing practices," and "housing patterns that had been stigmatized by the larger society" until the sixties allegedly made them legitimate. Among the approved "customs," he claims, was the formation of street gangs. This permissiveness extended to the illusion of some policymakers (he means the New Frontier, not the hippies) he says believed in "recognizing gangs as legitimate community groups" that should be funded with tax dollars. It was the children of the sixties who fostered this culture of tolerance. The sensationalist corporate media accelerated the trend by glorifying a "glamorous and rewarding" lifestyle.

This is where Miller's ideological leanings, and those of many in power, shape his social science. As the rest of this book will show, street gangs have their origins in nineteenth- and early-twentieth-century conditions that long preceded the sixties. When gangs like the Crips, Bloods, Latin Kings, and Blackstone Rangers exploded on the scene, it was in the vacuum left by two disastrous developments: the failure of the civil rights movement to achieve progress against northern poverty and discrimination, and the decision by the U.S. government to shelve the war on poverty for the war in Vietnam. Modern Vietnamese and Cambodian street gangs, composed largely of the children of boat people, demonstrate the cycle dramatically.[46] Street gangs have become what Jacob Riis called them a century earlier, "a distemper of the slum" telling us that "something has gone amiss in our social life."

The one explanation for the growth of gangs omitted from Miller's list is the continuation of extreme poverty and isolation among the generation labeled "at risk" in our nation's cities. This complete sundering of the subject of gangs from their roots in inner-city poverty is the political and intellectual accomplishment of American conservatives—with the gradual acquiescence of countless moderates and liberals over time. The redefinition of gangs as *criminal* per se, not a reflection of the institutionalized violence of life in the slums, did in fact begin in the sixties with government policies toward the turmoil of antiestablishment protests and the violent "civil unrest" that afflicted hundreds of cities as the Vietnam war escalated. The idea of a "war on gangs" emerged piecemeal, not as a conspiracy. It began with the vaunted special weapons and antiterrorist (SWAT) units in Los Angeles, then grew to the national level with the 1968 Crime Control and Safe Streets Act, allocating hundreds of millions of dollars for cities to toughen their law enforcement capacities. Richard Nixon expanded the secretive war, campaigning for an undefined "law and order" in 1968. The apparatus for fighting gangs was institutionalized steadily thereafter by the passage of six multibillon-dollar federal anticrime bills, the drug war's draconian penalties for possession of crack cocaine, mandatory minimum sentencing laws, three-strikes penalties, and the greatest splurge of prison construction in the nation's history. By the nineties, most police departments in America harbored an aggressive anti-gang unit and were busy stopping, frisking, profiling, and locking up hundreds of thousands of at-risk youth until the United States, with 5 percent of the world's population, contained perhaps 20 percent of the world's inmates.[47]

Miller's case, and that of modern neoconservatives, is that the permissiveness of the sixties toward drugs, single-parent families, and rebellions by the down-trodden led to the gang violence of the subsequent three decades. This is a classic case of scapegoating and denial on the part of those actually responsible for poli-cies that left millions of inner-city youth with nothing to live for.

To the extent that the current discussions of gang wars has roots in the sixties, parties on all sides should ponder the prophetic lyrics of the bard Bob Dylan:

> *Too much of nothin'*
> *Makes a fella mean.*

2

Roses in Concrete

Did u hear about the rose that grew from a crack
In the concrete
Proving nature's laws wrong it learned 2 walk
Without having feet
Funny it seems but by keeping its dreams
It learned 2 breathe fresh air
Long live the rose that grew from concrete
When no one else even cared!

—Tupac Shakur[1]

Without a gang you're an orphan.
—character in West Side Story

It's not us, it's everything around us!
—Maria in West Side Story[2]

After the 1992 Los Angeles riots I found myself outside the walls of main-stream perception. While the public was fed images of menacing and inexplicable violence, I was observing an alternative world of gang truces where, suddenly, Crips and Bloods tied their blue and red rags in knots of peace. Mexican and Salvadoran gangs tried to banish drive-by shootings at about the same time. Many of those who had created the madness were involved in efforts to end it.

This is a story about that decade, a time when it seemed possible to turn the corner against the scourge of gang violence, first, by adding the voices of these evolving gang members to an inclusionary process of restoring peace to the communities they had damaged and, second, by rethinking the wars on gangs, crime, and drugs that had become quagmires, and reviving a New Deal model of government leadership in rebuilding forgotten inner cities.

Those paths were not taken. Neither society nor the political leadership was ready for a major change of direction. As a result, the war on gangs went on, prisons were filled like never before, lives were lost, communities damaged, another decade wasted. Like a health problem untreated, the situation worsened. While established society clung to law-and-order solutions, however, a new generation of activism suggested to me there was hope for the future.

Books like Luis Rodriguez's *Always Running: La Vida Loca, Gang Days in L.A.*[3] and *Monster: The Autobiography of an L.A. Gang Member*[4] enjoyed a vast audience in the youth culture, from kids in juvenile halls to college classrooms, alongside such classics as *The Autobiography of Malcolm X.*[5] Gangster rap music soared on every chart, and rappers like the twenty-four-year-old Tupac Shakur became tragic folk heroes to millions.[6] As an unprecedented prison expansion unfolded, students and critics took up crusades against the "prison-industrial complex."[7] In hundreds of urban nooks and crannies, advocacy organizations made demands like "jobs, not jails." Films like *The Gangs of New York* exposed long-hidden chapters of American history. But ten years later, gang members were still social pariahs, doomed to hopelessness, imprisonment, or death. While opinion surveys revealed a public more willing to cut prisons than education spending,[8] the political class was deaf to calls for change. Liberals too often faltered in their historic commitments to social justice, playing defense against a conservative political juggernaut.

Why did I care, then, about the war on gangs? Some of us are born contrarians.

We question the status quo and make efforts to protect its scapegoats. We are nonconformists who think of "deviancy" as a response to social and psychological oppression, not a satanic gene. My favorite book as a kid was *The Catcher in the Rye,* about a disturbed young man seething at adult hypocrisy who wants to save kids from falling off cliffs. I came of age as a freedom rider in the civil rights movement. Hoping to end poverty, I served as a community organizer in Newark's ghetto in years of hope before the riots of July 1967. In those days, while we read Piri Thomas's *Down These Mean Streets* (1967) and Claude Brown's *Manchild in the Promised Land* (1965), America didn't sense a significant gang violence crisis. The white ethnic gangs of the past had diminished through assimilation into the middle class. Of course, there were gangs in minority communities, as viewers of *West Side Story* or followers of the New York's so-called "Capeman" killings, will remember.[9] Leonard Bernstein's musical was an archetypal presentation of the tragedy of gangs, with Puerto Ricans and white ethnics mirroring Shakespeare's feuding families in *Romeo and Juliet.* But these stories were seen at the time as relatively minor afflictions in urban life. Instead, most Americans recognized that we had a significant race and poverty crisis. In those times, those who became known as gangs were likely to call themselves "clubs" or "neighborhoods," taking on territorial and cultural identities to suit their status as outsiders. In Harlem, they were "hepcats"; in the Southwest, "pachucos." During World War II there was violent repression against the "zoot-suiters," Mexican-Americans who dressed in stylized suits, lengthy, draped coats, ballooning pants, and wide-brim hats. As Robin Kelley emphasizes, the zoot suits were subversive, even an "explicitly un-American style," forbidden by the War Production Board because of fabric rationing.[10] These pachucos frequented their own dance clubs, smoked marijuana, drove fine cars, and deeply irritated local police and navy sailors home on leave in Southern California. The zoot-suit riots and the murder trial known as the case of the Sleepy Lagoon are still etched in Southern California history, preludes to the gang wars of the future. In the seventies, Luis Valdez's play *Zoot Suit*[11] explored the pachuco era as primarily one of immigrant cultural defiance and urban survival rather than of criminal delinquency:

The Pachuco Style was an act in Life
And his language a new creation
His will to be was an awesome force eluding all documentation.

Valdez's hero, El Pachuco, attacked the racial demagoguery of the media, mainly the *Los Angeles Times*:

The press distorted the very meaning of the word "zoot suit."
All it is for you boys is another way to say Mexican.
But the ideal of the original chuco
Was to look sharp as a diamond
To look sharp
Hip
Bonaroo
Finding a style of urban survival
In the rural skirts and outskirts
Of the brown metropolis of Los, cabron.(2)

PRESS (yelling): You are trying to outdo the white man in exaggerated white man's clothes.
PACHUCO: Because everybody knows that Mexicans, Filipinos and blacks belong to the huarache the straw hat and the dirty overall.

Spike Lee's film *Malcolm X* opens with youthful Malcolm draped in an outrageous zoot suit in Detroit. The 1963 *Autobiography of Malcolm X* makes no mention of the "gang" phenomenon as such. In Malcolm's journey from Detroit to Boston to Harlem, there were plenty of hustlers, thieves, pimps, runners, prostitutes, and petty criminals, but they were not the African American gangs of the succeeding generation. This unorganized subculture of the street, however, attracted young Malcolm:

I spent my first month in town with my mouth hanging open.
The sharp-dressed young "cats" who hung on the corners and in the poolrooms, bars and restaurants, and who obviously didn't work anywhere, completely entranced me . . .

. . . I saw little black children, ten and twelve years old, shooting craps, playing
cards, fighting, getting grown-ups to put a penny or a nickel on their number for
them, things like that. And these children threw around swear words I'd never
heard before . . . such as "stud" and "cat" and "chick" and "cool" and "hip" . . . [12]

It was a time when "homeboy" meant just that: a bond between individuals
from the same place. When the young Malcolm sought work through a Roxbury
dance hall hustler named Shorty, he was asked about his previous employment.
Malcolm mentioned washing dishes in Macon, Michigan, leading Shorty to hap-
pily explode: "My homeboy! Man, gimme some skin! I'm from Lansing!"[13] Only
a few years later the question "Where you from?" would become a lethal challenge to claim and defend your neighborhood.

How long ago this seems, and how innocent a time. Yes, there was poverty
and racism, and gang stirrings, but in the early sixties hope was in the air and
movements were on the street corners. I remember, for example, the absolute
normalcy of boarding a bus in Harlem full of black people heading for the August 1963 March on Washington. As I remember, the media that day reported a
reduction of crime to zero levels in Harlem. The cause-and-effect seemed trans-
parent: crime was directly related to levels of economic hope and opportunity.
While youth committed most of the crimes—demography has always been
paramount—most of these young people individually acted mainly for economic reasons, not collectively as aspiring criminal syndicates. But we were on
the precipice. Violence simmered under the surface of things, waiting to erupt
when hope failed. The black prophet James Baldwin was writing of "the fire
next time," and Bob Moses, the civil rights organizer of the Mississippi Summer
Project, warned of the coming crisis as early as April 1964. It was the year of the
World's Fair, held in New York City, a futuristic extravaganza showcasing
"slumless cities" by the year 2000.[14] Meanwhile, black people in Mississippi were
being killed for registering to vote. Moses noted the contradictions, and spoke of
youth gangs forming in northern cities where unemployment rates were over
50 percent. It was invisible to the mainstream, he said, but "the country will know

about it" when the gangs turned from fighting each other to attacking property belonging to white people. That July, rioting broke out in Harlem and several other New York and New Jersey communities. Fifteen people were shot and hundreds arrested in police efforts to control what a city official called "the undermuck of Harlem."[15] Moses' prophesy was the first time I'd heard anyone predicting and linking the uprisings and gang wars of the next three decades.[16]

What happened? It's important to ask the question, especially today when there is a dominant consensus to shake our heads and treat violent crime as the work of incorrigible, even evil, psychopaths. To remember the early sixties is to remember that gang violence as we know it today was limited mainly to contained pockets of racketeering and hustling. My generation remembered gang violence as bloody shoot-outs in the Prohibition era by white ethnics with tommy guns. Suburban affluence had drained the earlier gang culture of its underlying pool of recruits, and the Great Society was widely expected to be a cleanup operation for the remaining pockets of poverty. The explosion known as "Watts" was just a year away.

As I look back, the slide into urban violence and, eventually gang violence, especially in black communities, began with the failure of the southern-based civil rights movement to achieve a breakthrough in the north, and with America's decision to escalate the Vietnam War in 1965 instead of the fledgling war on poverty at home.[17] Some, like Baldwin and Moses, sensed a need for rapid and radical change.[18] In Mississippi, on June 21 of that same summer, three civil rights workers—James Cheney, Andrew Goodman, and Mickey Schwerner—"disappeared" and were murdered, just as a grass-roots drive began to create a racially open Mississippi Freedom Democratic Party (MFDP) as an alternative to the officially segregated party of the time. During Freedom Summer in Mississippi, there were four murders, an estimated thousand arrests and eighty beatings of voter registration workers, and at least seventy-one incidents of church burnings, bombings, and shootings.[19] Despite the segregationist violence, the Freedom Democrats became the most significant model of participatory democracy built in the sixties. The project was the brightest alternative to the shoals of Vietnam and ghetto violence that were developing just beyond our perception.

On August 2, 1964, the U.S. government fabricated an incident in the Gulf of Tonkin ("a very delicate subject," Pentagon chief Robert McNamara called it at the time[20]), thus provoking the Vietnam War. While LBJ prepared his subsequent congressional war resolution on August 4, the FBI found three brutalized bodies buried in a Neshoba County, Mississippi, swamp. During an August 9 memorial service at the burned-out Mount Zion Church, Bob Moses questioned how the U.S. could fight for freedom in Vietnam but not in Mississippi. On August 20, LBJ declared an official war on poverty with a $947 million appropriation while also signing a defense augmentation fifty times greater as an initial Vietnam down payment.[21] The Democratic Convention began in Atlantic City at the same time.

If the inclusion of the Freedom Democrats had been taken up by the Democratic Party—Oval Office transcripts show that a majority of delegates favored the Freedom Democrats and were squelched only by the White House[22]—the Democrats still would have won the national election against the ultraconservative Barry Goldwater and recalcitrant southern Dixiecrats.

Looking back, this victory would have been a turning point with crucial multipliers. The Democrats would have been invigorated by the spirited, progressive MFDP and severed the influence of such Mississippi racists as Senator John Stennis, a leading Vietnam hawk who chaired the Senate armed services committee. The decision to seat the MFDP would have been a powerful impetus toward domestic priorities instead of the tragic Vietnam invasion in March 1965. In turn, a serious official commitment to ending racism and poverty might have prevented the several years of "urban disorder" that followed. The white backlash and political realignment that benefited Richard Nixon in 1968 would have been less likely. There can be no certainty about might-have-beens, of course. No one knows, for example, what the sixties might have been without the bloody trail of assassinations. But it seems clear in retrospect that the failure of Democratic liberal leadership in 1964 had the unforeseen consequence of ending the hopeful phase of the sixties and ushering in a time of violent chaos.

In the same era, hope was awakening in the Mexican-American barrios where the pachuco culture evolved among the immigrants of revolution and civil war in Mexico. By the late 1940s, the Community Service Organization (CSO) was formed by Saul Alinsky, Fred Ross, and Edward Roybal, to battle police brutality and disenfranchisement. Roybal was elected to the L.A. Council in 1949, and the community's first legal victories against LAPD brutality came in 1952. The mass deportations of the 1930s and the zoot-suit riots of the 1940s left a bitter legacy, however, and the pachucos evolved increasingly into a subculture of *cholos,* resisting the stigma of being categorized as permanent aliens. Then came political manipulations and forced evictions from the historic Chávez Ravine to make way for the new Los Angeles Dodgers. Amidst all the displacements, a new generation of homeboys—those like Luis Rodriguez—was born in the racial fissures of the U.S.A. The filmmaker and businessman Moctezuma Esparza, who grew up among those who became La Eme (the Mexican mafia) from the projects known as "Big Hazard," recalls an escalating police violence in the barrios that legitimized a rising counterviolence.[23] The SWAT teams were formed just as Chicano veterans were beginning to return from Vietnam. Where once the street gangs had occasional fistfights with the cops, viewing them as "another gang," the stakes swiftly became more lethal by the end of the sixties. These were the children of the immigrants of the forties and fifties, reinventing the pachuco style in the context of an emerging Chicano movement.[24]

Meanwhile, the CSO leadership recruited a former pachuco from Delano named César Chávez. Photos exist of Chávez in a zoot suit at age fifteen, during the era of the L.A. zoot-suit riots and the Sleepy Lagoon case. A longtime associate of Chávez recalls that:

> Cesar and [his brother] Richard used to talk a lot about being pachucos, cholos, hanging out, et cetera, but it was not so much organized gangs with all the ritual, hierarchy, weaponry, and so on, as street kids. Cesar always had the "street smarts" side to him which matches that picture of him and Richard and a buddy in "threads" and in which he used to take some delight.[25]

The young Chávez responded to the idea of a movement and joined with others, including Dolores Huerta from Stockton and longtime Filipino unionist Philip de la Cruz, to begin defending farmworkers. These immigrants performed stoop labor for little or no pay in nineteenth-century conditions. Like African Americans in the south, they were another large constituency excluded from the benefits of the New Deal. The historic National Labor Relations Act failed to include protections for migratory farm labor. Inspired in part by the black freedom struggle, Chávez began organizing farmworkers into a union of their own. The strikes, grape boycotts, fasts, and nonviolent marches to Sacramento helped stir an entire generation of Chicanos. But the failure of established political leadership in the sixties to embrace the union, and end the broader disenfranchisement of Chicanos, deepened the frustration of countless Chicano youth growing up in the barrios. They experienced moments of hope combined with angry helplessness. Those experiences contributed both to the growth of Chicano nationalism (Chicanismo, *la raza,* the concept of Aztlan) and barrio gangs in the late sixties, just as the failure of the civil rights movement and the repression of groups like the Black Panthers widened the door for African American gangs in northern ghettos.

Again, the promise of rapid and decisive reform, based on the surge of idealism in the early sixties, was not to be. In the case of Chicanos, what was needed was a serious completion of the labor reforms of the New Deal and the civil rights era for those left behind, like millions of migrant workers. Instead, the government went to war on the outer frontier of the American empire, in a place called Vietnam. It was in keeping with the analysis of historian William Appleman Williams, a major influence on the early sixties generation, who depicted America as a frontier society in denial, one that sought escape from domestic challenges by fantasizing demonic "others" and a manifest destiny.[26]

The hubris of assuming that America could fight on multiple fronts, one in the jungles of Vietnam and another against poverty at home, touched off the inner-city violence that spread to hundreds of ghettos in the next three years. Amidst this urban carnage emerged the Crips, Bloods, and much of the gang subculture of modern times, "the orphans of the civil rights movement," as one of them, named Twilight, later told the playwright Anna Deavere Smith.[27]

I experienced the urban violence that preceded this development of gangs in July 1967, when the Newark ghetto erupted. It began with the police beating of a cab driver, then quickly escalated. After five days, twenty-four black people were killed along with two firefighters (most likely killed by friendly fire). Hundreds were injured; 1,400 were arrested and detained. Most of the street confrontations with the heavily outfitted police and National Guard I witnessed were led by teenagers armed with nothing more than bottles or rocks. Most of the shootings by police, troopers, and Guardsmen that I recorded seemed intended to intimidate, and thus somehow control the disorder. My investigation concluded that all the victims were either innocent bystanders or, at most, looters. I wrote at the time of the surprising fearlessness that I saw on the faces of young people:

> The soldiers marched towards them, bayonets pointing. The kids kept coming, a few spreading out into the street or behind the cars. Face to face, ten soldiers with guns against 25 kids with two bottles. The guardsmen pushed the kids back with their bayonets. One bayonet went too far through the shirt and the victim turned around screaming into the soldier's face. Quickly the troops circled around him, and the rest of the kids moved into a wider circle. With the bayonet jabbing his skin, the young man continued yelling. Down the street troopers rushed with pistols and clubs swinging. The soldiers opened their circle to allow the trooper to crack the captured one across the back. Two blows and he fell to the street and twisted in convulsion. Rocks and bottles flew at the troops and four black men ran up to the writhing body. They sat on the victim to prevent his body from snapping . . .
>
> A neighborhood worker, encouraged by the police to cool people off, put down his microphone and swore. "If they're going to do this, fuck it. I can't do anything." After a moment, he picked up the bullhorn and started speaking: "Please, people, take your little children inside, take your children inside. Someone is going to get hurt out here."[28]

These young men facing the armed forces were seen at the time mostly as "children" or "angry young men," not "gangbangers" or "super-predators." But

the fierce confrontations amidst those hundreds of "urban disorders" were crucial in the formation of a future gang identity. The parents and grandparents of
most of these northern black people had migrated from the segregated south
only to discover that the "new promised land" was a slum with no exit. Claude
Brown wrote of their dashed hopes in *Manchild in the Promised Land*. Going
north was supposed to mean "goodbye to the cotton fields, goodbye to 'massa
charlie,' goodbye to the chain gang, and, most of all, goodbye to those sunup-to-
sundown working hours."[29] The children of those with migrant dreams,
whether black or brown, discovered "they had little hope for deliverance" since
they already were in the "promised land."[30] Their disillusionment, when it
came, was even deeper than their counterparts in the segregated south singing
"we shall overcome." That disillusionment was expressed as the difference between looting and sit-ins. Raging with humiliation, they discovered the power of
their color to strike fear. Their character was formed and tested in resistance to
the police and troops. Previously portrayed as "delinquent," they now drew
power from their "badness." Instead of seeking to integrate into America, they
accepted their exclusion and transformed it into a separate identity, even a country, they could belong to: the neighborhood ('hood), with its own names,
tattoos, slang, sign language, colors, dress, art forms (graffiti), and economy
(underground).

The Vietnam War made it all worse in a hurry. The young Americans who
were drafted or volunteered were disproportionately from those neighborhoods
where "disorders" erupted and gangs eventually followed. Second class in America, they were on the front lines in Vietnam, suffering the greatest percentage of
casualties, returning wounded, disoriented, and disrespected in the greatest numbers. Of the 600,000-plus Vietnam era soldiers with dishonorable discharges, for
drugs or insubordination, the highest percentage were black or brown.[31] Many
returned with heroin addictions, nightmares, unemployment, and wounded
pride that would not heal. For many of them the "urban disorders" were flash-
backs to Vietnam. At a minimum, they added new levels of instability to their
communities at a time when a younger generation badly needed role models.

There were important exceptions. Elmer "Geronimo" Pratt, for example, went from the Special Forces to the Black Panther Party. Another was Daniel "Nane" Alejandres, who recovered from both Vietnam and a heroin habit to found Barrios Unidos, a national gang intervention and violence prevention organization. "Almost nobody talks about the wars in Vietnam or later in El Salvador when they talk about the reasons for gangs," Nane recalled in a conversation at his Santa Cruz, California, headquarters in 2001.

> I had been experiencing that those that were falling into the lifestyle of the gang, the drugs, a lot of these youngsters' fathers were Vietnam vets. A lot of us vets who came back inflicted on people a lot of the violence that we brought back with us. The influence of vets, who were violence-prone and trained, when they came back, had an impact on the conflicts between gangs. The vets didn't come back into a movement, they came back addicted to drugs, they came back alcoholics, they came back with mental problems. Then all of a sudden you're back into a war with neighborhoods, and as a combat vet you would know all the ways to get back, to retaliate. And at the time there wasn't any violence prevention work or counseling available, so it just kept going on and on and on.

In 1992, when Los Angeles exploded in the largest urban rebellion of the century, I felt that the cycle was repeating itself, but in a downward path. By then I'd served ten years in the state assembly, representing a largely white, affluent west side district, spatially segregated at a "safe" distance from the inner city. When the riots broke out, I was in the midst of a closely fought Senate primary, speaking to white voters at lovely Pacific Palisades backyard events while clouds of smoke rose and hung over the inner city. I decided that, if elected, I had to do something about inner-city violence by stimulating the conscience of the affluent. For example, there was a need to challenge the economic system that had left the inner-city underdeveloped and the affluent neighborhoods so overdeveloped. But that wasn't enough. There was a gulf of perception and fear. Voters in my district thought of "East L.A." as anyplace east of UCLA. They never ventured south of the Santa Monica Freeway. They increasingly clustered their children in private schools. They saw private doctors while the poor stood in line at the county hospital. They drove SUVs while the poor waited for buses. They ordered take-out while poor neighborhoods lacked supermarkets. They purchased private alarm and security systems while the poor wondered if they should call the police when their safety was at risk. It was virtually impossible to find a racially inclusive gathering on the west side. My constituents were liberals increasingly sealed off from their early sixties, civil rights, antipoverty idealism. Their image of the inner city, fed mostly by commercialized television specializing in crime stories, was not unlike 1950s British colonial images of the Mau-Mau rebellion in Kenya.

I decided to challenge the stereotypes directly by hiring some allegedly "incorrigible" inner-city survivors to be outreach workers bridging the gap between South Central, east side and west side Los Angeles. There was Dewayne Holmes (aka "Snipe"), who spent half his life before the age of thirty behind bars, and who played a courageous role in ending the 1992 violence in Watts. There was his longtime homie John Heyman (aka, "whiteboy"), who became my driver in a political campaign immediately after his release from a decade in state prison. There was Silvia Beltran, raised in El Salvador, where she stepped over dead bodies on her way to school, who emigrated to the United States in the trunk of a car and who, though not a "loca" herself, spent six years bailing out her 18th Street boyfriend on weekends. There was Manny Lares, who described himself as a "fourth generation Santa Monica gang member" from the Pico neighborhood, a small barrio besieged by yuppie gentrification. There was the grieving Celina Martin, whose innocent teenaged son, Cesar, was murdered by west side gang members in a drive-by shooting. I asked the director of my local office, Sandy Brown, a white, middle-class homeowner, to learn to co-exist with this wild bunch. My statewide chief of staff, Rocky Jaramillo Rushing, was a straight-arrow former journalist who investigated prison conditions.

We created a loosely knit gang violence prevention project called the "peace process network," involving about fifty individuals from gang backgrounds. I had been inspired by the concept of an "urban peace movement" espoused by Luis

Rodriguez in a 1996 *Nation* magazine article. I visited Luis in Chicago, where he described his efforts to save lives not only in American cities but in a visit he'd made to El Salvador, where deported L.A. homeboys were trying to prevent gangbanging vendettas on the streets. His account of El Salvador made me recognize a paradox about the internationalizing of the gang problem. Having spent considerable time in Northern Ireland and the Middle East, I was aware that our government routinely invested resources in peace negotiations and conflict resolution. It was obvious that the U.S. government was prepared to send diplomats, security experts, and billions in aid packages to support efforts toward peace. I now wondered: if our government can support a peace process in Northern Ireland, why not South Central L.A.?, and if the Middle East, why not East L.A.? Was there not a war in our inner cities that had turned into a quagmire, wrecked thousands of lives, and undermined the possibilities of investment and development? Why should this unrecognized war at home be left only to local police departments, as if it were a decentralized public safety function? Did powerful interest groups care more about stability overseas than in our own cities? Were there no well-connected lobbyists or fat-cat contributors lobbying on behalf of the urban underclass?

Or had a profound and cynical weariness closed the window of hope when, in the early sixties, Americans were open to justice, to addressing the pent-up inequalities, poverty, and broken lives of our inner cities? Was James Baldwin our prophet after all when he, in *No Name in the Street,* diagnosed our deepest cultural need as that for a scapegoat:

> If Americans were not so terrified of their private selves, they would never have needed to invent and could never have become so dependent on what they still call "the Negro problem" . . . which they invented to safeguard their purity . . . [but] however the scapegoat may be made to suffer, his suffering cannot purify the sinner; it merely incriminates him the more, and it seals his damnation. The scapegoat, eventually, is released to his death: his murderer continues to live . . . The crucial thing, here, is that the sum of these individual abdications menaces life all over the world.[32]

The paramount objective of our experimental project was to build support for a crew of peacemakers—former or current gang members able to mediate and quell disputes before they turned violent, whether in the streets or state prisons. For years such individuals in Los Angeles and around the country had been having a quiet impact, measurable in the decline of gang homicides. The truce between Crips and Bloods in 1992 was a powerful symbol of potential change. It stimulated a National Peace and Justice Summit held in Kansas City, Missouri, in 1993, under the banner of "A Time to Heal, A Time to Build." There, hundreds of young men and women expressed a longing for reconciliation, symbolized when individuals from rival gangs approached a church pulpit to confess they had tried to kill each other in the past, then "dropped their colors" and tearfully embraced. In addition to these healing ceremonies, they adopted an urgent public call for 500,000 jobs for at-risk youth and community-based economic development.[33] According to a 1996 survey, there were suddenly 3,100 community-based peace organizations across the country, and that was only the tip of the iceberg.[34]

A central question this book asks is: what happened to that hopeful moment a decade ago? What happened to those young people who stopped banging and began building? What have they to show for their efforts, and what does that say about America? Having worked with or followed these efforts over a decade from the inner-city streets to government halls to college classrooms, I believe the answer is deeply troubling. The opportunity for a peace dividend has been lost. The jobs were not created. Prison construction outpaced school construction. The peacemakers themselves received little credit and fewer resources for their risky, mostly voluntary, efforts. Because of their own criminal backgrounds or tattooed appearances, they gained little trust or respect from established authorities. Instead of warm welcomes for changing their lives, they often were faced with skeptical questioners. How could such former criminals—and who was to know if their gangbanging had stopped?—be entrusted with peacemaking roles amidst a new generation of homeboys? Weren't the truces only momentary, not real alternatives to the trustworthy processes or the criminal justice system? Or worse, weren't the truces just facades to allow street "business" (drug dealing, carjackings) to continue with less heat from the police? And how could the peacemaking be measured? How do you measure a life saved in contrast to an arrest made? Wasn't the only sure path to ending the killing through a prison door? All the questions came down to one deeper question: weren't these people simply incorrigibles?

An official L.A. County gang task force in the mid-nineties readily acknowledged that for three years "thousands of rival gang members willingly participated in implementing gang truces. Gang members *down for the 'hood* [original in italics] were able to cooperate in preventing of violence despite the presence of a history of payback violence and rivalries."[35] But on the same page the report sabotaged its apparent good news, warning that "the impact of gang truces on communities can be negative. A truce can reinforce the gang's identity . . . at its worst, a truce serves to legitimize the identity of a gang and its members and lengthens its illegitimate reach."[36] On the street, such attitudes were a familiar refrain to homeboys: once a gang member, always a gang member. The *New York Times*'s Fox Butterfield found a similar pattern among those he interviewed. In 1997, at the height of the city's youth crime scare, Butterfield reported FBI data revealing that serious crimes had declined for the fifth consecutive year nationally, with murders at their lowest level since the late sixties.[37] The *Times* reporter found that young people on the streets had an explanation of their own, one backed by social workers, probation officers, and psychiatrists he interviewed. They disagreed that the lower violence rates were due to the aggressive stop-and-frisk tactics under Mayor Rudolph Giuliani. It was, Butterfield said, "a shift in attitudes among the young people themselves." One of those he interviewed, twenty-year-old Salahadeen Betts, on 144th Street, shot back with a crucial question for Butterfield, and the rest of America:

> How come when the violence goes down, it's because of the
> police, and when it goes up, it's us?

For Salahadeen, who was considered a "thug" by his teachers, the moment of change came when a close friend was murdered while rolling dice on a street corner. His sorrow at a preventable death, coupled with "getting smarter" himself about drugs and guns, began to turn Salahadeen around. He eventually became a college student and volunteer in a Harlem after-school program with 500 students ages six to twenty-two. Butterfield discovered similar attitudinal changes when he called probation workers in Chicago and Boston. "They remember their mothers crying and their older brothers not coming home, for no reason, and they don't want to be part of it," said one. Another key factor, Butterfield found, was the introduction of after-school programs with incentives for remedial and college degrees.

The peacemaker network in Los Angeles was composed of a lot of Salahadeens, and they rejected the skeptics and critics. They knew that everything else had been tried in the war on gangs except involving survivors to map a way out. They were, after all, living proof that gang violence is preventable, that redemption is possible. If formerly they had been gangbanging, shooting, stabbing, robbing, and selling drugs, they were now at the table urging peace and justice, demanding resources for their neighborhoods. If that disturbed some status quo assumptions, they felt, so be it.

Please come to the crossroads,
You can save the children, I know

They discovered a multilayered counterculture of violence prevention groups across the nation and world. They worked closely with national Barrios Unidos, the organization founded thirty years earlier by "Nane" Alejandres. There was the Jesuit priest Gregory Boyle, who had established the nation's only ministry to gangs, in East Los Angeles. There was former all-American football player Jim Brown's Amer-I-Can organization, rising from the ashes of Watts and prison cells. From Amer-I-Can emerged leaders like Aqeela and Daoud Sherrells, originally from the Grape Street Crips neighborhood in Watts, who were now building a self-determination institute in Watts and taking west siders on tours of the 'hood. There was "Blinky" Rodriguez, a kickboxing champion whose son was killed in the madness, who forgave the killers and dedicated his life to grass-roots peacemaking. Reflecting the globalization of gangs, there was Homies Unidos, organizing peacemakers from Pico-Union to the backstreets of San Salvador. There were other local groups like "Bo" Taylor's Unity One, Hector Marroquin's NOGUNS, Gilbert Sanchez's Gang Bridging Project at California State University—Los Angeles.

If these ghetto peacemakers were to form an inner circle, they would need the backing of an outer circle from civic society. So in addition to trying to legitimize peacemaking as a vocation (Gilbert Sanchez was educating, training, and credentialing peacemakers through Cal State L.A.), the network pursued the creation of a larger peace and justice movement. There were helpful civil rights attorneys like Connie Rice, and cultural personalities like Harry Belafonte. Dialogue was established with law enforcement officials from the police and sheriff's departments. The American Civil Liberties Union was urged to defend against police antigang personnel like the one in Washington, D.C., who declared, "this is the jungle . . . we rewrite the constitution every day down here."[38] The AFL-CIO was helping organize immigrant workers in sweatshops, often the parents of homeboys and homegirls with no economic futures. The clergy were asked to shelter groups like Homies Unidos against police and immigration officers. State legislators were lobbied to fund nonprofit, community-based organizations doing violence prevention work. Funding also was obtained for free tattoo removal for young people seeking jobs. The process of bringing busloads of ex-gang members to Sacramento to testify at hearings and meet one-on-one with elected officials was often more important than the results. The goal was to demonstrate that they had a right to be present in the halls of power, not simply behind prison walls.

The network's formal structure was altered when I left the state Senate and public funding dried up in 2000. But the participants have continued to carry on the work, as many others had done before and, undoubtedly, many will continue to do in the future. A few lost heart, some fell back to their old ways, but many more are digging in for the long haul. Their work was living proof that gang violence is preventable, that the seeming incorrigibles can become precious resources for change, that change, as Bob Moses once said, comes from the stones the builders left out.

3

The Peace Process

I've been defiled and refiled
Now I'm back to face facts with the strength of a juvenile smile . . .
Collapsed between a trigger-happy "fr-enemy"
And a loaded strap left to inter-be
I'm like a rose turned to garbage back to roses and back
Trying to convince my own eyes to see the beauty in me.
　　　　　　　　　—Daniel Cacho[1]

　　　I am a victim of the past, present and future
　　　My past hunts me like the boogie man in the closet
　　　Or monster under my bed
　　　Silence is powerful
　　　Cause I know you can feel all my emotions
　　　Even when I don't speak a word.
　　　　　　　　　—Maria Brown[2]

I am a lost soul floating in outer space screaming for help
But in space no one can hear you scream
I am like a ghost, I cause fear because I am in fear and I'm alone
I am like the moon, the only time I shine is in the dark.
　　　　　　　　　—David Mancillas[3]

Working Toward Inner Peace

The thrust of these street organizations differed in some respects from conventional liberal and conservative paradigms. Typically, the peacemakers stress a powerful role for personal transformation and healing in ending the violence; as our L.A. peace network brochures declared, "Those who had a role in starting the madness are best able to play a role in ending it." The violence does not inevitably or mechanically arise in every case from objective conditions like poverty, and cannot be ended solely by external public policy changes. Like veterans of any other wars, street activists face an *inner* peace struggle against countless demons, nightmares, guilt, and flashback traumas. Often these demons become real, in the form of rivals with scores to settle. The process, therefore, requires patient face-to-face interaction in peacemaking efforts, sometimes successful, sometimes not, and at a deeper level a process of creating trust-based groups, often combined with exercises in poetry, therapy, rapping, art, and meditation to help exorcise the demons. This inner process must occur in safe space, without fear of informants or law enforcement, so that hard truths can be acknowledged.

Some of the best writing I have seen on this subject is James Gilligan's *Violence: Our Deadly Epidemic and Its Causes* (1996). It is not a book about gang members per se, but about the backgrounds of convicted murderers in our penal system. Gilligan identifies the cause of the violence as an unbearable "shame and self-contempt"[4] perpetuated by a permanent *system of humiliations.* University of California criminologist Franklin Zimring says that "fear of being called chicken is almost certainly the major cause of death and injury from youth violence in the United States."[5] Friedrich Nietzsche, cited in Orlando Patterson's *Feast of Blood,* may have explained it most probingly: "When a man thinks it necessary to make for himself a memory, he never accomplishes it without blood, tortures and sacrifice . . . all these things originate from that instinct which found in pain its most potent mnemonic."[6] In *Why They Kill,* Richard Rhodes offers a potent example of how this Nietzschean sensibility takes root. A gang member who "fucked up a dude real bad," and was kicked out of school as a result, remembered that "it must have been right because nobody was giving me any shit any more . . . The way people acted *made me come alive.*"[7] The original humiliation at being oppressed incenses the victim either toward self-annihilation or the transference of rage to others. The resulting danger is either a civil war within the oppressed self or the oppressed communities, unless there is transformation.

Transformation can occur in key moments, or thresholds, when individuals are open to change. This explains the success of the Nation of Islam in recruiting so many adherents from prison. Monster Kody's book is one of many that describes the personal and educational intervention of a Muslim minister in changing his consciousness. For a humiliated, isolated inmate, the Muslims offer spiritual brotherhood combined with racial and masculine pride. It is no accident that Muslims sometimes function to defuse gang violence, as during the neighborhood meetings leading to the Watts truce in 1992. Or transformation can arise from the experience of trauma. One of our best peacemakers was George, from the Hazard neighborhood, who grew up hating whites and blacks. As a kid, George would draw a thrilling sense of empowerment from stabbing and robbing people. It was the fear in their eyes that turned him on. One day, however, his own brother came home bleeding from a stab wound. George was shaken. Not long after, George himself was stabbed and rushed to the emergency room at Martin Luther King hospital. Returning to consciousness after surgery, George was staring into the eyes of an African American doctor who had saved his life. As a result, George began to transform to a new way of seeing the world. His personal war was over. He continues to be a community street worker in the Hazard projects today.

The issue of transforming inner-city shame was addressed both clinically and politically in several works of the psychiatrist Frantz Fanon, who was born in the French colony of Martinique and died as an Algerian revolutionary in 1962. Fanon sometimes is oversimplified as a believer in a mystique of violence. But his clinical work gave Fanon important insights into the psychodynamics of colonialism, racism, and rage. The Algerian patients he treated in France, like most people of color, were profoundly ashamed of who they were in the eyes of

whites. The identities of colonial subjects were being stolen and replaced by categories of shame: niggers, spics, coolies, apes, and so on. "All this whiteness
burns me to ashes," Fanon once said of his own personal experience. He himself
was an educated professional with the tools to channel his rage into both medicine and politics. But among the poor he treated there were no avenues of escape. He came to identify a syndrome that was unclassified at the time, since
French psychiatry located the neurosis as an Algerian racial characteristic. In his
notes, he described his Algerian patients:

> Threatened in his affectivity, threatened in his social activity, threatened in his
> membership in the polis, the North African brings together all the conditions that
> create a sick man. With no family, no love, no human relations, no communion
> with the collectivity, *his first encounter with himself will take place in a neurotic mode*, in
> a pathological mode, he will feel empty, lifeless, fighting bodily against death, *a
> death that comes before death, death that exists in life*.[8] [my italics]

Fanon concluded that the only means at the disposal of this colonized individual to shake the "death that exists in life" was "to make myself known" (*me
faire connaître*) by a forceful act.[9] The confined existence of a ghetto, casbah, or
prison cell stimulated "muscular dreams, dreams of action, aggressive dreams"
that were mischanneled: "During colonization, the colonized man never stops
liberating himself between nine in the evening and six in the morning . . ."[10]
Fanon did not focus on the possibility that this mischanneled aggression could
become permanent in forms of collective self-destruction or intra-communal
feuds. He believed that individuals would overcome their condition through collective revolutionary action, negating the negation and birthing a new human
being. While his revolutionary solution was utopian, his diagnosis of individuals
combating the "death that comes before death" and acting out "to make themselves known" to an unknowing world still speaks to the experience of street
gang members.

Fanon was arguing against the tradition of (white) Marxism that classified the
"non-productive" classes as a dangerous rabble, the lumpen-proletariat. Fanon
asserted that the lumpen, by reclaiming themselves from self-destruction, could

become the agents of history. He was reacting to the heady events around him, including the Algerian and Cuban revolutions. Fanon did not live long enough to see these revolutions produce contradictions of their own, as the violence of the oppressed turned inward in power struggles, civil strife, and religious and ethnic wars. If Marx was too conservative in his reaction to the potential of the lumpen, Fanon was too uncritical, seeming to believe that the gang/lumpen lifestyle would be transcended through spontaneous violence against authority.[11] Had he lived, however, Fanon might have offered significant advice on the steps needed to heal self-hate and intra-tribal feuds. Instead, abandoned by the left and oppressed by the right, the lumpen of this country would have to forge their own analysis, remedies, and rehab programs.

After the 1992 uprisings and truces, gang members briefly gained an audience to explain their inner motivations in their own words. Former gang member Luis Rodriguez wrote in *Always Running* (published in 1993, it is one of the most widely read books in the gang and prison subculture) that young homeboys tend to murder their mirror reflections; "they're killing themselves over and over."[12] The "thirst for a reputation," even in death, is the purpose of all gang members, according to Monster Kody's *Monster: The Autobiography of an L.A. Gang Member*.[13] "The principle is respect, a lynchpin critical to relations between all people, but magnified by thirty in the ghettos and slums," where there is none, he writes.[14] By all accounts, what triggers most gang violence is *disrespect*—being "dissed"— and, according to Gilligan, "the more trivial the cause of the shame, the more intense the feeling of shame."[15] Male gang violence erupts frequently in competition over women. But it can be over any matter that is too embarrassing to reveal. For example, I recall a case where an individual blamed another neighborhood for stealing his money. It turned out that he'd lost the money gambling, was too ashamed to admit it, and wanted his homies to take revenge on those who'd taken his cash fair and square. A gang peace activist had to intervene to de-escalate the spiral.

The penal system is a concentrated environment for all this punishment and shame. It is no accident that so many gangs are born or perpetuated behind bars, among them La Eme, the Latin Kings, and the Blackstone Rangers. Those not literally born in prison settings are often consolidated there. Behind bars, the gang culture offers protection and connection; after release, the ex-offender feels indebted to his homeboys, and so it goes. L.A.'s juvenile hall is "our *heart*," says a sixteen-year-old member of 18th Street, the largest faction in the California Youth Authority (CYA).[16] The conditions in these facilities, rationalized by security rhetoric, almost seem designed to punish, humiliate, and sexually—and physically—threaten the inmate population into controlled submission. One 18th Streeter I know, whose street name is "Clever" (we used to call him "Not so Clever") was expelled from schools for fighting and sent to Youth Authority, where the fighting simply continued. Other wards kept coming at him, in a constant test of his growing manhood. One might have seen leadership potential in a young man like Clever, but he was defined only as trouble. When the whole facility was locked down for weeks, hundreds of young men like Clever were shut in tiny cells twenty-three hours a day. Many of them became ashen-skinned from the lack of sunlight, zombies from the deliberate overuse of sedatives to control inmates. In 1999, the state inspector general (an oversight office created by the legislature after numerous hearings on prison scandal) exposed a systemic pattern of abuse at the state's flagship CYA institution, finding that guards were

> slamming handcuffed inmates against walls; firing potentially lethal riot control guns at close range to remove inmates from cells; forcing unruly inmates to cells with urine and excrement on the floor; and ordering that disorderly inmates be injected with anti-psychotic drugs, [and forcing inmates] to confront other inmates, often rival gang members, in what where referred to as "the Friday night fights."[17]

In the state prison system, guards continued to kill and wound inmates in melees, a "practice unheard of in any other state."[18] Between 1989 and late 1994, California prison guards killed 24 inmates and wounded 175; after the resulting public clamor, another 12 inmates were shot dead and 32 wounded in the following four years, more than all the fatalities for those years in the entire national prison system.[19] The rationale given by the prison authorities was the "uniquely violent nature of California prison gangs," but of the 44 serious or fatal shootings between 1994 and 1999, only one of the inmates was found to be armed or inflicting serious harm, no guards were in peril, and none of the casualties occurred during an escape.[20] Though California's prison guards were more trigger-happy, the general policies of controlling prisoners by methods of dehumanizing, rather than rehabilitating, them was the pattern across the country. In prison as on the streets, the underlying assumption was that the inmate population was a caste of violent incorrigibles. Since the general public shares such assumptions, the implications for prison safety are ominous. At this writing, for example, California's high-security prisons are virtually on permanent lockdown. But since an atmosphere of violent intimidation only increases the potential for further violence, more riots and bloodshed are inevitable.

The culture of punishment persists long after inmates serve their time; for example, in New York State alone, ex-felons are prohibited from entering a hundred job categories, including barbering. Thirteen states provide for the disenfranchisement of felons, including Florida, where over 600,000 are disqualified for life. Felons are barred under federal law from public housing, even from visiting their parents. Drug felons are prohibited from seeking student loans if they return to school. Gradually a curtain of continuing punishment has fallen over ten million Americans who have done their time.[21]

Strangely, the punishment culture has expanded despite the nation's violent crime rate dropping to historic lows. Though Attorney General John Ashcroft fulminates against drug "kingpins" and "violent gun criminals," the truth is that a majority of federal inmates are convicted of "relatively unspectacular drug-related crimes." Only 5 percent are murderers or sex offenders, and 1 percent are considered major drug traffickers. Nevertheless, Ashcroft has ordered prosecutors to notify him whenever judges impose more lenient sentences than the federal guidelines.[22] The result is a huge number of young men, mainly black and brown, being classified and processed amidst the paranoid and violent environment of the prison system.

Take, for example, the crisis of unspoken sexual pressure and paranoia. By Gilligan's estimate, there were eighteen adult male rapes per minute in the country's prisons in the nineties, a total of 9 million sexual assaults yearly.[23] Sometimes these are guard-on-prisoner abuses; for example, in California's women's prisons, five employees resigned and another forty fell under investigation for sexual assault in 1999 after a class action prisoner lawsuit.[24] But most of the sexual aggression arises from conditions of prison life. Even assuming that Gilligan's sexual assault projections are high, the sexual acts are relentlessly repeated, not one-time incidents. In jails and prison, one becomes another's sexual slave or "bitch," permanently servicing his rapist's needs in silence. This is the subculture in which most gang members spend their formative years. To dominate or submit is the code, and violence is the penalty for weakness. In California's Corcoran prison, guards sometimes took inmates for "discipline" to 230-pound Wayne Jerome Robertson, known as "the Booty Bandit," who raped and beat them in his cell, often in exchange for extra food or sneakers.[25] One of his victims, 120-pound Eddie Dillard, now a college student in Northridge, California, said it felt "like you're being killed, just slowly."[26] During his confinement, he could not directly accuse "the Booty Bandit" because that would have violated the code against snitching, establishing "grounds for Robertson to kill him."[27] (I later interviewed Robertson in Pelican Bay prison, in a tiny high-security booth with a bulletproof separation. He was eager to describe a life of hard luck, petty crime, and lack of legal representation, but less willing to discuss his prison reputation. A resident of Compton, he said he "learned to be a criminal at Juvenile Hall." He considered himself a prisoner for "crimes I never got caught for." He didn't want extra security or protection, he insisted, because "I fight real good, without a knife. You come at me with a knife, I'll take it." He wanted me to leave a message with his mother for her not to worry about him. I wondered, as I left the cramped space, whether Robertson had become a greater menace through the experience of prison itself.)

Donald Garcia has many monikers—Big D, Pearly D, the Death Merchant, Stick-em-quick—from the days he helped found La Eme, the Mexican mafia, and the thirty-one years he spent in California penitentiaries. Now Big D is an esteemed gang peace counselor with his childhood friend "Blinky" Rodriguez in the San Fernando Valley. He was a force behind the peace treaty talks in Pacoima Park in 1992, where the slogan "no mothers crying, no children dying" was first heard. D and Blinky counted 172 sporting events they organized between gang rivals in those days. I met Big D at Blinky's office in 2003 to better understand his self-development. He was then sixty-two years old, powerfully built, still following a prison regimen of running, lifting, climbing, and doing push-ups everyday. A magnetic personality who continually waved his arms and punctuated his conversation by saying, "Check this out, bro," Big D had recently survived prostate cancer and was putting his faith in the Lord.

Big D's father was killed by a Pacoima gang when he was two years old. He grew up on the streets of San Fernando while his widowed mother worked in a tortilla factory. That was in 1943. D was mean and angry, always defending his family's honor, protecting little kids from bullies, and finally was sent to the Tracy correctional facility when he was seventeen. His crime was beating up three white guys with a blackjack he'd stolen from cops in Van Nuys. The white guys were taking advantage of a little kid by stealing his cigarettes, D says. When he entered the prison world in the mid-fifties, the majority of inmates were whites and they "had everything": the inmate clerks' positions, the flow of cigarettes and hard stuff. There weren't many blacks, he laughs, perhaps because "they were afraid of that needle, so they only pushed weed." Big D hated repeatedly being called "you dirty Mexican," so he and his partners decided to turn the tables, to make the whites afraid of *la raza*. "There's an old saying, you don't give a white man power, you don't give a black man knowledge, and you don't give a Mexican a knife." The Mexican mafia, as it soon was known, was formed to protect *la raza* in the prisons, but would grow over time into something "monstrous," a Frankenstein. Big D grew along with it, drawing convictions for manslaughter in 1958, second-degree murder in 1971, heroin smuggling, and gun possession as an ex-con. His longest single term was seven years. From experience, he learned how law enforcement manipulated gangs in prison. One time the guards encouraged him to "handle" a Black Guerrilla Family leader, but Big D knew the black inmate was about to be released and, out of respect, let the opportunity pass. On another occasion, when he had a murder charge, the narcs offered him justifiable homicide in exchange for giving up some of his connections. "It's just another Mexican," they said, but Big D passed that time as well. New values were stirring.

In 1982, Big D found Jesus Christ. It was timely, because "I was about to kill a dude." They had placed D into a Crip module, as the only Mexican, where he opened his "little store" of drugs and contraband. One day he learned that three black cell mates stole his goodies. That night, Big D planned to confront them, and kill the first one to get in his face. But the night before, Big D had a completely weird experience, a dream vision of his small grandson, who was already named Little D. Big D said that in his dream, "I seen his little face and what was gonna happen to him, he was gonna wind up on Death Row with me. I was raising him, he would wanna be like me, so we both would be on Death Row." Unexpectedly, Big D dissolved in tears, then began to wonder whether he wanted to kill his enemy. "I was tormented, saying 'I wanna do it,' 'I don't wanna do it.'" Right between his feet, he noticed, lay the Bible. "The only time I read it was in Tracy prison, because the paper was good for rolling cigarette papers." It was open to a passage from Luke.

> Love your enemies, do good to them which hate you
> Bless them that curse you . . .

By the morning, his torments had receded. "When I was gonna kill him, instead I felt a peace." He did his laundry instead. Now Big D was claiming both the mafia and Christianity. He knew he was straddling. In the Bible's Book of Revelation he read over and over the fate of the lukewarm:

> I would thou wert cold or hot, but because you are lukewarm and neither cold nor hot, I will vomit them out of my mouth.

Being lukewarm wasn't part of Big D's makeup, so he decided to commit himself further. At this point, his friends in La Eme thought D was going crazy. They dogged him in the yard when he turned up in Bible studies. He mocked them back, saying things like: "See them *nortenos* over there? I love 'em. See them *chiru-jos* [homosexuals] over there? I love 'em. The guards? I love 'em too. I'm supposed to love everybody equally. But you, *vatos*, I love especially, because you are deceived!"

When it became apparent over the next two years that the conversion was real, his homies left Big D alone. He eventually kicked heroin after a twenty-eight-year addiction. That was sixteen years ago. Even today, Big D is a man with huge respect in the Valley's streets and throughout the prisons. He might be a model for the Christian Right were it not for their Old Testament philosophy of punishment. Big D's story is one of survival in spite of the prison system. These days, Big D keeps a chaotic schedule of counseling young men individually, but when he talks, it's a chilling message about what prisons mean. When he talks in Youth Authority, he tells the wards that they are "the people they say will never amount to anything, but don't believe it." Big D cites as role models himself and his grandson, now in college, then asks if they are prepared for six challenges in prison:

Are you prepared to spend the rest of your life in prison? Are you prepared to kill? Are you prepared to get killed? Are you prepared to spend the rest of your life in SHU [Security Housing Unit—maximum security]?

Are you prepared to become a homosexual? I didn't suck no dick. I used to force suckers to suck my dick, I'm not proud of it, but I had to do it.

Finally, are you prepared to go insane? Are you prepared to commit suicide?

Big D's questions are challenging for a wider public than young inmates. What kinds of ideology, politics, and society have fostered such an atmosphere in its criminal justice system? Punishment is not about serving one's time, much less rehabilitation. Instead, it is about surviving systemic disrespect, physical and sexual assault, and an atmosphere of total paranoia where being perceived as weak has lethal consequences. The effect is to reinforce gang affiliations and harden whatever is left of the human spirit.

Survivors of these gulags like Big D, Monster Kody, Luis Rodriguez, and others often compare themselves to veterans suffering post-traumatic stress disorder (PTSD). The difference, as Monster points out, is that "there is no retreat to a place ten thousand miles away, where one can receive psychiatric attention with full benefits from the Veterans Administration. No, our problems are left to compound, and our traumatic stress thickens . . . is it any wonder our condition continues to worsen?"[28] For Rodriguez, "at 18 years old, I felt like a war veteran . . . I wanted the pain to end, the self-consuming hate to wither."[29] Tim O'Brien's description of Vietnam soldiers in his classic *The Things They Carried* contains a passage that would be familiar to veterans of our inner-city wars:

> They carried all the emotional baggage of men who might die . . . *They carried shameful memories.* They carried the common secret of cowardice barely restrained, the instinct to run or freeze or hide, and in many respects this was the heaviest burden of all, for it could never be put down, it required perfect balance and perfect posture. *They carried their reputations.* They carried the soldier's greatest fear, which was the fear of blushing. *Men killed, and died, because they were embarrassed not to.* It was what had brought them to the war in the first place, nothing positive, no dreams of glory, just to avoid the blush of dishonor. *They died so as not to die of embarrassment. . . . They were too frightened to be cowards.*[30]

When I once read this passage to a veteran of the Watts gang wars, he nodded affirmatively, saying: "Shit, that's growing up in a black neighborhood, afraid to blush. I had to prepare my son to fight like it was teaching reading and writing. I told him, don't let people punk you, put you in no headlock, or take your money. I taught my daughter how to fight, when they come up to you, hit 'em first. I am feeling bad because this is black on black. But once you get a rep as a buster or punk at school, it follows you your whole life."[31] A Crip who was interviewed for a class I taught made the point more succinctly: "Gotta keep it crippin for the dead ones, you got to."[32]

In the case of Korea, Vietnam, or Gulf War veterans, the cause was officially sanctioned, however demoralizing. For gang members, however, the killings are illegal acts in an illegal underworld, usually among people of the same race. Vietnam was an aggression against another people; gang wars are mainly intratribal, what the writer Wanda Coleman calls "the riot inside me."[33] In Vietnam, the hatred was channeled against an alien, officially sanctioned Other, while in gang wars the "enemy" is one's own kind, a reminder of oneself. Despite these fundamental differences, however, the centrality of reputation and shame is overwhelming.

For these reasons, the inner-peace process is integral to any solution to violence. Former gang member and professor at Cal State University—Long Beach Jose M. Lopez has studied post-traumatic stress disorders (PTSD) among Vietnam vets, Central American refugees, and inner-city youth, finding that traumas are perpetually reactivated by conditions on the streets.[34] Lopez discovered little children mimicking the violence-dominated world around them, acting out in games they called "county jail," "rock house," and "funeral" (in which some children took turns being a corpse, while others mourned or killed).[35] For similar reasons, Gilligan advocates and attempts to establish mental health counseling centers in prisons and jails.[36] As a result of such work, there were no riots or hostage-taking incidents during a five-year period in the Massachusetts penal system, and only one suicide and one homicide. Where prison guards routinely issued commands like, "Hey, shit-head! Time to go see the nut-doctor," Gilligan found that treating inmates with respect led directly to a reduction in violence. Later, in a San Francisco jailhouse experiment in anger management, Gilligan determined that violence was reduced simply by emphasizing inmate group discussions of the macho personality syndrome, programs of "restorative justice" involving meetings with victims' families, teaching of verbal and artistic self-expression, and other forms of therapeutic counseling. Gilligan frequently encountered the contradictions between good public policy and good politics, however. For example, among hundreds of inmates who obtained a college degree while in prison, none returned to prison over a period of twenty-five years. When the governor of Massachusetts heard the news, however, he held a press conference declaring his opposition to free college education for criminals.[37]

The Peace Process Network

Nothing stops a bullet like a job.
—*Father Gregory Boyle*

The need for an inner-peace process, led by former gang members or inmates with street knowledge, respect, and the capacity to be role models, must be reinforced by a peace movement in civil society demanding economic and social reform. While rare individuals occasionally triumph on their own—for example, the real-life story told in the film *Antwone Fisher*—the individualist dream is beyond realization for a majority of inner-city youth. The internal-peace process needs a transitional bridge to institutions that will support and open the doors to this generation of at-risk youth. As our network of activists found, their peace process sorely needed allies from mainstream religious, business, labor, and educational leaders to overcome isolation, prevent police harassment, and open up opportunities, including, most of all, remedial education, training, and employment at decent wages. Nothing could be worse than homeboys setting aside their weapons and distrust to explore options at the peace table only to learn, once again, that jail is a more likely future than jobs. As we visualized the peace process, it would develop organizationally in two circles: on the inside circle would be the peacemakers, working to end the madness they had begun, while the second circle, composed of civic leaders and peace advocates, would "watch their backs" against continued scapegoating.

The Peace Process Proposal

In July 2000, we offered a simplified, one-page "blueprint for gang peace" to local authorities, containing these specific provisions:

1. *The creation of a peace process coordinator.* The mayor should appoint a full-time peace process coordinator, someone like Father Gregory Boyle or Luis Rodriguez, to develop and implement a gang violence prevention plan.

2. *A peace council.* The mayor should appoint a peace council, to be chaired by the peace process coordinator, composed of individuals with a demonstrated record of effectiveness in working on gang truces and gang violence prevention programs, either on the streets, in CYA, or the state prison system. The peace council would have a staff of at least five full-time representatives (for the five subregions of L.A.).

3. *Violence prevention projects.* The peace council and coordinator should identify and become active in violence prevention efforts in at least three areas where gang tensions threaten to spiral out of control. The work should consist of mediation, identifying of grievances, and effective lobbying to bring needed resources to those communities.

4. *Education and skill training.* The coordinator should recommend to the mayor and city council a source of funding and an appropriate multi-agency task force to establish a certified program for education, remediation, job training, and life skills management implemented by former gang members who have changed their lives.

5. *Jobs.* The mayor and city council should require, as a condition of public subsidy or city permit, that all businesses over a certain size hire and retain at least one former gang member who has transitioned through the remedial program in item (4) and is qualified for work. This policy should apply to public agencies as well.

The purpose of the proposal was to begin elevating the violence prevention approach to a cornerstone of official policy. The point was to legitimize the peacemakers instead of demonize them, empower a class of disenfranchised youth, and to begin making institutions serve their needs using the powers of government. Along the way, we hoped, would come a transformation in police conduct as well. The core vision was to enact economic and social *policies that lessened shame.* We rejected the conservative market philosophy as bankrupt in its puritanical insistence that all that mattered was individual character and hard work. Obviously, by that measure, African slaves or Mexican farmworkers in California would have been richly rewarded for their generations of backbreaking labor. The conservative approach meant that homeboys or homegirls making $25,000 a year selling drugs should be grateful for $12,000 menial jobs at McDonald's ("slave jobs," they called them.) To stoke and reward the entrepreneurial spirit in the inner city still required such support mechanisms as education, training, loans, and credit. It was a cruel hoax to expect many former gang members to make it as entrepreneurs on their own, though many would try.

Reforming the New Deal

The traditional liberal model of job creation was more attractive. In the New Deal era, government recognized the right of industrial unions to collective bargaining and put millions of the unemployed to work directly, building such lasting structures as the L.A. County Hospital, where generations of elderly, the poor, and countless injured gang members have received their care. Great Society public employment programs made a difference in inner cities through the seventies, at least by absorbing the energies of many inner-city youth eight hours a day, and the paychecks included a powerful bonus of self-esteem.[38] Those public employment programs would have to be targeted to the gang subculture, and be more than a token New Deal in nature. The modest recommendations of William Julius Williams, originator of the "underclass" thesis, for public sector employment *below* the minimum wage is an example of how tepid liberalism has been forced to become.[39] The central notion of the New Deal was dignity for working people, as expressed in the Wagner Act—not simply low-wage jobs to keep the unemployed busy. Having extolled the nineties economic boom as good for black people because it enabled more of them to leave the ghetto for the suburbs, Williams later concluded that concentrated poverty was on the rise again, amidst the loss of 2.4 million jobs in 2001–2003, the first two years of George W. Bush's administration. However, he seemed reluctant to endorse bolder policies of targeted government intervention on grounds of political realism.[40]

A new New Deal would have to focus on at-risk youth, specifically gang members and former inmates, by creating public sector partnerships with community-based organizations working on the inner-peace process, empowering youth, and stabilizing neighborhoods. When I once tried reforming job training programs in California, I was shocked to discover that twenty-two separate agencies processed nearly $2 billion in public funds annually. Such programs tend toward "creaming," that is, targeting the job applicants most likely to succeed, thus producing good outcome numbers for oversight committees. But "creaming" by definition leaves the hard-core unemployed to curdle. Existing incentives would have to be reworked fundamentally to reward a focus on the most at-risk youth—that is, those most likely to fail. Nor could job creation be a stand-alone objective. The focus of most schools, community agencies, and the criminal justice system would have to change fundamentally as well, toward rehabilitating those now left behind. Perhaps the greatest single opportunity lies in restoring education, training, and community college programs in juvenile and state prisons (while assuring those same opportunities to law-abiding citizens as well). For instance, inmates in a rare California college program are intensely interested in business training "because parolees have trouble landing jobs and like the idea of working independently."[41] Instead, the punishment mentality dominates the correctional systems, and rehabilitation programs are steadily slashed.

The decades of the eighties and nineties, when gang strife was at its worst, were a time of deindustrialization, privatization, deregulation, and countless schemes to dismantle the New Deal tradition of government intervention. The New York City area lost 500,000 manufacturing jobs, resulting in drastic funding cuts for inner-city services.[42] South Central Los Angeles lost a net 50,000 jobs in the decade between 1992 and 2002.[43] In other cities across the country, manufacturing jobs that paid a middle-class wage to working-class people were slashed and replaced with low-wage service sector employment. The south, home of the sixties civil rights movement, led the country in manufacturing job losses in the nineties, and Atlanta became a crime capital.[44] The sociologist John Hagedorn studied how gangs reemerged in Milwaukee among African Americans and Latinos in response to this deindustrialization pattern.[45] Unlike previous generations who "matured out" of the gang lifestyle into working-class jobs, Hagedorn found there were no entry level manufacturing jobs to "mature" into. (The sociologist Joan Moore found the same pattern in East Los

Angeles in a 1991 study.[46]) Hagedorn observed that the former Milwaukee jobs were being replaced by an "abundance of part-time jobs in the illegal drug economy."[47] In addition, he found a shocking withdrawal of government-sponsored social programs from the inner-city neighborhoods they were intended to serve; for example, zip code 53206, in the heart of the Milwaukee ghetto, lacked even a single alcohol/drug treatment facility.[48] More broadly, a study done of the national labor market for sixteen-to-twenty-four-year olds showed that, in 1999, only fifty-four of every 100 young adults lacking a high school diploma were employed at all; and only 23 percent of black high school dropouts were employed full-time.[49] A *New York Times* headline summarized their status as "on the way to nowhere."[50]

The Drug War and Gang Violence

In formulating an economic development approach to peace, coming to terms with the war on drugs cannot be avoided. First, what I have called the inner-peace process requires a greater shift to treatment for addicted gang members and inmates. The war on drugs is currently weighted lopsidedly toward war and suppression. Prisons and jails are filled with drug offenders, few of whom receive any treatment before being returned to the streets. Nationally, only 1 in 6 of the 800,000 inmates incarcerated for drugs receives treatment.[51] New York City has some 200,000 heroin addicts but only 38,000 in methadone treatment.[52] In California, the typical drug offender is released to the streets in eighteen to twenty-four months, although a voter-passed initiative now mandates rehabilitation for first-time offenders.[53] The discrepancy in sentencing between users of crack versus powder cocaine deeply aggravates the racial double standards applied to African American and Latino inmates.[54] But in addition to more treatment and reform of sentencing laws, the glaring need is to create jobs in the inner city that are more lucrative than the drug trade. Why have our leaders so disinvested from jobs and training for low-skilled inner-city youth at a time when the underground economy beckons the same youth with real, if illegitimate, income? Drug dealing and illegal sweatshop employment have become key economic engines for marginalized inner-city youth. In a rational society, a strategy of fighting crime by driving young people into the underground economy should be a nonstarter.

Consider the intersection of the gang wars and drug wars during the height of the killings starting in the late eighties through the nineties in Los Angeles. First, nineteen elite narcotics officers in the L.A. sheriff's department were convicted in the early nineties for involvement in the crack cocaine market. They skimmed thousands of dollars, beat up suspects, planted drugs, and falsified affidavits. Some of the ill-gotten funds were used to buy vacation homes, big-screen televisions, and, in one instance, a buttocks liposuction.[55] Then two city council members were forced to resign amidst charges and allegations of heavy cocaine use. One of them, Mike Hernandez, with an alleged $150-a-day cocaine habit, represented the immigrant Pico-Union community, a major "safe zone" for receiving, cutting, and bundling cocaine for large-scale buyers. Not by coincidence, Pico-Union is where the Rampart police scandal unfolded.[56] Despite his flaws, Hernandez was the council's most outspoken advocate of inner-city jobs and critic of police brutality. He was surveilled and taken down in 1997 by a secretive LAPD task force known as IMPACT (Inter-agency Metropolitan Police Apprehension Taskforce). At about the same time, officers in the LAPD's Rampart division, which covers Pico-Union, were involved in a pattern of planting and selling drugs themselves, which led to the Rampart scandal (to be described in full in chapter five). Not long after, it was charged that an LAPD deputy chief helping direct the official inquiry into Rampart had laundered hundreds of thousands of dollars in the cocaine profits of his own incarcerated son.[57] The pervasive culture of officials' drug corruption was reminiscent of alcohol Prohibition in the twenties.[58]

Specifically, the parallels between recent gang violence and the bloodshed during Prohibition are striking but hardly mentioned in most debates over the drug war. The modern drug trade is not the underlying cause of gang feuds—" 'gangs equals drugs' is a myth," says a RAND researcher, among many others[59]—but homicides steadily escalated when crack cocaine was introduced in the eighties. The FBI's national data on gang-related homicides show the pattern: 288 (1985),

357 (1986), 395 (1987), 428 (1988), 678 (1989), 905 (1990), 1192 (1991), 994 (1992), 1362 (1993).[60] What happened was described in 1997 by Fox Butterfield in a *New York Times* series.[61] The legislative war on crack began in 1986 after the death of basketball star Len Bias, though it was learned one year later that Bias had died of *powder* cocaine, not crack. William Bennett, the chief of the nation's drug war, was calling it "World War III," and he warned that crack soon would invade every American home. Crack became the only drug that carried a five-year mandatory sentence for possession. James Q. Wilson declared approvingly that "putting people in prison has been the single most important thing we've done to reduce crime" as the U.S. began to imprison more people on drug charges than all the prisoners in England, France, Germany, and Japan combined. Only 5 percent of those swept away were high-level drug dealers, according to the Sentencing Commission, while the rest were small-time, street-level dealers loosely affiliated with street gangs or crews. Many were homeboys trying to survive, but there also came a new, armed breed of hustlers seeking quick fortunes by any means necessary. When Monster Kody returned from prison, for example, the streets were different. As a close homeboy told him,

> It's the dope, man, it has tore the 'hood up. Check this out, there are some homies who got a grip from slangin', but they don't come around 'cause they think the homies who ain't got nothin' gonna jack 'em. And the homies who ain't got nothin' feel like those who do got a grip have left them behind. So there is a lot of backbiting, snitchin' and animosity around here now.[62]

The most famous case was that of "Freeway" Ricky Ross, who grew up in a Crip neighborhood to become a multimillionaire crack dealer and central figure in a controversy still mired in ambiguity. Ross, who is serving a life sentence in federal prison, obtained his heroin from Nicaraguan dealers who partly funded the Reagan administration's illegal Contra wars with the proceeds. When Gary Webb, a *San Jose Mercury-News* reporter, revealed that the Nicaraguans were CIA "assets," the controversy exploded. Three major newspapers—the *New York Times,* the

Los Angeles Times, and the *Washington Post*—published massive articles, all rebutting any conspiratorial allegations about the CIA flooding ghettos with crack. The CIA director, John Deutsch, spoke to angry African American audiences in L.A., again dismissing the rumor. Congresswoman Maxine Waters relentlessly pressed for deeper explanations. I attended one meeting between Deutsch and some twenty-five black leaders where he promised that the agency would get to the bottom of the charges. The audience was understandably puzzled, never having received a briefing from a spy before. Peacemaker "Bo" Taylor asked how such an agency could investigate itself, since the institution was committed to deception. Deutsch promised unconvincingly that the agency's inspector-general was independent. Someone next asked, "If you do answer us, how can we know you're telling the truth, since you are supposed to lie for a living?"

Gary Webb's reputation as a reporter was destroyed, even though he himself never published the conspiracy theory. Lost in the journalistic furor about Webb was the fact that the U.S. General Accounting Office (GAO) had written in 1989 that "the lucrative crack market changed the black gangs from traditional neighborhood street gangs to extremely violent criminal groups."[63] The CIA later acknowledged that it had failed to "cut off relationships with individuals supporting the Contra program who were alleged to have engaged in drug trafficking activity."[64] Further, the agency revealed that from 1982 to 1995 there was an internal agreement not to report on allegations of drug trafficking by "agents, assets [and] non-staff employees" of the agency.[65]

I never met Ricky Ross, but I interviewed his closest homeboy, Chico Brown, just after Chico's release from an eight-year conspiracy conviction in federal prison in 2002. He was the first inmate in the new privatized federal prison in Taft, California, run by a corporation—Wackenhut—which, by coincidence, was involved with murky security operations in El Salvador during the Contra wars in Nicaragua.[66] Dark-skinned, well-dressed, and slightly uneasy amidst his new freedom, Brown became a counselor at A Place Called Home, a gang intervention center in South Central. Still known as "Chico from the Pocket," a Corner Pocket Crip, he wanted to set some history straight. In the early eighties, "when the drug money was big, gang shootings were down. Everybody was happy, everybody was into making money," millions of dollars. A wave of drug conspiracy prosecutions later in the eighties, however, meant that "everybody and their momma could go to jail for conspiracy. Nobody I knew got caught with cocaine, it was wiretaps or somebody telling on them." The street killings rose when the raids and arrests came down, because prices went up "and you couldn't make any money." The drug warriors' onslaught pushed the dealers elsewhere for better prices, even out of state. These individuals were primarily drug dealers, not gang members, but they recruited according to gang territories. "Once you're a drug dealer, you don't be active [in a gang], but the younger ones be active."

Chico grew up in Compton, saw his best friend killed by Bloods in school, and was a pallbearer by age fifteen. Like Ricky Ross, Chico's favorite film was Al Pacino's *Scarface,* which came out as a 1983 remake just in time for the crack cocaine epidemic. Now, while taking his own life one day at a time, Chico counsels neighborhood kids that they could face adult time, and he takes them on visits to prisons, hospitals, and morgues. He is still troubled by questions he can't answer: "The US makes it hard to get Cuban cigars into the country. We got technology to find caves in Afghanistan. So how do tons of cocaine get here?"

A similar kind of preventable mayhem broke out eighty years ago when liquor was banned by the Harrison Narcotics Act and the Volstead Act, which enforced the Eighteenth Amendment. While conservative preachers like Billy Sunday were claiming that "the reign of tears is over" and "the slums will soon be a memory," street gangs became organized crime syndicates during Prohibition, the nation's prisons filled to capacity, a two-tier system of justice was rampant,[67] and homicide rates grew to ten per 10,000 of the population, a 78 percent jump over the pre-Prohibition period.[68] When Prohibition was repealed in 1933, gang homicide rates began declining to pre-Prohibition levels. The New Deal simultaneously began to provide work opportunities for America's then-army of the unemployed.[69]

The free-market economist Milton Friedman has noted that national homicide rates started climbing again "after Nixon introduced his drug war," and believes that "a reduction in the homicide rate from its average during the eighties to its average during the fifties would, with our current population, mean a saving in excess of 10,000 lives a year."[70] Elaborating Friedman's model, the economist Jeffrey Miron published research in 1999 concluding that prohibitions "create black markets, and in black markets participants use violence to resolve commercial disputes." Obviously, some of Friedman's contemporary neoconservative disciples part company with their philosopher-king because of the greater emphasis they place on enforcing Puritan morality. Governor Jeb Bush, whose daughter suffers from crack cocaine addiction, declared in 2002 that he would "like to wave a magic wand and have this *devil* be, you know, *exorcised* from her, from her life, from her soul . . . But I can't. She has to do it." (As punishment, his daughter received a ten-day sentence in 2002 for concealing crack in her shoe in violation of a court-ordered rehab program. It seemed more a public relations exercise than an exorcism.)[71]

In summary, if alcohol prohibition and the first New Deal are any model, a revived New Deal for inner cities will have to offer better alternatives than drug wars for possession and street dealing. Instead of allowing the drug trade or McDonald's to set wage standards, government will need to enforce a strategy of living wages and benefits in the inner city if Americans—including Jeb Bush—want to beat the devil of the drug economy. In addition, targeted drug treatment programs will have to be boosted. Whether legalizing drugs is the trade-off necessary to end the violence should be a matter of open inquiry, not the pretext for a new Inquisition. Friedman's pure free-market model cannot be an ultimate solution to the crisis of drugs, gangs, and violence. The legalization of alcohol created a liquor lobby with enormous political power, a culture that glamorized drinking through advertising and entertainment, budgets that underfunded treatment programs, and woeful laws against drunk driving for several decades. Legalizing drugs on a laissez-faire basis would lead to similar disasters. But the drug war, like the gang war, can be shifted from a military paradigm to a medical one. Starting with marijuana, certain drugs could be decriminalized, dispensed through approved outlets, forbidden to be advertised, their revenues prohibited as a source of campaign contributions, and taxed to fund prevention and treatment programs. Such sweeping reforms would not end the gang phenomenon, which originates from a deeper alienation, but they certainly would remove a major factor in gang violence.

In summary, the proposed peace process would include not only a return to rehabilitation, with a new emphasis on counseling for war traumas, but a return to the New Deal tradition of government leadership, with a new emphasis on targeting those currently trapped in the streets, pushed into the drug trade, or scarred by repeated incarceration. These are enormous challenges in a period of triumphal market fundamentalism, but they must be faced one way or another. The question is not whether government should intervene in the economy, but whether it only intervenes to police inner cities, construct prisons, and manage the outsourcing of jobs. The result of such law-and-order priorities will be a deepening racial polarization of American society and our increased isolation from global standards of social justice. Until the national political climate changes, there is plenty of work in saving lives at community levels all over the country and, increasingly, all over the world.

The 1998 Santa Monica–Culver City Gang Truce

Unexpectedly, the chance to stop gang violence arose in my neighborhood in Santa Monica in 1998. Like most Santa Monicans, I had been blind to the history of gangs in the Pico barrio on the south side of the coastal city until the realities exploded in a sudden rash of killings. Then I began to learn the history of this other Santa Monica.

Gang formation and warfare had a long history on the west side of Los Angeles, in Santa Monica, West L.A., Culver City, and Venice. Its roots lay in the U.S.–Mexico conflict going back to the nineteenth century (some would say to the Conquest of the indigenous, as depicted on contemporary barrio murals). A long tradition of "social banditry" (criminals to the Anglos, folk heroes to the Mexicans) preceded the formation of twentieth-century gangs. In the immediate wake of the Mexican Revolution, nearly 400 Mexicans were killed in El Paso, Texas, where the term *pachuco* originated, between 1911 and 1919.[1] In the wake of the revolution, several million Mexican refugees began arriving in the Southwest, creating small barrios and laboring mostly in agriculture as exploited seasonal workers. Their lives turned upside down once again in the thirties when over 1 million were deported back to Mexico. Known as *repatriadas*, tens of thousands were placed on trains from Los Angeles after a campaign of fear generated by the L.A. Chamber of Commerce. Since most of them were born in the U.S., they lived as stigmatized strangers in Mexico, learning the Spanish language that was prohibited in L.A.'s schools. Amidst this turmoil, which shredded families and reshaped identity, new bonds emerged among young people on the streets.[2] One tradition, known as *palomilla*, or adolescent male bonding for mere "mischief and adventure," became a cultural basis of Mexican street gangs.[3]

Manny Lares was a thirty-year-old, fourth-generation gang member in Santa Monica who inherited the hidden history. The earliest gang formation in Santa Monica was known as "the tomato gang," for the early fieldworkers. Each of Manny's uncles, on his mother's side, were attached to gangs, car clubs, and "whatever" in the Santa Monica area. There also were nephews of his grandfather, cousins, and their brothers; and, on his father's side, a younger brother and three nephews. "There's a whole bunch of us, and most of them have been in prison," he says of his family.[4]

Few outside the area understand the historic tradition of west side gangs in the state's prison system. Based on the car clubs' tradition, members refer to their gangs as "cars" in which they ride. In prison, "if you are in the Westside car, you are all right, you have a lot of clout, it has a certain style to it, that car has a strong presence in the prison system."

So it was that Manny Lares, in 1992, at age twenty, inherited a leadership role as L.A.'s gang wars were reaching their peak. "What happened was, things were getting wild. Pipe bombs were being used. Women being hit. People being assaulted with their parents at the mall. The old code of ethics we had all lived by had broken down. Drive bys were the talk of the town." In 1992, someone in the Venice neighborhood named Rick Mejia called Manny. Things had gone so far that three women from Santa Monica, and one from Venice, were shot. Manny took part in his first negotiations to stop the violence. It was an important rite of passage. A year later, at a huge meeting in Elysian Park, the Mexican mafia (La Eme) would call a cease-fire on drive-bys among Latino gangs. But the earliest decisions to prevent the violence, according to Manny, were "decisions made by the guys on the street," from the bottom up, not by shot-callers in prisons.

Manny had never met Rick before. They talked at the Lares' family restaurant on Pico Boulevard, not far from Santa Monica College. Rick brought along Manny Flores from Culver City, who had negotiated a Christmas season cease-fire. The possibility of a broader end to the violence was in the air. Soon, all four west side neighborhoods were meeting regularly, trying to deal with crises on the street. Representatives of other neighborhoods, like Lennox or Inglewood, would sometimes show up, saying, "We wanna get in the car, too, you know what I mean?" Manny's fledgling notion was to focus only on the west side con-flicts, but he was overridden. So many newcomers wanted to get in the "car" that sensitive discussions about squashing the local shootings were derailed. The meet-ings stalled, but the grass-roots pressure to reduce the violence rose.

Across town, an Eme leader named Ernest "Chuco" Castro, who later proved to be an LAPD informant, was coordinating efforts to manage the widening war. La Eme had placed a "green light" on a growing Salvadoran gang, called Mara Salvatrucha (MS), which included a young man named Alex Sanchez who would play a historic role during the L.A. Rampart scandal a few years later. The green light meant that all neighborhoods with an Eme allegiance should attack the green-lighted MS neighborhoods, whose offenses might be refusing to pay "taxes" to La Eme from local drugs sales, robberies, or extortion. To turn off the green light required doing something significant, like turning over $5,000 in cash and a dozen guns to whomever was taxing them.[5] When the "taxes" were paid, the neighborhood would get a "red light," which meant "no one could fuck with MS." Lifting the green light meant that the first tentative "moment of inclusion" was allowed by Mexican gangs toward their rivals among Salvadoran immigrants in places like Pico-Union.

When "Chuco" (the future police informant) helped mobilize more than 1,000 gang members to the big gathering in Elysian Park on September 18, 1993, Manny arrived in a vanguard "car" filled with peacemakers from west side gangs. The total crew consisted of four or five carloads from Venice, Culver City, and Santa Monica, who had been still trucing for some eighteen months. They were jittery as they approached the park, which happens to be only a short walk from the Los Angeles police academy. "We didn't know what was gonna go down. So we are coming down a hill and see an undercover [police] car with one of those hand-held sound catchers you see at football games, so I see this and I am thinking this is really stupid, we shouldn't be here." Alex Sanchez was arriving, too, with a carload of nervous Salvadorans, as hundreds of rival homies occupied the park in a virtual congress of gangs from East L.A., Mexico, and Central America.

When he arrived on the grounds, Manny noticed the individual named Chuco talking "a lot of high-powered bullshit," which triggered Manny's paranoia, since "he knows the cops are here, how could he not know? The cops are all over the place." People kept arriving by the hundreds, including many just released from prison. Manny remembers walking through thirty guys in a parking lot "with only six bullets in your gun, fifteen if you're rich, but everyone was cool." The message of the day was to stop the violence, which Manny's neighborhoods already had begun to do. Chuco grew louder and louder, naming or asking about key leaders from different neighborhoods. Later, when it became known that Chuco had been an informant, many wondered if the rumors he spread had caused distrust and divisions among gang members trying to bring peace between Monica and Culver City. "Who knows, maybe he settled a lot of scores for the LAPD," Manny observed.

Who could know? Law enforcement's long struggle to destroy this supergang, not to mention La Eme itself, is shrouded in secrecy, rumor, and intentional deceit. What is known is that La Eme was formed in the California high-security prison system in the 1950s among Mexican Americans who came of age in the earlier zoot-suit era. It was a time of intense discrimination preceding the rise of Chicano power in the sixties. The pressures included hostility from African American inmates in addition to the dominant Anglo culture. A combination of angry nationalism and gangster dreams created a tightly knit network of *carnales* (brothers) inside and outside the penal colonies. A surviving founder of La Eme, Donald "Big D" Garcia, told me the original purpose was to protect *la raza* behind bars, then, like Frankenstein, it took on a life of its own. Films like *Blood In, Blood Out* and *American Me* depicted some of the history. From the dominant law enforcement perspective, La Eme was nothing but an organized syndicate of street gangs. Such a vision suited prosecutors and stoked public fears, but the truth of the Mexican gang experience was more complicated. One of the key distinctions, according to a veteran of L.A. County's antigang unit, was that "the Mexican Mafia is a business, [while] street gangs are a lifestyle . . . the Mexican Mafia tends to be structured, with an identified leadership and codified rules of conduct. Street gangs come purely from emotion. They rebel against any authority, even among their own."[6] "If the Mexican Mafia tells you to kill your mother, you kill your mother—or else. [But] that is totally alien to the street gangs."[7] As the *Los Angeles Times* later wrote, there was "growing resistance on the streets to Eme,"[8] truce ventures were emerging like Manny's, and others were reported in San Diego, Riverside, San Bernadino, and Santa Ana.[9] In Pacoima Park in the Valley, "Blinky" Rodriguez and "Big D," now a born-again Christian, organized sports events between rivals and opened and closed their events in prayer, with La Eme watching but not controlling.[10]

La Eme's purpose in calling the Elysian Park meeting was to reassert authority on the streets by issuing a "no drive-by" edict with warnings that any offenders would be "dealt with" in prison. There were to be no more killings of women and children. If there was "business to take care of," it would follow the older tradition of one-on-one battles. The change was articulated as *"por la raza"* and for honor. There were other factors, of course. The rampant drive-bys were bad for the business of drug trafficking because they brought down police heat. Also, the African American truce established in Watts the previous year served as an example and an implicit challenge. With race wars expanding in the prisons, if the blacks were coming together in a united front, perhaps it was unity time for Mexicans as well. "Something that big," Manny remarked later, "you never know what the motives are. You kind of feed into arguments to justify what people want. If it's the blacks—we gotta be prepared. If it's money—this is a better way to get your dope sales on. If it's cultural nationalists—the argument was, we shouldn't be killing our people." In the end, Manny said, the result was less killing for the first time since his childhood (a reduction confirmed by police statistics as well).[11] The *Los Angeles Times* reported that "gang members seem almost relieved that they have been given an honorable way to let tensions cool."[12] La Eme was "credited with decelerating one of the bloodiest cycles" in L.A.'s gang history.[13] Brother Modesto Leon, director of a Pico-Union school for troubled youths, told the media that "regardless of how the message is getting out, I think it's something positive."[14]

Was it possible the Elysian Park event was also a setup? Until the unlikely day that police files are disclosed, there can be no certain answer. Certainly the pressure for truces came from the bottom up, not simply the top down. Given all their means of surveillance, did the police know, exploit, or channel the sentiment as it evolved? In November 1993, shortly after the Elysian Park gathering, police raided Chuco's Alhambra home, shovels in hand, and dug up guns buried beneath the place. Perhaps the guns were his, perhaps not, but Chuco was in big trouble as an ex-con, drug addict, and active member of La Eme since 1983.[15] But his bail was mysteriously lowered from $500,000 to $100,000, and he used $10,000 from a drug sale to buy his freedom.[16] At that point, according to official police claims, Chuco turned informant against a score of his Eme *carnales*. Or the arrest might have been a cover story to create the appearance that his previous activity, such as the Elysian Park convention, was genuine. The federal charge on Chuco—illegal possession of weapons—was dropped. Instead, the FBI placed him in a government protection program, and paid him as much as $200,000.[17]

It was the first time that the federal government had employed the Racketeer Influenced and Corrupt Organizations (RICO) Act in Los Angeles.[18] Under the law, which assumes a vertically structured organizational conspiracy, prosecutors can utilize previous convictions in state courts as evidence of a conspiratorial criminal enterprise. The landmark 1997 Eme case, built on Chuco's testimony, lasted six months, resulting in convictions for seven murders, seven attempted murders, and several lesser findings of guilt. Ten reputed La Eme figures were given life sentences, two received thirty-two-year terms, and seven pled guilty to lesser charges.[19] Three of those murders were of consultants to Edward James Olmos's movie *American Me,* which had been filmed in East L.A.'s Ramona Gardens housing projects and which portrayed sodomy and betrayal. Chuco testified for two months about Eme meetings he'd secretly videotaped or recorded with an FBI wire. In one meeting, he raised the question whether a hit should be placed on Olmos; in another, he seemed to order an attack on African American inmates. Some of the testimony confirmed the complexity of the La Eme's structure; according to the *Times*'s account, Chuco stated that "no one is really in charge of the Eme. It has a loose command structure with no 'generals,' making it difficult to determine if the word of one *carnal*—the term Eme members use to refer to themselves—carries any real authority within the group. It's hard to confirm who really is a *carnal*. Government tapes show that at some of the videotaped hotel meetings, even some of the Eme *carnales* present couldn't figure out who was a member."[20]

The truce process on the west side lasted from 1993 (which began with the talk between Manny Lares and Rick Mejia at the Lares' family restaurant on Pico Boulevard) to approximately 1998. As a result of the Eme indictments and revelations of FBI undercover operations, Manny and many others stopped going to truce meetings at all. In the late nineties, a six-month war broke out between Latinos and the black Shoreline Crips in Venice, which finally ended though negotiations again involving Rick Mejia. Meanwhile, in Santa Monica, "everything was cool," according to Manny, due to the truces mediated at neighborhood levels. There were some shootings, Manny recalled, but "they were from outside neighborhoods who would come in and shoot, and you didn't know who they were, about once a year is all." Manny turned to strategies of community organizing, eventually taking an outreach job with the L.A. Housing Authority's Youth in Action program. "I learned how to speak my mind, but nothing concrete, nothing about how to make programs work." He became interested in forming a chapter of Barrios Unidos, the gang intervention project started by Nane Alejandes in Santa Cruz. He liked the spirituality component of Barrios Unidos, "which was lacking in our lives." I attended the founding meeting of the Santa Monica chapter; of the thirty to forty people in attendance, many were members of Manny's extended family, many of them former convicts.

I asked Manny once about his estrangement from his father, the owner of the Lares' restaurant and another property on Pico. As a teenager, he said, he once tried to kill him with a knife.

My dad used to come home drunk at two or three in the morning, and think of things to get off his chest, right there on the spot. This one night while I was on the couch, he went in to say some shit to one of my brothers. So I said, why don't you shut the fuck up and be a father. I was swinging, and just before I stabbed him in the neck my brother hit my arm with a judo hold. That was the last time my father and I had a confrontation. It was like a right of passage thing.

Despite the incarceration of so many family members, who sometimes even shared the same cells, Manny had managed to avoid anything more than brief juvenile detention. What was the difference? I asked him. Does it make you proud or doomed or both? "I don't know how it makes me feel," he admitted.

It doesn't make me feel anything, just that that's my family, it's my life. I can't be proud of it, 'cuz it's stupid. But I can't feel ashamed of it, 'cuz it's my family, you know, straight up. It's just the way it is. I'd like to take some of that misdirected energy and use it to advantage, to build something that will last long past all this. All that waste in prison. We have to be smart in what we're doing. Learn how to play the game like those who are winning play it. When we get in the game and control some piece of it, maybe then we can change the rules. But it's hard when you're on the outside. You feel so vulnerable.

When I hired Manny, he was about twenty-eight and pony-tailed, light-skinned with indigenous features, an aggressive, self-taught intellectual of the streets. He was learning rapidly how to "get in the game," and I believed in his growth. He was struggling every day, too, with a shaky marriage to his high school sweetheart, Belinda, trying to raise two kids, fighting off a drinking problem that had landed him an occasional DUI. But he was a visionary leader, hungry for analysis, one of the few who could thrive in the contradictory environments of the street and the legislature.

My understanding of Santa Monica's hidden street crisis tragically deepened when Cesar Martin, a high school friend of my son Troy, and a player on the junior varsity baseball team I coached, was gunned down in January 1996. Cesar was a life-of-the-party young man who had just turned twenty years old. He was at a party in Mar Vista on January 20 when some young men from a West L.A. neighborhood, known as the Sotels, arrived on the scene. There might have been an insult exchanged over a young woman—nothing more. Cesar and his friends left the party to drive back to Santa Monica, but were followed by the Sotels, who fired several rounds into the back of the vehicle carrying Cesar. By a horrific act of fate, a bullet passed through the trunk, backseat, and passenger seat before lodging in Cesar's vital organs. He died at the hospital. Another rider in the car was critically wounded. It was the twentieth killing of a young man in the Pico neighborhood since the mid-eighties.

This was a personal introduction to the tragedy of gang violence and the beginning of a long association with Cesar's mother, Celina (whom I eventually hired to manage my office). That it happened in the Santa Monica area, not far from the school my son Troy attended, brought home the impact in a way that hearing about street killings never could. Cesar had not been a gang member, but in the end it didn't matter. He was part of a youth culture in which neighborhood gangs, guns, drugs and alcohol, and hair-trigger macho rituals and rivalries were ever-present. It was the world where the only experts were unrecognized young men like Manny.

Troy and his friends were part of an overlapping world. They hung out every night in an apartment that served as a club house, attached to my bungalow home in Sunset Park, a few blocks from Santa Monica High and the Pico neighborhood. It was a time when rap tapes and graffiti were the emergent currency of hip-hop culture. Troy's "gang" called itself Payback. It was somewhere between a graffiti crew and a pack of wannabees. They tended to be artists drawn to the outlaw style. Troy's surreptitious moniker was "Despo," and it was appearing on freeway bridges and phone booths across L.A. County.

I could warn them, ask them questions, but stopping them seemed like trying to stop testosterone itself. I racked my brain for an answer, but there was none. To physically crack down on my son would have no greater effect than a police sweep through a neighborhood. And, after all, he was the seed of rebellious parents. Was my divorce from his mother, Jane Fonda, when Troy was turning sixteen, the cause, or was the outlaw gene implanted long before? Maybe I was a blind enabler, but maybe, too, he was right to rage against the hypocrisy of the society we had bequeathed him. I decided to not only counsel but to listen to my son, and through that decision I began to learn about hip-hop, gangs, and what he already defiantly called "my generation." Troy carried rap music, recorded on pirate tapes, in his jacket pocket. He showed me photographs of amazing murals painted overnight on walls downtown. Since crews routinely painted over each others' murals, all that remained was the creative moment recorded in memory and photograph. The point was that creativity could never be institutionalized, he said. The pure act was all that mattered. Turning private property into live graffiti displays was a statement against a society that would not listen to its young people. He lobbied me to make the government set aside public walls for graffiti crews.

Finally, inevitably, Troy and his friends were arrested with spray paint on a dark stretch of the Mulholland Hills. Though he was underage, his name (and that of his parents) was published coast-to-coast. He now felt bad for the embarrassment he felt he'd visited on his parents. His mother and I wondered what else he would learn from the experience. The deterrent effect of his arrest was offset by the "rep" it secured him in graffiti circles at the time. I felt I could be nothing more than a guardian angel. What finally diminished his nocturnal activity was the passage of time and, in particular, the evolution of the subculture into both commercialization (selling out) and dangerous destruction (as crews turned violent, Troy received threatening messages on his answering machine from challengers). Over time, he still identified with hip-hop as the religion of his generation, and evolved into an actor-artist. Many others could have made the same transition if the jobs were available.

He was lucky. Troy could have been Cesar Martin on that night in January 1996. Few Santa Monica parents at the time knew what their teenagers were doing in cars, at parties, on the streets, over weekends. The very nature of adolescent rebellion required coming of age without parental consent. If the safer rebellions of middle-class youth included such elements of danger, how much greater the risk for kids growing up in zip codes of hardship? It was no accident that the Mexican-American kids on Troy's baseball teams might suffer the fate of Cesar. Manny Lares knew this, that the gang truces of the nineties were temporary fixes in the race against fate. He was quick to understand, where the authorities were clueless, that the shooting of Cesar Martin was a sign that the west side truce would not hold. The Sotels had carried out a blatant drive-by against an innocent group from Santa Monica. Fortunately, the two shooters were immediately arrested and eventually convicted. But law enforcement could not arrest the dynamic that was beginning to unravel.

Manny was trying his best. Before I hired him, he'd continued to search for ways to design his new-style gang "car" that could save lives. At the housing authority job, he observed and learned from programs that failed. He took young homies on trips to Disneyland, helped them with their homework, and concluded that "nothing was coming of it." He attended and watched residents' assemblies where "they just spun their wheels." He found himself "chasing kids down and saying, hey, you signed up for this program, and watching kids not believe in themselves." Manny started to build his own theory of organizing.

> A lot of kids can't shut up. They just run their fucking mouth. Which is a bad thing in school, you get thrown out. But what I started to do is put them in front of the class, fill them with information, have them start spitting it out, see if I could turn them into leaders. Build on what they have to offer. So all of a sudden the same kid who is drawing all over his desk, which was a bad thing for the school turned into a good thing as I saw it—we could put him on the computer, or get him to make flyers or posters. Or a kid that intimidates or bullies, because he can manipulate kids to feel bad about themselves, can also be taught to manipulate people to do good and feel good about themselves.

Manny started discovering that he had a talent for turning the "baddest" into natural-born leaders, a "gang" of troublemaking community activists. He started his chapter of Barrios Unidos with four primary principles he believed necessary "to be successful in life":

First, the lesson of generating constructive self-discipline. "Finishing what you start—most kids never finish. You have to honor your commitments. They never finish school, they never even finish their prison terms."

Second, positive self-image or esteem. "Understanding what your talent is, how it contributes to building the community in general, and what your role is."

Third, concrete tangible skills. "That's what education is supposed to teach, but if they fail to have the first two principles, all the skills in the world won't make them successful."

Fourth and hardest, "What you do to implement these skills has to be real." For example, "If we are teaching kids to speak out for themselves, we have to organize opportunities for them to be heard. If we are teaching business skills, there must be money out there when you are ready to open a business."

Manny wanted me to see these hard-learned principles in action. He invited me to a hip-hop clothing store opening on Lincoln Boulevard, several blocks from my house, the creation of "guys from the neighborhood," particularly one named Frank Juarez. They were maturing out of trouble, thought they could make some money and "give back to the neighborhood." Their store, called Westside, was a model of what Barrios Unidos defined as community-based economic development, an alternative to both government welfare and demeaning "McJobs" in the private sector. Interested in how a state senator could help this local enterprise, I readily agreed to visit.

They say in the neighborhoods "laugh today, cry tomorrow" because it always happens. No gang-related killings had occurred in Santa Monica in the nineties, and gang-related crimes reported to the local Santa Monica police had been dropping from 150 to 250 per year in the late eighties to 50 to 75 per year in the period from 1993 to 1997.[21]

The end of the five-year truce between Culver City and Santa Monica began when someone considered a "psycho renegade" from Culver City shot someone from Venice in early 1998, which provoked a "green light" on his whole neighborhood. (For the record, the gang known as the Culver City Boys—or Boyz—comes from the Mar Vista Gardens, a housing project in West Los Angeles. This is a matter of great importance to the image of Culver City, according to officials I met not long after. They prided themselves on an urban image of being "gang-free." When I sought to clarify this with members of the Culver City Boys, they laughingly told me that the Culver City police once offered them free, high-quality jackets, but only if they were emblazoned with "Mar Vista.")

On October 12, 1998, which celebrated Christopher Columbus's "discovery" of America, twenty-two-year-old Omar Sevilla, known as "Sugar Bear," from Culver City, was shot in Santa Monica. Just released from prison, he was walking along Pico Boulevard to the Clare drug and alcohol treatment center when the shots took his life. I was told that Sugar Bear's family, which was "deep into Culver City," went crazy over the shooting. News of the fatality was eclipsed, however, by the robbery murder of a German tourist, Horst Fietze, who was leisurely strolling with his wife by Loew's Santa Monica Hotel, only a few blocks away. While Sugar Bear's killing went unnoticed in the media, the death of the German tourist made national headlines. Santa Monicans suddenly experienced an urban fear they had never known. Tourist-conscious officials noted that only one homicide had occurred in the entire previous year, and there had been no deaths from gang violence since 1985.[22] (The death of Cesar Martin evidently didn't count, because the drive-by shooting occurred while his car was heading *toward* Santa Monica.)

The death of Sugar Bear might have activated city efforts, however difficult and late, to salvage a truce between Culver City and Santa Monica. But intelligence sources said "no one has been able to determine why Sevilla was killed or by whom."[23] Official police practices may even have stirred the pot. Santa Monica Police Chief James Butts, a conservative African American appointed by a progressive council majority, considered it a "success" if aggressive police sweeps in the Pico neighborhood resulted in driving gang members and drug dealers into Culver City or Venice.[24]

Manny Lares knew what was about to happen, however. Sure enough, on October 17, a posse of Culver City Boys chased Juan "Marty" Campos, twenty-eight, into Eddy's liquor store on Pico and Twentieth, emptying ten shots into him as he scrambled to find shelter. Marty was employed in a Santa Monica jobs program and, according to Manny, was "an interesting character, halfway in and halfway out," not really from the neighborhood, but the kind of guy who, "if someone's getting beat up, will jump in and help out."

The next day, the Culver City Boys struck again, attempting to murder Jaime Cruz, twenty-five, as he stepped out of his car in the Pico neighborhood. He was picked out for random retaliation because he was muscular, bald-headed, and a visible target on an open street. Santa Monica gang members with police scanners heard the whole episode via a police car tailing the shooters. Jaime, whose moniker was Rebel, was a well-known, highly regarded example of a developing peacemaker. The year previous to his shooting, Rebel testified at my Senate hearings on the increased need for community service programs at universities, like tutoring inner-city youth. Rebel himself was part of the Pico Partnership, an innovative program started by Santa Monica College that offered community college education and part-time jobs for young people from the adjacent Pico neighborhood. As a living example of this transitional program, Rebel was enrolled at UCLA when he was shot. Governor Pete Wilson vetoed my bill on expanded tutoring programs after it passed the legislature. After recovering at the UCLA Medical Center, Rebel continued his studies at the university.

Someone from Santa Monica next tried to retaliate, shooting a homeboy in Mar Vista Gardens in the leg, triggering a high-speed chase on the San Diego Freeway and two arrests for attempted murder.

Then, on October 27, the vengeful reaper arrived at the door of the new west side hip-hop shop on Lincoln Boulevard near my home, before I could ever pay my first visit. The store's owner, twenty-five-year-old Frank Juarez, was inside, enjoying a visit from his cousins, nineteen-year-old Anthony and twenty-seven-year-old Michael, who had moved to Northern California several years before to escape the culture of violence. During that Tuesday noon hour, someone walked in firing an SKS assault weapon all over the one-room store. The two cousins from San Luis Obispo died immediately. Frank, the owner, was seriously wounded, as was a twenty-one-year-old customer.[25]

The Santa Monica police put their officers on twelve-hour shifts and leased a helicopter equipped with an infrared detection system. But undetected by the authorities, a peace process was initiated in an urgent effort to stop the violence. Manny, with my authorization, started talking with Santa Monica (gang members), sometimes at his home or in restaurants. To reach out to Culver City, we found Hector Marroquin, an older veteran of gang wars who owned a roofing business and was deeply involved in a violence prevention group called NO-GUNS. I knew Hector from the citywide peace process dialogues and respected his street savvy. He was a regular target of police and occasional media harassment for purported connections to La Eme, but in my experience he was sincerely interested in ending the violence. Years before, he'd sought a blessing in a family safety matter from an individual known to be "connected," a relationship that might now be helpful. Hector talked with Manny about trying to bring both sides to the table before the slaughter deepened. It was about out-of-control egos now; both neighborhoods, it was felt, were feeling defenseless and motivated to attack first. But a point would come when either the bloodlust would dissipate or the deadly score would be even. In addition, gang veterans who could help "squash it" were expected to be released from prison in two weeks. The climate was ripe for intermediaries like Manny and Hector. The immediate opportunity was the approaching Halloween weekend when, according to Manny, "no one wanted to run around with masks on." A behind-the-scenes meeting quickly established a weekend cease-fire. So far, so good.

We were concerned about a possible police overreaction. The negative publicity about the image of Santa Monica was causing them to step up aggressive tactics. They were successful in arresting the two assailants of Rebel, an incident they happened to observe firsthand. But Chief Butts was also activating a task force with city, county, and federal agents to crack down on parole violators. "Any gang members are very aware that we are conducting probation and parole searches and they're very aware there will be consequences to their actions," he declared.[26] These were reassuring words to a panicked public, but in fact it was problematic. What the public didn't know is that there are thousands of parole violators in the Los Angeles area on any given day. About 90,000 parolees are sent back to California prisons annually, at twice the national rate.[27] They are the "engine of the state's prison industry, generating jobs for guards," according to a

caustic *Los Angeles Times* editorial in 2002. Those who re-offend are usually technical violators who drive without insurance or fail to show up for meetings with
their parole officers. Despite the everyday tolerance of tens of thousands of violators out on the streets, the police can't afford to let their secret out, since their
image is based on upholding every law, not on admitting that chasing parole violators is a low priority.

Our concern was about Michael Herrara, aka Pee Wee, a parole violator released from confinement on August 31, now hiding in Riverside County, who had
influence in Santa Monica and was needed for the secret truce negotiations.
Troubled by drug addiction, Pee Wee had chosen to live underground rather
than see his parole officer at the appointed times. He had a wife, children, and,
most important for our purposes, respect in the Pico neighborhood. No one can
precisely define "respect," but it usually means having "put in work for the neighborhood," defending it against rivals, serving time, collaborating in gang activity,
never snitching, showing loyalty, "representing" faithfully. One could grow out of
"the neighborhood," be no longer active but still have respect. Michael Herrara,
for whatever reasons, had respect. But could he enter Santa Monica without being picked up? The issue quickened when we heard that a Culver City Boy had
visited Corcoran state prison to discuss the cease-fire with one of their older
homeboys who had a personal stake in the long-standing neighborhood feud.
Word came on Sunday, November 1, that Culver City was ready to come to the
table. We had to bring in Pee Wee.

That weekend I had a long phone conversation with Chief Butts, urging him to
relax the hard-line policy in order to give peace a chance. I suggested that he visit
Rebel in UCLA's Medical Center, as I had, to express sympathy and support. Rebel
had been misidentified as a Santa Monica gang member in the local press, and it
was important for the chief to convey that that was not law enforcement's attitude. He agreed. Then I asked if he would allow Pee Wee to come in for the weekend. He cautiously supported the peace gesture as I outlined it. Manny Lares
called the chief to confirm the understanding, then phoned Pee Wee in Riverside,
who in turn called a Santa Monica antigang detective and thought he received a

"red light," which meant the police would not obstruct or arrest him while in Santa Monica. In Manny's scenario, Pee Wee might facilitate the cease-fire agreement, then turn himself over to his parole officer, hoping for lenient treatment in light of his good deed. Manny called the chief again to confirm arrangements and invite him to a Monday press conference, which Butts declined.

Monday, November 2, was the Day of the Dead, a time when many Mexican people take to the streets, carrying candles, attired as skeletal ghosts. The presence of death in the affairs of the living is acknowledged, respected, and simultaneously mocked, a ritual far different from the American tendency to avoid and deny death since it exists only "after" life. Late that morning, two carloads of homeboys converged on my Senate office in West L.A. from Santa Monica and Culver City. Riding with them were Manny, Hector, and a third individual with respect, "Blinky" Rodriguez, from the San Fernando Valley. Blinky, along with his wife, Lilly, had lost a sixteen-year-old son to gang violence. He dedicated himself to community services, amateur sports programs, and evangelizing for peace through Christian ministries. Since many young gang members participated in his programs, which included football and baseball games (played all-out with no pads, which somehow remained incident-free), Blinky's magic was attributed by certain law enforcement officials as evidence of ties to La Eme. From my viewpoint, he was a spiritual role model, an incredibly effective supporter of the Peace Process Network. The Valley peace treaty he had fostered in 1993 had resulted in a reduction of gang-related murders from fifty-six to two in its first year,[28] and he was honored by Arnold Schwarzenegger, Governor Pete Wilson's chairman of a state council on sports and fitness.

Undoubtedly, it was the first time these homeboys ever felt welcomed into a government office. My title of "El Senador" perhaps lent a sense of promise to the negotiations at hand. Since the matters to be discussed were not my business, I shook their hands, left the room, and closed the door. I took careful notice of Pee Wee, who had a shaved head and wore a white T-shirt. He smiled broadly, but displayed a nervousness that could have been simply his personality, or a wariness of the police. The central decision, to negotiate a cease-fire, already had

been made at pre-meetings in private homes, so the key issues besides an affirma-
tion involved implementing the process: how many days would it take to get the
word out through the streets and prisons so there were no spontaneous provoca-
tions? Who was taking responsibility for unresolved grievances in the past? How
would it be announced to the press and public? After an hour or two, it was settled. I returned to the room as a witness to a circle of individuals burning sage
and solemnly praying. Then they disappeared from the premises, and we informed the media waiting outside that an agreement had been reached, that it
was fragile and would take a few days to be consolidated. "Gang Truce Could
Stop Killing," the headlines read.[29]

   That night several hundred shaken and grieving residents of the Pico neighborhood gathered at St. Anne's church to hold a vigil for peace. I attended with
Cesar Martin's parents, Celina and Jesus, his older brother Jesse and his girlfriend
Monica, and his little sister Amy. Few Anglos were present for this emotional gathering in the city's invisible barrio. One of the organizers, Oscar de la Torre, from
Sixteenth Street, told of growing up always looking at a "graveyard wall" where
dead homeboys were memorialized. In planning the vigil, he identified the spots
where eighteen had been killed in a seven-block radius in the Pico neighborhood
alone, not counting gunshot victims like Jaime "Rebel" Cruz. In those eighteen
places, the organizers placed flowers, votive candles, and crosses with the victims'
names and dates of death. As we marched, small knots of people would pause at
the memorials for someone they knew, or, like myself, would slowly read the roll
of these many forgotten dead for the first time. I stood with Cesar's silent family
for a long time at the flowered asphalt spot that claimed his name.

   Manny was going slightly crazy. In the last three days he'd negotiated the
truce, represented Pee Wee's delicate situation to the chief, held a press conference, and helped organize the candlelight vigil. The Day of the Dead was turned
into the day of the truce. But would it hold?

   He was worried about the police. Would they permit the cease-fire to be implemented, which would mean acknowledging that those they considered a
criminal element could achieve what law enforcement could not? Manny had
asked the police for a seven-day "red light" for Michael Herrera, but the response

was inconclusive. "I talked to the detectives and got no indication whether they were going to pick him up. We said we would walk him straight into the parole office afterwards and maybe his efforts to stop this would get him consideration." On Friday, my office sent a letter to Pee Wee's parole officer proposing a meeting.

That same Friday night, Pee Wee went to bed with his wife, Leticia, and their kids. All told, it was a productive week. It felt good to him to be useful, good to be in bed with Leticia, good to be in the old neighborhood. Around 6 A.M., some twenty police agents hammered on the apartment door, ordering him to come out. Before Pee Wee and Leticia could dress, the officers bounded in. Kids were screaming; Pee Wee remembers "going crazy" when the police grabbed his wife. He and Leticia were thrown down and handcuffed. He was charged with a state parole violation for failure to report as a drug offender. Leticia was hit with three charges: harboring a fugitive, resisting arrest, and possession of a usable amount of drugs.[30]

I bailed Leticia out fifteen hours later and drove her back to the apartment. Pee Wee was not eligible for bail. He returned to county jail, where he would spend at least ninety days. Parolees like Pee Wee have turned the language of the law upside down; instead of "violating parole," they describe themselves as being "violated," as in "the parole officer violated me." In this case, at least, it was certainly true.

Were the police and state agents trying to wreck the fragile peace? Send a message that taking risks for peace would get you no leniency? Or, simply, as I suspected, reasserting the image of absolute control in circumstances where the killings were stopped without them? Certainly their word was no good. The peace was destabilized. It would be a long time before another person like Pee Wee would be willing to assist a truce. In weeks to come, Chief Butts repeatedly credited the end of the violence to the saturation tactics of an interagency law enforcement task force. I never heard from him again. Later, Pee Wee told Manny that the only thing he was angry about was that he was duped, that the Santa Monica police said they would not "dime" (arrest) him if he came into Santa Monica.

With a successful truce in place, the next step was to create a peace dividend with steps to empower the Pico neighborhood, especially the youth, and invest in jobs and social programs. With Santa Monica's reputation as a progressive bastion in mind, I held hearings on the causes and possible solutions to the crisis that had taken five lives (including the German tourist) and wounded at least four people in fifteen days in one of the nation's most peaceful, affluent towns.[31]

Before the Senate hearings began, I received an unexpected jobs proposal from a longtime friend of mine, Michael Dieden, a former radical activist who had joined the ranks of developers. Barely over the truce negotiations, I was now to experience the dilemmas of political compromise in a society that lacks a public sector jobs program. It happened that Michael represented the nearby Playa Vista development that I strongly opposed. Playa Vista, once owned by Howard Hughes, had become the property of Steven Spielberg, David Geffen, and Jeffrey Katzenberg, and happened to be the largest open wetlands in Southern California. Michael's clients—liberal Hollywood powerhouses who were used to having their way—wanted the wetlands converted to twenty-first-century studios, complete with an affluent development the size of a small city. It had become one of the hottest controversies in California, with many environmentalists who were dependent on Hollywood largesse compromised as fence-sitters. I was on record against the wetlands destruction for environmental and traffic reasons, but also opposed because of its less noticed effects on the inner city. I wanted development to target inner-city communities, but instead the pattern was to underdevelop those areas while overdeveloping the affluent suburban rings around Los Angeles. By an official estimate, for example, the Playa Vista development would bring 220,000 new car trips *daily* to a region already choked with traffic.[32]

But Michael had a big heart, and was a shrewd strategist. Hearing of the cease-fire negotiations, he immediately called with an offer to employ actual gang members, or former gang members, on the construction site. There would be a specific number of set-aside jobs, 10 percent. He subsidized a jobs-for-peace initiative already being created by an African American probation officer, Brad Carson, which would serve as a hiring hall for homeboys—recruiting, training, and preparing them for the jobs. Michael promised that Playa Vista would set an example for other corporations in the region, formally proposing that they "step up" and hire these unemployed gang members and convicts as a far-ranging peace dividend.

Most people think compromise is crude and ugly, but in politics I have found it more often subtle, untraceable, almost unconscious. Was I being asked to sell out my environmental beliefs in exchange for a few jobs for gang members? Or asked to relax my principles to save the peace? The question was never put to me. It wasn't necessary. By cooperating with Michael, I would be sending to the environmentalists a compromising message that saving gang members was more important than saving birds. It was even more complicated: what if approval of Playa Vista was absolutely inevitable, given the friendships of Spielberg, Geffen, and Katzenberg that reached from L.A. city hall all the way to Bill Clinton, who socialized frequently at Geffen's Malibu estate? Would I be bypassing an urgent goal that was achievable in order to hold out for a principle that wasn't?

I greatly respected Spielberg as an artist (he later withdrew from the project). I knew Geffen only from his outlaw hippie days, not in his corporate incarnation. I had tangled once with Katzenberg when he had called me after seeing a quote in which I was critical of Playa Vista in the *Los Angeles Times*. He had objected fiercely to my characterization that the project was a subsidy for the affluent that would leave the inner city behind. He reminded me that he devotes considerable resources to inner-city charities, "as I'm sure you do yourself, Tom." (I don't.) Then he said that Playa Vista would make as many inner-city hires as possible, for example as security guards, and asked me to encourage as many job applications as possible. "You know," Katzenberg confided, "there just aren't many qualified people over there." I was struck silent by his comment, knowing of numerous instances where literally thousands of inner-city residents stood in long lines to apply for a handful of jobs. "You know what I mean," Katzenberg broke in finally.

Dieden's offer was, therefore, a breakthrough of sorts, and I wanted to consider it carefully. I took the proposal to Manny, Dewayne Holmes, John Heyman, and violence prevention groups like NOGUNS and Unity One. Never having received such an offer, they were confounded and divided. Considering compromise seemed unreal in a world where they had never been at the table. But, instinctively, several of them resented anything that smacked of divide-and-conquer tactics from "the Man."

With no time to waste, I invited Playa Vista to the Senate hearings to make their proposal. I supported the hiring of homeboys from the Culver City–Santa Monica area and the wider proposal of Playa Vista to the L.A. corporate community. As for the development itself, I reserved the right to continue opposing it. But in the areas already permitted, where job creation was already inevitable, I supported the hiring of gang crews, starting with about twenty jobs immediately. We were on the threshold of a historic moment, I believed. A sense of excitement was in the air as the hearings began. It would not return again.

The hearings, held at the Santa Monica Pier, a few blocks from the Pico neighborhood, were a demonstration of how contending voices can talk past one another despite a good-faith effort. City officials, including four past and present Santa Monica mayors, presented a litany of all the good things they already were doing for the Pico neighborhood.[33] Like most local officials everywhere, these representatives placed the blame on the state legislature for failing to fund cities.

But none of them answered the question posed by young Josefina Santiago of the Pico neighborhood:

> The problem is that our business community will not hire a youth with a criminal background. We will get them up and to the point of an interview, almost with their foot in the door, and then it's closed in their face. So what am I left with? How do I inspire again? You know what? We live in a contradiction.

As if it were a teach-in, Manny narrated the hidden history of the "four corners" of Santa Monica, West Los Angeles, Culver City, and Venice. He described a process of neglect and exclusion going back to his grandfather's time in the 1920s, when "young Latino men and women, usually labeled as criminals, delinquent at best, were targeted by police for what by today's standards would be considered gangs." He described growing up in a gang culture, which meant for persons like himself that "you just live on the streets, you operate, and that's the way you live." He spoke of the 33 percent drop in violent youth crime since the 1992 "relative peace." Unfortunately, he concluded, "as in any situation, stagnation will create a hostile environment." He itemized the repeal of Santa Monica rent control and the spiraling pressures of gentrification on the working-class Pico neighborhood. Despite the growth of the tourist industry in Santa Monica, he concluded, none of the wealth had filtered down.

Concrete alternatives were praised. The Santa Monica College president spoke of the Pico Partnership with a 70 percent retention rate among students holding jobs while studying at the same time. The Venice Community Development Project described building low-income housing and hiring ex-gang members for construction and security. But these were small steps in what seemed like a desert. Lucia Diaz, of the Mar Vista community center, had words of wisdom on hiring:

I understand it can be scary for some people to say, "How can I offer a job to someone I don't really know? It can be a risk for us" . . . we need to create a plan. Before they're being hired by anyone, there are certain skills they need to learn. They need to start by learning the most important skills, the life skills, that help us keep a job.

We want to see how we can bring different representatives from the different gangs and to really allow them, to give them the space for them to come up with their own plan and I would facilitate the process . . .

If you have a mind to hire one of these guys, I think that you won't regret it. I had two of them working with me for over two years and they're doing a wonderful job. They're very respectful, and they never, I don't think, for a whole year . . . have not come to work, or they maybe had to show up late twice.[34]

As for the police, she noted that her relationships with the Culver City Boys had to remain confidential:

When people come to me and they trust me, they see me as a private counselor, and so I cannot go to the police and say "this is what happened." The police do their work in one way, and centers like mine work in a different way. It's not really trying

to get in the way of the police but finding a way to get to the kids so they can look
at something different than jail.[35]

Brad Carson's testimony was even more specific about a peace dividend. The
probation officer recognized peacemakers not only from Santa Monica and Culver City, but also from Venice. He noted that the county's Proposition A, a safe
neighborhood parks act, required that 10 percent of all jobs go to at-risk youth.
He helped organize 200 "shot-calling gang members" from seventy-five different
sets who lobbied the county to implement the measure. Santa Monica, he noted,
had obtained $7.1 million in Prop A funds but had not hired the requisite per-
centage of at-risk youth. If necessary, he said, the grass-roots coalition would sue
the county for enforcement. The vast majority of the county's eighty-eight municipalities were resisting the obligation to hire homeboys.[36] As the several-hour
hearing ended, there was a palpable sense that lives were being saved and a model
was being established for urban peace and justice.

Five years later, however, the results were decidedly mixed. The good news
was that Oscar de la Torre's community center, funded for $300,000 (less than
1 percent of the city budget),[37] was thriving, and Oscar himself was elected to the
Santa Monica school board. The County of Los Angeles settled the Prop A legal
case for a projected $100 million in 2003, ten years after the election that had
promised 10 percent of the jobs would go to homeboys. Playa Vista came through
with some 900 jobs for at-risk youth, including many gang members, at $12 an
hour, although there was trouble making the training work. Hector finally
formed his own Youth at Risk General Contractor and Labor company to take
over much of the training and mentoring.

Though some violence broke out despite the truce, the Pico neighborhood itself avoided gang homicides. Manny set up his own Barrios Unidos office on
Pico, not far from Oscar, obtained some foundation funding, was invited to speak
at Harvard, then fell into funding woes again. Depression took over his life for
months, but the last time we talked he was ready to resume his brilliant but unfunded crusade. He was finishing up a community organizational model, based

on the four directions of an Indian medicine wheel, and was looking for backers.

Pee Wee the peacemaker was the real loser. After the 1998 cease-fire and his arrest, he served a few months before being released, but then he rolled back and forth through the prison doors on more drug violations, none of them violent. But in late 2001, a crew in a West L.A. "car" drove into Santa Monica looking for trouble, were intercepted by Santa Monica homeboys, chased, caught, and shot up, and then crashed, by coincidence, two doors down the street from Pee Wee's house. Pee Wee dashed out, helped someone out of a wrecked vehicle, then found himself staring straight into the faces of his rivals. He sprinted back into his house, but three days later was arrested at home as a felon in possession of a gun. Why was he carrying a gun? "Everyone pretty much knows where he was living," Manny said, and "there was always fear of retaliation." Pee Wee took a six-year plea bargain on the possession of a weapons charge, not knowing what was coming next. Not long after, he was charged with murder by the same Santa Monica police who had arrested him before. When Leticia and his lawyers came looking to me for help, I was a retired senator with little advice. Pee Wee remains in prison with an addiction problem after a cycle of events that began with his involvement in the peace process.

The Santa Monica police, headquartered in a sparse facility built long before the crime wars of the nineties, were rewarded by the public with a $63 million structure capable of holding ninety-six inmates.[38]

The Demonization Crusade

> Maybe we've already made our decision. Those that can be advanced to
> the middle class, let them be advanced. The rest? Well, we do our best
> by them. We don't have to do any more. They kill some of us. Mostly
> they kill themselves.
> —*character in Saul Bellow's novel* The Dean's December[1]

The major obstacle to ending gang violence is perception, or, as gang members
might say, "word." Power and prejudice, filtering what we see, acknowledge, respect and fear, determines the climate that dominates politics. No one is more vili-
fied today than a "gang member," with the exception of an "international terrorist"
or a "narco-terrorist," and, as we shall see, these shadowy personas are increasingly
morphed into a single archenemy of society. The mainstream perceptions of order
and well-being depend on the projection of an opposite, the barbarian.

Take the example of a 1993 nonfiction book on gang violence, *Baby Insane and
the Buddha: How a Crip and a Cop Joined Forces to Shut Down a Street Gang*. The author
is a Pulitzer Prize–winning *Los Angeles Times* writer, Bob Sipchen, whose account
implies that mythic action-hero personalities may be the solution to the gang
violence crisis.[2] Sipchen's tale features an unorthodox San Diego cop, the "Buddha"

(because of weight problems, not wisdom), who turns a Crip gang member named "Baby Insane" into an undercover informer. In 1989, they become the nucleus of an aggressive antigang police unit, the kind that became infamous in Los Angeles's Rampart scandal ten years later, where secretive, paramilitary police outfits frequently take the law into their own hands in a war against gangs.

It's a juicy read about the eighty-eight-member Special Enforcement Division (SED), inspired by the LAPD's Community Resources against Street Hoodlums (CRASH) units, which "swept into southeast San Diego like marines storming a Vietcong stronghold," led by a commander who declared that "whenever two gang members get together on a street corner to plot illegal activities, they are going to have a police officer standing next to them, in their face . . ."[3] In a similar macho vein, the police chief compared himself to Arnold Schwarzenegger in *The Terminator*.[4] The hero of Sipchen's book, the Buddha, became part of "Operation Blue Rag," targeting Crips who identified themselves by the same color.

According to the author, violent crime statistics plunged,[5] and "no one could deny that the neighborhood Crip and west coast strongholds were more peaceful than they'd been in years."[6]

Baby Insane and the Buddha was optioned for a Hollywood movie, a contract was signed, but the film was never made.[7]

But at least the good guys won—or did they? Sipchen admitted that his book was based on court records, official transcripts, conversations "when I was not present," and selective dialogue.[8] Sipchen nowhere explains the omission of the following significant information, all of which occurred before the book's 1993 publication date:

In April 1989, two months after the ass-kicking squads of the SED were created, the very community residents who had demanded the police crackdown were marching against a fatal police shooting. A local resident spoke of regretting that "the police gang unit that we encouraged the mobilization of has now caused this particular death," referring to the killing of thirty-two-year-old Stanley Buchanan, who allegedly grabbed a flashlight before being shot six times by an officer named in four previous police brutality lawsuits. The dead man was said to have rock cocaine in his pocket.[9]

According to the *Los Angeles Times*, there was an "outcry from citizens and civil rights groups" in 1990 due to a "perception that police officers are somewhat trigger-happy."[10] Indeed, by the end of 1990, police had shot twenty-eight people in San Diego, killing twelve, compared to nineteen, eighteen, eighteen, and twenty-one shootings in the years before SED was unleashed.[11] "You can't please everyone," San Diego's chief replied to a media inquiry.[12]

During the five-year period from 1985 to 1990, of 110 police shootings there were only five cases of discipline, but no firings or prosecutions of officers.[13] An internal review was ordered after police killed three people from May to June in 1990 for allegedly wielding a plastering tool and two baseball bats.[14]

When a citizens' advisory board recommended that officers shoot to wound or fire warning shots instead of shooting to kill, the San Diego police chief said police might put themselves in danger by trying to pinpoint their shots. "Nobody shoots to wound in this country," he said.[15]

In 1991, the press reported that, despite the pervasive street presence of the SED, "gang violence remained as common in 1990 as it was in 1989."[16]

The controversial and centralized SED was shut down in February 1992, and replaced by a decentralized "gang suppression team" half its size.[17]

A few years later, I checked with Roberto Martinez, a longtime Quaker representative in the Logan Barrio, on community perceptions of the SED. He wrote back that one associate remembered filing grievances by two young Chicanos against the SED that resulted in the officers being disciplined. "Nobody else seems to remember much about the unit," he added. "Speaking for myself, I only remember what I read in the newspaper. However, the reason I didn't make much of it was because back then there was so much police violence, including shootings of blacks and Chicanos, it was hard for me to separate what SED did with what the other cops were doing."[18]

Sipchen took after my views in 2003, a decade later, after a panel discussion at the University of Southern California, where I questioned the demonizing logic of the unsuccessful war on gangs. He was responsible for an editorial in the *Los Angeles*

Times condemning my "familiar fretting about how the police and media sow needless panic by 'demonizing' gangs."[19] The editorial lashed out at "the city's Haydens" for being "infatuated with their tired rants,"[20] even suggesting that many critics "express more sympathy for the shooters than for those shot."[21] For anyone with a memory, the *Times* was sounding the call once again for a war on gangs: "Now seems a good time to finally stand up to the street gangs that terrorize communities" declared a typical 2002 editorial.[22] Six decades before, the *Times* had routinely described Mexican youth on the streets as "hoodlums" (including "girl hoodlums") and had printed triumphal headlines like "Zoot Suiters Learn Lesson in Fights with Servicemen."[23] While the *Times* has been the best source of critical information in subsequent decades, and was responsible for exposing the Rampart scandal by its tireless reporters Matt Lait and Scott Glover, its editorial calls for "finally standing up" reflect an amnesia about the ineffectiveness of the city's long war on gangs.

As for the *Times*'s carping against "tired rants" about demonization, one purpose of this book is to question the most "tired rant" of all: the thirty-year call by many conservatives and increasing numbers of liberals for a permanent war on gangs and the belittling of any alternatives as being "soft on crime." This "neoconservative" thinking has left a legacy of hardening poverty in our inner cities, an unprecedented rate of youth incarceration, a permanent growth of the police-and-prisons budget, an unquestioning acceptance of conservative ideology cloaked in academic chatter, and a political culture that offers little or no exit for an entire generation of inner-city youth. No one likes to explore their institutionalized racism or question whether the police themselves are lawbreakers, but it will take a more questioning journalism to cause a public rethinking of this long and bloody war. It was such critical journalism that finally forced a reappraisal of the Vietnam War. Unlike the Vietnam tragedy, no editorialists have called for an end to the war on gangs—nor even an agonizing reappraisal.

Baby Insane and the Buddha was just one example of journalism sensationalizing the war on gangs while failing to weigh the human costs or note the deepening socioeconomic quagmire that the war has become. I cite *Baby Insane and the Buddha*, however, because the author continues to be a prominent perpetrator of the official logic that propels the permanent war on gangs and disparages its critics, including myself and a number of former gang members who are trying to build a peace process in the inner cities. As long as such pundits stoke public panic against gangs, the politics of law-and-order will prevail over any proposals to turn toward peace by dealing with the root causes of inner-city violence. In fact, as we shall see, the academic policy guru of the war-on-gangs establishment, James Q. Wilson, questions whether there are any root causes at all,[24] and dismisses root-cause thinking as simply a way to avoid taking aggressive action against crime.

In the decade since 1993, American society has been provoked into panic by rising levels of gang violence and "urban disorder." Starting in the sixties, accelerating in the eighties and nineties, the nation sponsored overlapping wars against gangs and drugs that have resulted in prison terms for over 2 million people, the largest percentage of them black, brown, tattooed, and gang-affiliated.[25] As already noted, in Los Angeles alone, over 11,000 young men died in gang wars between 1980 and 2000.[26] The excesses of police antigang units, starting with the heavily militarized SWAT teams of the Los Angeles police department in the 1960s, led eventually to scandals, federal investigations, civil rights lawsuits, blue-ribbon commissions, and vague promises of reform. The gang menace became a staple of law-and-order politics across the country, leading to the election of Republican mayors in such overwhelmingly Democratic cities as New York and Los Angeles.

But a decade after the 1992 peak of gang violence, the gang problem is still with us, and the prisons overflow with hundreds of thousands of homeboys, addicted, uneducated, unskilled, the new incorrigibles. The Los Angeles police chief, William Bratton, fresh from crime-fighting successes in New York (and lesser-known failures in race relations), declares yet another war to take back the streets from what he labels the "homeland terrorism" of street gangs. Bratton's declaration was only the latest echo in a war launched at least sixty years before, in 1942, when the LAPD pledged to jail every gang member in the city and "take them out of circulation until they realize that the authorities will not tolerate gangsterism."[27] It is worth briefly outlining some of the major conflicts over the decades between the L.A. police and sheriffs' departments and inner-city communities, as compiled by Robert Garcia, a former U.S. prosecutor under Rudolph Giuliani and a long-time civil rights litigator in Los Angeles:

August 11, 1965—Watts uprising. After six days of rioting, 45 people lay dead, over 1,000 are hurt, 4,000 arrested, and property damage is estimated at $40 million.

December 16, 1965. The McCone Commision issues its blue-ribbon report, citing community hostility toward police, unemployment, and lack of good schools as the causes of the Watts riots.

1968–69—SWAT created. Former chief Darryl Gates wanted to name them Special Weapons Attack Teams, but the acronym was changed to stand for Special Weapons and Tactics teams. These warrior assault units were armed with MP5 9mm submachine guns, Cold CAR-15 5.56mm assault rifles with double banana-clip magazines, Benelli 121-M-1 semiautomatic shotguns, scoped bolt-action sniper rifles, flash-bang devices, and other advanced weaponry. The SWAT model spread quickly across the country.[28]

December 8, 1969—LAPD assault on Panther offices. SWAT units launched dawn raids using armored personnel carriers, helicopters, and dynamite charges against three Panther offices four days after the Chicago police shootings of Panthers Fred Hampton and Mark Clark. Thirteen Panthers were exonerated in the L.A. case on December 24, 1971.[29]

July 1972—Elmer "Geronimo" Pratt is convicted for murdering a woman in Santa Monica. Pratt serves twenty-seven years in prison proclaiming his innocence before a state habeas court vacates his conviction and life sentence on May 29, 1997. The chief witness against Pratt is revealed to be an LAPD undercover agent with close ties to the city's most prominent African American church.[30]

April 1975—LAPD spying scandal. The department destroys 2 million dossiers on 55,000 individuals and organizations. In 1978, when the secretary of the Coalition against Police Abuse (CAPA) was exposed as an LAPD agent, 120 plaintiffs sued the department for illegal spying, including eavesdropping on numerous elected officials.[31] Darryl Gates warned on *Nightline* that, "If I really laid it on the line, and it may come down to that, watch out."[32]

1977—CRASH begins. With an initial federal grant, LAPD creates its first antigang unit, a forty-four-officer team called Total Resources against Street Hoodlums (TRASH). After criticism from civic leaders, the name is changed to Community Resources against Street Hoodlums, and the CRASH units are born. Their official mission: total suppression of gangs and, as they tell the *Times,* to " 'jam,' or harass gang members wherever they find them."[33] In 1979, the L.A. County sheriffs receive funding for a similar suppression team called Operation Safe Streets (OSS), who will arrest gang members for loitering, curfew violations, and even swearing in public.[34]

1983—Lyons chokehold decree (461 U.S. 95, 1983). The U.S. Supreme Court finds that police chokeholds are justified in a case where a black motorist was placed in a chokehold after a routine traffic stop. In 1982, however, the City of Los Angeles bans chokeholds after finding that LAPD officers killed sixteen people, including twelve black men, during routine arrests.

1988–93—Corruption in L.A. Sherriff's Department. As a result of an undercover investigation, nineteen deputies are convicted in drugs and money cases by 1993.

April 1988, 1989—police sweeps. Under the title "Operation Hammer," the LAPD undertakes massive police sweeps with 1,000 officers in a ten-square-mile zone of South Central, making arrests on minor violations and using vehicle-mounted battering rams against suspected crack houses. The purpose of "Hammer," according to Chief Gates, is "to make life miserable for gang members." But, according to a *Los Angeles Times* analysis, the operation "alienated large segments of the community while doing little to reduce crime."[35] In one raid on Dalton Street, eighty-eight LAPD officers smashed apartments during a drug raid that yielded two minor arrests. Chief Gates admits the raid "got out of hand."[36]

1990—Thomas case. In a revival of the earlier *Lyons* case, the NAACP Legal Defense Fund alleges that LASD deputies in Lynwood systematically used excessive force, racial harassment, and illegal searches and seizures. The accused were known as the "Grim Reapers," a fraternity of deputies who tattooed death skulls on their ankles. In September 1991, a federal judge in the *Thomas* matter favors a public examination of the LASD and issues a preliminary injunction that is stayed by the U.S. Ninth Circuit Court.

March 3, 1991—Rodney King beating. Four LAPD officers beat and arrest Rodney King while twenty-three others stand by and do nothing. The video is broadcast around the world. The four officers are charged with felony assault.

April 1, 1991—Christopher Commission. Mayor Tom Bradley appoints corporate lawyer and future Secretary of State Warren Christopher to investigate the LAPD. On April 4, Bradley's police commission puts Chief Darryl Gates on a sixty-day leave.

July 9, 1991—Christopher findings. The report documents the systemic use of excessive force and racial harassment in the LAPD, including a finding that 70 percent of police canine searches and bites occurred in minority communities. The commission also releases tapes recording officer remarks such as these:[37]

"Well . . . I'm back over here in the projects pissing off the natives."

"I would love to drive down Slauson with a flame thrower . . . we would have a barbeque."

"Sounds like monkey-slapping time."

"If you encounter these Negroes shoot first and ask questions later."

"Hi . . . I just got mexercise for the night."

"Okay, people . . . pls . . . don't transfer me any orientals . . . I had two already."

"I almost got me a Mexican last night but he dropped the gun too dam quick."

July 22, 1991—Gates announces resignation. The deadline is set in 1992.

November 15, 1991—Latasha Harlins verdict. In March, Soon Ja Du, a Korean-American grocery store owner, shot to death a fifteen-year-old African American girl, Latasha Harlins, after accusing her of stealing a $1.79 bottle of orange juice. Facing a potential eleven years in prison, the Korean grocer is sentenced in November to probation, community service, and a $500 fine.

November 26, 1991—Simi Valley decision. The Rodney King case is moved to Simi Valley, a virtually white suburb with a high proportion of law enforcement officers as residents.

December 1991—Kolts Commission created. The County Board of Supervisors appoints retired judge James Kolts to investigate the LASD.

April 29, 1992—Rodney King verdict. The Simi Valley jury finds the four LAPD officers not guilty. Riots begin in Los Angeles. Forty-two people are killed, 700 structures destroyed, 5,000 are arrested, and $1 billion in property damage is inflicted.

May 8, 1992—Crips-Bloods truce is official. Negotiated and achieved just before the Rodney King verdict, the historic truce is announced after the National Guard leaves the city.

May 11, 1992—Webster Commission created. The L.A. Board of Police Commissioners appoints William Webster, former head of both the FBI and CIA, to review the LAPD's performance during the riots.

May 14, 1992—Darryl Gates resigns. After fourteen years' tenure, Gates is replaced by Willie Williams, an African American police official from Philadelphia.

June 4, 1992—Charter Reform Amendment passes. By a large majority, L.A. voters support limiting the police chief to two five-year terms combined with greater civilian controls.

July 20, 1992—Kolts findings. The LASD is described as systematically guilty of excessive force, racial harassment, and lax discipline. A monitor is recommended.

October 21, 1992—Webster Commission Report. Calls for further reforms of the LAPD are announced. At the same time, the U.S. Ninth Circuit rules that plaintiffs in the 1990–91 *Thomas* litigation against the LASD may seek injunctive relief.

April 17, 1993—King case convictions. Two officers are convicted of violating Rodney King's civil rights, and two are acquitted, by a federal jury. In August, the two officers are sentenced to thirty months in prison. They will be released after twenty-four months.

June 8, 1993—Republican Richard Riordan elected mayor. Multimillionaire Republican venture capitalist Richard Riordan is elected mayor over Democrat Michael Woo, an Asian American council member, who led the call for Darryl Gates's resignation.

December 1993—LASD drug scandal. Nineteen elite LASD deputies, known as "the majors," are convicted of drug money skimming and widespread brutality, including beatings and flushing inmates' heads into toilets, as well as lying, falsifying search warrants, and planting cocaine.[38]

December 7, 1993—Sentencing of Damian Williams. Gang member Damian

Williams, convicted in October 1993 of beating Reginald Denny on the first day of the riots, is sentenced to ten years in prison.

April 19, 1994—Rodney King civil settlement. A jury awards King $3.8 million in actual damages for loss of work, medical costs, and pain and suffering. Punitive damages are denied in June.

1995—Largest crackdown ever. Under Willie Williams, the LAPD carries out the largest sweeps in its history in an 800-officer joint antigang operation with the FBI. Of 63 individuals arrested by the 800 officers, only 1 is charged with a violent felony.[39] Another task force that year, designed to destroy the 18th Street organization, "also fell far short of its goals."[40]

December 1995—Thomas litigation settled. The LASD agrees to pay $7.5 million for injuries and attorney's fees. The county is required to spend $1.5 million for officer training and a computerized tracking system. A federal court describes the deputies known as "the Vikings" as a "neo-Nazi, white supremacist gang" operating under cover of law enforcement. A tattoo displayed in court reveals the number "998," code for officer-involved shooting.[41] The same deputy gangs would enjoy "renewed popularity among young deputies" in 1999, until the newly elected sheriff, Lee Baca, himself a former head of the Lynwood station, ordered an end to the practice.

These were intense times for the police and sheriffs, the residents of Los Angeles, and the country itself. No less than four blue-ribbon commissions, headed by individuals from the highest levels of diplomacy, law enforcement, and national security, investigated the role of the L.A. police and sheriffs. They discovered profound antagonisms between the police and inner-city communities. They recommended substantial reforms, some of which were carried out.

But the most difficult reforms, those involving civilian control of the department and an end to the militarized culture of secrecy, seemed impossible to achieve. One must conclude that whatever was wrong with the LAPD was in all probability wrong with policing in America. Not only was the LAPD a self-avowed vanguard of aggressive policing, a pioneer in the use of SWAT teams and CRASH units, but its paramilitary behavior was mirrored by departments across the country.

The Rampart Scandal

Then came the Rampart scandal, acknowledged to be the largest Los Angeles police corruption crisis in the sixty years since the police vowed to drive "gangsterism"
out of town. Named for a police precinct in Pico-Union, the Rampart scandal laid
bare the most secret levels of the undeclared war. The revelations began in 1998
quite by chance and not because effective preventive mechanisms were in place. A
Rampart CRASH officer named Rafael Perez was charged on August 25 for pilfer-
ing eight pounds of confiscated cocaine from a police locker. Facing a long prison
sentence for his misconduct, Perez decided to break the organization's code of silence and begin naming names.[42] His testimony revealed a glimpse of the secretive
structures of the undeclared war on gangs.

The FBI and related agencies like the Immigration and Naturalization Service
(INS) and the Bureau of Alcohol, Tobacco, Firearms and Explosives (ATF) had
organized joint task forces with local police antigang units to share secret data
culled from street frisks and target individuals for arrest or deportation. In effect,
the CRASH suppression program was being replicated on a national scale, with
little or no accountability.

In Los Angeles, the Rampart scandal opened a momentary window into the
secret war, because it created tensions among law enforcement personnel themselves. For one thing, Rafael Perez testified under oath that the LAPD turned
over potential witnesses in police misconduct cases to the INS for deportation,
and that police and immigration officers worked in violation of city policy. At the
time, the LAPD was forbidden to cooperate with the INS to avoid alienating undocumented immigrants who would not cooperate with police for fear of deportation. The zeal of the FBI and CRASH became too much for some long-time
professionals in the INS. Anonymous phone calls were made to *Times* reporter
Anne-Marie O'Connor from federal sources alleging that there was "a lot more
where that came from." One call instructed her to wait in the paper's downstairs
lobby at a certain time and date. When she did so, O'Connor was met by a lone
individual, casually dressed in jeans, whom she didn't recognize and whose voice
did not match those she heard on the phone calls. The stranger handed her a

pile of FBI and INS documents the size of two phone books, then walked out the door.

The documents, which were stamped confidential and may have been illegally transmitted, confirmed the suspicion that the Rampart scandal was a window into a larger picture of collusion and cover-up in order to circumvent constitutional rights.

The documents included a charge by one INS office that the police crackdown and deportations of 18th Street members were a "political move" initiated by Mayor Richard Riordan's office.[43] Subsequent street sweeps in 1997–98 were based on a special list of 10,000 alleged gang members, 160 of whom were deported while another 40 were prosecuted on felony charges for illegally reentering the United States after being deported.[44] The sweeps had triggered objections from the U.S. Attorney's office, who said the assignments were "rammed down our throats" by the FBI.[45] One dismayed INS officer complained that the LAPD was "targeting a whole race of people."[46] Another agent wrote that his agency was waging "an undeclared war on individuals purported to be members of the 18th Street gang."[47] He went on to describe many victims as "working people on the way home when they were picked up by LAPD CRASH. Some were cooking or had just come from work. A lot of them were just getting off the bus."[48] In one document, the INS drug enforcement task force coordinator noted that "only a very small portion of those arrested were actually hard-core gang members," and recalled interviewing one individual who was an assistant manager at McDonald's and married with children.[49]

Officer Perez admitted that in 1996, along with his CRASH partner Nino Durden, he had violently abused a twenty-two-year-old Pico-Union gang member named Javier Francisco Ovando, who was arrested, handcuffed, shot point-blank in the head by the officers, then framed by the planting of the weapon and drugs near his fallen body.[50] It was never clear what Durden and Perez were doing in that particular neighborhood that night, since, according to one source,[51] they usually were assigned to another stakeout area. Why did they shoot Ovando not once but twice? Were they supplying him with drugs? Was he ripping them off for money? Was he a witness to anything? As a result of Perez's admission, the paraplegic, brain-damaged Ovando, who had no previous criminal record but had been criticized by the original trial judge for showing no "remorse," was released from state prison during the third year of a twenty-three-year sentence. Well, not released immediately. In an unprecedented step, the LAPD met him at the prison gate and flew him to a secret debriefing location for over two weeks without any contact with his family or friends. Like a scene from a Soviet spy novel, the LAPD's unexplained holding of Ovando showed the extent to which the department would go to control the story. Chief Bernard Parks wrote that my concerns were misplaced, that Ovando was "free to come and go."[52] It was not true. If anything, Ovando was suffering from the Stockholm syndrome, reportedly saying through third parties that the police were his friends. Taking "protect and serve" to a new level, the LAPD saw nothing inappropriate in secretly interrogating and trying to bond with an individual who had been framed and nearly assassinated by their officers. Ovando eventually was freed, and settled his grievance with the department for $15 million. But he made few public accusations, and soon disappeared into obscurity.

There were other oddities in the Perez story. Some of the cocaine Perez stole was from the locker of a white officer, Frank Lyga, who shot a black officer, Kevin Gaines, during a bizarre confrontation in 1997. Gaines was dating the estranged wife of Death Row Records founder, Suge Knight, and apparently living with her in Knight's Malibu home. Gaine's Mercedes' license plate declared "ITS OK IA," a dissing of the department's own Internal Affairs (IA) division.[53] Was it a coincidence? Immediately, rumors flew that Gaines was a Blood-affiliated intimate of Death Row Records, along with several other moonlighting cops. A photo surfaced of Rafael Perez partying in Lake Tahoe with an LAPD partner, David Mack, who had ripped off a Bank of America for hundreds of thousands of dollars. Mack was draped in an extravagant Blood-style red suit. As with most major scandals, fact and fiction bred conspiracy theories and obscure tips that exhausted most reporters or threatened to drive them to paranoid isolation.[54]

The Rampart issue proved uncontrollable and unending. While LAPD public statements and later investigations attempted to limit the scandal to a handful of rogue officers in a single precinct, the allegations of a wider problem continued to mount. As Perez kept spilling secrets about "a cancer . . . that has gone on a long time untreated,"[55] public defenders started reviewing 3,000 cases potentially tainted by false police testimony.[56] According to one attorney, Gregory Yates, handling a mountain of Rampart cases, Perez talked of framing some 100 defendants, and implicated 70 officers as being in the loop or not reporting what they knew. If those 70 officers each made 200 wrongful arrests—a reasonable number to Yates—the total number of tainted cases would be 14,000.[57] While those estimates could well be inflated, Chief Parks himself eventually called for the mass dismissal of tainted cases against 99 defendants in 57 cases where individuals were framed by his own officers.[58] Antigang injunctions were suspended temporarily across the city due to false police testimony (nearly half the approximately 140 18th Streeters named in restrictive injunctions were identified by LAPD officers caught up in Rampart).[59] One former assistant LAPD chief, David D. Dotson, accused the department of covering up extra-legal policing measures by "rogue units," based on his own experience.[60] As late as 2003, the scandal continued to erupt. The federal monitor appointed to oversee reform complained of inadequate supervision of gang units and retarded investigation of brutality complaints.[61] Investigators continued to pursue a former Rampart officer who, according to federal authorities, "organized friends, relatives and police officers into a network of thieves who stole drugs, money and property during home-invasion robberies, sometimes while in uniform."[62] Next it was admitted that ninety-six LAPD officers had avoided possible prosecution because department investigators waited until the statute of limitations had passed before sending the cases to the district attorney, including one instance where a cop beat up his girlfriend's ex-lover and made him walk barefoot on broken glass.[63]

Five years after it began, the Rampart scandal still reflected what the *Los Angeles Times* had declared in a bold February 2000 headline: "Police in Secret Group Broke Law Routinely, Transcripts Say," and went on to report that:

> An organized criminal subculture thrived within the Los Angeles Police Department, where a secret fraternity of anti-gang officers and supervisors committed crimes and celebrated shootings by awarding plaques to officers who killed or wounded people.[64]

One only had to visit LAPDGEAR.com on the cops' own Web site to experience a whiff of this paramilitary culture. The skull-and-crossbones insignia, with a rook on the cowboy hat, overlaid with aces and eights on the officers' Rampart patches, said it all. Describing themselves as "some of the finest officers on the job," even during the Rampart probe, the CRASH officers proudly described themselves as "ruthless regulators." Since they never knew what hand they would be dealt in "routing out the predators," they selected the "dead man's hand" of aces and eights.

As evidence that the Rampart scandal extended to other LAPD divisions, LAPDGEAR.com also advertised a skull image from the "Shootin' Newton" division, the chest of skulls logo representing the Harbor division, the skull image of the 77th Street division with the motto "77th Street Eat Their Dead," or the "hired guns" patch of the Southwest division. Perez ventured the opinion under oath that other CRASH units were implicated.[65] The department claimed it was an isolated incident due to management breakdowns, but internal interviews by a UCLA team suggested otherwise. One CRASH officer, faced with several misconduct complaints from gang members, said "Our job is to put assholes in jail. Gang members are pieces of shit as far as I'm concerned. They don't belong in this city!" The interviewers concluded after a meeting with rank-and-file officers at the 77th division that "they felt these kids had no fucking rights."[66]

The causes of the Rampart scandal were many layered. At the broadest civic leadership level, there was little resistance to the war on gangs scenario that permitted the anything-goes mentality. Checks and balances had broken down. Within the department itself, the paramilitary ethos had always dominated. Structurally the CRASH units were either beyond supervision or were given a green light to implement street justice as they saw it. Citizen complaints were "routinely dismissed or stonewalled," according to federal monitors.[67] Symbolically, the CRASH unit office at the Rampart division was located outside the overcrowded precinct's walls. From there, members of the fraternity-like units recruited themselves, formed a closed circle, even partied together at their favorite police bars. One original CRASH officer I interviewed noted the high proportion of Marines (like Rafael Perez) and other military veterans recruited to the Rampart CRASH unit.[68] When I once accompanied the Rampart CRASH unit on an undercover surveillance mission at the drug-dealing corner of Bonnie Brae and Fourth, the esprit and excitement were palpable as officers drove up alleys, entered their own stakeout building, hid behind venetian blinds, radioed their undercover buyers, and made three arrests. The targets were immigrant boys who appeared to be less than eighteen years of age.

However, there was a price to the macho paramilitarism. One officer described a post-traumatic stress disorder that he and, he believed, many other officers silently suffered. In his case, Officer Alex Sandoval started in the mid-eighties as an eighteen-year-old soldier stationed in Honduras during the Central American wars. He remembers doing security for Congresswoman Pat Schroeder when she visited. It was bloody business, and it psyched Alex to sign up for the LAPD CRASH units on his return. In 1991, when he was a twenty-four-year-old rookie, Alex got caught up in an off-duty confrontation with 18th Streeters not far from the Rampart precinct. He stopped his car to help a woman with a child who was being hassled, and soon was surrounded by hostile gang members who smashed his car. As they took off their belts and approached him, he pulled his gun and shouted at them to stop. As he remembers, an approaching gang member grinned and coldly said in Spanish, *"Mata me, mata me"* ("Kill me, kill me"). Alex decided not to pull the trigger, and then was run over by a car, which broke his leg. When he returned to duty from the hospital, an undefined anger had taken over his life. His partners jeered at him for not having "blown away his fucking ass." He kept replaying the scene until he decided he would never let it happen again. He signed up as an undercover narcotics agent, consciously wanting to inflict payback on any gang members he could. He was told by a department psychologist that he probably was the victim of a traumatic stress disorder. Under the circumstances, he couldn't rid himself of the images plaguing him. He was stuck emotionally. He chose to do high-risk drug deals, which meant being trained to lie for a living in conditions of extreme danger. He dropped thirteen- or fourteen-year-old gang members in rival neighborhoods after spreading rumors about them. He was out of control, having nightmares, sleeping around, abusing his wife, who left him for a sheriff's deputy. In therapy, he began to pull his life together, and eventually became a private investigator. Sandoval became convinced that his irrational, aggressive behavior was based on a fear that he was losing control. The behavior was a cry for help, but the message he kept receiving at work was to suck it up. Today he is a strong believer in mandatory evaluation and treatment for the traumas that too many officers, lacking treatment, transfer to others in various forms of brutality. "Subpoena the psychologists and make them disclose what they know," he says, or "we'll all keep going to doomsday with our little self-destructive mechanisms."[69]

One question is whether the Rampart syndrome is tied inextricably to a rigid form of warrior masculinity. While some 18.5 percent of LAPD officers were women at the time of the scandal, one review showed only one woman's name among seventy officers then implicated.[70] A decade earlier, during the Christopher Commission hearings, the Feminist Majority Foundation showed studies indicating that female police officers were equally effective but less authoritarian and more able to defuse potentially violent situations. The Christopher Commission itself echoed the feminist argument, finding that "female LAPD officers are involved in excessive use of force rates substantially below those of male officers."[71]

In essence, Rampart symbolized *sanctioned* aggression against gang members who were stigmatized as a class, as aliens from another planet without the rights belonging to other Americans. If there were 350 gang-related homicides by 100,000 gang members in L.A. County, clearly only a small percentage of gang members were committing murder. Yet they were all treated as accomplices. An experienced law enforcement insider, Merrick Bobb, said that "what happened in Rampart would not be tolerated in other parts of town. Gang profiling is a variant of racial profiling. Like New York, the dragnet policy to stop-and-frisk leads to wildly disproportionate numbers of African-American and Latino males enmeshed. [They] get kids on small charges, then warrants for not showing up, then tickets for trivial things until there are so many that a warrant is issued and they go to jail. Now they have a record for whatever purposes, and their name comes up every time the police run the records. You should narrow the dragnet by insisting that all stops be preceded by articulated reasonable suspicion and all arrests by proper probable cause, combined with audits of stops."[72] But few were listening, or motivated to respond, including some customary watchdogs. For example, before the scandal broke, even the local ACLU, long a critic of the LAPD, participated in ride-alongs with Rampart officers, and were quoted as feeling that "in terms of community relations, [the Rampart commander] did a good job, at least from our perspective."[73]

Those views would change when Perez began to talk. Many of the city's longtime civil rights leaders were relatively silent as well as the Rampart revelations unfolded, perhaps because their voting middle classes were distanced from the gang and immigrant subculture, which in many ways was an angry unfocused revolt against perceived failures of the older generation. Liberal state officials were quiet too, choosing not to hold oversight hearings. Only the *Times*'s coverage kept the issue alive. Then the ACLU, along with the National Lawyers Guild, threw itself behind the call for an independent investigation. Several community-based coalitions with immigrant constituencies began protesting. Some significant public officials, such as former Assembly speaker Antonio Villaraigosa and Senate Majority Leader Richard Polonco, raised their voices. Longtime civil rights attorneys Paul Hoffman, Robert Garcia, and I wrote the U.S. Justice Department's civil rights division to complain of a "pattern and practice" of violations that should trigger federal action. Eventually, the assistant U.S. attorney general, William Lan Lee, a former law partner of Garcia and Connie Rice at the Legal Defense Fund, launched just such an action, finding that the department was guilty of the unconstitutional use of force, including improper shootings, as well as a pattern of unconstitutional stop-and-frisks and arrests not based on reasonable suspicion or probable cause.[74] Rather than endure a jury trial, city officials would finally accept a federal consent decree outlining a path to reform under judicial supervision.

The notion of "pattern and practice" was a trade-off provision in hard-line federal crime control laws. It arose with the Rodney King incident in mind, Lee later told me.[75] Previously, civil rights attorneys were hamstrung in obtaining legal standing unless there was a specific police "policy" in question. The new "pattern and practice" formulation allowed the U.S. Justice Department to litigate "practices," not simply policies. It was still difficult to prod the feds to action. President Clinton enjoyed being seen among uniformed police officers, and was supported by their conservative, law-and-order unions. Attorney General Janet Reno was a lifelong prosecutor who wanted to ensure that any "pattern and practice" cases were beyond question. She also wanted the police chiefs on board for any Justice Department action. But things were heating up. The torture of Abner Louima and the killing of Amadou Diallo made national headlines. At a national gathering of police chiefs and community activists, Clinton was questioned roughly by the Reverend Al Sharpton about the Diallo case. When the Reverend Jesse Jackson started calling the White House, the newly installed Lee finally got a call from the West Wing asking what might be done. The White House was "pleasantly surprised" that Lee already had a special litigation unit working on police misconduct and, it just happened, had submitted a budget request for more funding. The White House caller was "very relieved," Lee added, to learn that they already were in support of the request, which increased the civil rights division's budget by 45 percent.

At the first news reports of Rampart, the LAPD message to Justice Department investigators was, in effect, "don't worry, we're doing a great job." However, the Justice Department already knew otherwise. In the wake of the 1992 Christopher Commission report, the LAPD had promised to set up a computerized monitoring system for "problem officers," but contrary to their statements, the city had done nothing to get it up and running. According to Lee, "had the tracking system been up and running, Rampart might never have happened." His lawyers felt they were misled.

Lee's office sent a "pattern and practice" notification letter to the City of Los Angeles, indicating that legal action would be taken unless a package of police reforms was implemented. At a subsequent meeting in Los Angeles, Mayor Riordan and Chief Parks were "pretty tepid," Lee recalled. Other city officials saw a chance to incorporate the Christopher reforms into a consent decree. But from the very beginning of the discussions, no one was questioning the policy of "gang suppression" that justified a range of legally questionable police behaviors. Instead, the central reforms on the table, in Los Angeles and around the country, had to do with racial profiling, which was "more palatable for middle class black communities."

The talks went on for months. Riordan and Parks dragged their feet and lobbied in Washington against the decree. "They would come in to see us, then get tired of seeing me, then they'd go to someone else," said Lee. Whatever conversations were being held in the White House, Lee was unaware of any pressure to rein in his investigation. Given the president's desire for photo-ops with cops in blue, Lee thought his crusade might be "inexpedient" but he continued, anyway. "We felt we were responding to an enforcement need." Lee was just in time. In the 2000 presidential race, candidate George Bush promised to lessen federal interference in local police controversies. Finally, however, L.A.'s resistance withered as Riordan was replaced as mayor in 2001 by City Attorney James Hahn, who supported the decree. Hahn removed Parks and brought in William Bratton as the new chief, who promised to abide by the decree.

While it was a sensational example, Los Angeles was not an isolated case. In any community he visited, Lee heard complaints of police misconduct. "It was very strange to go city to city and have people tell you the same thing." When he left office with the Clinton administration, Bill Lan Lee was investigating scandals in over twenty jurisdictions across the U.S. Under the Clinton Justice Department, the number of police sent to federal prison increased by 600 percent, to 668, and many experts agreed that "much of what has been revealed in Los Angeles . . . is being played out in cities and towns across America."[76]

Chicago. A secret antigang unit was described by a federal judge in 1999 as having "regularly engaged in the physical abuse and torture of prisoners to extract confessions."[77] One victim won a $1.1 million civil suit over claims that he was "tortured with electric shocks and handcuffed to a hot radiator."[78]

Miami. Federal authorities charged thirteen SWAT officers called the "Jump Out Boys" in 2001 with shooting unarmed people and planting guns as evidence. One was a seventy-three-year-old man in a two-room house where 123 bullets were fired.[79] Four officers eventually were convicted by juries, and the Jump Out unit was disbanded. The scandal followed one in the previous decade when two dozen police were found guilty of forming a gang of their own to tap drug proceeds.

Cincinnati. After antipolice riots in 2001, the federal government initiated pressure for police reform. One black minister urged a national boycott, writing that the "police are killing, raping [and] planting false evidence."[80]

Wilmington, Delaware. Using claims of reasonable suspicion, police formed a "jump out squad" to burst out of patrol cars to photograph, question, and search individuals. The campaign, called "Operation Bold Eagle," stopped 658 individuals in a three-month period. "If you're not a criminal, you don't have anything to worry about," explained one officer. "It's for future reference."[81]

Oakland, California. Federal authorities charged four officers known as "the Riders" (a play on the Raiders) with faking evidence, planting drugs, and beating up suspects in 2000. Their alleged leader, known as "Choker," disappeared underground and may have left the country. Prosecutors threw out eighty-two arrests in their review of cases filed by "the Riders."[82]

Detroit, Michigan. Habitual patterns of false arrests and illegal detentions, the highest rate in the nation of fatal police shootings, and the shooting of a teenager in the face by officers who mistook his chili fries for a gun led the Justice Department in 2003 to negotiate a five-year consent decree with an outside monitor.[83]

Houston, Texas. The police chief resigned in 2003 after troubles that included the shooting death of a resident in a drug raid, hundreds of police searches without warrants, shakedowns from cantina owners, protection of prostitution rings, and mass arrests of innocent people.[84]

State of Georgia. In 1998, the federal authorities indicted the State of Georgia for operating "paramilitary boot camps" containing "widespread neglect and abuses." Colorado, North Carolina, and Arizona also were forced to eliminate and reform their juvenile justice camps. In South Dakota, Justice Department investigators found children "handcuffed spread-eagled to beds."[85]

The New York City Police Scandals

New York City deserves special attention because its law-and-order issues led to Republican electoral victories in the nineties and because its chief of police,

William Bratton, also became the chief in L.A. after the Rampart scandal. The modern history of the NYPD is filled with corruption and brutality scandals, beginning with the revelations of an honest officer, Frank Serpico, in the early seventies. The subsequent Knapp Commission found widespread police involvement in the drug trade, including kidnapping of witnesses to prevent their testimony at trials, and providing armed protection for dealers. There was the "Buddy Boys" scandal in the eighties, which again involved drug dealing by police. Then came the Mollen Commission in the early nineties, which uncovered "clusters of officers," especially in Harlem, who protected friendly drug traffickers, beat up the uncooperative ones, falsified evidence, and "testilied" in court.[86] An Amnesty International study of ninety cases of police shootings in the late eighties to mid-nineties in New York City identified thirty instances in which fatal shootings "did not warrant the use of lethal force."[87]

Most commentators on public safety will celebrate the "miracle" reductions of violent crime during that decade, which will be analyzed shortly. But it is well to remember that during the nineties, New York City experienced a slow-motion Rampart scandal, as documented by the investigations of Michael Jacobson and J. Phillip Thompson.[88] Hundreds of thousands of indigent African American and Latino youth were detained individually for up to nineteen days following arraignment on misdemeanor charges. Misdemeanor arrests escalated from 129,404 in 1993 to 197,320 by 1999. Some 900,000 people were incarcerated in city jails in those same years, 92 percent of them Latino or African American. The city finally paid upward of $50 million to settle a lawsuit on behalf of 50,000 of those individuals who claimed to have been strip-searched, the largest such monetary settlement in New York history. Citizen complaints and civil rights claims rose by 75 percent between 1992 and 1996, mostly in nine precincts out of the city's seventy-six. The torture-rape of Abner Louima in an NYPD precinct on August 9, 1997, and the shooting of an immigrant named Amadou Diallo on February 4, 1999, with forty-one bullets while he was reaching for his wallet, became international scandals. The police shooting of Patrick Dorismond, twenty-six, on March 16, 2000, was particularly revealing. Dorismond, a security guard, was shot while refusing to buy crack cocaine from an undercover NYPD officer. Mayor Giuliani "violated legal ethics" by releasing Dorismond's juvenile arrest records in order to discredit him. His only arrest was a violation punishable by a summons when Dorismond was thirteen. Nevertheless, Giuliani declared that he was "no altar boy" (although it turned out that Dorismond actually had been an altar boy).[89]

While the *New York Times* reported that most white residents were comfortable with the police behavior they saw, nine out of ten blacks felt that "the police often engaged in brutality against blacks [and] almost two-thirds said that police brutality against members of minority groups is widespread." The state attorney general in 1999 reviewed and condemned the stop-and-frisk policies, finding that 90 percent of those targeted were Latino or African American, and that the requirement of "reasonable suspicion" was not articulated in one-fourth of the stops. After the Diallo murder, civil rights attorneys sued the NYPD in a case that closely mirrored the Rampart scandal. The NYPD's Street Crime Units (SCUs) were front-line paramilitary police who routinely violated constitutional rights by "tossing" any street corner youth they encountered. Giuliani argued— as William Bratton would do in Los Angeles a few years later—that the protests over Diallo's killing caused NYPD officers to retreat from aggressive tactics, thus allowing killings to rise.[90] The litigation was settled with an agreement to disband the SCUs and adopt new policies to avoid racial profiling.[91]

This was about *gang*-profiling more than racial profiling. The rationale was that against an elusive, invisible "terrorist" enemy it was necessary to take preemptive action to bend the laws and procedures in order to capture the teenage predators who often proved too difficult to catch in the felonious act. *Paramilitarism* became the dirty secret of a dirty war against an allegedly dirty enemy. Middle-class leadership looked away.[92]

Back in my high school days in 1954, by comparison, the black and white rates of youth unemployment were close to equal, with sixteen-to-nineteen-year-old blacks slightly *more* employed. By the 1980s, black youth unemployment had almost quadrupled while the rate for white young people remained the same.[93] Similarly, fifty years ago, whites were 77 percent of all prison inmates compared to blacks who constituted 22 percent. But by the 1990s, blacks were 45 percent of all those in state and federal prisons.[94] In California, two-thirds of all state and local inmates were black or brown, with the same percentage identified as gang members.[95]

According to Professor Troy Duster, writing in 1997, "during the past two decades, we have seen the greatest shift in the racial composition of the inmates in our prisons in all of US history."[96] Led by California, the United States imprisoned more people—and built more prisons—in the period from 1980 to 2000 than at any time in the nation's history.[97] In the 1970s, the national rate of imprisonment per 100,000 people had been slightly over 100, a ratio little changed since the time of my birth in the thirties.[98] By 1998, the rates were an astonishing 690 per 100,000 and growing.[99] By comparison, the rates in England and Japan that year were only 125 and 45, respectively.[100] According to Anthony Platt, by the year 2000 the United States had 5 percent of the world's population but 25 percent of its inmates.[101] Most of those inmates were black and brown and, significant numbers were identified as gang members. According to one survey during the era,[102] in California alone, there were 1,100 "tough on crime" changes in the penal codes, such as the lengthening of sentences. Twenty-four new state prisons were built in California between 1980 and 2000, with the number of state inmates shooting up from some 28,000 when I was elected in 1982 to over 150,000 when I retired in 2000. Three-quarters of those entering California prisons were technical parole violators (compared to one-third nationally). The revolving door was spinning madly: 36,000 parolees were released in L.A. County in 2001, 98 per day, with $200 in their pockets. A federal study showed that of 270,000 released inmates, two-thirds were rearrested within three years. Youth of color were 2.8 times as likely to be arrested for violent crime as white youth, 6.2 percent more likely to be transferred to adult courts, and seven times as likely to be sent to prison by those adult courts. Under Attorney General John Ashcroft, these trends were reinforced by Ashcroft's order that prosecutors notify his office whenever judges handed down lenient sentences.[103]

Somewhere between the 1960s and 1990s, sympathy-provoking public images of racial and civil rights injustices had been morphed into frightening ones of crime, violence, and gangs. A 1987 study in the California Attorney General's office revealed that two-thirds of adult nonwhite males were arrested before age twenty-nine.[104] The analysis excluded juvenile arrests and arrests after age thirty, which, had they been included, would have meant a risk of arrest surpassing 85 percent.[105] If limited to inner-city males, excluding their rural counterparts, the range would have been over 90 percent.[106] A follow-up 1993 study sponsored by the California State Assembly indicated that one-sixth of black men age sixteen and older are arrested each year (and that 81 percent of Latinos and 92 percent of black men arrested on drug charges were released for lack of evidence or inadmissible evidence).[107] A 1990 study by the Sentencing Project indicated that "on an average day in the United States, one in every four African American men ages twenty to twenty-nine was either in prison, jail, or on probation/parole.[108] Another survey showed that on a typical day in the nation's capital, Washington, D.C., 42 percent of all eighteen-to-thirty-five-year-old African American males were in jail, in prison, on probation/parole, on bond, or being sought on warrants.[109] This escalation of race-related incarceration continued even while the nation's violent crime rate reached its lowest level since 1973 and property crimes dropped by 70 percent.[110]

I have argued that gangs and the "thug" lifestyle escalated from the vacuum left by the failure of the civil rights movement to change America. With official racism discredited, not enough Americans have been willing to face the new, unconscious, crime-coded, institutional racism. Instead, the blame for urban crime is focused on the scapegoat, white guilt is lifted, and the urban racial and class divides grow far beyond what I imagined possible as a freedom rider in the early sixties. Worse, the nightmare is being globalized.

The Globalization of Gangs

The much heralded process of globalization includes the globalization of gangs as a tragic and little noticed corollary. The process is not simply due to global communications technologies spreading the word from South Central to the global south, nor simply because drug networks cross continental boundaries. The primary reason for the globalization of gangs is that the dominant Western development model leaves unemployment, child and sweatshop labor, and cultural uprootedness for billions of young people in its wake. By 2003, engaged academics at New York's John Jay College of Criminal Justice and the University of Illinois—Chicago were holding international symposiums on the globalization of street gangs, with research papers produced from every continent.[111]

Mainly in this book I will focus on the example of Homies Unidos, a group of gang peacemakers originally from El Salvador. As war refugees, they grew up on the streets of L.A. forming gangs for all the usual reasons: identity, territory, protection against existing gangs, access to the underground economy. When they were ultimately arrested and deported, the gang subculture was deported/exported with them. I have interviewed tattooed L.A. gangsters on the streets of El Salvador, in Mexican villages, in Belize, and in Jamaica. In the wake of America's Central American wars of intervention in the 1970s, these deportees have become a primary security problem for Latin American authorities. They are, in the words of a Homies Unidos rap song, *las frutas de la guerra* (the fruits of war).

While there is no systematic overview of this globalizing process, news items and academic papers abound. Some examples provide flavor. In Chiapas, according to James Diego Vigil, urban gangs have formed as a result of the dislocation of thousands of indigenous people in the past decade.[112] In Mexico City, *los chavos banda* (kids of the gang) began appearing in the eighties, wearing painted faces, long hair, and platform shoes.[113] In Honduras, 700 alleged gang members were killed on city streets between 1997 and 2002.[114] Brazil's street gangs have been depicted brilliantly in *City of God*, the 2002 Academy Award–nominated film.[115] Street corner gangs in Kingston, Jamaica, are the focus of Laurie Gunst's 1995 work, *Born Fi' Dead*.[116] In post-apartheid South Africa, gangs of young men are called "The Americans" and "The Hard Livings," and they put up murals of Tupac and Snoop Dogg. "Of course, the boys here dream of being gangsters, it's their only hope for becoming somebody," says a school principal.[117] Similar groupings have arisen in the Muslim suburbs of Paris, the all-white housing projects of post-communist Poland, and among Maori youth in New Zealand.[118]

The phenomenon of anarchic, dispossessed urban youth has created a harsh reaction. Leading globalization (and militarization) advocates like Robert Kaplan stir public fear with apocalyptic images of a future filled with "barely manageable turmoil," where huge countries like India and Mexico will be "undermined by a volcano of unemployed youth in urban slums," while "armies of murderous teenagers [emerge] in West Africa," and terrorists multiply among "hundreds of millions of unemployed young males in the developing world, angered by the income disparities that accompany globalization."[119]

Does Kaplan offer a plan to reduce these "income disparities that accompany globalization"? Does he support the United Nations anti-poverty program that addresses the needs of "homeless children [who] are neglected by society and denied shelter, food, clothing and education [and who] in sheer desperation are often forced into a life of crime and prostitution in order to survive"?[120] Does he consider the future from the viewpoint of those without futures? No, because globalization is "Darwinian," he proclaims:

> It means economic survival of the fittest—those groups and individuals that are disciplined, dynamic and ingenious will float to the top, while cultures that do not compete well technologically will produce an inordinate number of warriors [animated by] the thrill of violence.[121]

The gang menace in Kaplan's grim scenario flows like lava into a larger field of frightening terrorist images: "armies of murderous teenagers in West Africa, Russian and Albanian Mafiosi, Latin American drug kingpins, West Bank suicide bombers, and associates of Osama bin Laden who communicate by e-mail." What they crave, like Achilles, he claims, is "slaughter and blood and the choking groans of men."[122]

Kaplan is far from alone in projecting such apocalyptic futures. A more balanced analyst of empires, Michael Ignatieff, defends military imperialism as a last resort to preserve global order when nation states fail. Markets cannot create order, but they require order "where it breaks down, and crime, chaos and terror take root in the rotten, unpoliced interstices,"[123] which are the common spawning grounds for street gangs. Ignatieff is addressing a very real global issue, the break-down of order in most inner-city neighborhoods (although he locates the problem in epicenters like Bosnia, failing to notice its appearance in American cities as well). As a self-defined liberal realist, he endorses military action as a necessary condition of nation-building or social reconstruction. What is missing from his global analysis, like that of law-and-order advocates domestically, is any sense that the economy matters as both a contributing cause and solution to the chaos afflicting poor communities. Like Kaplan, Ignatieff's book *Empire Lite* never advocates increasing the American contribution to United Nations' antipoverty programs (which was ten times greater during the first Kennedy administration than currently), or supporting mandatory antisweatshop measures in the global economy. In his view, order must be reestablished first, as if millions of the young, poor, and disenfranchised will be rewarded if first they behave themselves. This glaring analytical omission permits the conclusion that global anarchy is rooted in fanaticisms that have no relation to the divide between rich and poor.

The hysterical view of inexplicable terrorism gained credence in 2002 when federal authorities arrested Jose Padilla, a former member of the Chicago Latin Disciples, for conspiring with al-Qaeda to detonate a "dirty" radioactive bomb.[124] White House officials, classifying Padilla as an "enemy combatant," denied any access to lawyers or the media, arguing that "any effort to ascertain the facts concerning Padilla's conduct while amongst the nation's enemies would entail an unacceptable risk of obstructing war efforts," thus elevating the former gang member to the status of symbolic demon.[125] Coincidentally, the arrest occurred in the same week that thousands turned out in Queens for the funeral of Italian mobster John Gotti. It seemed that as one faded symbol of gangsterism was buried, another was resurrected. It was not the first fusion of street gangs and terrorism, but the most dramatic. In 1987, four El Rukn members were convicted of taking $2.5 million from Libya, allegedly to plan terrorism, leading *The Economist* to opine that "there is a curious and disturbing link between such gangs and terrorism."[126] In the 1990s, after the fall of the Soviet Union, the White House reassigned 100 top FBI agents to the war against street gangs, and followed up by

integrating the antigang strategy into the war against narco-terrorism.[127] That
organized and sophisticated conspiracy and cartel models hardly fit the disorganized character of street gangs did not seem to matter. The law-and-order establishment was finding a new enemy to replace the old ones of the Cold War.
Anyone who doubted these connections and paradigms was soft on terrorism,
narco-trafficking, gangs, the works.

The law-and-order globalists adopt the Darwinian assumption that the present form of the world economy and distribution of privileges is the only rational
one, reflecting the survival-of-the-fittest. The same worldview was propagated
during slavery times, and by the American robber barons, who claimed that
African Americans, Indians, Mexicans, as well as immigrant industrial workers,
lacked discipline, dynamism, and ingenuity. White ethnic gang members (mostly
Irish, Italian, and Jewish) were characterized as incorrigible and inferior. It turned
out that the "permanent underclass" of those times fought its way out of slavery
and into the middle class through rebellions, union drives, community action,
and political parties, sharply altering the Darwinian balance and achieving
middle-class status. The same possibilities await Kaplan's "hundreds of millions
of unemployed young males . . . angered by the income disparities that accompany globalization." Many can and do join social movements aimed at abolishing
slave and sweatshop labor. Others battle for human rights, safe workplaces, clean
water and air, insisting on a globalization that includes the same legal protections
for workers that are reserved for investors in Kaplan's model of globalization. If
the Kaplans of the world resist these aspirations for justice, this anger will grow
into further violence and pathology, a global "distemper of the slum" that Riis
identified a century earlier.

The second inflated claim, that the gang threat equals "homeland terrorism,"
and that these terrorists are centrally organized cartels, is equally dubious. Those
making the assertions are not marginal fanatics, but responsible people like
William Bratton, who has been a police chief in Boston, New York, and Los Angeles.[128] Bratton says that L.A. street gangs are "homeland terrorists," that they
are "worse than the Mafia," and that they are "the head that needs to be cut off"
to stop the gang menace from spreading to the world. A Bratton aide pledges to

use the "full force" of RICO (Racketeer Influenced and Corrupt Organizations Act) against gang members, because "that's what got Al Capone."[129] In response, Father Gregory Boyle, who has buried over 100 gang members during decades of ministry in East Los Angeles, says from experience that gang members are essentially *"disorganized* crime."[130] Criticizing Bratton for creating a "mythic enemy," Father Boyle adds, "Gangs rarely have a Tony Soprano–type leader . . . if gangs are run at all, they are only loosely managed by an ever-changing politburo or informal 'board of directors' that is fluid and unstable."[131] The vertical law enforcement model of gangs as "syndicates" meets the needs of prosecutors, however. Both federal RICO laws and the 1986 California Street Terrorism Enforcement and Prevention (STEP) act make prosecutions possible without requiring evidence that targeted individuals actually broke an existing law, only that they served a "hierarchy" that was responsible for law-breaking behavior. Malcolm Klein, a longtime researcher on street gangs, describes the prosecutorial logic this way:

> (1) These agencies know and understand organized crime; (2) they do not know street gangs; and (3) they often assume the two are similar, when in fact they are not. The DEA in particular gets confused because drug distribution organizations such as Colombian cartels and Jamaican posses share an interest in drugs with some street gangs. Calling each kind of group a gang leads to the application of cartel thinking to street gangs.[132]

The terrorism charge is equally distorted. Certainly a drive-by shooting is a terrorist act, defined as the killing of innocent civilian life. But terrorist *organizations* go far beyond the usual capacity of street gangs. In the first place, they usually have an ideology, however twisted, where the typical street gang has none whatsoever. Secondly, they have training camps, safe houses, weapons dumps, intelligence operatives, military technicians, disciplined and clandestine organizational structures often spanning the globe. In terms of lifestyle, terrorists rarely drink or act out in public. Gang members display all the opposite characteristics. The association between gangs and terrorism is made for political reasons, to hype the threat, and also for convenience of prosecution. For example, under the antiterrorism STEP act, evidence of association with a gang is presented to the judge *after* a criminal conviction for purposes of adding three, five, or seven years to the sentence. That is, a conviction for armed robbery by a *gang* member (as opposed to a *non-gang* career criminal) receives up to three years longer incarceration for the same crime, as well as permanent inclusion in a secret gang database for use in the event of future cases. Much of the information is inaccurate and out-of-date. There is no notification or appeals mechanism for de-listing. In some cases, school kids have been rounded up, identified, and told if there was a fight they would all be expelled as gang members. "I don't think the police *know* what people are using the database for," says civil liberties lawyer Carol Sobel.[133] According to one knowledgeable investigator, the database includes only gangs of color, not white Aryan or skin head groups.[134] The database is the template of a new McCarthyism.

The Neoconservative Dream of a New Victorian Order

The war on gangs, and the larger war on terrorism have been pursued by the neoconservatives who first came to power during the Ronald Reagan presidency and later realized their ambitions in the second George Bush presidency.

The ubiquitous James Q. Wilson led the charge in 1995 by asserting that a teenage crime wave was inevitable. By the end of the 1990s there would be 30,000 more "young muggers, killers, and thieves than we now have," he claimed, admonishing Americans to *"get ready."*[135] In *Body Count* (1996), Reagan's drug and education czar William Bennett, drug warrior John P. Walters, and a number-crunching protégé of Wilson's, John J. DiIulio, elaborated the same thesis: "a new generation of street criminals is upon us—*the youngest, biggest and baddest generation any society has ever known."*[136] DiIulio, writing an article entitled "The Coming of the Super-Predators" in the *Weekly Standard*, the house organ of the neoconservatives,[137] enlarged on Wilson's previous prophecy, claiming there would be an additional 270,000 *"juvenile super-predators," raised in "practically perfect criminogenic environments"* who would *"terrorize our nation"* by 2010.[138]

The declared purpose of these neoconservative alarms was to discredit two liberal ideas: first, that the purpose of punishment should be rehabilitation ("a false premise that has emasculated the criminal justice system"). Instead, the authors argued that super-predators were incorrigibles, beyond rehabilitation, afflicted with "moral poverty," perhaps requiring transfer to Christian-oriented orphanages. The second intention was to "demolish as politically correct myths the ideas that economic poverty causes crime or that the United States imprisons a disproportionate number of its citizens."[139] As the foremost political representative of these neoconservatives, former Mayor Rudolph Giuliani of New York City bluntly declared, "There has never been a proven connection between the state of the economy and crime, and there is absolutely no correlation between unemployment and crime."[140]

"liberal myths"

There may be no causal chain between a specific cigarette and a single case of lung cancer either, but that doesn't mean there are no correlations. Most of those arrested for murder are drawn from the ranks of the "desperately down-and-out," who lack the resources to settle disputes nonviolently.[141] As for imprisoning a "disproportionate" number of citizens, the incarceration rate in the U.S. is five to ten times higher than any other developed nation.[142]

Wilson first articulated his claim that there are no root causes of crime in 1975. The argument was reiterated in *The Moral Sense* (1993), with the accusation that sixties-style moral relativism replaced "the belief in personal responsibility with the notion of social causation and by supplying to those marginal persons at risk for crime a justification for doing what they might have done anyway."[143] The same themes were amplified by the writings of Charles Murray, a self-identified Whig, in two bestsellers, *Losing Ground* and *The Bell Curve*.[144] The first work blamed welfare programs for creating a degenerative culture of fatherless families and shiftless dependency, making no connections with the culture of capitalism and greed. The second work, with Richard Herrnstein, revived genetic theories of black inferiority. For Murray and many neoconservatives, solutions required a renewal of nineteenth-century morals and institutions. Only a heightened priority on punishment would protect these New Victorians from the New

Rabble.[145] Murray and Herrnstein proposed an apartheid-like "custodial state" in which the dangerous classes would be controlled in "a high-tech and more lavish version of the Indian reservation . . . while the rest of America tries to go about its business."[146]

The theme of a "coming storm of super-predators" swept the nation politically. Republicans like Representative Bill McCollum, chairman of the House subcommittee on crime, warned in 1996 that *"Now, here is the really bad news: this nation will soon have more teenagers than it has had in decades. Brace yourself for the coming generation of super-predators."*[147] On the Democratic end of the spectrum, President Bill Clinton invoked the same demographic time bomb theory: "We have about *six years* to get ahead of this juvenile crime and drug problem that will be almost unbearable, unmanageable, and painful."[148] Backed by a bipartisan majority, the nation accelerated its prison building, expanded penalties on juvenile crimes in forty-seven states, and lowered the age at which juveniles could be tried as adults (to fourteen in liberal California, and ten in even more liberal Wisconsin).[149]

One emerging politician who embraced the neoconservative crime theories was George W. Bush in his successful 1994 gubernatorial campaign against Texas Governor Ann Richards. His campaign consultant, Karl Rove, decided to focus on the theme "that we faced this generation of juvenile criminals," despite the fact that most crime rates had fallen in Texas and Governor Richards already had implemented a historic prison-building program.[150] Bush's consultants ran basically identical law-and-order commercials to those used in two other governors' races that year, California and Illinois.[151] Bush already was grounded in hostility to sixties "permissiveness" (he was a Yale football team cheerleader during that era) and, on Rove's suggestion, now became a devotee of Marvin Olasky, a University of Texas professor, who rejected social welfare and jobs programs. A Communist until the seventies, Olasky became a born-again Christian and the godfather of Bush's doctrine of "compassionate conservatism." Like Bennett's work, Olasky's *The Tragedy of American Compassion* identified with nineteenth-century religious orphanages and charities rather than jobs or antipoverty programs.[152] Whatever

had to get
ahead of
the prob -
prisons
ext. penalties
↓ age adult

else may be said of returning to the nineteenth century, the notions worked politically. Bush's consultant described juvenile crime as "a way to open up a new front on the crime issue and it worked very well"; the voting public, according to two Bush biographers, was "terrified at the prospect of violent young thugs with guns, stealing cars, committing murder."[153]

The great fallacy in the super-predator thesis was that demography is destiny, that one's fate is determined essentially by the date and zip code of birth. The Wilson-Bennett-DiIulio triumvirate forecast an *increase* in super-predators simply because there would be an *increase of teenagers*. But there was no clear causal relation between youth violence and demographics, according to University of California Franklin Zimring in *American Youth Violence* (1988).[154] DiIulio said he regretted promoting the super-predator notion and confessed that he had experienced a "conversion of heart."[155] Specifically, Zimring's data showed an increasing rate of youth violence in the late 1980s while the size of the youth population declined, and a decrease in such violence after 1993 when the youth population was growing.[156] It wasn't the demographic threat of more young people on the loose, Zimring contended, but instead the crack cocaine epidemic, socioeconomic frustrations, and greater gun use. Nor was it the "moral poverty" the neoconservatives claimed arose from single-parent fatherless families. Large decreases in youth crime occurred on two occasions since 1980—1980–84 and 1993–96—Zimring found, without any shift in family structure to explain them.[157]

Further challenge to the Wilson-Bennett-DiIulio doctrine came from Michael Males, a statistician at the University of California—Irvine.[158] For perspective, Males noted that young people faced far greater hazards at home or work than in the streets or schools, based on federal statistics from hospital emergency rooms.[159] Of reported injuries, 48 percent occurred at home, 29 percent in the workplace, 15 percent in the streets, and 6 percent at school. As for the predictions of exploding teen carnage, Males found a 53 percent decline in teen homicide rates in the 1990–96 period, the period when *Body Count* was written.[160]

In a volume published by Harvard University Press (2001), Bernard Harcourt further disputed the neoconservative's evidence that clear causal links existed between "disorder" and crime.[161] He argued that the crime declines in New York City were likely influenced by factors such as the 25 percent increase in police hirings (to a phenomenal 40,000) and the fall of the crack cocaine trade. According to a study of seventeen cities nationally during eight consecutive years between 1991 and 1999, homicide rates declined independent of whether tough neoconservative policing doctrines had been implemented.[162] Interestingly, San Francisco, long attacked by neoconservatives as a symbol of liberal permissiveness, maintained high levels of social programs, eliminated its youth curfew policy, and nonetheless showed the sharpest declines in total violent felony crime for any city between 1992 and 1998.[163]

Zimring ridiculed the neoconservatives for "blaming the toddler" as being a future predator, a conclusion that could only be based on believing that "the causes of serious juvenile violence are fixed and objective circumstances, such as the number of children in a population group, family status, place of residence, and characteristics determined at a very early age."[164] The neoconservative doctrine of demographic fatalism would become a "manifesto for disinvestments" in the inner city, Zimring warned, for if the problem was moral poverty, if future violence was preordained, "why waste efforts and resources in trying to stop it?"[165] The neoconservatives took no notice of *socioeconomic* demographics such as the labor market studies finding that 5 million sixteen-to-twenty-four-year-olds were both out of work and out of school.[166] Thus, corporate deindustrialization or public disinvestment from inner cities could be rationalized as unrelated to the problems of at-risk youth, which, according to the neoconservatives, were moral rather than economic. In fact, the whole architecture of the New Deal and Great Society could be dismantled because crime, to William Bennett, was a problem of sin, not injustice.[167] Bush's guru Olasky provided much the same rationalization, arguing that the greatest need of poor people was redemption, not reform.[168] The great corporate downsizing of the 1980s and 1990s, which stripped away working-class jobs from metropolitan areas all across the country and left crack cocaine as the main economic opportunity for many in the inner city, was not to blame for the gang violence that arose in its wake. The homeboys were supposed to just say no.

The notion of moral poverty as root cause was articulated primarily by Bennett, one of many neoconservatives influenced by conservative philosophies that upheld the value of "moral absolutes" against what they perceived as the "moral relativism" of the sixties generation.[169] In this view, articulated in Bennett's best-selling *Book of Virtues*,[170] the root of America's crisis was the failure of parents to firmly educate their children in absolute rights and wrongs. As a result, the sixties generation allegedly was conditioned to believe that truth and morality were relative, to tolerate different viewpoints as equally legitimate, and to search for underlying causes to evils that could only be banished by force. Thus, permissive liberalism, the sixties counterculture, and the so-called death of God were to blame for the rise of the super-predator.

There always was a hidden double standard in the neoconservative ideology; they were more tolerant of corporate wrongdoing like tax cheating or insider trading than toward street crimes, for example. In Bennett's case, the moral absolutes came to an abrupt suspension when the issue was his personal gambling addiction, where he failed to follow his moral orders to set boundaries on his own appetites. In 2003, Bennett was exposed by *Newsweek* and the *Washington Monthly* as having lost $8 million during his "virtuous" years playing slot machines and video poker from Atlantic City to Las Vegas.[171] The casino industry that gave Bennett "preferred customer" status (limousines, free hotel rooms, revolving lines of credit, etc.) was the focus of numerous investigations of drug funding, as Bennett, the former U.S. drug czar, knew well. Federal indictments in the mid-nineties, when Bennett was writing his moral manifestos, uncovered "crimes in the hundreds of billions of dollars amid international corruption at the highest levels of business and government" with Las Vegas as the nexus.[172] Thus Bennett's personal gambling habit compromised his integrity as a public official. At first, Bennett tried to defend himself against the embarrassing press reports, even dredging up Catholic teachings on bingo as a rationale for his casino binging. Shortly after, however, Bennett announced he was quitting gambling,[173] having experienced either moral conversion or stern lectures from his fellow neoconservatives. Whatever the reason, it wasn't viable any longer for Bennett to receive $50,000 honorariums for speeches on morality and then use the money to repay his gambing debts. The depth of his conversion remained suspect, however. For example, on the same day that Bennett retreated, I received a mailed fundraising appeal from Bennett on Heritage Foundation letterhead warning against "radicals" who have been "increasingly successful at recruiting young people who have been steeped in moral relativism all their lives."

While Bennett was gambling away his virtue, the conservative radio commentator Rush Limbaugh, who "regularly told his listeners that drug users should be jailed,"[174] was buying illegal drugs apparently supplied by his maid. The voice of the Republican revolution, the man who said "if people are violating the law by doing drugs, they ought to be accused and they ought to be convicted and they ought to be sent up,"[175] was popping OxyContins, "a particularly potent narcotic," which he pathetically purchased in parking lots with cigar boxes filled with cash. "Notorious for skewering politicians who waffle, [Limbaugh] played coy with his audience for a week about the pill-popping scandal," the *Daily News* noted wryly.[176] Limbaugh finally checked himself into a rehabilitation center and solicited prayers from the faithful. In any other case, Limbaugh would have been denouncing the dealer and addict as nothing but street scum, calling for their prosecution, and deriding tax-subsidized treatment programs. The man who warned that "we're becoming too tolerant, folks,"[177] asked for the same understanding he had always denied others. One can only hope that his rehabilitation will lead to greater empathy with the other homies on the streets.

"Broken Windows" or Broken Promises?

The most effective instance of neoconservative ideology packaged as popular politics was the "broken windows" theory, which first appeared in a 1982 *Atlantic Monthly* article by James Q. Wilson and a Harvard researcher named George Kelling, also associated with the Manhattan Institute, a conservative think tank. The "broken windows" argument rapidly became incorporated in the successful Republican mayoral efforts of Riordan in Los Angeles and Giuliani in New York, and the statements of the police chief who served both cities, William Bratton.

In their 1982 *Atlantic* essay, the authors wrote that "if a window in a building is broken and is left unrepaired, all the rest of the windows will soon be broken . . . one unrepaired broken window is a signal that no one cares, and so breaking more windows costs nothing."[178] The theory swiftly became gospel among politicians and the media, and the NYPD a magnet for consultants, with as many as 200 police officials from over 100 countries receiving briefings in 1998 alone.[179] It was an ideological crusade as well, attacking anyone associated with a liberal concern over root causes. Solid academics like Dr. Andrew Karmen at John Jay College, who tried dispassionately to understand why crime was declining, were beaten up editorially as "professors" and "double-domes" who allegedly believed that " 'social forces' or lunar cycles of some such nonsense are the most important factors affecting crime . . . [or believe that] crime trends are influenced far more by demographics and social forces and yadda, yadda, yadda than by police work."[180] New York governor George Pataki boasted that "we, as servants of the people, are not charged with carrying out a sociological study." In Pataki's account, "criminals cause crime."[181] Bratton added his own ridicule of sociological theories: "We'll knock them down like ducks in a row."[182]

In part the theory fortified the argument for foot patrols and a greater emphasis on community policing, with which few reformers could quarrel. In addition, developers and business interests backed Kelling's argument that "restoring order is key to revitalizing our cities" through gentrification and office development, "regardless of whether a reduction in crime results."[183] But the doctrine's political popularity arose from deeper roots in the realignment of liberalism that was accelerating in the nineties. For Republican strategists like the late Lee Atwater, urban crime was a "wedge issue" to split the Democratic electorate.[184] Feeling that twenty-five years of civil rights policies had failed to restore urban peace, battered by ugly conflicts between Orthodox Jews and African Americans in places like Crown Heights, fearful of drug addicts and panhandlers increasingly appearing in urban space, large numbers of cosmopolitan Democrat voters decided to give law-and-order a try. Even if there were root causes of street violence, they seemed to reason, it first was necessary to reclaim the streets for the middle class. As just one example, friends of mine in Greenwich Village, who might be described as left-wingers with children, were puzzled when I complained that Gramercy Park was closed at midnight by NYPD units driving small armored vehicles with powerful headbeams. My friends supported Mayor Giuliani's policy of such midnight sweeps because it made them feel a greater sense of overall safety. It was easy to understand the popularity of these policies.

But the questionable issue was whether making aggressive sweeps of juveniles for petty "broken windows" offenses (parole violations, driving without a license, panhandling, etc.) was indeed a deterrent against more serious crimes in the future. To the extent that "broken windows" was about stopping and frisking "undesirables" without reasonable cause, the police were sure to obtain *some* evidence related to other crimes. For the police it was a "bonanza," Bratton said.[185] According to police data, one out of every seven subway fare evaders had prior warrants, one out of twenty-one was carrying a handgun, and several thousand of the *hundreds* of thousands frisked in 1997 were found with other weapons too.[186] For many New Yorkers, the *results*—less anxiety on the streets—more than justified the *means*: collaring thousands of innocent people or petty offenders. The underlying notion, shared by police and large numbers of the public, was that if a street youth happened to be innocent of an immediate offense, they were either guilty of something in the past or would be guilty of something in the future. Mayor Giuliani apparently spoke for the majority when he proclaimed without any evidence that *"murder and graffiti are two vastly different crimes, but they are part of the same continuum."*[187]

George Kelling and Catherine Coles cited DiIulio and Wilson's "superpredator" theory to make their case. "The feared future—of marauding bands of armed and vicious youths—is already with us . . . Citizens and neighborhoods are in trouble *now*, they need help *today*."[188] The authors approvingly cited another neocon professor, Nathan Glazer, who, echoing Giuliani, claimed that graffiti artists and those "who rob, rape, assault and murder [transit] passengers . . . are part of one world of uncontrollable *predators*."[189]

They agreed with Wilson that it was time to "crack the whip," to send a "message to 'wannabes' and those guilty of committing marginal crimes that their actions will no longer be tolerated."[190] A crucial notion was that stern punishment for marginal crimes would deter the wannabes, who were said to have "important information about who is dealing drugs from where; about who carries weapons, and when; about who is planning to commit crimes or who has; about who has been 'dissed'—humiliated—and intends to strike back."[191] The authors were certain that the so-called wannabes (the term was never defined) would be willing to snitch—"strike a deal"—and thus cede control of their troubled neighborhoods.[192] They conceded that the wannabes "certainly need help: education, training, jobs. [But] to use help, however, they need control first."[193]

I was elected to the state assembly in 1982, the same year that the "broken windows" article appeared, and can testify to its resonance with ordinary voters. In walking door to door, I recognized this fear of street crime as a dominating issue. In fact, my own home was invaded by a violent, mentally disturbed individual on one occasion. While some voters blamed the Reagan administration for the budget cuts that closed the state's mental hospitals and cast thousands of individuals onto the streets with nowhere to go, the majority of voters simply wanted the restoration of order instead of more talk of underlying causes. That meant more police on the streets and tougher sentencing. I supported more community policing and tougher sentences for burglary. But I could not find any Republican or many Democratic colleagues to support rent control, affordable housing, drug and alcohol treatment centers, or job training. Budget dollars flowed to law enforcement and prisons at the expense of social programs. Clearly the neoconservatives understood voter sentiment—and liberal weakness—accurately. But their rhetoric that anxious middle-class citizens were in trouble "now" and need help "today" could be applied even more tellingly to the condition of inner-city youth. The blame instead was laid on "liberal" court decisions handed down in the sixties: that illegally seized evidence couldn't be used against defendants in state courts (the so-called exclusionary rule); the right to counsel during interrogation, prior to indictment; and the right to remain silent (*Miranda*, 1966). At the height of the gang wars, the LAPD and many other departments were training their officers to circumvent *Miranda*, policies that received strong rebuke in 2003.[194]

The strongest neoconservative claims were based on the falling homicide and crime rates in New York City. There was no doubt about the trend: a 50 percent reduction in reported violent crimes in a decade. This was based in part on the more than 1 million stop-and-frisks by a police force numbering over 40,000, four times the number in Los Angeles.[195] In a city as congested as New York, the securing of public space even from "nuisance" offenders was welcomed. My left-wing friends in Greenwich Village supported the midnight sweeps of Washington Square Park, even if it meant a handful of homeless addicts were dragged repeatedly through the revolving doors of the jail system. Everyone breathed more easily. But there were questions. The neoconservatives claimed that 60,000 violent crimes were *not* committed in the 1988–98 decade because "broken windows" policing was implemented.[196] This assertion correlated the rates of decline on a one-to-one basis with implementation of more aggressive tactics at the precinct level. But the problem was that crime and violence, including gang violence, were falling *nationally* during the same decade, including declines in cities where the "broken windows" policing model was not in operation. Another problem was that the neoconservative analysis failed to note the deep revulsion at the community level toward the crack cocaine trauma. The *New York Times*'s columnist Bob Herbert, who was pleasantly "astonished" at the falling rate of crime, noted that "young New Yorkers have gotten too little credit for the changes in their behavior that have contributed to the curtailment of crime in the city."[197] Fox Butterfield also noted that a 1997 Justice Department study "found that the most important reason for the decline may be the waning of the crack cocaine epidemic."[198]

The criminologist Andrew Karmen developed an objective, multicausal explanation in an exhaustively researched book cleverly called *New York Murder Mystery: The True Story Behind the Crime Crash of the 1990s*. Karmen readily credited Bratton's computer-based crime tracking program (Comstat) but questioned the police orthodoxy that it was the sole reason for the dropping rate of crime. First, he noted that with a police force twice the per capita size of other cities, New York was a skewed model. Second, he said, while police might claim credit for reducing murders committed outdoors, the murder rate behind closed doors was dropping at the same rate. Despite the NYPD lagging behind other departments studied, auto theft was declining, too. The quality of arrests was shabby, with one out of every three cases dismissed in 1995 and half of misdemeanor convictions resulting in no jail time.[199] Despite zero-tolerance policies, gun arrests did not rise, but kept falling after a 1990 peak. The proportion of felony arrests leading to indictment, conviction, and imprisonment declined after 1993.[200] Nor did liberal explanations satisfy Karmen's scrutiny. Crime fell in poor areas despite the fact that poverty rates of blacks and Latinos did not decline, even in the nineties boom.[201] Like Butterfield and Herbert, Karmen did credit neighborhoods with healing themselves "through informal mechanisms of social control," especially where the label "crackhead" denoted destruction of self and community. Many "little brothers" learned how lives were ruined, and adjusted accordingly, but they were "still treated indiscriminately as potentially dangerous persons by the NYPD," and were "not given any credit for turning their backs on hard drugs and violence by commentators in positions of authority and influence."[202] In summary, he said, a " 'teachable' moment materialized but was largely missed."[203]

By 2003, while crime levels were still down in New York City as a whole, the murder rate in one Brownsville precinct had increased by 50 percent; in another nearby precinct, by 62.5 percent, and in September in Crown Heights there was a 400 percent homicide jump from the year before.[204] Alone among the city's papers, the *Village Voice* headlined the killings as "bloodshed and tears all over again." A special court was appointed to manage the felony gun cases sprouting from five Brooklyn neighborhoods which once again were accounting for a disproportionate percentage of the city's overall shootings. Though New York remained a safer city than the decade before, it was an ominous sign that policing alone cannot stop the violence that arises from the perpetual misery. As Bakari Kitwana, former editor of *The Source*, told the *Voice*, "The tension on the street, in the 'hood, is very much like it was in the early '80s and '90s, and that is largely due not to rap music but to the changing economics—close to 3 million jobs have

been lost in the last two years. As usual we make up the bulk of the people unemployed. . . . I mean, people are ready to explode."[205]

What the neoconservatives completely ignored was the profound polarization
of race relations in the wake of the "broken windows" model. Notions marketed
to the middle class as "broken windows," "zero tolerance," and "quality of life
policing" looked like old-fashioned, discriminatory, and brutal "street justice" to
inner-city residents. In fact, Chief Bratton called the sweeps "frontal assault" and
the "juggernaut," and defended racial profiling and the stop-and-frisk tactic as
"absolutely essential."[206] From 1980 to 1989, felony arrests nearly doubled in
New York City, mainly in response to crack cocaine; however, the implementation of "broken windows" shifted the emphasis from felony arrests, which lev-
eled off after 1994, to misdemeanor arrests, which mushroomed by 53 percent
between 1993 and 1998.[207] The massive numbers of African American and Latino
youth incarcerated on misdemeanors only later to be found innocent, and the
death-squad behavior of officers in the cases of Diallo, Louima, and Dorismond,
were apparently unimportant collateral damage. According to Amy Wilentz,
only about one-fifth of actual searches were being reported by the Street Crimes
Units.[208] She posed this question: "Imagine what it would mean if 225,000 Jews
had been stopped and searched on New York City's streets in the past eight years.
The African American neighborhoods were like occupied territory."[209] In Operation Condor, launched in 2000, a total of 21,445 arrests were made by 500 officers
in only its first two months, 75 percent of them for misdemeanors or even lesser
violations.[210] A third of the total were for possession of marijuana, trespassing,
drinking in public, or sneaking onto subways.[211] Police and neoconservatives
claim the sweeps turn up people sought for more serious offenses like murder,
but should homicide detectives arrest people at random as the preferred way to
investigate specific killings? The neat paradigm of establishing "order" against
"disorder" veiled the hidden interaction. Low-keyed but routinized police misconduct was becoming part of an "order" that so humiliated an entire class of
young minority males, it was sure to foster a defiant "disorder" as a result. In a
closed feedback loop, George Kelling's "order maintenance" policing contributed
to the very "disorder" it claimed to be preventing. It was perfect.

"Broken windows" policing is *punishment*—directed deliberately and *disproportionately* toward young inner-city males, using *minor* infractions to detain and criminalize these individuals in a *selective* manner that would never be employed in the white suburbs—and, as Gilligan has shown in a lifetime of research, the emphasis on greater and greater punishment is more likely to alienate and harden offenders than rehabilitate them to Christian virtue. "Nothing stimulates crime as powerfully and as effectively as punishment does (since punishment stimulates shame and diminishes guilt, and shame stimulates violence, especially when it is not inhibited by guilt)."[212] Hard-line "broken windows" policies risked exactly such an outcome. Cracking down on young people for marginal infractions was likely to alienate street youth from the unfair double standards of the justice system, not turn gang wannabes into snitches for the police. The doctrine of aggressive frisks and repeated misdemeanor arrests was based on a prejudice that perceived gang members, even if innocent of the specific charge, were destined to be guilty of something, anyway. Thus, targeting and incarcerating young people because of their identity, instead of their specific acts, became an acceptable norm. Even if there was scant evidence to connect loitering or tagging to homicidal behavior, the association was rooted as dogma in public and law enforcement perceptions. There would be one set of constitutional protections covering white-collar crimes and police discretion when it came to administering street justice.

Kelling's work seemed to rest on a "haunting experience" in Boston in 1995, while working on a contract to a mass transit agency. In the company of uniformed police officers one day, he chose to stare at four tough-looking young black men near a transit stop, "something he would not have done had the officers not accompanied him."[213] He felt himself face-to-face with the super-predator enemy. They were thirteen to fourteen years old, he estimated, and not more than 140 pounds. Each wore a "dark sweatshirt" and "dark baggy pants" and appeared "vulture-like." They refused to shrink back from Kelling's stare, even though the police stood by. Later, after Kelling and the police had driven away, there occurred a mugging at the train station. When the police troop returned, there was no sign of the four "vulture-like" youth. What are we to make of this "haunting experience"? Without a doubt, most readers would share Kelling's perception of a "marauding band," and assume them guilty of remorseless assault. The assumption might be correct. It is also possible that the four youths departed from their bench after the police left. Kelling offers no evidence aside from their "vulture-like" appearance and the fact that they refused to be intimidated by his stare. On the basis of that evidence, they were guilty of staring back at white authority, nothing more or less than "mad-dogging" the cops. The notion that a lifetime of being stared at by authority figures might contribute to black rage is not mentioned. But since, in Kelling's theory, these young men need "control, first," they will be denied education, training, and jobs until they submit—which simply perpetuates the cycle.

We have seen this pattern before, in the nineteenth-century civic horror at "the dangerous classes," the urban vagabonds depicted in Victor Hugo's *Les Miserables*, the immigrant slum dwellers who represented a "distemper" to Jacob Riis, and always the blacks and Mexicans who threatened the dominant order. Behind their street crimes, as Diana Gordon has argued, "lay the shadows of a greater danger—the [progressive] challenge to conditions that bred robbers and vagabonds."[214] Labeling these "dangerous classes" as incorrigible social pariahs and moral zombies "reduced the likelihood that respectable people would perceive social disorder as a reminder of the ways in which the social and economic arrangements of their society were failing them . . . Control supplied the solution."[215] Even Karl Marx and Friedrich Engels shared the Victorian view in denouncing those they labeled the "dangerous class" of "social scum," as they described the *lumpenproletariat* (slum proletariet) in *The Communist Manifesto*. For the conservative Victorians, the lumpen represented a violent threat to civilized values such as the work ethic; for Marx and Engels they represented a potential tool of reactionary movements. In either perspective, the slum-dwelling classes were demonized.

Gordon's book on the dangerous classes is about the contemporary drug war, which, she writes, has "become like the issue of communism in the Cold War years in its evocation of a great range of public fears."[216] But her analysis applies as well to minority gangs, whether African American, Mexican, or Chinese, who are said to be particularly dangerous when intoxicated or high, even when empirical evidence is lacking. Cocaine, for example, was a "medical blessing" during the Civil War, but became a "dangerous stimulant" in the early twentieth century when associated with blacks, "despite contemporary evidence that African Americans were rarely users." The pattern was to continue through the double standards of the crack cocaine crisis of the nineties when (middle-class) powder cocaine use was hardly penalized in comparison with its cheaper ghetto form. The wars on gangs and drugs were milestones in the Cultural Right's campaign to discredit and subsequently dismantle any programs to equalize opportunities for justice.

The Wilson-Kelling-Coles thesis was dedicated to the memory of Robert Peel, the nineteenth-century architect of British policing. Peel wrote his vision in 1829 that "the police are the public and the public are the police," a statement cited on the opening page of *Broken Windows*. The slightest research would have raised questions about Peel's noble goal, however. Meant to declare an impartiality not unlike the modern neoconservatives' vision of a "color-blind" America, Peel's vision was founded on the double standards required by the British Empire. Peel's police were the harsh colonial overseers of the nationalist and Catholic communities in Ireland. To this day, the nationalists of Northern Ireland derisively label the police as "the peelers" and accuse them of collusion with the British state and loyalist paramilitaries. Recently, the British Prime Minister John Major even restated the essence of this colonial policing doctrine when he said, "It is time to understand less and condemn more."[217]

The point, however, is that there can be no "zero tolerance" in a social order split by socioeconomic divisions. The police will be harsher toward "the dangerous classes" than toward white collar criminals; the sweeps will be of the mean streets rather than the corporate suites; the victims of brutality will be people of color more than white Aryan vigilantes. In Kelling's own words, the needs of "the citizens" must be addressed today, superimposed above the needs of the "vulture-like" others.

To take a blatant example, government officials are routinely "soft" on white-collar corporate lawbreaking that results in such workplace suffering as being de-capitated, electrocuted, and buried alive, even where intentional wrongdoing has been established. Over the same decades as the gang wars, from 1982 to 2002, federal investigators looked into 1,242 officially described "horror stories" where willful employer safety violations led to workplace deaths. A *New York Times* re-view found a pervasive official reluctance to seek prosecution "even when em-ployers had been cited before for the very same safety violation [and it] persisted even when the violations caused multiple deaths, or when the victims were teenagers." Clearly the doctrines of moral poverty and stern punishment are ap-plied selectively, reflecting deep disparities in the social order. Far from maintain-ing absolute standards of virtue and morality, the neoconservative approach to crime is based on a moral relativism of its own. Punishment is most severe when directed against officially constructed scapegoats, and most lenient towards rep-resentatives of wealth and status.[218]

This is an argument tracing back to the biblical era. But as Gilligan and many others ask, if the core theory of punishment—that more punishment ("order") is necessary to end violence—has failed for 3,000 years, it surely is time for recon-sideration. The alternative, for prison experts like Gilligan as well as homeboys on the streets, is to better understand the cry, *no justice, no peace.*

New York City: The War on the Latin Kings

Some of the Latin Kings were children of Young Lords. The Kings had a lot of the same sort of radical wrath that we had back then. The Kings had the same problems as the Chicago Young Lords. They were really a gang that leaders tried to turn into a political group, and could never master the transformation. The police and politicians were against the transformation too.

—Juan Gonzáles, New York Daily News *columnist,*
former Young Lord[219]

In the expressed opinions of some of those present, a number of whom presented themselves as "terrorist experts," the most troubling development about the gang was its turn to radicalism.

As one person at the meeting phrased it, "There's no way we're gonna let a bunch of
gang-bangers think they're the Panthers or the Young Lords."
    —quote from New York police official[220]

The story of the Latin Kings, a mainly Puerto Rican street gang, is very much a counterpoint to the narratives fostered by neoconservative intellectuals like Wilson and Kelling, politicians like Giuliani, and law enforcement officials like Bratton. The Kings are historical successors to the gangs described by Jacob Riis as a "distemper" of the slums, warning that "something is amiss" in the social order.

Formally described as the Almighty Latin King/Queen Nation (ALKQN)— the Kings are among the most significant examples in the nineties of the struggle of a street gang to overcome the inner and outer obstacles to transformation. Despite the massive efforts of politicians and law enforcement to classify and crush them as merely a criminal syndicate, the story of the Kings is far richer and more complicated, as evidenced by widespread community support, occasional in-depth media coverage, documentary films, and the scholarly work *Between Black and Gold,* produced by researchers at John Jay College and published by Columbia University.[221]

The first Latin Kings banded together in the Chicago penal system in the 1940s, in response to the isolated condition of Puerto Rican inmates threatened by white and black inmate prison gangs. Their initial vision, expressed in a manifesto still in circulation, was dimmed and derailed by gangbanging, but the group was revitalized in 1986 by a Chicago-born inmate, Luis Felipe, in the upstate New York Collins Correctional Facility. The first passage of the ALKQN's manifesto is obviously political, echoing and redefining *The Communist Manifesto*, and focuses on the key problem of tribal bloodletting:

> The history of all hitherto existing gang feuds is the history of label struggles for the sake of clique recognition. It is this egotistical force for recognition which leads to rivalry and senseless disputes which often cost the high price of human life, the life of our people, the oppressed third world people.[222]

Instead, the Kings called for the creation of "the new King," dedicated to a "life of service to our fellow man," who would live according to five points on the organization's crown symbol: respect, honesty, unity, knowledge, and love. Their colors were to be black and gold, symbolizing the polarity of "the darkness of the immense night" of the universe and the "brilliant sun" of the "glow of hope in oppressed people." The colors are displayed in elaborately woven beads worn as a rosary. The King sign is a three-finger crown (thumb, index and little fingers) used in greetings (held to the heart), toward superiors (fingers joined and pointed up), and for prayer (hands together, forefingers touching, held to the chest). Their meetings, known as "universals," are organized in circles with each member touching, symbolizing that the group was "360 degrees unbreakable."

The philosophy of "Kingism" was a direct antidote to feelings of worthlessness generated in marginal communities of inmates and immigrants. Rooted in the memory of Inca and Taino ancestors, and particularly in Puerto Rican nationalism, Kingism takes pride in "the blood of royalty in our veins" and defines its "divine mission" as the awakening of oppressed people from submission, ignorance, and self-destruction. Father Luis Barrios, an East Harlem priest who advises the Kings, has described them as "a form of self-organized therapy for the poor and marginalized," borrowing from Christianity, native religions, and twelve-step programs.[223] The King's customary greeting, identifying expression, and street chant is: *"Amor de rey!"* (King love!)

The Kings' fundamental character evolved from the gang culture in prisons and the streets, struggling to elevate its existence from crime, drug dealing, and "label struggles for clique recognition." A good example is a thirty-two-year-old King now living in Los Angeles named Filthee (Forever In Love Thanking Highest Eternal Existence).[224] When he was twelve years old in New York, he was making $3,000 per day dealing drugs in the projects, keeping $500 for himself. His family was deeply immersed in the King subculture, and he rose rapidly in the organization. "I did things one hundred percent," he says quietly. When a close friend was shot in the head in front of him, however, Filthee's life changed. He was fifteen years old and about to have his first son. Eventually, having done jail time for drug trafficking, having robbed supplies even from military bases, increasingly tangled in dangerous "dramas" involving law enforcement, Filthee became a hip-hop artist and graphics specialist in L.A. He remains a King, wears his beads proudly, but has retired from gangbanging. "My son was the turning point." He hopes the Kings will further evolve as a revolutionary Puerto Rican movement in the tradition of the militants of an earlier generation, the *macheteros*.

The Kings' prison manifesto describes three stages in the hard ascent from the gang life to spiritual and political emancipation. In the first, or "primitive stage," the future King is gangbanging, getting high, and "being recognized as big and bad." Despite the self-destructiveness of this primitive stage, "it is not wasteful in the sense that the environment conditions this type of behavior in order for one to survive the hardships of ghetto life." At this point "one either breaks or becomes strong," opening the way toward the second, or "conservative," stage, sometimes known as the "mummy stage." Here, the future warrior becomes tired of the senseless gangbanging, hanging on street corners, searching for ego recognition. The gangbanger often gets married and retires from the life. In doing so, however, the mummy King separates himself from the larger King Nation, ignoring the ultimate responsibility to free the Nation and his or her people. To overcome this unconscious neglect is the mission of the third stage, that of becoming the "new King," who selflessly and fearlessly devotes himself to his community's advancement through building a Latino "brown force."

By the early nineties, the Kings embarked on a plan of organizing gangbangers, by stages, into cultural and political revolutionaries. One can immediately sense the hazardous ambiguities of the journey. The possibility of transformation was real, but so, too, was the danger of backsliding. The contradictions in building a social movement out of a gangbanging street culture would be explosive in any context, but especially when opposed by law enforcement and the political establishment. When I met with a King representative at John Jay College in 2001, a young man enrolled in community college, the organization had been battered from all directions.

In 1994, thirty-six Kings were indicted by federal authorities on racketeering charges, based on the same RICO law used against La Eme in Los Angeles, a legal instrument by which top leaders could be indicted for any and all acts of their members. In this case, it was charged that Luis Felipe, the Cuban-born founder known as King Blood, had orchestrated murders from inside prison through commands to either "BOS" (beat on sight) or "TOS" (terminate on sight). His conviction led to a unique punishment, 150 years in prison, with the first forty-five years to be spent in complete solitary confinement. King Blood was thirty-six years old at the time. Sent to a "supermax" prison in Colorado, he was denied permission to submit his poems, writings, and sketches to magazines, send letters to prisoners' rights groups, or even contact religious organizations. He was placed in a sensory-deprivation cell designed so that inmates cannot see one another's eyes. A black-and-white television set beamed educational and religious programs into King Blood's seven-by-twelve-foot structure, where he spent twenty-three hours each day, seven days per week. These conditions, according to the *New York Times,* were "virtually unprecedented," an "extreme example of a penological trend to make prison more punitive," and a foreshadowing, one might add, of the later war on terrorism.

The impact of King Blood's confinement on the Kings was not the deterrence the authorities apparently expected. "Kings don't die, they multiply," became the war cry as news of the harsh treatment spread through the barrios. While most might agree that the organization had failed to transcend its gang heritage, the extreme punishment galvanized a nationalist response. "Why they sentence Blood like that?" one King asked, and answered, "because he was Puerto Rican, a Latino. They saying, 'We'll put you in a box, we'll bury you alive, nigger.' " The case became a turning point. The Kings were determined to prove that they had rights. At King Blood's sentencing, the leader asked the judge not to let the Nation "live in the shadow of my mistake, let them begin over."

A new leader, or Inca, now inherited the organization's leadership with the blessing of King Blood. He was King Tone—born Antonio Fernandez in one of the poorest sections of the barrio, a school dropout, former drug dealer, and crack addict, who felt Kingism to be a transformative doctrine in his own life and potentially that of the whole barrio. "Nobody could tell me what to do," he said of his adolescent years. At Rikers Island in the early nineties, an older inmate, named King Mafia, told Antonio to "lock down" and read the Kings' lessons materials "cuz you real stupid." He ultimately did so, and began to change. "When I was growing up, I didn't know who I was, and if you don't know who you are you don't know where you are going. The reason is that you are colonized, you don't got a voice. Why they never told me this in high school? I wouldn't have done crack. All we had to look up to was Michael Jordan or somebody and you gotta buy a $150 pair of sneakers to believe you're like them. But you don't need no money for pride."

Tone rose to a leadership role in the Kings after he left Rikers, becoming a charismatic teacher somewhat akin to the young Malcolm X in relation to Elijah Muhammed. He already had respect due to his crazy ways, but now he became inspired with vision. As he expressed, or "broke it down," for youngsters on the street,

> To get to eternal life you must be righteous. So what I'm telling the Kings is in the three stages of Kingism, I tell them: "you already been there. You already killed each other" . . . all of you are in the second stage. Now you don't kill each other, but you still recognize the enemy, but you still not be able to get your eternal life gift . . . I tell them to get eternal life and not be a coward and not to die, you must fulfill the righteousness that the Lord wants so you can sit amongst Kings . . .

Tone attempted to move the Kings in directions that would bring community support. They marched against police brutality, joined AIDs walks, and sent a contingent to the Puerto Rican Day parade every year. Tone envisioned the Kings becoming a political force creating avenues for young people to become judges, lawyers, businessmen, teachers, politicians, "not by leaving the barrio, but by transforming it":

> so either me and the ghetto make it together, or me and the ghetto die together. And I think that if more people would take that concept into the street and the schools and everything, there wouldn't be a ghetto. Because the Kings are starting to recognize that it isn't a ghetto, it's home. All you gotta do is not shoot each other, not sell drugs, and walk each other's kids to school. You just make this no more ghetto. So that's where I'm at. I want to beat this ghetto.[225]

In Tone's long-term vision, the society that was oppressing the ghetto had to become part of the solution:

> I already got the Kings to stop killing each other. And if I'm telling the drug dealers to stop, too, then I've got to replace that money with a job where they can make a living.[226]

By most accounts, King Tone was making a difference, drawing support from a variety of community-based organizations. An Episcopal priest, the Reverend Gordon Duggins, said, "I'm reluctant to use this word, but in many ways I think he's a prophet. He's certainly a leader and a social critic."[227] His impact in changing the ways of other Kings was measurable, too. For example, in a long interview, "King Montana" (the name echoes the hero of *Scarface*) described Tone's influence on his violent tendencies. This painfully honest statement summarizes the immense challenge and volatility of what I have called the inner struggle for peace:

> I would get pissed when a brother get hurt, so we go out with drugs, let's go kill him, get revenge, but King Tone always told me, no it's not like that, you don't want to go to jail for 25 to life, and the kid that got shot, he'll be out on the street and you'll be 25 to life. So he changed my lifestyle a lot, a lot. Consider him a father and mom. Why? Cuz I don't got a mom, my mom died when I was four years old, she got killed, shot up like ten times, my father got shot in the head, my sister got shot too, all my life, my brother's got gun holes all over his body . . .
>
> I got so much pain inside that when a brother got hurt, I want to go and go crazy, why, because the people that killed my mother they didn't care who she was, she had kids, they let me watch when they were killing my mother, so when I start fighting I have flashbacks, all the anger comes out, I keep on trying to hurt the kid real badly. Everytime I do that, there's always a brother telling me to take it to another level . . . this is my family right here.[228]

At the same time that one feels empathy and hope in response to King Montana's raw emotions, it becomes obvious why the impressive process of transformation is far from perfect and subject to constant backsliding, trials, and tribulations. As Gilligan puts it, violence is a public health problem that requires ongoing treatment in a safe, therapeutic environment. As with drugs and alcohol, the treatment of violence will include relapses as well as recovery. The problem is that while these relapses are understandable in a therapeutic context, they are unacceptable in a law enforcement context. Helping someone like King Montana recover from his wounded life risks the charge of being "soft on crime." But without the effort, which can only succeed with the involvement of others who share his secrets, his wounds, and his street experience, the remaining options are a cell or tomb (which is what New York City's oldest jail is called, the Tombs).

Fortunately, the research team at John Jay College has provided a treasure of interviews with Kings and Queens that document the potential transformation of such a group and rubbish any notion that gang members are frozen in incorrigible criminal identities. John Jay College's David Brotherton and Luis Barrios, in hundreds of interviews with Kings and Queens, discovered a fluidity in their consciousness of possibilities. The role of leadership on the inside, and especially the opportunities or barriers presented on the outside, would determine the direction of this consciousness. For instance, the Kings who were interviewed believed unhesitatingly that powerful social forces were out to destroy them, based on their firsthand experiences. But, at the same time, while complaining that negotiating with these hostile forces was next to impossible, according to Brotherton, "they continually sought to respond to and reach out to those same forces in search of an illusory middle ground." These Kings were optimistic in their approach to a community peace process and social reform, almost despite themselves.

Brotherton and Barrios found other internal complexities between Kings and Queens. Like most gangs originating in the dangerous confines of prison, the Kings were the "epitome of in-your-face barrio masculinity," or the "social dynamite" feared by established society. Following the inmate subculture, homosexuality was at first banned by the Kings' organization, and women were treated as more or less auxiliary sex objects. Eventually, however, the name was changed to include Queens, women formed meetings of their own, became more assertive, and launched an internal dialogue that had consequences for the outside world. For example, the John Jay College interviews show a clear gender difference in the definition of the Nation's enemies. For men interviewed, the primary problem was the police, who threatened the barrio's culture of masculinity with a "working class street masculinity" of their own. For Queens, on the other hand, the chief enemy was the media, which was seen as disrespecting and ignoring any positive initiatives of the Nation, often in collusion with the police. To oversimplify, the Kings were locked into a masculinity struggle that required confrontation, while the Queens were seeking better public understanding. This was not an either-or division since the Kings still remained predominantly patriarchal in nature, and the Queens were not lacking in hostility toward the police, too. But the dynamic again illustrates the absurdity of considering the gang identity fixed and frozen forever. From a public policy perspective, the data suggests that the authorities might try to deescalate aggressive behavior that provokes threats to masculinity while also strengthens the opportunities for negotiations and better access for the Kings' viewpoints in public forums. Thus a rational public policy should encourage the maximum avoidance of punitive "dissing" approaches that only fuel the desire to lash back. As Brotherton and Barrios described the bind, the Kings learned that "no matter how hard members tried to reform, as long as they were associated with the organization they would always be singled out as criminal deviants. It was an impossible contradiction since, as we have seen, the very key to members' resolving many of their 'issues' was the organization that was causing them to be labeled."

In perspective, "some of the Latin Kings were children of the Young Lords," says Juan Gonzáles, a former defense minister of the Panther-style Puerto Rican organization, and now a Latino historian and radio journalist. "The Kings had a lot of the same sort of radical wrath we had back then. The Kings had the same problems as the Chicago Young Lords. They were really a gang that leaders tried to turn into a political group, and they could never master the transformation. The police and politicians were totally against the transformation too."[229]

No enlightened responses were forthcoming from the establishment, however, raising the question of which side in the gang wars was "incorrigible" and which was not. The *New York Times* published an article on Tone's attempted transformation with the headlined question "Man of Vision or of Violence?"[230]

The headline suggested that Tone's commitment to violence prevention was in question. Perhaps it was a ruse, a front. Or perhaps Tone's personal commitment wasn't good enough, that he was responsible for the behavior of all Kings, former Kings, and renegade Kings. By comparison, no such standard was imposed on the police. (A headline might have asked, for example, "Police Reform, Real or Deception?" or "Police Killings: Accidents or Intentional?")[231]

Other New York papers like the *New York Post* engaged in full-scale demonizing of the Kings, denouncing any effort to "legitimize these wolf packs" and "thugs in sheep's clothing."[232] In this superheated climate, which they themselves helped to generate, the police and politicians went after the Kings with no holds barred. King Tone's attorney, Ron Kuby, described his client as "falsely arrested and charged more often than any human being I've ever known."[233] In one case cited by Kuby, Tone was found with a tiny amount of marijuana during a police pat-down and was brought into jail, where police mysteriously found a loaded gun they had somehow missed during the pat-down that turned up the speck of weed. The gun charge was dismissed in court, then resurrected in a federal indictment and dismissed again. "This meant daily harassment for three years, including a year and a half in jail awaiting trial on charges that were dismissed," Kuby says.

In 1997, Mayor Giuliani announced a war on gangs in the New York City public schools amidst media claims that the "Latin Kings Infiltrate Our Schools," based on the apparent discovery that a single King was being employed as a school security guard at one of the city's several hundred schools. In response to the mayor's goading, the school system adopted sweeping rules, including a prohibition on "gang-related graffiti," "gangwear," and "other elements essential to gang recruiting and intimidation," as well as giving special priority to penalties for "gang-related offenses." Especially significant was a prohibition against any school officials, including safety officers, from meeting with gang members to mediate gang-related disputes. While mediation was endorsed as a method of handling other kinds of disputes, it was specifically prohibited in gang-related matters because it "lends an air of legitimacy to these criminal organizations." Rather than solicit the Kings to prevent a violent dispute from erupting between children, the rules were rigid enough to make it highly difficult for an eight-year-old "King" to attend public school, or, for that matter, anyone else dressed in "gangwear." The crusade coincided with Giuliani's reelection campaign against city council member Ruth Messenger, who had been campaigning on the need for education reform. Messenger might have tried arguing that underfunded schools, high dropout rates, and strong-arm police tactics only contributed to the gang subculture, but instead, Giuliani's tactic worked. Messenger backed down, agreeing that the mayor's initiative "makes sense."

Then came a massive police raid code-named "Operation Crown" (evidently for its purpose of taking down the Latin Kings' sacred symbol), on May 14, 1998. One thousand police and federal agents descended on the Kings at five A.M., the largest raid in New York City since the 1920s.[234] Over 100 alleged Latin Kings, including Tone, were arrested on charges varying from drug dealing and firearms possession to parole violations. No guns or drugs were found in their houses, and not one resisted arrest. Taken in police buses to Fort Hamilton for processing, the Kings were "welcomed" by celebrating police with displays of black and gold balloons and doughnuts. In the end, only two Kings were even prosecuted: a King named "Lalo," and Tone himself. Less than half the total number arrested turned out to be Kings at all. But as the city's police commissioner boasted, "In spite of the Latin Kings attempts to portray themselves as a benign, community-oriented organization, this gang has always been and continues to this day to be, a dangerous group of criminals," adding that "today's arrests have effectively dismantled the command structure of the Latin Kings organization by effectively removing the so-called Supreme King."[235]

Tone was sentenced to thirteen years in federal prison on June 3, 1999. The conviction stemmed from an incident going back to 1996, two years before "Operation Crown," in which Tone was filmed by police while coming out of a drug distribution location on Coney Island. Tone sat next to an informant who was wired, where he was recorded saying, "This is rock." According to the trial judge, Tone at the time was apparently a low-level bagger who was set up by another Latin King who had become an informant for the FBI and the NYPD. (The use of informants has never been disclosed in detail, but in one 1999 court case against the Kings it was revealed that an informant, "King B," was paid $55,000, and two others

$21,000.) Tone fought the charges to the end, when he emotionally pled guilty to avoid trial, where he faced a mandatory twenty-five-year sentence. The harsh sentence was determined by the state's guidelines based on Tone's two prior convictions in 1993 and 1994. Tone was two months from coming off probation when Operation Crown netted him. By pleading guilty, he lessened his sentence to thirteen years from twenty-five. Ironically, the federal prosecutors acknowledged in court that the key underlying premise of RICO was mistaken, that Tone did not use his leadership position in the Latin Kings to further his criminal goals. Tone's lawyer described him as having "succumbed to the streets." He was guilty of his past. The outcome was more tragedy than triumph.

What sort of justice was served by Giuliani's mayoral campaign and Operation Crown? Was an automatic twenty-five-year sentence for a low-level bagger on a three-year-old case an appropriate remedy and, if so, to what problem? Was it better to imprison the reform-minded leader of the Kings who was trying to turn lives around, including his own, or to drop the petty charge and offer him treatment, counseling, and incentives to remain a peacekeeper in the organization? The ruthless politics of law and order were to prevail, with the antigang units, bedecked in black and gold, appearing more like a gang of their own than impartial dispensers of the law.

The Kings were not destroyed, however—at least not in the short time frame expected by the police. When I met with a young King member in New York two years later, he was still reminiscing proudly over the Kings' response to Giuliani during the 1999 Puerto Rican Day parade. "We marched in five rows of long columns, five or six hundred brothers and sisters. This was *after* Operation Crown, so at every church along the way we knelt down for Tone. We were totally quiet, kneeling. When we got to Giuliani at the reviewing stand, we knelt down in front of him and threw him the crown, and you could hear him say, 'I thought we got rid of these fuckers.' "[236]

Father Barrios put the matter in perspective at a church meeting with the Kings:

> . . . for 33 years Jesus stayed in a place like this, *uptown* [emphasis] . . . in Galillee. They knew he was there but nobody care about that. Then came a moment when Jesus say,

"I'm going *downtown*," and he took all his nation downtown. After 33 years he finally
went from uptown to downtown. It took them one week to kill him.[237]

The John Jay researchers conclude that street gangs hold the potential of value
transcendence, of evolving to challenge the society that marginalizes them.
Brotherton and Barrios reject "the self-fulfilling prophecies of orthodox criminology," affirming instead the notion that the human condition is unpredictable and
uneven "when it is understood as a struggle for justice and dignity rather than as
a cycle of adaptation and functional interdependence."[238] They offer the following definition of a "street political organization" to the debate over gang identity:

> . . . a group formed largely by youth and adults of a marginalized social class
> which aims to provide its members with a resistant identity, an opportunity to be
> individually and collectively empowered, a voice to speak back to the dominant
> culture, a refuge from the stresses and strains of barrio or ghetto life and a spiritual
> enclave within which its sacred rituals can be generated and practiced.[239]

Challenging the conventional discourse depicting gangs as proto-criminal enterprises, these John Jay College authors propose the possibility of youth with
criminal backgrounds instead being drawn to oppositional movements. It is a
conceptually liberating alternative to the self-fulfilling definition of gang membership as inevitably violent and criminal.

Of signal importance in this broadened definition is the notion of a "spiritual
enclave" where sacred and historic rituals can be generated and practiced. There
is sometimes a powerful spiritual dimension within the gang subculture, manifest most obviously in ceremonial funerals, wall murals depicting La Virgen de
Guadalupe, African spiritual figures, and Native American symbols. Almost all
gang peacemakers are engaged spiritually, in an eclectic range of traditions from
indigenous medicine men to the Nation of Islam. The 1993 Kansas City gang
summit was noteworthy for its inclusion of religious rituals at every turn. The
work of Father Boyle in East L.A. and Father Luis Barrios in Spanish Harlem is a
local form of the liberation theology created in Latin America in the sixties. In an

essay on "the spirituality of resistance," Barrios describes the complex doctrines of the Latin Kings in great detail. King Tone consciously utilized Bible stories in his preaching to Kings' children and members. The black-and-gold beads are taken from the rosary tradition. The Kings' children have been baptized jointly by priests like Barrios and leaders like Tone. The King's "bible," or "way of knowing," contains 366 prayers. The Kings' constitution requires fasting two days per month. Their salutations are similar in style to the Christian prayer gestures. The result is more than simply a form of organized therapy. For the Kings and many such groups, spirituality offers a connection with the larger Creation, a legacy of rituals linking them with their pre-Conquest ancestors, a source of self-worth, a sense that their practice is sacred, and an internal solidarity against a harsh, hostile, and long-uncomprehending world. While these attributes are hardly present in all forms of the gang culture, they may be decisive in any attempts at transformation.

The Response to Rampart: Bratton to the Rescue

By 2002, the "broken windows" coalition was enjoying almost uncontested support. George Kelling was writing pieces in the *New York Post* emblazoned with headlines like "Tough Cops Matter."[240] While a few like Amy Wilentz derided the "broken windows" approach as "the Batman theory of criminal analysis" ("if the superhero is performing, crime goes down") and worried that it was only "quick-fix urban beautification" for tourists and investors, the theory was attracting big consulting fees for Rudolph Giuliani, Kelling, and others at the conservative Manhattan Institute.[241] The Giuliani Group netted $4.3 million to advise Mexico City, while the Institute focused on Latin America as a whole.[242] Meanwhile, Bratton ran afoul of power and ego conflicts with Giuliani and thus made a lateral career move in 2002 to the battlefields of Los Angeles as the new chief of police. Could he restore the reputation of the LAPD after Rampart? Could he suppress gang violence without a return to the Rampart tactics? Would the political magic of "broken windows" policing continue to resonate, or might there be a new awareness that solutions required more than locking up unprecedented numbers of homeboys for temporary stays in the "universities of crime," as the state prisons were known? An opinion piece by one of the city's foremost civil rights litigators, Connie Rice, welcomed Bratton to the "Wild West," but advised him to "get a new playbook."[243] Hurling the ultimate challenge, she wrote that *"our emergency isn't broken windows; it's broken communities. And broken children."*[244]

Bratton declared what the *Los Angeles Times* called a "war on gangs"[245] virtually before he finished his search for a new home in Los Angeles. After objections from the mayor and several African American leaders, Bratton touchily denied using the phrase. He would not "raise gang members to the level of going to war with them." He was quoted accurately, however, in declaring the gang threat "the head that needs to be cut off," "much more of a national threat than the Mafia was,"[246] a menace that called for "an internal war on terrorism."[247] Because of the Rampart scandal, he said, "for three or four months, our gang units were not on the street, and the gang-bangers were just doing what they wanted."[248] He promised to take his victory in New York to the streets of Los Angeles, starting with a war on graffiti, somehow without repeating the illegalities of Rampart.

Just as he denied that his pronouncements amounted to "war," Bratton seemed to retain a selective memory about his New York City tenure. Only well after litigation and protests had questioned the NYPD's tactics in claiming that "we own the night" did Bratton reflect on the brutal side of what were otherwise seen as the "glory years." He wrote in 2000 that the "glorification in which the end justifies the means" cannot be tolerated.[249] But what was "broken windows" policing if it wasn't about the end (public order) justifying the means (racial profiling, double standards)? As for solutions to the contradiction, he made a vague suggestion in *Time* magazine for "greater dialogue" between police and affected communities, an approach that he appeared to follow in the New York years, to uncertain ends.[250] The *Los Angeles Times* provided virtually no coverage of the Rampart-like controversies that accompanied "broken windows" policing in New York. A lengthy *Times* piece, datelined Bedford-Stuyvesant, began with a presumed homeboy wearing a leather jacket and a miniature assault rifle on a chain, declaring that "Bratton's *the Man.*"[251]

Bratton's new rhetoric may have been welcome to officers feeling besieged by the Rampart accusations. If the government and the public were concerned about heavy-handed tactics against homeboys, the "cops' solution," according to one LAPD commander, was to "stop being a cop."[252] But was Bratton's war rhetoric sending the wrong message? The chief was sending at least a mixed message, urging his troops to roll out and cut off the heads of a terrorist threat worse than the mafia while still complying with the federal consent decree in Rampart that required ending the code of silence, disciplining brutal officers, and implementing other reforms sought since 1965.

Bratton's initial campaign was against graffiti, the issue that had built his reputation as transit chief in New York. It was a perfect example of good politics disconnected from rational policy, however. There was nothing that offended voters, homeowners, and small businesspeople more than the tagging that seemed to announce the existence of the hidden nation of vandals in the city's midst. The relationship between graffiti artists, muralists, taggers, gangs, and violence, however, was deeply complicated. A muralist named "Toomer," one of Bratton's early targets for arrest, considered himself a "piecer," neither a scrawling tagger nor an inspiring museum muralist. "It's for us," he said of his work. "I'll tell you what graffiti is about. It's about respect. People write graffiti for respect. People write graffiti for fame. People write graffiti to mark territory, or for the rush."[253]

According to a *Times* report, L.A. is home to 250 graffiti crews as well as hundreds of gangs that use graffiti to mark turf, many complete with their own Web sites, digital cameras, and computer drives—the instruments of the illegal information economy. "Still," the *Times* noted, "investigators know there are criminals, and *criminals*."[254] In Bratton's New York, the taggers could be found around subway stops and train tracks. In L.A., by contrast, the tags and murals could be found anywhere amidst the thousands of alleys, school properties, bridge crossings, and junkyards across a space of 400 square miles. In New York, three mayors spent $250 million over fifteen years to wipe out graffiti on 7,000 train cars.[255] No estimate was placed on the cost or time line for Bratton's removal campaign in L.A. The official struggle to reclaim the streets apparently had no boundaries. The radical historian Mike Davis compared the antigraffiti plan to invading Moscow in winter.[256]

But there was possibly a more sinister implication to the antigraffiti strategy. It might be a quagmire, but the numbers could be made to look good. As part of the permanent effort to appear tough on crime, the state of California had defined any property damage from graffiti worth $400 as a felony, a sharp reduction from the previous felony threshold of $2,000 of damage.[257] As a result, starting well before Bratton's war on graffiti, felony prosecutions of juveniles in L.A. grew from 160 in 1999 to 546 through the first nine months of 2002.[258] California, unlike New York, is a "three strikes" state, which means that a third conviction for a felony, even nonviolent property damage, results in an automatic twenty-five-years-to-life term in state prison. By 1999 there already were 50,000 individuals sentenced to second and third strikes in California, about 65 percent for property or drug crimes. By arresting thousands of graffiti taggers, therefore, Bratton could demonstrate huge numeric results to a threatened public, but with the potential collateral effect of locking away for life thousands of young people whose threat to society was unauthorized painting on walls. So much for punishment fitting the crime. The stated purpose of the "three strikes" law, passed overwhelmingly in 1994 at the height of public panic, was to put away *repeat violent offenders*. But it swiftly became an instrument to put away countless individuals from "the dangerous classes" for life. An analysis of third-strike cases from 1994 to 1997 revealed that less than *1 percent* involved murder and only one-fifth other violent offenses, while two-thirds were property, drug, and alcohol offenses.[259] For those who believed "three strikes" was necessary to prevent violent crime, the fact remained that violent crime declined in the period after 1994 in many states that had no "three strikes" law like California's.

Bratton's strategy in fighting "broken windows" was to use a computerized analysis of crime patterns combined with tough requirements for precinct commanders to target hot spots and reduce the number of crimes. The system, known as Compstat (comparative statistics) was effective as a tool for concentrating officers at locations with high-crime densities, but it encouraged a worship of numbers and delusions of mastery not unlike the computer models made famous by Defense Secretary Robert McNamara during the Vietnam War. The numbers fostered a sense of control at the computer screen, but were no substitute for understanding the street. The definition of who was a gang member or a "gang associate" (an unknown term on the street) was left usually to an individual officer in the course of a stop-and-frisk. That data, compiled on three-by-five cards and sent to the division headquarters, was so subjective that L.A. County Sheriff Lee Baca, the man in charge of gang data collection for the entire county, called much of it "junk."[260] Merrick Bobb, an expert police monitor, called the process "goofy."[261] The bits of subjective information, including photographs, cars driven by gang members, "known associates," nicknames, and tattoos, were filed in a system of stand-alone dial-up servers available to 125 agencies designed by the Orion Scientific Systems corporation in Orange County. It was a "virtual office" shared with police and prison officials anywhere in the world.[262]

This Orwellian intelligence net included no mechanism for an individual to appeal his or her designation. Nor is the list open to any form of public scrutiny. According to a CAL/GANG spokesman, there was no reason to worry, since the names were being collected for "information," not as the basis of probable cause for arrest. Of 20,221 names kept in Orange County, more than 90 percent were Latinos, Asians, and African Americans.[263] At Senate hearings I sponsored, one witness, a gang member in his youth and now a married father of two and a FedEx employee, testified that he had lost his job because his employer learned of his listing on the database.

As a result of this pseudo-scientific data collection, no one really knew how many "gang members" Bratton was up against. Some researchers used the figure 200,000 for the L.A. area.[264] Bratton claimed publicly to be outnumbered ten to one, which translated into a gang menace 100,000 strong.[265] After public criticism of inflated numbers, the *Times* began using the lower figure of 52,000 in the city amidst a wider sea of 100,000.[266] Simply by removing the "junk" names from the database, officials could have proclaimed a victory, relieving public anxiety, and focused more resources on an identifiable hard-core (if only they knew who they were). But who wanted to reduce the scale of the menace? After all, the more gang members there were, the more public panic there would be, the more votes for law and order candidates, and the more funding for the outgunned police. If not intentional, it was the logic of the system in place.

More specifically, internal LAPD data showed there was no increase in gang violence during 2002, the first year of the Rampart reforms and the period when the
new chief announced his "war" on gangs. It is quite true, as Bratton claimed, that
Los Angeles led the United States in overall homicides in 2002, and that those
numbers rose by 10 percent against the previous year, after a long decline (from
596 in 2001 to 658 in 2002). But the number of *gang* homicides in 2002 was the
same number as 2001 (347, or 53 percent of all homicides), and there was only a
0.4 percent increase in "gang-related" crimes such as aggravated assault and arson
in the same one-year period.[267] All the scare talk of increased gang violence generated by Bratton's early remarks wasn't justified by the department's own data for
the first year of his tenure. (For 2003, gang homicides plunged 28 percent, although attempted homicides were 22 percent higher than the five-year average.)

But who cares? the outraged citizen might shout. Wasn't *any* gang violence in-
tolerable? Should anyone be satisfied if the levels of gangbanging merely stay the
same? Angry questions like these boil up from the deepest levels of the voter psy-
che, and make rational debate all but impossible. But Bratton could just as easily
have said: "Our level of violent crime is too great, and I intend to support every
effort to reduce the killing. Thankfully, gang homicides have declined by half
since 1993, so something's been working before I arrived here, the numbers remained level last year, and I intend working to keep those numbers going down."
Why didn't he? Surely such an approach would have defused the momentum behind the "juggernaut" solutions Bratton favored. It would have required giving
credit for gang violence reduction to factors beyond the jurisdiction of law enforcement. It would have opened doors that some forces wanted closed.

For example, Bratton was quite right to declare his concern at the death toll in
minority communities. In the nineties, 4,193 African American men were murdered in Los Angeles County, primarily by other African Americans.[268] The pattern
was similar in cities around the country. Recall that the overall homicide rate in the
Los Angeles inner city jumped by 10 percent in 2002, while the gang-related homicide numbers remained the same. Here is an astonishing fact: since January 2001,
during the apex of the Rampart scandal, the South Bureau of the LAPD (running
from South Central to East Los Angeles) lost 106 officers through attrition, or

almost the same number who left the city's three other police bureaus combined.[269] This was an area containing 40 percent of the city's homicides, with streets where the murder rate is double that of Bogota.[270] Furthermore, in the 77th Street Division, which generally leads the city in homicides, LAPD detectives "hit a low point in 2001," closing only 17 percent of their cases with arrests.[271] A *Times* analysis of twelve years of LAPD data concluded that the department had "for years assigned more detectives per homicide in safer, more affluent parts of the city than in Central and South L.A., where the murder problem is most acute."[272] In response, Bratton began shifting more resources to the 77th in 2003.

Some police insiders blamed the Rampart scandal itself for diverting valuable manpower to deskwork on reforms. Others blamed an incomprehensible computer-driven system that allocated officers on the basis of twenty-five variables such as calls for service, time of day, travel time to respond, and so forth. Community cries for equal protection of the law had been voiced since the eighties to little avail. The data showed that police responded to false burglar alarms in the San Fernando Valley more often than to violent crime calls in the inner city.[273]

The police war on gangs consumed a disproportionate amount of energy, resources, and manpower, compared to the pursuit of other homicides. The gang wars reinforced public fears and grabbed media attention, while "mere" homicide cases were little reported and tough to solve. In the war on gangs, the LAPD was the thin blue line saving civilization, while homicide prevention seemed a less-glamorous mission. In addition, the pressures of San Fernando Valley homeowner associations were greater than the pressures from the powerless depths of the inner city. The police perhaps could relate culturally to middle-class Valley residents who, like the police themselves, chose to live as far as possible from the inner city. The distrust of police in the inner city, which impeded collaboration in finding witnesses, arose from long years of the LAPD beating the Rodney Kings of the world. The highest concentration of homicides was in the LAPD's 77th Division, where the police symbol was a skull-and-crossbones over the motto "The 77th Eat Their Dead." Who would want to be a cooperating witness for cops like that? The war on gangs, based on threat and intimidation, was inhibiting good detective work based on cooperation and trust. There was an explanation that was understood on the streets: the deaths of inner-city residents, of black and brown people, were simply not as important as the deaths of white or middle-class people.

This was the world Bratton inherited as he tried to draw attention to the city's shockingly high crime rate. Not penetrable by Compstat data, it was a world that depended on denial in large amounts.

Hidden Histories: The Watts Truce Between Crips and Bloods

> *In these bloody days and frightful nights when an urban*
> *warrior can find no face more despicable than his own, no*
> *ammunition more deadly than self-hate and no target more*
> *deserving of his true aim than his brother, we must wonder*
> *how we came so late and lonely to this place.*
> —*Maya Angelou, 1991*[1]

From the second-floor window of his Jordan Café, Oscar Niel surveys the Watts he has known for fifty years. At 114th and Wilmington, his "down home" place is nestled next to Watts's famous housing projects and near the new light rail line that divides Watts from Compton. "We came from a pain generation," Oscar recalls. "We were two generations from slavery, traditional people from the South where they never had migrated one hundred yards." The fathers would arrive first, find a room, take a job, and eventually bring the rest of their families to Los Angeles. It was the process known to African Americans as the first "great migration." For Oscar, who graduated from Jordan High School in 1955 with a UCLA track scholarship, the journey was similar to that which the young Claude Brown described in his 1965 classic *Manchild in the Promised Land*.

These migrants were told that unlimited opportunities for prosperity existed in New York and that there was no "color problem" there . . . this was the "promised land" that Mammy had been singing about in the cotton fields for many years . . . Even while planning the trip, they sang spirituals such as "Jesus Take My Hand" and "I'm On My Way," and chanted "Hallelujah, I'm on My Way to the Promised Land."

It seems that Cousin Willie, in his lying haste, had neglected to tell the folks down home about one of the most important aspects of the promised land: it was a slum ghetto. There was a tremendous difference in the way life was lived up North. There were too many people full of hate and bitterness crowded into a dirty, stinky, uncared-for closet-size section of a great city . . .

The children of these disillusioned colored pioneers inherited the total lot of their parents—the disappointments, the anger. To add to their misery, they had little hope of deliverance. *For where does one run to when he's already in the promised land?*[2]

Like other communities where gangs appeared, the African Americans were immigrants, too, and doubly so, first as slaves ripped from their native lands, then as uprooted people from the South. These immigrants to Los Angeles found themselves in an old barrio of Watts called Mudtown. In the white working-class city of Compton, just over the railroad tracks from Watts, public signs ordered "Negroes" out by sundown. Blacks faced a new segregation of broken promises.

But for Oscar, life included vibrant moments, too. "When I wanted to see a musician or athlete, all I'd do is look over the fence," he recalls fondly. Jordan High sent champions to the Olympics. George Brown beat Jesse Owens's long-jump record. Ed Sanders bested Ingmar Johanneson. Buddy Collete, the Platters, Big J McNeely, the blues music of Central Avenue, and Johnny Otis's Barrel House on Wilmington and Santa Ana were magnets of energy, and 103rd Street had theaters, banks, a post office, and markets that did home delivery.

Originating in a Spanish land grant, which became a village of Mexican railroad workers—people like Luis Rodriguez's family—Watts evolved in the forties into a majority-black town. Like Pico-Union for Latino immigrants a generation later, Watts swiftly became the most cramped center of population density in Los Angeles County.[3] For another of its native sons, Eldridge Cleaver, "Watts was a place of shame."[4] The future Black Panther and heralded author wrote from Soledad prison in 1968, "We used to use Watts as an epithet in much the same way as city boys used 'country' as a term of derision . . . the in-crowd of the time from L.A. would bring a cat down by saying that he had just left Watts, that he ought to go back to Watts until he had learned what was happening, or that he had just stolen enough money to move out of Watts . . ."[5]

Discriminatory housing covenants hemmed the residents in; a "cotton curtain" excluded them from higher-wage industrial jobs; most of the city's 100 labor union locals shunned blacks; until the sixties, there was no bus or rail service.[6] On every border were white racist gangs like the "Spook Hunters" that attacked blacks who dared cross boundaries, or white cliques in public schools who attacked black students or burned them in effigy.[7] "White people wouldn't let bands of blacks hang out on corners," Oscar remembers, "and the police would back them up."

The first "gang" Oscar recalls in Watts began in the twenties and was known as "the Farmers." It was one of a loose-knit network of "clubs" that came into existence for solidarity in the face of threats and exclusion. The Farmers didn't identify with the label of a "gang" but adopted identifying jackets, worked proudly on their cars and, more generally, on "being cool." By the fifties they became what the sociologist James Diego Vigil described as "architects of social space in the new, usually hostile, settings" across South Central L.A., with monikers like Businessmen, Gladiators, and Slausons.[8] They mushroomed in the packed public housing projects built in the fifties a few blocks from Oscar's restaurant—the Jordan Downs, the Nickerson Gardens, and the Imperial Courts, which enclosed one-third of the residents of Watts. These apparently were called "projects" because they were an urban planner's experiment. Like identical structures that birthed gangs in every northern city, these projects contained and institutionalized the low-income and welfare classes. The effect was to spur middle-class blacks to seek life opportunities beyond Watts when the California courts banned discriminatory housing covenants in 1952.

Vigil, like other gang experts, notes that the phenomenon of black gangs is "relatively recent," "is not a part of African culture, nor a part of the South's African American culture."[9] In Oscar's own street history, gangbanging started with the pachucos in East L.A. and the Italians who preceded the blacks in Watts. In this narrative, black gangs were a product of the uprooting and disillusioning experiences of the great migrations. But there is more to the story. The notion that black gangs are only a recent urban immigrant phenomenon erases the profound impact of African slavery. The pattern of absence of African American fathers, cited by neoconservatives as the cause of "moral poverty," did not begin with the New Deal welfare state but with the deliberate attempts by slaveholders to strip black men of their families and their dignity. Another legacy is a culture that stresses an extreme preparedness for protection of self and honor. "If you were a black father around here, you taught your son how to knock a nigger down with one punch," Oscar says, describing how "preparing your son for toughness came from slavery times." If your son was in a fight, he added, you "taught your son to hurt him bad so he'll never want to fight you anymore. You can't run away, 'cuz your daddy will beat you up and send you back out on the street."

According to some street observers, gangs and the broader rap culture are a "residue of the freedom struggles of the 20th century in the African American community." The gang culture is rooted in a choice to be "runaway Africans" as an alternative to either being a "house Negro" or a "field Negro."[10] Histories are rich with descriptions of this runaway slave tradition. According to John Hope Franklin and Loren Schweninger, in their 1999 book *Runaway Slaves: Rebels on the Plantation,* up to 80 percent of runaways were field hands in their teens and twenties.[11] "Death came early to slaves," and funerals were omnipresent. Only one of six held any skills as artisans or house servants. The African-born runaways often bore tribal markings from their original villages. These runaways often were described in the white press as "gangs" on the run from racist posses. "A considerable gang of runaway Negroes" was a typical nineteenth-century media description of runaways hidden in forests or bayous. Some became "outlaw gangs" building a clandestine underground economy, on rare occasions joining with gangs of whites. These "runaway gangs," according to the authors, "were a constant source of fear and anxiety for whites."[12] Murder, assault, arson, rape, pillage, burglary, and theft were "frequent occurrences."[13] Most of the violence was spontaneous and directed against whites, but a Virginia study revealed the lethal effects of self-hatred and intratribal bloodletting: among those convicted of murder, one-third of the killings between 1785 and 1864 were black-on-black.[14]

Fox Butterfield provides a fascinating example of how these experiences still echo today, in his Pulitzer Prize–winning 1995 work, *All God's Children,* a family history of twenty-five-year-old Willie Bosket, considered "the most dangerous inmate in the history of the New York penal system," whose spree of robberies, stabbings, and shootings earned him the desciption of "a mad dog killer" by New York's mayor and caused the state legislature to pass the first statute in the country allowing the trial of thirteen-year-olds for murder.[15] Shackled in a specially designed isolation cage, Bosket described himself as a "monster created by the system" and pleaded with Butterfield to research his family origins. The subsequent research told the story of a long sucession of "bad black men" in the Bosket family going back to slavery and Jim Crow.

In a finding that could describe today's gang members, Butterfield tells of a Southern code of honor that bred violence not only in the white culture but that of African American slaves: "they had been stripped of all their earthly possessions, even their families and their humanity. For many of the slaves, all that was left was personal honor," which he notes was an "ancient warrior's code," not based on rational calculation so much as a personal imperative.[16] Under the slavery/segregation systems, punishment was "no disgrace" for black men, but a test of will. Respect under this system could be achieved by being "bad," by resisting the overseer's lash, by refusing work, by "crimes" of defiance against the owners. The bad black man became an icon. Living amidst absolute degradation, without a name or possessions, the path to honor could only be through warrior will and prowess. Names like John Henry, Railroad Bill, and Stagolee became legendary in songs and folklore. Richard Wright summed up their stance as "despairing rebellion," or "rebellion turned inward."[17] Perhaps the most enduring is Stagolee, or "Stag" Lee Shelton, a nineteenth-century hipster of the type known as a "mack," who lived in an underworld of black social clubs, saloons, and whorehouses. "Stag" or "Stack" were references to male sexual potency and cardplaying. These outlaws were well-versed in competitive street toasts known as "the dozens" or the "dirty dozens," an antecedent to modern rap, whose uninhibited intent was to "jeer at life."[18] The dress code of the "macks" consisted of full-cut imported suits and stylized Stetson hats with silk-covered brims. In an incident symbolic of thousands of future homicides, Stagolee shot another black man named Billy Lyons in a St. Louis bar in 1895. Lyons had disrespected Stagolee by grabbing his five-dollar Stetson hat while the two were having words. As Lyons sprawled on the floor, Stagolee leaned down and said, "Nigger, I told you to give me my hat," and walked away.[19] Later, Stagolee was hung, and his legend was born. Sixty years later, when the Crips and Bloods were rolling, Melvin Van Peeble's 1971 film *Sweet Sweetback's Bad Ass Song* made the tale a modern revolutionary one. The Stagolees were violent, macho, sexually potent romantic heroes who materialized as icons whenever improvement in the black condition seemed most hopeless. Under a white-controlled law enforcement system, the only sanctions for many African American disputes involved violence or its threat. Butterfield quotes the historian Lawrence Levine's description of the bad nigger: "They were pure force, pure vengeance; explosions of fury and futility. They were not given any socially redeeming characteristics simply because in them there was no hope of social redemption."[20]

At the high point of Van Peeble's 1971 film, with Sweet Sweetback on the run, there is a musical exchange between the writer-director's "Colored Angels" and the runaway Stagolee. The Angels first quote the timeless advice of certain black leaders who have accommodated to their masters: "By and by, By and By, Progress, Sweetback." To which Sweetback answers: "That's what he wants you to believe." The Colored Angels, protective now of Sweetback, respond that "They bled your brother, They bled your sister, They bled your momma, They bled your poppa." Sweetback asks: "How come it took me so long to see . . . How he gets us to use each other?" At the end of the sequence, the Colored Angels are singing urgently: "Run Sweetback, Run motherfucker." In Van Peeble's account of the film, he writes that "these lines are not a homage to brutality that this artist has invented, but a hymn from the mouth of reality."

There is a direct line from Stagolee and the dozens to Sweet Sweetback's Baadaasss Song and the rap music that became ghetto anthems in places like Watts by the eighties. The lyrics of Tupac Shakur are reprinted in law enforcement guidebooks as alleged calls to war to against the police. In one police training manual, the words of Tupac Shakur's "Words of Wisdom," an echo of Stagolee, are taken literally rather than as history-laden symbolism by a gang expert:

Killing us one by one. In one way or another America will find a way to eliminate the problem one by one.
The problem is the troublesome black youth of the ghetto,
And one by one we are being wiped off the face of this earth at an alarming rate
Niggas what are we gonna do? Walk blind into a lie? Or fight and die if we must, like niggas?
[America] I charge you with robbery, for robbing me of my history. I charge you with false imprisonment for keeping me trapped in the projects . . .
Nightmare, that's what I am, America's nightmare. I am what you made me. The hate and evil that you gave me.
You should be scared. You should be running. You should be trying to silence me. Just as you rose, you will fall, by my hands.[21]

Butterfield argues that the "great migrations" from the South might have lessened the pull toward violent, *honor-based codes* learned in the Confederacy, replacing them with *dignity-based codes* in which an individual's respect and worth no longer depended on the opinion of others. By holding that every person is born equal, an internalized sense of dignity could allow one to "ignore the slights and insults that precipitated fights in the South."[22] However, the demoralizing new segregation that greeted migrants to the North undercut any such feelings of self-worth, and the "Southern-born honor code found a new spawning ground," Butterfield concludes.[23] Stripped of respect again and again, confronted by police and prison codes that carried reminders of plantation justice, the seeds of violent rebellion were redistributed wherever the northward migration reached a dead end.

Conditions in Watts and the South Central ghetto reproduced the culture of "bad" black men. Between 1963 and 1965 alone, the LAPD killed sixty black people, twenty-five of them unarmed.[24] As Martin Luther King said after visiting Watts in 1965, "Los Angeles could have expected riots because it is the luxurious symbol of luxurious living for whites. Watts is closer to it and yet further from it than any other Negro community in the country."[25] An additional explanation, in the view of David Wyatt, lay in the artificial expectations literally manufactured by the Los Angeles entertainment industry; he cites the 1944 study by Theodor Adorno and Max Horkheimer that "the culture industry perpetually cheats its customers of what it perpetually promises."[26]

In Watts, the typical person arrested during the August 1965 uprising was a seventeen-year-old black male "with little or no previous contact with the police"; and was "not a gang member."[27] The Los Angeles Times reported that "teenage gangs had nothing to do with the outbreak of the rioting."[28] Despite these clear findings, there were widespread alarms, some from law enforcement, that black gangs and the Nation of Islam had plotted the uprising months before and even engaged in guerrilla warfare. There were plenty of gangs in Los Angeles, of course, and gang members certainly participated in the uprising, though not as an organized vanguard. In fact, the rebellion had more effect on the gangs than the other way around, by creating a militant new cohesion among alienated young men on the streets of Los Angeles.

Until that time, the Gladiators, the Businessmen, the Slausons, and others were engaged in relatively low-level rumbles. The news of the southern civil rights movement shaped a more political consciousness, however, and the Watts uprising crystallized black pride, nationalism, and radicalism. Some in the gang known as the Slausons, for example, started defining themselves through face-to-face engagement with the LAPD's occupying army. Prison was often the teacher. One of the Slauson sets, known as the Renegades, was led by a street activist named Alprentice "Bunchy" Carter. He had been incarcerated in Soledad prison, where he became close to Eldridge Cleaver, a convicted rapist who was writing his best-selling autobiography, *Soul on Ice.* Bunchy Carter's transformation had begun; it would be lethally short-circuited in January 1969, when he was gunned down with another Panther, Jon Huggins, at a black studies meeting on the UCLA campus in a conflict with a rival nationalist group, United Slaves (US), while FBI counterintelligence agents were actively manipulating what they termed "an aura of gang warfare" between the groups.[29] Both organizations at the time were trying, with some success, to recruit gang members, or street people, to their ranks.[30]

On the cover of Gerald Horne's 1995 history of the Watts uprising, *Fire This Time,* is a photo taken on the second night of the 1965 uprising, showing a young black man staring with cold fury into a police line, surrounded by attentive, even enthusiastic, young "rioters." He has just finished declaring that "it's not about the neighborhood you're from, it's about us against these white cops!" Thirty-eight years later, in 2003, I interviewed that young militant, Ron Wilkins, a still-charismatic, gray-bearded instructor at several Los Angeles colleges. He was wearing a new T-shirt emblazoned "SLAUSON village," which he had picked up at the neighborhood's fiftieth anniversary. Ron recalled growing up in "the neighborhood" as a baby Slauson, with his mentor known as Bird, when the primary purpose was not to commit crimes but to claim an identity. "We resisted the term 'gang.' We saw the police as a gang, we saw ourselves as a club formed because of discrimination. You couldn't get into the Boy Scouts, you couldn't go to the public swimming pools, you couldn't go into Inglewood. Southgate was off limits." The Slausons sponsored their own social activities and beach parties in response to the exclusion. The Slauson "V" hand sign, meaning "victory" and taken from Viceroy cigarette commercials, was believed to be the first hand sign to represent an L.A. neighborhood. The Slauson "Shuffle," created at the Savoy Skating Rink on 78th and Central Avenue, was shown on national television. The homburg hat, like Stagolee's Stetson or the modern Godfather style, was adopted as the neighborhood look. The early territorial segregation also inspired a desire to become territorial themselves, not unlike nationalism developing under colonial rule. The Slausons fought rival neighborhoods, even fought each other over the streets they claimed. Typically, they fought over women. "I would be delighted to have a girlfriend in another neighborhood, so I could brag about it. If it became a pattern, we could brag to our rivals that the girls in your neighborhood like us more. Or tensions could break out when people said about an outside girlfriend that she's not from the neighborhood. That's how rooted it was."

Ron recalls the Slausons as "so damn defiant," they wanted conflict, thrived on conflict, grew their reputations and manhood on conflict. Over time, they would develop a reputation as the oldest and first "gang" to begin influencing other areas. They did "the wildest stuff" to demonstrate their prowess. Once when the police took someone down to the 77th police precinct, carloads of Slausons pulled into the parking lot reserved for police cars and barged through the private back door of the precinct "talking stuff." Another time they went after white gangs like the Spook-Hunters from Maywood, Lynwood, Huntington Park, and Southgate and routed them. "We wore those white boys out and took over their park. It was big news, the Slausons whipped the Spook Hunters. We took their jackets and drove all over in their cars."

The Slausons were formed not solely for criminal or political reasons but as a "cultural" response to exclusion and deprivation, in the phrase of Bird, who still maintains an office in the neighborhood. The prolonged existence of Los Angeles racial segregation combined with the growth of the civil rights movement fostered a nationalist militancy by the mid-sixties. "We would talk all the time about wanting to have been on those slave ships, and the hell we would have caused the slave owners."

The incident that ignited the Watts uprising on August 11, 1965, was the arrest and mistreatment of a high school dropout with a juvenile record, Marquette Frye, five seven in height and 130 pounds. "Technically, I was living in Watts, not the Slauson neighborhood," Ron Wilkins remembers. "So I called the Slausons and said 'it's on.'" Bird and Marquette Frye were distantly related, so the Slausons rolled into Watts. They didn't get along with the neighborhoods/gangs in Watts, "but even though we didn't like those guys we hated the police even more." On August 12, Ron found himself at Imperial and Avalon, haranging the crowds toward unity. "The rebellion did a lot, it was a unifying event, it helped us put aside squabbles and divisions and come together to fight the system." During the rioting, the simmering neighborhood rivalries were sublimated toward goals that seemed like the destruction of a prison by its inmates. "We started seeing how much we could destroy in our neighborhoods, or go out each night and count how many cars were overturned." There was also human destruction. On the first night, Ron was standing next to twenty-one-year-old Leon Posey as he walked out of a barbershop at 89th and Broadway. Suddenly a police bullet felled Posey, who became the first officially recorded death of the week."Oh shit, they're shooting at us," Ron recalls himself thinking.

In the immediate aftermath of the uprising, revolutionary street organizing began in earnest. Ron became a leader of Los Angeles Student Nonviolent Coordinating Committee (SNCC) and its liaison to the emerging Black Panther Party. The Slausons began a Community Alert Patrol (CAP), following the police with cameras and notebooks, a tactic that the Panthers escalated a year later to carrying guns and lawbooks (which cited the requirements of reasonable suspicion for stops and the right of citizens to bear arms in self-defense). Former rivals from different neighbhorhoods joined such organizations in a burst of angry hope. "I think if those organizations had lasted, they would have channeled the gang instinct. But the system didn't want that. Gangs are more useful to justify a big budget for suppression. Whenever it gets political, it's harder to justify the suppression."

An ideological group behind the community patrols was the emerging US (United Slaves) organization, led by Maulana Karenga (Ron Everett), which engaged in intense debates over the role of street people, or lumpen. Nearly all black nationalists at the time were recruiting from the street, like Malcolm X, or reading Fanon, and celebrating the element the Panthers called the "brothers on the block." US, the Panthers, the Nation of Islam, and numerous local groups had developed a paramilitary capacity as well. Often remembered for bitter feuds with the Panthers, Karenga later became a professor of black studies at California State University—Long Beach, the author of a widely used university textbook on the subject, and credited with creating Kwanzaa, the African American spiritual celebration. His recall of the late sixties debates about the recruitment of gang members, or "brothers off the block," remains important. Interviewed in his South Central office in 2003, Karenga noted the attractions of the gang world from which nationalists had tried to recruit: protection, self-respect, a sense of belonging, and profit (which became more important with the expansion of the drug trade). According to nationalists, the lumpen had an admirable fighting spirit, but Karenga felt they had a dual character. Living on the edge, they were extremely individualistic and, therefore, vulnerable. Having no positive ideological stance except individualism, they would break, or sell out, if captured. It was more likely they would carry their lumpen ideology into groups like the Panthers than the other way around. In Karenga's view, they needed to be uprooted from the context of the gang, and provided ideological grounding and new opportunities. The Muslims, who recruited half their members from prisons, had been successful in planting a new religion and worldview. Karenga believed the solution was in-depth training for social action and employment.

Kumasi, who still lives in the neighborhood, joined the Slausons at age ten. At fourteen, he was in the Youth Authority for attempted murder, where he met Brother Crook. Kumasi was bounced to foster homes in San Diego until finding himself in the streets during the 1965 Watts rebellion. "I always tried to incite, not to back away," he told me thirty-five years later at a restaurant near the University of Southern California. Before the rebellion, he had tried to keep one foot in the world of the federal Jobs Corps as a screening agent. But even there, along with Crook, he was arrested by the Compton police for postering a telephone pole. "We were pushing their fucking program when we could have been out robbing and murdering," he recalls. A call from a federal official caused the charges to be rescinded, but it was too late. Not long after the heady nights of the August 1965 rebellion, when the gang culture might have become political, even revolutionary, Kumasi instead found himself in a classic circumstance that officials describe as "gang-related violence," a Stagolee-style murder.

It was December 21, 1965, when "a dude made me kill him in front of 500 people" on Adams near Victoria. The dude was drunk, and "our eyes locked, that's all it was." Kumasi actually was backing up, or shadowing, a partner at a street party. There had been a fight over a girl. Kumasi took his partner's gun "'cuz I was supposed to have a level head." Kumasi tried to pull the partner out of an argument, telling him it was time to go, when the eyes locked. "You backing somebody's play? Me and you, me and you." Kumasi backed away at first, and the enemy drew a gun. Kumasi said, "Brother, we don't have no business," but warned that if guns were out, he was "not gonna be the loser." The enemy's partners now got into it, warning "that youngster [Kumasi] gonna kill you." But now the enemy was striding forward like John Wayne, and Kumasi started firing, trying to make him turn away. Finally, when the enemy closed the gap, "Bam, he was dead before he hit the ground." Kumasi thought, Now I'm dead. He was nineteen years old and destined for the state prison system. He didn't even know the name of the brother he had killed.

The prison system was where Kumasi grew up politically. As he reflected on his Slauson days, carrying guns, representing the neighborhood, looking for girls, he remembered that Crook spent one hour every day reading in the library. He decided to emulate his partner. During the early sixties, you couldn't read *Jet* or *Ebony* in the Paso Robles facility, you couldn't watch television news until after the Kennedy assassination, and prison officials carefully clipped news of Martin Luther King out of *Look, Life,* and *Time.* So inmates like Kumasi found *Reader's Digest,* an unlikely consciousness-raising journal, and "we'd read the fuck out of it." They read "30 Days to a More Powerful Vocabulary," and held their own discussions of the history withheld from them. They were organizing study groups on Booker T. Washington and W.E.B. Dubois, the revolutions in France, Russia, and Cuba, the Mensheviks and Bolsheviks. There emerged a prisoners' union in 1970, with the newly conscious Kumasi in the lead. Frightened at the prospect of a prisoners' rights movement led by convicted followers of Franz Fanon, the authorities refused to recognize the union or make any concessions. Instead, the prison system fostered and reinforced the brutalizing gang culture, constantly disgorging more Kumasis onto the streets. Unlike a revolutionary organization, the gangs reinforced what Kumasi called "misplaced aggression . . . You know, Curley slaps Moe, Moe slaps Joe, but they don't slap the guy that hit them first."

Thirty years later, with a UCLA grant, Kumasi was still pushing for an independent study of whether prisoner unions with education, training, and jobs programs would lessen crime and recidivism.

Crook, too, remembered how the shadow side of the gang life emerged after Watts as the alternative to revolutionary politics. "You started seeing more drugs, and drugs impacting people who were part of the movement." With the underground economy as their entry point, there came "pimping, robbing—some of the best bank robbers came out of the neighborhood—mostly people doing it themselves for the money, not for the neighborhood." In a famous instance, a carload of Slausons drove through Wilson's House of Suede and grabbed a storeful of leather jackets, which they distributed cut rate in the neighborhood according to the rank of members. This was "before the Panthers adopted their leather jackets," Crook said proudly. In addition, sometimes "cold killers, just sick" ravaged among those on the streets, one of whom drove around for weeks with the body of his slain girlfriend in his car trunk.

The Slausons may have supplied more people for movements ranging from the Panthers to the Fruit of Islam than any other neighborhood in Los Angeles. Several lost their lives in shootouts with the police or rival organizations. Yet many others, according to Bird, "became more successful than their critics," as Vietnam veterans, judges, lawyers, school principals, teachers, clergy, businessmen, recording artists, and top athletes. To the establishment, including many older blacks, says Bird, they were "considered as delinquent, incorrigible, and rebellious, which was true in some cases." But, he concludes, they were also "the defiant ones, the soul brothers and sisters, who were the chosen few that stepped forward to take a stand." As evidence, he needed only to point to Slauson Village's fiftieth reunion in 2002, attended by hundreds. The legacy of the Slausons thus cannot be reduced simply to a tale of violent criminality, but one of a mischanneled freedom struggle by a street organization flawed by internal ego rivalries and thwarted by the hostility of outside power structures. "Those who create the spark wind up as ashes," Kumasi lamented.

In the wake of the 1965 Watts uprising, a Blood leader named "General Robert E. Lee" declared that "there was no longer a need for us to fight each

other. That's when the Gladiators, the Businessmen, the Ditalians and Blood Alleys came to peace. That was from August '65 to the end of '68. There weren't
any gangs fighting each other at that time. It was a black thing."[31] Unfortunately
the same period saw the destruction of radical and black power organizations
springing up from the streets, as well as cutbacks on promised employment and
social service efforts.

When the Panthers were demolished, nonpolitical fighting gangs symbolized
by the Crips emerged in the vacuum. "This is where Crippin' began and don't
you forget it. In the embers of the Watts riots," says a character in *Inhale*, Donald
Bakeer's novel about the uprising.[32]

Crippin', Bloods, and Dyin'

Like most gang history, the origin of the Crips, including the name itself, is
shrouded in street lore. What is clear is that the Crips, the largest gang of the era,
emerged between the 1965 Watts uprising and the decline of civil rights and black
power movements in the late sixties. The failure of radicalism bred nihilism. The
constructive imploded into Richard Wright's "despairing rebellion," or, in the
phrase of Riis, a "distemper of the slums." Those who claim that the first Crips
were originally political in nature say the name stood for "Continuing Revolution
in Progress." Others say that the term evolved from "cribs," slang for babies in
cribs. Still others assert the name simply arose as shorthand for "cripple" when an
elderly Asian victim of the gang told police in fractured English that she had been
attacked by a "crip with a stick," or cane. In any event the fearsome gang known as
the Crips started to appear forcefully in late 1968 and early 1969 around Fremont
High School in Watts, symbolized in a teenager named Raymond Washington, and
around Washington High School around a youngster named "Tookie," or Stanley
Williams. Wearing prison-style blue bandannas, they started gangbanging. A
twelve-year-old named Kody Scott was typical of the youngsters Tookie and the
others appealed to. Later, as Monster Kody Scott (or Sanyika Shakur), he would
write of the glory days when James Brown's "The Payback" seemed like the Crip
Nation theme song:

I can do wheelin', I can do the dealin',
But I don't do no damn squealin'.
I can dig rappin'; I'm ready, I can dig rappin',
But I can't dig that back stabbin'.[33]

For those youngsters, Tookie was royalty. "He gave the Crip name a certain majesty and was a magnificent storyteller," Kody remembered years later. "For hours at a time he'd give us blow-by-blow rundowns on the old Tom Cross record hops at Sportsman's Park. Or he'd tell us about slain members who would have loved meeting us, cats like Buddha, Li'l Rock, and Moe, to name a few. He had a Cadillac and never drove it, preferring to walk everywhere . . . His entire living room was filled with weights. No furniture whatever, just pig iron. Tookie was huge, beyond belief at that time: twenty-two-inch arms, fifty-eight-inch chest, and huge tree-trunk legs. And he was dark, Marcus Garvey dark, shiny, slick and strong. He had the physique, complexion and attitude that intimidated most American people."[34]

Rivals of the Crips emerged in places like Piru Street and Nickerson Gardens. They called themselves Brims, or Brim Army, and finally Bloods—a name that some say originated among African American soldiers in Vietnam.[35] Confrontations were frequent, escalating to gunshot wounds, deaths, and fights during funerals. At one point, the Crips upended the casket of a Brim named L'il Country, and the bloodletting became unstoppable.

Raymond Washington was shot and killed in gang violence in the seventies, but Stanley "Tookie" Williams still survived, in a manner of speaking. I found him in the twentieth year of his solitary confinement on San Quentin's Death Row in late 2001. Never having visited Quentin's old death house blocks, I was taken aback as I made my way through the penitentiary's successive security checkpoints. In the parking lot I met a woman who had just returned from visiting her loved one. She happened to be a former prison guard who had married an inmate the day he was sentenced to Death Row. She met him first in prison, where he was awaiting execution for a robbery homicide. She thought I would understand why she was livid. "I don't have a problem with his doing time for the robbery, he knew he was doing it. But he has no memory of the killing. He tied some people up, and killed them execution-style, the way they taught him in the military. So now he's on Death Row for doing what they trained him to do in Vietnam." She was my welcome to the gulag, where truth is subjective, evasions and paranoia commonplace, and reality often a slippery slope in a world of informants, interrogators, provocateurs, and walls with ears.

After inspecting my belt, shoes, and wallet, after taking away all my possessions, including pencils and paper (not allowed), I passed through the security entrance and walked along the walls beneath the execution room. I was struck also by the painful contradiction between the gloomy structures on my right and, only a few yards away, the breathtaking freedom and beauty of San Francisco Bay. In the visitors' center I found myself in a room filled with cages where family members and lawyers could meet the accused, always under the watchful eye of armed guards. Along one side were vending machines where one could buy an armful of soft drinks, barbecued chicken, and other fast foods. My companion for the day, Barbara Becnel, busily began injecting a roll of quarters into the slot for chicken, and soon held several boxes on her lap. "It's the food Stanley craves," she said, "compared to the standard prison diet." Barbara, an African American journalist, was Stanley's conduit to the outside world, having met him several years before while researching a book on the Crips and the Bloods. Now she was coordinating his legal defense while also helping direct a community center in the heart of the nearby North Richmond ghetto. They are now intensely connected, working together on legal arguments, public relations, and the distribution of Tookie's children's books and Internet Web site (www.tookie.com) that urge peaceful alternatives to gang violence.

From the streets to the *New York Times,* the word was that Tookie is a reformed man, that he is helping kids stay out of gangs and prison, that his messages have been heard respectfully by Crips and Bloods alike. Swiss parliamentarians had even nominated him for the Nobel Peace Prize in 2001.[36] But the prison authorities and guards weren't buying any talk of conversion. They had captured their mortal enemy. This was the Godfather—the founder of the Crips!—and a leopard never changes its spots (at his trial, the prosecution used another jungle analogy, referring to him as a "Bengal tiger").[37] In the first years of his confinement, Tookie told me, guards with loaded shotguns regularly surrounded him as he was escorted in full-body chains the few feet from his cell to the cage where his lawyers awaited him. The overkill was not based on pure paranoia, since this was the place where revolutionary prison gangs had killed and died in brutal confrontations in the late sixties. On a national level, Death Row was a final battleground, legally, between the state and accused gang members, with more than forty African American and Latino gang figures facing execution among the total 211 nationally authorized by the U.S. Department of Justice as of 2001.[38]

Tookie was convicted of four killings related to two robberies in February 1979, when he was twenty-six years old. He denied the killings, and little direct evidence linked him to the crimes. During his trial, he sat in a courtroom restrained by heavy shackles and surrounded by armed guards while several dubious eyewitnesses testified against him. One, a declared co-participant in one of the murders, received a deal from the prosecution in exchange for all charges being dropped. Another witness said later that he was beaten and coerced into testifying. Two more, also admitted felons, received a deal from the prosecution. A fifth was a jailhouse informant facing the death penalty himself who had sought a deal in exchange for testimony. The government managed to suppress evidence that one of the witnesses had been prompted by law enforcement to elicit incriminating statements from Tookie. The original defense lawyer apparently failed to solicit investigators or witnesses for the guilt and penalty phases of the case, similarly failed to present an opening argument, gave only a forty-eight-line closing argument, and failed to present mitigating evidence or make an appeal that the court spare Tookie's life. The jury that convicted him was all white, the three black people in the eligible jury pool having been removed.[39]

After reading the voluminous appellate briefs, I could form no conclusive opinion as to what happened on the night of the murders. What leaped from the pages, however, was chilling evidence of the enormous obstacles for gang members—especially a founder of the Crips—to receive a fair trial. Inadequate representation at the trial court is only where the obstacles begin. Further, under California state law, it is not until the federal appellate level that resources are available to an indigent defendant to employ investigators to explore the original evidence and witnesses, which means many years after the crime itself.

According to prison procedures, Barbara Becnel and I first were locked into the cage we would share with Tookie. We did so, carrying boxes of the dark red barbecued chicken. After a couple of minutes, a heavy metal door leading from Tookie's cell block to the interview cage swung open. Accompanied by armed guards, the prisoner appeared at last, in chains that shackled his ankles and hands while also circling his groin and chest, meant to tighten the restraints if he struggled against them. Tookie was reduced to walking backward in baby steps toward our cage, which then was opened. Once inside, he placed his shackled hands backward through a slit in the cage door, where they were uncuffed. Only then did he give Barbara a brief hug, look straight at me, and shake hands. He had been confined this way, with a death sentence pending, for twenty years. I couldn't imagine surviving a single week in this condition, and wondered where he contained his rage.

First things first. Stanley was ravenous for the cold pieces of barbecued chicken and began gnawing on them, one at a time, until nothing was left but bones. He exchanged a subtle verbal message with Barbara about their correspondence with a publisher. For writing purposes, he used a typewriter presented to him by his mother in Los Angeles. He placed the machine on his metal bed while sitting against the opposite wall of his nine-by-four-foot cell. Tookie had tapped out twelve short books aimed at young people, describing the hellishness of prison, drugs, violence, and gangs in concise, self-taught prose. With Barbara's expertise, he also directed an Internet Project for Street Peace, which communicates with youngsters through chat rooms around the world.

Tookie was still as powerfully built as young Monster Kody had described him, though his twenty-two-inch biceps had softened with the passage of time and poor diet. He spoke clearly and directly, in a voice lowered from many years in the presence of guards and informants. He smiled frequently and easily, somewhat to my surprise. He was glad to help me with my research into the Crips and the gang phenomenon, which he was writing about himself. When I explained how difficult it was to interview him without a notepad or tape recorder, he asked his guard and received one of those short pencils that golfers carry on their rounds. Amused, he pushed a soiled napkin in my direction for the taking of notes. "Just put the napkin in your pocket when you go, and it'll probably be all right. Otherwise, you have to listen and remember."

It was impossible to make any serious or readable notes—state policy under Governors Wilson and Davis forbade interviews with prison inmates on the grounds that it might create unwarranted public sympathy for their stories—but Tookie's most powerful points stayed with me.

On my most mundane question about the origins of the name, Tookie claimed that Crips evolved from "cribs." The organization, he said, started in response to other gangs, then emulated the gang model. The Crips began, as he remembered, with a meeting with Raymond Washington at the Rio Motel on Imperial. When I asked him whether he thought his gang career was inevitable, he paused, then said, "There was a Bill Simmons, he operated a foster home, and was an ex-gang member. He might have made a difference if I could have stayed there . . . but probably not." Why did he form the Crips? He remembered telling a Youth Authority hearing as a teenager that his goal "was to create the biggest gang in the world." They let him go. Why the ambition? I asked. "I was a megalomaniac. I wanted to smash everyone. I wanted to make a rep, get respect and dignity. I wanted my name on everything, to be known everywhere." It was in a setting, he said, where "violence was the only answer to everything." He reflected again, then said something that I found stunning. "Do you know the word 'anachronism'?" he asked. "Yep," I said, realizing that Tookie had studied the dictionary in prison. "I think we were a kind of anachronism. We were meant to be born in a warrior era."

I confess that I believe in ancestral echoes, traumas, and hidden personas that affect us in the present day. Therapists acknowledge the role of paternal influence, which opens the door to influences stretching further back, say, to slavery time. What if individuals like Tookie are misplaced warriors, filled with a rage that stems from an experience in the hold of a slave ship that has never been acknowledged, addressed, or respected? The "anachronism" before me carefully described his evolution away from violence.

The change began after six consecutive years in the hole, a dark Death Row dungeon based on deathlike confinement. In that darkness, analogous to Plato's cave, Tookie's solitude led to the "discovery of how to reason." With reason and a dictionary, he studied the history of black people and learned "we're not worthless individuals driven by self-hate." Next he found that he was endowed with a conscience. From that realization came remorse, and finally a quest for redemption, resulting in the spate of children's books and the Internet peace work.

Of course his captors saw this evolution as the ultimate act of a con artist facing execution. "What a swell message to kids," sneered a *San Francisco Chronicle* writer, that "you can gun down four people and turn your life around."[40] But what was the alternative?

After our second hour, I found myself easily believing that Tookie was a changed man. What convinced me most was his grace under a pressure that I couldn't bear. There also was a decisive moment when he looked at me and said, "I'm not doing all this to improve my case. I'm not guilty and I want a new trial. But I'm doing this for my redemption." It seemed clear that he felt his work with young children formed a legacy that would enable him to face death.

On September 10, 2002, the U.S. Ninth Circuit Court of Appeals upheld Stanley Williams's death sentence, almost sealing his fate. But in a "rare move," according to the *Los Angeles Times*'s legal writer, the court asserted that "Williams's good works and accomplishments since incarceration make him a worthy candidate for the exercise of gubernatorial discretion," or clemency. The state's prosecutor, in response to the court's statement, said, "I have never seen anything like this, certainly nothing so blatant or specific."[41] A subsequent *Times* editorial acknowledged that if Tookie was "no candidate for sainthood, he is one for clemency. The effort that he has since put into undoing that harm is a powerful argument for saving his life."[42] The criminologist Lewis Yablonsky penned an endorsement essay as well.[43] In November 2002, an ACLU chapter filed a friend-of-the-court appeal to the Ninth Circuit to reconsider.[44]

If Attorney General Bill Lockyer, and California's prison officials and prosecutors, finally have their way, Tookie's enormous body will be strapped down and injected with lethal chemicals—soon. If that happens, a majority may think good riddance—if they reflect on the matter at all. But what is at stake is more than Tookie's guilt or innocence in the specific case. It is his claim of transformation that challenges our society's deepest assumption about gang members. If a founder of the Crips could transform, why not others presently considered incorrigible and deserving of death by injection? Why kill a reformed Stanley Williams to demonstrate that killing other people is wrong? Why not release him from his living death, or transfer him to quarters where he can continue his Internet peace process, or counsel inmates, or meet busloads of youngsters who might learn something from him? If he is executed, the war on gangs may declare victory, but what message will be sent to the next generation of homeboys coming out of the projects?

Peace in Watts, 1992

Dewayne Holmes was born in 1967, in the wake of the first Watts uprising. He and his longtime sidekick, John "Whiteboy" Heyman, remembered Tookie only as a fading legend. They were both from the Imperial Courts, where they jumped off the next phase of gangbanging and survived it, with Dewayne playing a key role in the peacemaking process that emanated from Watts at the very time of the 1992 uprising. I offered Dewayne a Senate staff job in 1995 while he was serving a seven-year sentence in Wasco state prison on dubious charges involving the theft of ten dollars during a party celebrating peace in the projects. I hired John, also twenty-nine, virtually the day he was released from ten years in state penitentiaries on a teenage drug violence conviction.

Before we met, Dewayne was already known as an important peacemaker by writers close to the scene, such as L.A. historian Mike Davis, who believed that Dewayne was framed at a key time when peace efforts seemed fragile. Former governor Edmund G. "Jerry" Brown even attended Dewayne's trial on the ten-dollar theft charge as a character witness. His chief advocate was his passionate and believable mother, Teresa, who formed a group in the projects called Mothers' ROC (Reclaiming Our Children). At the urgings of Teresa and the coalition, I went to meet Dewayne at the prison in the badlands of Kern County. My friend and chief-of-staff, Rocky Rushing, a former investigative reporter with both savvy and idealism, accompanied me to the forsaken facility. I was impressed at Dewayne's style the moment he sauntered into the visitors' room to shake hands.

Though he maintained a certain reserve, his charisma was astounding. His perfectly white teeth arced in a wide smile, matching the glow in his eyes. Short, buff at perhaps 200 pounds, he wore pressed prison-issue garb, including black shoes that sparkled. He had become a street intellectual who plowed through numerous books on subjects like the "prison industrial complex." We sat down at a round cafeteria table and talked, uninterruptedly, for two hours.

Dewayne's first contact with juvenile hall occurred when he was ten years old, in 1978, in a case involving a robbery of tools from the back of a truck. He remembered that when the sherriffs' deputies slammed his cell door closed, he beat the walls with his fists and cried all night for his mother. When he woke up, he was curled in a ball with the knuckles on both hands smeared with blood. Dewayne was arrested four more times as a juvenile, spending nearly five years in the Youth Authority from 1983 to 1988.

This wasn't summer camp, but a friendly counselor or two could be found. Over the coming decade, the original mission of juvenile rehabilitation was replaced in the Youth Authority with "a culture of punishment, control and, sometimes, brutality."[45] Wards were overdosed with unprescribed medications for population control. Many were locked up twenty-three hours per day, seven days per week. Guards encouraged "Friday Night Fights" between rival gang members. Punishment included "gym TD," in which wards were handcuffed and forced to kneel around the clock or until "their legs went numb."[46] Eventually, the system's own inspector general, a position created after legislative hearings in the nineties, condemned the systematic abuses, but not before Dewayne's generation of homeboys were hardened in adolescence.

Dewayne's twin brother died at birth. What might that loss have to do with his later loyalties and fatalism? Dewayne counted himself lucky. Having three sisters, a father, and mother under one roof made him, in his words, "one of the fortunate individuals in our community." His father served in the military, where he "incorporated a lot of that GI Joe attitude, you know?"

> He was real into commands or whatever and he didn't know how to, like, express his self in any other way. I think he viewed sensitivity as being something that was

like, feminine or whatever. So he wasn't best with that. It was never, "I love you, son," or whatever. It was, like, "Boy!," you know what I'm saying?

You know you see your mother and father get into it, and pops is whipping your mom's ass or whatever. You know what I'm saying? And me being the only boy in the family, I grew up to resent that shit. And there never was any real show of affection.

But Dewayne's father tried to provide money and clothes, keeping a roof over the family's head. The father was a hustler, a jack of all trades, a style Dewayne would grow into himself. His father gambled in clubs, played the horses, sold real estate for a friend. Later Dewayne would respect his father's commitment, but

As a kid, growing up, I didn't give a damn about that. I wanted attention and shit, you know, time, those type of things . . . some affection from the only male role model in my immediate household. And I really didn't receive that. So that pushed me out onto the streets, where I found the understanding and identity that I was looking for. Something I could identify with in a neighborhood when I hung out with the fellas. We grouped up, cliqued up. All of us had our personal situations that we didn't really talk about, but we knew. You know what I'm saying? I knew who's father was molesting them, you know, who's mother was beating them and shit because she hated the father so she took it out on the son. We didn't have to talk about it, it was already understood.

For Dewayne, then, his new circle of homeboys was a tight-knit club of silent, wounded individuals who never spoke of the conflicts going on in their households that had molded their aggression by the day. His friends called his father "Smiley" because "the guy never had a fucking smile on his face."

Dewayne's mother, Teresa, was a former model who was employed at the time in a clothing store at the Magic Johnson Mall on Crenshaw Boulevard. "She's real ladylike, you know what I'm saying, the way she dresses, the way she talks, all that shit, it's like, *woman!*" Intensely loyal to her son, Teresa would become an activist leader among women in the projects.

Dewayne grew up after the passing of the civil rights and black power movements. Everything by then, he recalled, was "about individualism, me, me, me,
me, how can I get up out of these goddamned projects, how can I get up from being dirt poor to just poor." Entry into the gang culture seemed a natural part of
growing up. Where Dewayne and his "partner" John Heyman lived, the "gang"
and "the neighborhood" were synonymous. In Dewayne's projects, it was the
Crips, subdivided into numerous sets reflecting street names like the Hoovers,
the Rolling 60s, or Grape Street. In those days, there was no "courting in" or
"jumping in." "We never really did say, okay, now we're in a gang. We represented. Today the gang is something totally different from the neighborhood, but
when we grew up, it was, like, 'you from the neighborhood,' everyone had a
common interest in the neighborhood, trying to protect the neighborhood."

Dewayne remembers a childhood rage at being denied material things that
bombarded him on television. Dewayne Holmes wasn't having it. "It's one thing
to not have things, you know, but it's something totally different to have shit
waved in your face and you can't get to it!" When Dewayne wanted a bike, he
got one by nailing an old skate to the bottom of a milk crate, shoved an old
shirt inside the crate, and presto, he and his friends had go-carts. For a time there
also were teen posts, created after the Watts uprising, which channeled Dewayne's
energy toward sporting events, camping trips, drill teams, and girls. "It kept us out
of trouble, as long as we had that, we were cool, we always had something to do."
But funding for the teen posts dried up as the riots faded from memory.

The set developed a rampant delinquent style, which included stealing brand-
new mopeds off trains inexplicably stationed on the tracks that bisected Watts.
Next, "Sherman," or PCP, the liquid form of a hallucinogen, became a local craze
and source of easy cash. Dewayne's friends schemed to make fake PCP in A-1
bottles with quick-start lighter fluid that smelled like the drug. Mixed with butter
or baby oil, "shermans," or cigarettes, could be dipped into the concoction, netting Dewayne $30 a pop.[47]

After the trauma at the juvenile camp, he never cried again. The camp experience "was about being able to survive, so I had to become more aggressive. It was
a lot of fighting for shit that I didn't really have to fight about, but I was picking at

it just to kick some ass." While the Crips may not have been born behind bars, they were the prison system's foster children. "It used to be if you were a Crip, that's all you had to say, man, I'm a Crip, and along with that came a lot of respect, you know, people would move out of your way. You'd be all shackled up and shit, and the police be like, 'Crip module coming through!', they'd make everyone turn and face the wall." The LAPD gang database shows Dewayne as "an admitted Project Crip, in file since 06-16-83."[48]

At the same time, a political seed was growing in Dewayne's mind. The Crips had come out of a "whole other movement," which was born and died before his time, an offshoot of the Panthers and "Bunchy" Carter, which "was to fight against all these outside forces and enemies that was inflicting harm on the community." As Dewayne understood it, those movements had failed. The residue was a raw appetite for respect. Dewayne, John, and their homeboys were, after the fashion of Tookie, undeveloped warriors, misplaced in time.

For his first serious juvenile offense, Dewayne wound up spending eighteen months in the camp after an initial sentence of five months. By the time he hit the streets again, he was a grown gangbanger with the moniker "Snipe." Two months after release, he engaged in a dangerously impulsive assault with a deadly weapon. The fight erupted from jealousy over a girl. One of Dewayne's homies was raging at a young man from Inglewood coming into the neighborhood to see a former girlfriend. "So my homie wanted to fight the dude, which was shit, cool, all right, you wanna fight. He wanted me to come to watch his back."

Then fifteen years old, Dewayne was high on marijuana and Old English when the time came. When his homeboy knocked on the door of the enemy suitor, he found himself confronted by the father, mother, and sister of his enemy. The father marched on Dewayne, holding one hand behind his back, screaming, "You young fuck, you don't know who you're messing with." The man was bluffing, but Dewayne pulled a gun and "shot his ass, I was mad, so I shot his son, shot the car up and shit. I wasn't trying to shoot his wife, I didn't really mess with her. She was outside of the car with the baby." Arrested a few days later, Dewayne was sentenced to eleven years in Youth Authority, where he served eight. From age thirteen to twenty-one, then, he was behind bars, learning manhood, building his reputation. "I had acquired the respect of my peers, which was good, that's what you're in the game for. I stayed true, never told on no one, never ratted out anyone, did my time and got out, name still intact, no smut on it."

Dewayne's favorite movie, and that of most homeboys in that era, was Al Pacino's *Scarface*, a film so memorable that it was rereleased in 2003. By now it is described in the mainstream media as "an iconic film in an urban landscape," which had shaped the identity of the hip-hop generation (Sean "P. Diddy" Combs saw it sixty-three times).[49] In Dewayne's day, it was the reigning fantasy of the streets, with Scarface's code of conduct memorized and recited in all the neighborhoods:

> All I have in this world are my balls and my word, and I don't break 'em for no one . . . It's those guys, the fucking bankers and politicians, they want to make the coke illegal so they can make the fucking money and get the fucking votes . . . You don't have the guts to be what you want to be. You need people like me so you can point your fucking fingers, "that's the bad guy." You just know how to hide, how to lie. Me? I don't. I always tell the truth, even when I lie.

By the beginning of the nineties, Crenshaw Boulevard—"the Shaw"—was a dangerous, high-energy carnival of Scarface wannabees on Saturday nights, rival sets displaying everything from cars to women. One night in 1991, after his release, Dewayne pulled up with his homies at Manchester and Crenshaw in the midnight hours. He was on a daredevil "mission."[50] Wearing a blue Crips T-shirt, Dewayne proceeded to drive a convertible straight into a parking lot filled with scores of Bloods. His plan was to force the Bloods to yield ground or do battle. Holding a gun on his lap, Dewayne mad-dogged a Blood in a champagne-colored Monte Carlo. "Whassup Blood?" The challenge delivered, now a crowd formed in front of Dewayne's vehicle, then opened up to reveal a Blood pointing a 9mm directly at Dewayne. "He starts 'boom, boom, boom.' He remembers the windshield cracking. Dewayne reached to grab the shooter, his adrenaline flowing, then yanked his car onto Manchester at high speed. The homeboy with him was laughing. "Them fools tried to kill us." Dewayne realized the car was full of bullets, and that some were in his chest. "Cuz, I am hit," he told his homie. The blood was pumping out of Dewayne, so he stuck two fingers into the holes in his chest and let his partner drive. They were close to Daniel Freeman Hospital, which would be dangerously near any vengeful Bloods, so Dewayne's partner raced across the city to Martin Luther King Hospital while Dewayne slumped on the car floor. When they arrived at MLK, a homegirl saw the crumpled Dewayne bleeding from the chest and alerted the neighborhood.

Dewayne was rushed into the emergency ward while doctors cut open his side to remove the possible lead poisoning. A fist-size hole was opened under his right armpit, another over his right chest. Meanwhile, Dewayne's homies, believing the hospital had allowed their brother to die, started attacking and destroying the emergency room. Next the LAPD arrived, fought and arrested the homeboys, and finally marched into intensive care with an uncle to verify that Dewayne was alive. Tell your homies you're okay, the officers demanded. "I didn't say shit, I wasn't okay." Dewayne remained in the hospital for two or three days before checking himself out. Once home, he planned a new round of vengeance on Crenshaw, a sortie that was prevented by chance when police in a routine stop discovered a loaded weapon in his car. (According to probation records, Dewayne declared "he did not have a gun. The gun was in the car in which he was riding.") The case was dismissed.[51]

By this time, in his mid-twenties, Dewayne Holmes would have seemed an incorrigible menace to anyone in his path. The decade of incarceration in camps and YA facilities sharpened his manipulative skills, toughened his physical prowess, and enlarged his legend. However, other traits were surfacing, because the Dewayne Holmes I met in prison five years later had transformed into a self-controlled, curious, humorous, and increasingly political person.

Partly it was a simple maturation process; his adolescence was over. But his transformation seemed to grow from a disillusionment with what gangs had turned into by the nineties. As an example, a young friend of Dewayne's named Little Peter was murdered by rivals who "blew his head off, man, brains and shit was all in the parking lot." Such tragedies, he began to acknowledge, were not the original intent of the homies he grew up with. In his idealized memory of their origins, there was a shared sense of neighborhood solidarity, though it was outside the boundaries of the law and mainstream society. "We did a lot of destructive shit, but that wasn't our intent, it just happened that way because we were experimenting with shit. Our intentions were to put protection on the women and children in our neighborhood, that was our thing," he said. "I used to come running in anybody's house in our neighborhood when the police was chasing me, I could run in any door and they'd hide me, or let me run through and wouldn't tell the police I ran through and went out the door. Because we were like a family, there was a sense of belonging, we shared and struggled, that was the atmosphere. But in '90 when Little Peter got killed, that was no more. And I began asking, how the fuck did it ever go down like this?"

Locking up Dewayne and his generation of homies forced an abrupt transition in leadership on the street. The original, idealized bond of solidarity was replaced with a meaner mystique. It was the era of the crack cocaine epidemic. The vacuum was filled by the "sort of dude who could only get in front of the television and watch 'Scarface'" and say, that's how you're supposed to do it, but never really instilling the values and principles that made us acceptable in the neighborhood. Even though we were out there doing a lot of shit, we were accepted in the neighborhood because we wasn't really doing it to the people of the neighborhood. We weren't robbing the homeboys' mothers or raping the homeboys' sisters, we weren't into that." The new dudes embarked on a rampage of indiscriminate destruction. A war between the Imperial Courts and the adjacent Jordan Downs projects, inflamed during Dewayne's incarceration, for example, "could have been resolved and saved a lot of lives," Dewayne said, "but an asshole was pushing it because it was beneficial to him to have the whole neighborhood at war instead of himself alone."

The rechanneling of Dewayne Holmes's restless rage occurred when his uncle Henry Pico died at the hands of the LAPD. Henry was shot amidst a power outage caused by a fierce storm (some still insist it was a deliberate blackout), when LAPD units entered the projects dressed in black body armor with high-powered flashlights on a search mission. Curiously, just days before the blackouts,

Dewayne was stopped by two LAPD officers who demanded to know if gang members were planning to fire on police. If that was going down, they said, "it's King's X from now on," referring to a game of tag based on a medieval monarch's stamping a wax seal on messages. It meant anything goes. In the police version of Henry Pico's death, Henry had an AK-47, though the weapon was never recovered. Dewayne says Henry, the father of a large family, was shot while "helping kids get out of the line of gunfire."

Though it was little noted outside the projects, the shooting of Henry Pico became an intense focal point of antipolice hostility, and a turning point for Dewayne. Along with his mom, he joined the neighborhood's Henry Pico Defense Committee. A fruit tree was planted on the spot where Henry had died, where it still grows today. Dewayne told the press that he was urging the homeboys "not to retaliate against the police and instead channel their energies towards nonviolent protest."[52] The defense committee raised his awareness of the potential that lay in community mobilization, connecting across ethnic lines with similar police reform groups in East Los Angeles's Chicano community. But it also posed the question of how gang members could cross their own boundaries to collaborate on police abuse issues. "The natural question became how do we get together but still have these conflicts," Dewayne said. For example, Dewayne began participating in meetings at a Muslim mosque across the street from Nickerson Gardens, the turf of the Bounty Hunter Bloods. Paranoid about even crossing the street—much less attending a meeting with deadly rivals—he and others sometimes brought guns. The Fruit of Islam disarmed them at the door and guaranteed security.

For Dewayne, the moment had arrived for thinking about the unthinkable, a pause in the violence that gripped the projects. With Henry Pico's murder, following that of Little Peter, the carnage had come home. "Our family was in a lot of pain and he just wanted to stop the war," said Teresa. "Sometimes, when you lose someone who's so special to you, it helps you make up your mind to do what you should have been doing long ago."[53] Dewayne had to rechannel his courage. Teresa can still remember "her baby," unarmed and all alone, walking down the street to the rival Jordan Downs projects to propose a

peace

truce, then making the same walk over to the Bounty Hunter Bloods at the Nickerson Gardens.[54] Only someone with Dewayne's reputation could extend the offer.

> Kids today can't articulate why they're feeling what they feel, but those same kind of rebellious emotions are getting them in trouble because they have no way to vent the pressure. So they end up hating those things that have put them in that position, and if what has put you there is the fact that you're black, you end up hating that. You don't kill yourself but you kill others who are like you.
> —A.C. Jones, L.A. County probation camp officer[55]

> Today I know what that weight was, but then I didn't. It was my conscience struggling under the weight of constant wrongdoing. Not wrongdoing in any religious sense, but doing things that were morally wrong based on the human code of ethics. Also, it was my subconscious telling me that my time was up . . . At nineteen, I felt like thirty.
> —Monster Kody[56]

Just across that border from Dewayne Holmes, Aqeela Sherrells was growing up in the Jordan Downs housing projects, one of ten children in a family that migrated from Monroe, Louisiana. Born in 1969, Aqeela, along with his brother Daude, two years older, was another orphan of the civil rights period. The Jordan Downs neighborhood was a rival of Dewayne Holmes's neighborhood, although everyone caught in the "set trippin'" was a Crip. The violence only intensified when crack cocaine hit the scene in the early eighties. In ninth grade, Aqeela saw one of his best friends, named Ronzelle, shot and killed in a schoolyard. The neighborhoods no longer were settling their rivalries by "going heads up," he realized, but with a lethal escalation of weapons. Aqeela decided to "stop claiming the set" and gangbanging after the shock of his friend's murder, although he still hung out with his homies. Their parents, professional cooks by trade and community activists as well, succeeded in encouraging most of the kids to enroll in college, which

meant California State University—Northridge, for Aqeela. But even before mi-
grating to the San Fernando Valley, his discovery of girls led him to wander beyond
the confines of the projects. Just when it seemed to Aqeela that "all the beautiful
girls from grade school were running around all night looking for the next hit," destroying themselves before his eyes, he met a girl from the west side of Los Angeles. "I learned that I had to change the way I dressed and looked to get these kind of
girls," he said, "and also I had to be camouflaged to travel through enemy neighborhoods to get there." A strikingly handsome, self-described "party animal,"
Aqeela fathered five children with four women by the time he was eighteen.

Daude continued to gangbang even after enrolling in Bakersfield College, not
stopping until he had fathered his first child. Aqeela depended on other brothers'
and sisters' gang activities to provide "enough money so I wouldn't starve getting
through college." But he escaped the worst of the drug-related violence of the
eighties and found refuge at Northridge with a black studies professor named Dr.
Johnny Scott, who had grown up in Jordan Downs during the time of the civil
rights movement, attended Harvard and Stanford, and now was mentoring and
protecting any black students who succeeded in making it to the university.
Aqeela found himself falling in love with ideas, writers, and black history. He
read *The Evidence of Things Not Seen,* by James Baldwin, about the murders of
black children in Atlanta in 1979–80, in which Baldwin writes of terrors that
memory blots out, and concludes that "only love can help you recognize what
you do not remember."[57] Aqeela realized he had to come to terms with the repressed fact of his molestation as a young man. At first he searched for blame,
trying on a menu of ideologies, from black nationalism to the Shiite version of Islam. For a while he prayed five times a day, starting at 4:44 A.M., then started wondering what he was doing. Was it because he feared God, as prescribed in the
Scriptures? A voice told him no, that God is love. He wound up next at the Aquarius Spiritual Center at Martin Luther King Boulevard and Normandy. Then, in
1989, at age twenty, he attended a huge rally to stop the killing, sponsored by
Minister Louis Farrakhan at the L.A. Sports Arena, where he met the football
great Jim Brown. A controversial icon of black male masculinity, Brown was living the good life in the Hollywood Hills, a lifestyle every gangster aspired to, and

exploring new forms of rehabilitation for black men in the prisons. The effort would widen into the Amer-I-Can program aimed at fostering self-esteem and "life management skills" among disenfranchised inmates and at-risk youth. He was hanging out, too, with members of Public Enemy, the rappers who were dramatizing the "gangsta" lifestyle to millions of young people. Aqeela was impressed with Jim Brown. The party animal was becoming a dreamer, one with college training and skills. He decided to gather up his dreams and return to Jordan Downs.

Tony Perry was a few years older than Daude, Aqeela, and Dewayne Holmes. He grew up in Newark, New Jersey, during the 1967 riots and deaths. Tony's mother never recovered from all the violence, so the family fled for Southern California, ending up in San Diego just as Crips were emerging there. Because of the influence of black consciousness, Tony couldn't countenance black-on-black violence, despite all his anger. Neither did it seem possible to escape the ghetto. So he tailored a gangster lifestyle within the underground economy. Tony, a tall, slender man of forty in 2002, described the process vividly:

> My father divorced my mother. She tried to commit suicide. So we lived with our grandparents. My mother came back, took two jobs and refused welfare. So we were hungry, struggling for clothes. My thing became survival and struggle. My mom looked the other way while we stole. We were into the need and not the greed. I kept enough to pay for clothes and lunch money. I was a petty thief, but I was an honorable petty thief. I didn't buy nothing flashy.[58]

Young Tony admired people who returned from jail buffed up. He studied television shows like *It Takes a Thief* to learn how to break into houses without breaking windows. "I didn't operate on ignorance." His sister's boyfriend used him to sell drugs but also taught Tony about "coolness." In those days, he recalled, the gang lifestyle was more about being cool than violent, never showing fear no matter what the pressure. Coolness also was about approaching girls. Tony in fact became cool, that is, overcame fear, in order to learn how to talk to girls. There was a lesson in this about violence. "What I learned was that the cats that could not talk to girls were more aggressive than other males, but the cats who could talk to girls came into the 'player' category." They were focused on the women, while the others, he thought, were getting attention through violence. It wasn't that the players were wimps who couldn't defend themselves, it was that "they didn't have to be in an all-male group about who was the most violent." Tony wanted the girls, not the violence, so he mastered being cool.

Tony was still a cool but nonpolitical young man in the neighborhood when Aqeela and Daude went off to college. Tony rejected "the white man's education." He thought educated blacks were selling out, leaving the community. But he was on a quest for identity, too, in the vacuum that followed the civil rights movement, so he became a street intellectual sampling African, Muslim, Rastafarian, and Mayan religions. When Aqeela, and then Daude, returned to the neighborhood in pursuit of their undefined dreams, Tony took notice and began to listen.

By this time, Aqeela and Daude were deep into gnosticism and esoteric studies in addition to black power. In Aqeela's vision, he flashed on the mathematical angles that underlay his world of housing projects. They sat at a perfect ninety-degree angle, a hypotenus if you traveled from the Nickerson Gardens down to the Imperial Courts, turned left, and reached Jordan Downs. The hypotenus, he knew, was an infinite line that crossed the axis of x and y, which Aqeela now saw as "the line of God" because it had no beginning and no end. Eureka: the bottom of the ghetto was holy ground, where something sacred was meant to happen.

Aqeela and Daude began organizing marches inside the projects against both the killing spree and the LAPD. Some of it was political: "black power/gets stronger by the hour," "no justice/no peace!" Sometimes the style was paramilitary: green and black camouflaged military outfits, African *kufis* (crown hats), high black boots with steel toes. At other times they wore white robes and preached the Age of Aquarius. They began promoting the color purple, the color of valor, the mixture of red (blood) and blue (crip). They developed a following. In time, they ventured across the street. "I had a dream we were going to get into a shoot-out in the Nickerson Gardens. I didn't want to go, but we prayed, and I went. First thing that happened when we got to Nickerson, I saw this guy Droopy and he said it was cool."

Dewayne Holmes was suspicious. Who were these college graduates working with Jim Brown, bringing tidings of peace? As the meetings in the mosque developed momentum, other interested outsiders and dignitaries began to appear, including ministers and Congresswoman Maxine Waters. Dewayne and his crowd weren't having any of it at first. They were homeboys, while the others were organizers. Dewayne's whole world was the street. He even objected to the spreading story that the intermittent truce talks were "Muslim-sponsored." While he expressed appreciation for the use of the mosque, "we didn't want to take our shoes off, we had guns and shit." In reality, the meetings were far from promising, bogged down in heated discussions of what rival homies had done to each other. They couldn't get past the foul air of suspicion and vengeance. Who was accountable to whom? How could any cease-fire be enforced? Then they realized that those responsible for the madness had to become responsible for ending it. At one meeting, when some people asked, How do we know this shit is real?, "the guys from the Nickersons stood up and said if we wasn't here you wouldn't be here," meaning they were providing security for the enemies of their own homeboys. At each painful step, guys like Dewayne took the peace proposals back to their homies, especially to people who had lost loved ones in the war.

It was a moment of truth for Stanley "Tookie" Williams on Death Row in San Quentin, too. What had seemed a dream—a transition from revenge to forgiveness—was beginning to happen. It was now or never. Voices for peace would either prevail or be buried, perhaps for another generation. Concerned community leaders in South Central arranged a televised closed-circuit message from Tookie in prison to a deadly serious roomful of Crips and Bloods. Tookie lamented a "legacy of black on black genocide" created by the gang wars, and urged his audience to channel their "do or die attitudes as street warriors" into rebuilding their own communities. The meeting ended with peace signs and embraces among lifelong enemies.

Meanwhile, Tony Perry was awed. He believed that Aqeela and Daude were fulfilling a Mayan prophecy. Tony was reading a book by Jose Aguillar predicting that the year 1992 heralded a new age. "I thought, here's the people of Watts in the worse condition but fulfilling an ancient prophecy." While the private truce meetings were continuing in the mosque, churches, and homes, Daude asked Tony to write up the gang truce idea being discussed, and Tony said sure. "I never wrote one before, but I knew I could do it." First, he needed to research a precedent in history, and thought the parallel might be the Middle East. "I knew from the Bible and Koran that the Jews and Arabs were Semitic, they were related, both children of Abraham, it was tribal bloodletting, and I knew from gang members the same thing, that they were saying, 'man, he's my cousin' about their enemies in another gang."

Treaty

Tony visited the UCLA library on his research mission, but was turned away. Next he visited the Von Kleinschmidt Library at the University of Southern California, where a helpful staff member directed him to a basement filing room holding papers on the Arab-Israeli conflict. There, Tony found what he was looking for: a twelve-page document entitled "The Arab-Israeli Armistice Agreements," signed on February 24, 1949, by Walter Eytan for Israel, Seif El Dine for the Egyptians, and Ralph J. Bunche as acting United Nations mediator. When Tony realized that Ralph Bunche was born in South Central, he took it as another sign.

"What was in my mind was to use the Israeli-Arab treaty because they were related people and the gangs in Watts are related people. There were fights over land rights, turf, and grudges people just won't let go." Tony studied the 1949 pact with its details of cease-fires, safe corridors, and the like, then applied the text to the tribes in the four Watts housing projects, and handed the finished draft to Daude. After some redrafting by Daude, the finished version closely matched the 1949 armistice document. For example, the Israeli-Arab version declared that "the establishment of an armistice between the armed forces of the two Parties is accepted as an indispensable step toward the liquidation of armed conflict and the restoration of peace in Palestine." Daude's version declared that "the establishment of a cease-fire between the armed gangs of all parties is accepted as a necessary step toward the renewal of peace in Watts, California." Where the 1949 treaty assured that "no element of the land, sea or air military or paramilitary forces of either parties, including non-regular forces, shall commit any warlike or hostile act against the military or paramilitary forces of the other party . . . ," the Watts treaty announced that "no element of the land drive-by shootings and random slayings of any organization shall commit any warlike or hostile act against the other parties, or against civilians under the influences of that gang." Handwritten notes by Daude and Alisunn Walker emphasized that the purpose was to "plan to create a better environment for children, parents and for economic development, bringing jobs and business back to the community [and that the] quality of education is going down, kids are scared to come to school."

Of course, the draft peace treaty could not be a formal or official document. Most in the projects never sat down and read it. But it perfectly expressed an aspiration that already was taking hold at the time, project by project, individual by individual. The meetings in the mosque, the churches, and at Jim Brown's home provided space for building trust. The truce was truly a movement, needing individual steps of courage from the bottom up. If there was an exact moment when peace was declared, it probably was April 26, 1992, when a van load of Grape Street Crips including Aqeela and Daude drove to the Imperial Courts, home of Dewayne and the PJ Crips. The atmosphere was tense as the PJs uneasily surrounded the dozen or so unexpected visitors from Jordan Downs. One of Aqeela's homeboys, named Playmate, pulled out a video camera and turned on music in the van. Dewayne Holmes, then twenty-four, remembers wondering what would happen next, when Tony Bogard, a key player from Imperial Courts, said "let's take this in the gym." Older gang members, taken aback by the suddenness of the gesture from Jordan Downs, headed into the Imperial Courts rec center, where lingering suspicions and questions would be aired. But the process couldn't be delayed by more meetings. The younger homies, whose entire lives had been dictated by a war with their own neighbors that none of them really understood, began to fraternize and socialize with the visitors. People who had known of each other their whole lives were shaking hands for the first time. As word spread, more started showing up. As the sun went down, they started partying. The peace was on.

The next day brought another first. Weeks before, Jim Brown had obtained buses to transport a cross-section of homeboys from Watts to lobby the L.A. City Council for greater resources, and it happened that the council meeting was the

Peace declared

morning after the cease-fire took effect. Over 200 young people, already high on
"trucing," climbed aboard the bus for their first exposure to the world of politicians. Perhaps not since Rosa Parks or the freedom rides had there been a more
important bus caravan. Upon arriving and climbing the steps to the ornate city
chambers, Dewayne Holmes and Aqeela and Daude Sherrills were among those
who spoke in an official setting for the first time in their lives. Police took up positions around the hall as the phalanx of gang members moved toward the mi-
crophone to speak. There is no record to show whether council members paid
attention, but the time for public comment was shorter than usual. Dewayne
and others articulated a platform for peace, calling for council resources to rebuild
the communities they had damaged. They wanted the hiring of gang members
as security guards for children on their way to school, or for grandparents walking to the market. A nervous Council brushed them off with perfunctory promises, and they took their buses back to the ghetto, where the truce parties were
spreading to the Nickerson Gardens.

The following day, April 29, a Simi Valley jury announced not-guilty verdicts
for four LAPD officers on trial for the March 3, 1991, beating of Rodney King. By
the afternoon, one of the most significant riots of twentieth-century America
was under way. Within six days, as many as forty-five people were killed, over 700
businesses were burned, and $1 billion in property damage was incurred.[59] Any
inclination of civic leaders to respond to the Watts peace process evaporated in
the panic to restore order. Police were quick to blame gangs for the outbreak of
violence, including Crips at the intersection of Florence and Normandie. However, a leading historian of police and the 1992 uprising, Lou Cannon, wrote that
"the riots were neither a gang conspiracy nor a revolt against harsh conditions
but a cry of black rage" against the verdicts in the Rodney King case, the final
straw in a series of affronts well documented before the beating.[60] Similar con-
clusions were reached by the official blue-ribbon Christopher and Webster commissions convened to assess the aftermath. The newborn Watts truce efforts
were ignored or discredited during and after the spring riots. According to a *Los
Angeles Times* investigation completed five years later, however, "in Watts the infant truce held" during the 1992 week of rioting. Of the forty-five deaths that

April week, only three occurred in Watts, all attributable to the LAPD.[61] While the *Times* acknowledged (without examples) that gang members might have used the chaos to kill rivals elsewhere, the pattern of vendetta failed to erupt in Watts itself. Maps of buildings damaged in 1992 showed little destruction in Watts compared to the hard-hit areas of Western and Vernon, Western and Slauson, Vermont and Manchester, and Central and Vernon.[62]

Understandably, city officials were too busy to respond creatively to the Watts truce at the time, but nothing explains the subsequent pattern of official indifference in the years that followed. On a macro-scale, significant post-riot promises of reform went unfulfilled. A private-sector initiative known as "Rebuild L.A." was launched by Peter Ueberroth, an Orange County Republican businessman and architect of the successful 1984 Olympic Games in L.A., with an objective of $6 billion in investments in South Central to create approximately 74,000 jobs in the coming five years.[63] "Our goals are long-term, systemic change," he declared in July 1992. "The last thing we need is to get a lot of people to rush out with goody-goody gestures that will not last."[64] A year after the initial hoopla, Ueberroth withdrew, saying "the obstacles are much more formidable than I thought."[65] The project simply folded up. In 1997, the *Times* reported that Hands Across Watts, a nonprofit corporation founded to create business ventures in the projects, died as well. Even though the truce was still holding—"police and residents of Watts confirm that gang-on-gang slayings over emotional issues of turf boundaries or gang clothing have virtually disappeared"—the hope for entrepreneurial opportunities was gone.[66] Like the nation as a whole, Los Angeles seemed bewitched by privatization as a model of urban development.

The city budget for 2000–2001 mirrored the lopsided priorities on policing versus social and economic development, a microcosm of the mini-citadels that big cities were becoming. There was subsidized excess, starting with a $239,849 salary for the city's top bureaucrat, making L.A. the biggest spender on top executive salaries among American cities.[67] The police chief was paid $228,678, far more than chiefs in New York, Chicago, or Philadelphia.[68] The LAPD budget for that fiscal year was $898 million, or 33.3 percent of the city's General Fund budget of $2.9 billion.[69] The LAPD received another $300 million from bonds and state or

Rebuild LA [margin annotation]

federal grants, lifting its overall budget to $1.2 billion.[70] By comparison, just $1 million was budgeted for "L.A.'s Best," an after-school program for at-risk youth, and less than $2 million for gang intervention work.[71] In that same year, the city was accused of environmental racism for having the lowest ratio of parks to people in America, with the worst ratios in communities with the highest numbers of at-risk youth.[72] The most elementary general services were sacrificed to the police budget; for example, funds to fix potholes in the car-dependent city were so paltry that it would take an estimated seventy-seven years to fix those listed for repair.[73]

The *Times* took another look at the Watts truce in January 1998, in an article titled "Ex-Gang Members Work to Bring Peace to the Streets."[74] Slayings in the South Los Angeles sector of the LAPD had declined from 466 in 1992 to 223 by 1998. Drive-by shootings were down 27 percent citywide, and gang-related homicides by 36.7 percent compared to the previous five-year average. A homeboy named Raymond "Mad Dog" Lafayette told the reporter he had quit the thug life because "a group of older, retired gang members convinced him of the futility of it all." One LAPD patrol commander gave credit to the truce efforts for reducing shootings over gang colors.

The *Times* looked again in 2002, the tenth anniversary of the Watts truce, and headlined its conclusion that the truces were "All But Forgotten as Homicides Soar."[75] It should have been no surprise that gang violence would resume in the double vacuum of economic and political hopelessness left by the riots of 1965 and 1992. By now, a new generation of gang members were out to make their reputations, with only the dimmest memory of the truce era and nothing to show for it. "Yeah, I remember hearing about the truce," said twenty-year-old Jose "Chuy" Gonzales. "I remember hearing about JFK getting killed too."

Men like "Chuy" had never received a peace dividend. Instead, deindustrialization and corporate downsizing had eliminated the manufacturing jobs in South Central. Wages in South Central had failed to keep pace with the rest of Los Angeles County. Instead of 50,000 new jobs in rebuilding, South Central lost 55,000 jobs between 1992 and 1999, and was turning into a local Rust Belt.[76] Of the 600 properties damaged in the 1992 riots, 100 were still not rebuilt, almost all them in South Central. As for "Rebuild L.A.," its promise of $6 billion in new investment turned out to be only $389 million, with "millions spent outside the riot-torn neighborhoods."[77]

Despite the bleak assessments, however, the *Times* acknowledged in 2002 that "only a treaty in Watts is still functioning." It was as if the fragile Watts peace was an unexplainable aberration created by unidentified forces. Instead, it could have been examined as a remarkable achievement against the odds, worth serious credit and further study. Despite the brutal toll of economic downsizing, the truce was holding—barely, but holding—in Watts. For how much longer could it last, given the despair and the continued disinvestment? With the Watts truce generation aging, what could they show for their efforts?

No one has calculated the cost of thwarting the hopes of so many of the peacemakers who threw down their colors and hugged former enemies a decade ago. "High T" was dead, so was Tony Bogard, and many more. Others were in jail or in despair, feeling their lives were wasted. Almost ten years later, I watched a video showing hundreds of Crips and Bloods trotting and marching enthusiastically, at the height of the 1992 truce. A veteran peacemaker, "Bo" Taylor, recited in rapid fire those on the screen he recognized: "He's dead, dead, in prison, he was stabbed, dead, in prison."

Dewayne Holmes faced new punishment even as he was engaged in the emerging truce efforts. In February 1992, he was arrested after breaking up a fight at a dance where he headed security. According to Dewayne and his eyewitnesses, the altercation occurred when two individuals were turned away for lacking the $3.50 needed to purchase tickets. One later said Dewayne had stuck a gun in his ribs and forced him to leave, a claim Dewayne denied. He was charged with robbing the individual of two five-dollar bills, but was sentenced to prison for seven years as "a danger to society."[78] (That is where I first met him three years later.) The *Times* correspondent took the unusual license to describe him as "launching a remarkable transformation that continues to serve as a healing force."[79] But the seven-year sentence was an extreme rebuke to any notion of redemption. Nevertheless, Dewayne served his time and joined my staff upon his release in 1996. He continued working on violence prevention initiatives, learned to lobby the legislature, traveled on a peace delegation to El Salvador, supported his mother's "reclaiming children"

projects, married his girlfriend Cindy from the projects, and had a baby boy, Dewayne Jr. After my legislative retirement in 2000, Dewayne continued working
with other gang intervention programs before developing a licensed business serving disabled people in the Watts area. He moved his family to Riverside and tries to
keep his son, Dewayne Jr., as far from gang culture as possible.

His partner John had a harder time adjusting to freedom after ten years in
prison. He performed extremely well for me in the high-pressure role of driver
and advance man after his release. The structure of a political campaign, with its
hyper energy, seemed to suit him well. But there were underlying problems I
didn't understand, perhaps symbolized by the saying tattooed across his chest
that read "Love Don't Love Nobody." One of those problems was his sexual drive
after a decade in cells. Within two nights of John's release from Quentin, I received
a screaming phone call from his attorney asking where he was hiding. She was under the illusion that she and John had a "relationship." From the moment of his
freedom, John couldn't meet enough women, and many couldn't get enough of
John. One night at an outdoor party in Watts, John was shot in the knee in a drive-
by. I rushed to the local hospital to cheer him and found a lovely young woman already nursing him, beneath the covers. Eventually, John made an underage young
lady pregnant, took responsibility, and became the proud father of DaeJohn.

There were other problems of adjustment. Perhaps the sudden freedom was
too much. John was always in debt, always behind on car insurance, always frustrated with confusing "constituency service" work that trapped him in trying to
cope with bureaucracies like the state prisons that had confined him for so long.
Once, the police made an (unauthorized) stop of a car with John inside and discovered a stolen cell phone. John had purchased the phone on the street for $60
because he couldn't afford a store-bought one. It took just one phone call from a
well-connected Westwood lawyer to the prosecutors to prevent John from receiving a third-strike felony on the cell phone charge. But the problems continued. When he had to take the bus to work because his broken-down car was in
the shop because he was behind on payments, he stayed home, depressed. He felt
himself being sucked back into the cycles that had dominated his life. I failed to
create a counter-magnet powerful enough to keep him going. On September 22,

2001, a police unit stopped John while he was riding a bicycle through the projects. The police had neither reasonable nor probable cause for the stop, but they found a gun nearby on the ground. Under the law, convicted felons can receive enhanced sentences if convicted again within five years. In this case, John was five years, one month, and nineteen days past his last discharge from prison. But he received enhancements anyway, and is serving a five-and-one-half-year sentence in Delano state prison. Dewayne Holmes tries to look after little DaeJohn. John's prison letters describe a heart-wrenching guilt and depression.

As the millennium turned, Aqeela and Daude opened the Community Self-Determination Institute in Watts. Evolved from the Amer-I-Can program, they managed a staff of up to eighty young people in social programs funded by Los Angeles County. Eighty-eight percent of their trainees increased their grade point averages, and 80 percent of those on probation are not returned to custody.[80] The brothers still dream of Watts as the birthplace of peace, declaring that "our efforts to bring an end to urban gang warfare, which has claimed more lives than some international wars, has set a precedent in redefining what it means to create peace and sustain it over a significant period of time."[81] On a daily basis they tend to the wounds of war. "It's all about post-traumatic stress," Aqeela says, "and the need for a safe haven, a sanctuary, a promise of a place in the future." They mentor and tutor young people, operate a community center, and sponsor weekly bus tours to engage middle-class professionals and business people firsthand in the realities of the projects. They envision a network of community councils, including genuine representatives of the street, to broker local peace efforts and push for private and public resources, a sort of parallel structure to official bureaucracies. Having seen the college world and tasted the lures of the west side, they plan to remain in the neighborhood indefinitely, preferring to "work with the uneducated than the mis-educated." Aqeela's faith is that personal and community wounds, once unearthed, have positive, recuperative powers. To any audience that will listen, he repeats the mantra "your wounds are your gifts." His favorite book remains James Baldwin's *Evidence of Things Not Seen*.

Sure enough, the 2003 election of a new city councilman, Martin Ludlow, revived the peace process in South Central. A longtime labor and civil rights activist,

Ludlow immediately realized the gravity of the long, hot summer ahead. He hired "Bo" Taylor to hit the streets with a mandate to try mediating disputes before they turned into killings. He paid students from Dorsey High School to walk door-to-door with job opportunity brochures, and began pulling together a grass-roots Olympics. Perhaps most importantly, he kept his council doors open from Thursday through Sundays, 8 P.M. to 3 A.M., the most likely hours for violence to break out. Ludlow also planned to demand of developers seeking permits in his district that they hire some homeboys. Playa Vista was one of the first to make an offer. It was evidence that sparks of the peace process continued to flicker.

But the cycle, the karma, could not be broken, not yet. On January 10, 2004, Aqeela's eldest child, eighteen-year-old Terrell, was home between semesters at Humboldt State University. Terrell, who mirrored his father's handsome looks, was to Aqeela the archetype of the lover, the child who saw joy in everything. That day, Terrell attended a party where he was shot eight times and killed. It apparently started over dancing with the wrong girl. But everyone knew it was really about the deeper madness growing in the hopelessness of the world. At the funeral, Aqeela spoke of the strength to "live into the eternal truth of the power of the resurrection."

Tupac Amaru Shakur, R.I.P.

The life and death of Tupac Shakur describe the arc of events in Watts, and most other African American communities, during the period since 1965. The story of Tupac is one of tragedy, about individuals who exhibit a greatness while succumbing to inner demons in the face of others either helpless or unwilling to intervene. The gang culture during Tupac's short life (1971–96) was torn by the same polarization.

Tupac's mother was a Black Panther, Afeni Shakur, but Tupac grew up in the "post-revolution,"[82] when the Panthers disintegrated and the gang culture was growing on the streets. Afeni (originally Alice Faye Williams) was part of the New York 21, a group of Panthers charged with conspiracy in 1969 to attack commercial outlets and police stations. After the longest criminal trial in New York history, the jury acquitted thirteen defendants facing a total of 156 charges.[83] Afeni was pregnant with Tupac in jail, and gave birth to him shortly after her release. His godfather was Elmer "Geronimo" Pratt, a Panther hero who survived twenty-seven years in prison, mostly in solitary confinement. His murder conviction was finally reversed when it was revealed that the key witness was an LAPD informant. Geronimo also was one of thirteen Panthers exonerated after a 1969 shootout with the Los Angeles police, the verdicts coming shortly after the New York 21 acquittals.[84] Tupac's aunt is Assata Shakur (Joanne Chesimard), another Panther icon who survived a near fatal shooting by highway patrol in New Jersey and was nevertheless convicted of conspiracy to murder. She escaped from a high-security New Jersey prison to Cuba. For a short while, Tupac's mother, Afeni, and her Panther comrades were shining stars on lecture circuits, but repression and internal struggles brought the organization down. Tupac grew up as a child of the Panther legend in a world increasingly without the Panthers. His mother was crushed for some years by poverty, homelessness, and crack cocaine.

Tupac embraced the Panther principles in his own political thinking. But like Tookie, he was out of sync in space and time. The Panthers, and the brief revolutionary moment they heralded, were already an anachronism when Tupac was growing up. In a postrevolutionary time, his contribution would be cultural. He was an intellectual, a voracious reader, a student of music and acting. At fifteen, he performed in Lorraine Hansberry's *Raisin in the Sun* as a fundraiser for Jesse Jackson's presidential campaign. But in the same postrevolutionary time, the "thug life" was woven into his being. He understood "thug life" to be a form of resistance by the damned, perhaps a more outrageous form than the Panthers. "It's not thugging like I'm robbing people, 'cause that's not what I'm doing. I mean like I'm not scared to say how I feel." He also said the letters spelling "thug life" meant "The Hate You Gave Little Infants Fucks Everyone." But this child of war also was struggling with nightmares and addictions. Tupac was continually stoned, drinking, and frequently around weapons. He engaged in battles with police and rival rappers that shifted suddenly from the symbolic to the real. Tupac reflected all these contradictions in his spirit, lyrics, and performances—and in the danger, violence, self-destructiveness, harassment, and imprisonment that filled a short life. The rap artist Mos Def told Michael Eric Dyson that "the bewildered children of the movement" were heavily impacted by its repression and demise.

> It is not the nuclear holocaust, the dropping of the bomb, that is terrible, the fallout is the real bullshit. *Tupac represents the fallout generation.* That is my generation. Pac represents something that is heroic and tragic, not just for black society but for American society.[85]

The poet Sonia Sanchez harbored similar feelings. When her sons first played Tupac's tapes for her, she was shocked. "Shakur? Do you know that all the Shakurs are in jail, dead, or in exile? Does that young man know he's at risk? Is someone protecting him?"[86] No one was. If anything, they were profiting off him.

"I am hopeless," Tupac declared. He stayed connected to those he called the "niggas in the gutter," a caste now considered lower than the Panthers' "brothers on the block," "the nobodies" who, defined by Dyson, were "tragic figure[s] embroiled in violence, a violence that was both conscientiously lamented and vigorously embraced."[87] Tupac instinctively knew that the death of the civil rights movement, with all its redemptive potential, was a death sentence for his homeboys and himself. As Tookie put it, they were meant to be born in a warrior era. Tupac rapped his "urge to die" as if the embrace of death was a final rebuke to all fear, and to a system that made the civil rights dream impossible.

Fruits of War: Homies Unidos and the Globalization of Gangs

Thoughts of a Prisoner

The days, I feel them so long
what my heart feels, and what my eyes see
I am not the same one
my sun no longer shines
the sky is gray
everything vanishes away, and yet
my face does not know how to smile
I wish not to wake up in the morning
I wish to sleep for ever
fleeing from the reality of pain
loneliness
sadness
and the memory of love.

Locked-in with my feelings, and man's pride
and I look to life for encouragement

to escape and find the sun
to nourish the existence of a lifeless flower
loneliness that lives within so many of us
and takes over, it builds a fortress of emotions
that hurts
and fear prevents us from talking to others
caused by anything
sometimes it directs us to tragedy
at times to sorrow and
all of us fear to accept our loneliness

we lose little by little
and become apart from what helps us
many times everything is sorrow
and the fear that is being born brings only problems to humanity

loneliness is something that will always exist
it does not matter what you have
a moment will come when it will own you
and you will never know when or how it will happen.

—*Boobee (Amilcar Rodriguez), Homies Unidos, 1994*

It is conveniently forgotten that the sources of most street gangs lie in violent oppression, dispossession, and migration. The African slave trade disrupted the lives of millions, disintegrated their families, and spawned a bitter legacy that continued down through Stagolees, Crips, Bloods, and Blackstone Rangers. The colonization of Puerto Rico eventually produced the Latin Kings. British colonial rule in Ireland uprooted 2 million refugees in the mid-nineteenth century who became Martin Scorcese's fabled gangs of New York. The Sicilians who became mafia were victims of invasion and displacement, as were Jews from the Pale of Settlement who turned into bootleggers and killers. During the Mexican Revolution (1910–21), 1 million were killed and another million emigrated to the new "neighborhoods" and labor camps of El Norte. The Vietnam War led to the rise of Vietnamese (and Cambodian) street gangs from the ranks of the "boat people." Out of this violent

chaos came countless outlaws, *macheteros,* bandidos, any number of sociopaths, celebrated bad men, and occasional revolutionaries, whose dramatic lives provided
"secret vicarious revenge" for the newcomers to America.[1] Gangs thus are an integral part of what Juan Gonzáles calls the "harvest of empire."[2]

The most notorious new gangs of the nineties, measured by sensational front-
page series in the *New York Times* and *Los Angeles Times,* describing them as "wearing their tattoos like a sneer,"[3] were those of Salvadoran youth who formed Mara
Salvatrucha (MS) and joined 18th Street. Prior to the U.S. military intervention
and refugee flight, street gangs were scarcely a presence in El Salvador, although
the country's longtime revolutionaries were frequently labelled "delinquents."[4]
The sudden emergence of these *pandillas* (gangs) was due entirely to U.S. military intervention in El Salvador in the eighties. The same neoconservatives who
promoted the wars on gangs and drugs at home were champions of the military
policies, which, ironically, would import those wars to the streets of Los Angeles
and other cities. When Ronald Reagan was elected in 1980, the civil war in El Salvador was stalemated, with Jimmy Carter's ambassador reporting that Salvadoran leaders wished a political and economic settlement instead of further war. At
the time, many Salvadorans I would come to know—specifically Alex Sanchez
and Silvia Beltran—were children of war, stepping over dead bodies on their way
to school. Right-wing death squads linked to the Salvadoran army were killing
1,000 people a month.[5] Twenty-three people were killed on the steps of the historic cathedral in San Salvador in May 1979.[6] Many youngsters witnessed their fathers being shot or dragged away never to be seen again. Few were spared.
Archbishop Oscar Romero was assassinated during mass in his cathedral on
March 24, 1980.[7] On December 2 of the same year, four American churchwomen
were kidnapped, raped, and murdered.[8]

The incoming Reagan administration ignored Jimmy Carter's negotiations-
oriented U.S. Ambassador Robert White, announced a doubling of military aid to
El Salvador in March 1981, and unleashed an official change of priorities that fore-
shadowed larger events in years to come: the greatest problem facing the world,
according to the Reagan team, was "rampant international terrorism."[9] Jeanne
Kirkpatrick, a neoconservative from the American Enterprise Institute, became

Reagan's controversial UN Ambassador, promoting alliances with "traditional au-tocrats" instead of the Carter administration's defense of human rights.[10] The per-ceived enemy now included Catholic proponents of "liberation theology," a doctrine proclaimed in 1968 that inspired many Latin American priests to form "base communities" among the poorest of the poor. The new Reagan doctrine, summarized in the 1980 "Santa Fe Document," accused "Marxist Leninist forces" of conspiring to infiltrate the Church "with ideas that are less Christian than Com-munist."[11] This fabricated charge was meant to discredit Catholic activists in El Sal-vador as well as the growing sanctuary movement for Salvadorans in the U.S., and it emboldened the right-wing death squads.

The Salvadorans already had suffered under a military despotism going back fifty years, since the massacre of an Indian-based peasant uprising in 1932. There had been coups in 1944, 1948, 1960, 1961, and 1971, all either directly or tacitly ap-proved by the U.S.[12] The people had remained strikingly poor during the century since the Spanish empire's demise in 1821, which was followed by Mexico's failed attempt to annex them, and finally the rise of a coffee oligopoly known as "the fourteen families." Collective village landholding was abolished in the late nine-teenth century, and by the 1970s, 30 to 40 percent of Salvadoran families were landless.[13] As if things couldn't be worse, a border conflict with Honduras in the late 1960s resulted in the forced relocation of 130,000 Salvadorans.[14] By the 1980s war, therefore, many Salvadorans found it impossible to survive. The Reagan de-cision to escalate rather than negotiate was the final blow. What followed was forced emigration on an unprecedented scale. In 1980, there were only 94,000 Salvadoran-born people in the entire U.S., according to census figures; in four years the number quadrupled to 400,000, mostly in Los Angeles; in ten years there were 701,000; by 2000, the number was 1.2 million, or 40 percent of the 1980 pop-ulation of El Salvador itself.[15] The largest number lived in the Pico-Union neigh-borhood of Los Angeles, but the Salvadorans also spread out to Adams-Morgan in Washington, D.C., and the suburbs of New York City and Maryland.

By most estimates, 75,000 Salvadorans died in the conflict, mostly at the hands of soldiers trained or supplied by the U.S. military.[16] Not counting other casualties and torture victims, the Salvadoran death toll was *the equivalent of 4.2 million Americans.*

Not only were they traumatized by war, by family separation, and by the perils of flight, their status was largely illegal. Carter's 1980 legislation provided asylum or at least nondeportation status to anyone with a "well-founded fear of persecution" based, among other factors, on "membership in a particular social group or political opinion."[17] This language would prove unexpectedly important to Alex Sanchez almost twenty years later, but its immediate value was narrowed by the Reagan administration's decision to hold thousands of captured undocumented (illegal) Salvadoran immigrants in packed INS detention centers for months at a time, frequently followed by deportation back to the land of the death squads. By comparison, most Cuban or Nicaraguan refugees from Fidel Castro or the Sandinistas were granted legal status and benefits with relative ease.

Alexander Antonio Sanchez-Enriquez—Alex Sanchez—who became a central character in the Rampart scandal almost three decades later, was born in these circumstances in San Salvador in 1971.[18] He was soon nicknamed *el rebelde* (rebel) by his mom. He grew up to be short, powerfully built, brown-skinned, with indigenous features. Alex's parents were forced to become refugees to Los Angeles in the seventies, leaving Alex and his brother, Oscar, one year younger, with their next-door neighbors, as temporary war orphans. Alex never learned why his father left El Salvador, but soon he was caught, deported back, then slipped north again.

Silvia Beltran was born two years after Alex, in 1973.[19] Her mother left for El Norte shortly afterward, and there was no contact with her father. As a child she witnessed the FMLN's offensive on the streets of San Salvador. The guerrillas were teaching kids to make molotov cocktails while the army was conscripting them for war. She still remembers the bodies in the streets. Parents were on the run from the police while others disappeared with the guerrillas into the mountains. Death squads prepared lists, and children without parents were traumatized. Finally, in 1979, as he was turning eight, Alex and his little brother were flown to Mexico, placed on a train, and ultimately crossed the border at San Ysidro to join their parents, who feared "that we would get stuck due to the war that was beginning."[20] Silvia, a petite teenager, was packed in the trunk of a car and smuggled over the border to L.A. to rejoin her mom. There she would obediently practice her

Catholicism and study hard in school, while also being drawn to the edges of the crazy life. She would meet Alex Sanchez and help found Homies Unidos a decade later.

These new immigrant youth in Los Angeles started calling themselves the *la mara loca,* which roughly means "the crazy neighborhood." Soon they were known as *mara Salvatrucha stoners,* and finally *mara salvatrucha,* the "Salvadoran neighborhood," or simply MS. In a larger sense, they were *las frutas de la guerra,* the fruits of the war, a description that would become a rap anthem of Homies Unidos a few years later. Written by Marvin Novoa Escobar, a one-armed dynamo I would meet in San Salvador, the long Spanish rhyme went like this:

> *Saludando a mi patria y a mi gente nativa,*
> *Me dejo caer con una rola productivo.*
> (Saluting my country and my native people,
> Coming at you with a productive rhyme.)

> *Guanacos* do corazon y pipiles** de el Salvador*
> *Ayudando a mi pueblo, mejor que embajador.*
> (Guanacos from the heart and pipiles from El Salvador
> Helping my people better than an ambassador.)

> *Empezando esta vez, desde la raíz,*
> *De una historia de Guerra que enpeso en nuestro pais.*
> (This time beginning from the root,
> From a history of war started in our country.)

> *Doce anos, fueron, los que se sufrieron,*
> *Almas inocentes que la vida perdieron*
> *Por gente demente que sin pensar combatieron.*
> (Twelve years of suffering, it's what it was,
> Innocent souls that lost their lives
> Because of demented people that fought without a thought.)

˙A national bird emblematic of being Salvadoran.
˙˙An indigenous person.

Varias familias, se tuvieron que dividir,
Buscando una forma de sobrevivir,
De su patria asi mismo obligados a salir.
(So many families had to be divided,
Trying to find a way to survive,
From their homeland they were forced to flee.)

A otro país con cultura diferente,
Algo que no era usual para nuestra gente.
(To a different land, a different culture,
Sometimes so strange to our people.)

Adaptandose al sistema sin ninguna opción,
Trabajando como burros sin tener decisión,
Descuidando al igual, lo comunicación,
Dejando a los hijos sin orientación.
(Adapting ourselves to the system with no real option,
Working like donkeys with no power to decide,
Neglecting at the same time our communication,
Leaving the children with no orientation.)

Empezando esto fue, como una semilla,
Trayendo como fruto la formación de pandillas.
(This started as a seed,
Gangs were its fruits.)

Trataremos este tema con mucha seriedad,
Es algo sin sentido pero esto es realidad,
La realidad que se vive, como frutos de una guerra.
(Let's deal with this topic with all its seriousness,
It's something that's senseless but it's a reality,
The reality we live, it's the fruit of a war.)

Many of these *pandilleros* were alone on the streets, while others lived in families fragmented by war. Most were socialized outside the norms of institutions, on the streets, a process well described by James Diego Vigil.[21] Shadowing them was a war experience, in which many were forcibly recruited at age twelve. Some had been in combat. They didn't talk about it, but some had raped girls in villages. Any uniformed policeman in Salvador was to be avoided as an unapproachable abuser, or worse. Now they found themselves in an urban world, the most congested barrio west of the Mississippi, surrounded by new enemies, the foremost being Chicanos and other U.S.-born Latinos at school. It was the little things. From Alex's juvenile perspective, the more assimilated kids were into disco, breakdancing, wearing flat-top haircuts, baggy clothes. Many distanced themselves from soccer, preferring American sports like football and baseball. They called the Salvadorans wetbacks and worse. They were better off and wanted the newcomers to know it. They had nice shoes with the big laces that were in style. The poorer immigrant kids had to buy their gear at a place catering to the very poor called El Pio Jito (the little lice), which was even cheaper than Payless. "They were differing themselves from us immigrants to feel better about themselves," Alex recalled. "We just hated it."

MS became a haven for homeless, unemployed Salvadorans on the streets. The 18th Streeters, located from Venice up Hoover to Alvarado, originally were Mexican, though eventually they opened their spreading ranks to Salvadorans, too. MS was born in Alex's own neighborhood, on Westmoreland and Ninth, with a first clique known as the 7 11 Locos (for the 7-Eleven where they hung out). Then they expanded toward Leeward and Hollywood, forming the Normandy Locos, the Berendo Locos, then on down Western, Martin Luther King, and Vermont, then east siders and south siders joined, and it spread to San Francisco, New York, Long Island, Reno, and Texas. It was potent medicine for raging victims of war and nothingness.

MS were stoners, wearing long hair, listening to Metallica, some even worshipping the devil, cultural tastes stimulated by the export of American culture. The sign of MS was also the sign of the devil, two fingers up. In some of their initial rituals, they would eat rats, hang out in cemeteries, vow to take nobody's shit. That included La Eme, who expected "rent" from the newcomers as well as respect. "The heavy metal thing was very popular in El Salvador because of the military," Silvia said. She started hanging out with an 18th Streeter, a romance that consisted of bailing him out of the Rampart station on weekends.

Alex was fourteen when he was initiated into the *mara salvatrucha stoners* in 1985. The initiation, typical in the gang subculture, was a beating that lasted thirteen seconds, because thirteen was "kind of an evil number," not because MS affiliated with other gangs using the same numeral. The purpose of the beating was "being accepted into what this world was," a submission like a blood oath "to protect and defend your brothers, your neighborhood, even if it costs your life." Once the beating ended, everyone hugged each other, even crying to seal their unity.

As with all gangs, MS was male-centered, especially in the early days. Women were objects who could be initiated in one of two ways: "the easy way" was by having sex with the leadership of the gang, while "the hard way" was being beaten up by the rest of the gang. Many thought "the easy way" was rape, and never joined. Alex believed that since the girls "had the choice" it wasn't exactly rape, but acknowledged that "in the long run we respected more the women who got jumped in the hard way." Silvia didn't let herself get jumped in either way. Those young women who became members found themselves experiencing a triple burden: as Salvadoran immigrants, as gang members, and as women. Though a minority, many women submitted to the rituals, joined the gang, grew in confidence and respect, or formed *loca* cliques of their own. What attracted them, if not multiple forms of self-hate? One Homies Unidos member who joined 18th Street at age twelve explains the process this way:

> I came here when I was four years old. My parents were fighting and protesting the war. The homies accepted me for who I was. They celebrated my birthday. They provided me with milk and pampers for my first son. I felt safe. The only thing is that I had to prove myself, I had be willing to "represent." Be one hundred percent. Don't let the guys push you over. Kick ass at whoever.[22]

It is necessary to dwell on these unpleasant, even grotesque, details for several reasons. First, to acknowledge that the public has credible reason to loathe aspects of the gang culture. Second, to note at the same time how the gang subculture *mimics in an extreme form* the sexual abuse and violence that is frequently exposed in our military and entertainment cultures despite all efforts to civilize and regulate them. And finally, as a prelude to showing that, over time, many gang members can come to transcend the most degrading behavior in measurable ways.

Alex loved Pink Floyd, Judas Priest, Ozzie Osborne, King Diamond, and Metallica. He brought the music home as part of his rebellion against a mother who was a Jehovah's Witness. "I had this religion driven down my throat all the time, so I was going to do the opposite. I was not like a Devil worshipper even though some of the guys would try to do stuff like, let's draw some blood and let's drink it all and all this bullshit . . ." The music also "got in a lot of girls." They flaunted sexiness in tight Levi's and heavy metal shirts. The promised land was a heavy metal concert, and Alex would do anything to attend. He wanted more than anything to be in the slam pit.

The music also reflected their anger at the different culture around them, which pressured them to sit in the back of the class as the new unwanteds. His mother worked in a factory cleaning hospital garments, his father delivered newspapers at three in the morning. Gradually Alex got in trouble at Hobart Elementary School. It was the fourth grade, and he was playing with a paper airplane. Running to catch it, Alex encountered a Mexican kid, the school bully, holding it in his hand. Gimme the plane, Alex said. Come and get it, he was told, and then the Mexican kid crushed the plane in his hand and threw it down. So Alex blew up, broke his enemy's tooth, spilled blood all over, and was suspended from school. He hid the shame from his parents. He began living more and more on the streets.

Alex's street clique was a circle of undocumented kids, seven in all, averaging fifteen years old, including two girls, all runaways from home. The only way to survive and eat was to steal from shopping carts. "It was straight survival, not like a racket." They tried to do their business outside the neighborhood, which required stealing a car for the round trip. They were frequently stopped, frisked, and arrested. But they kept on getting money off the streets by stealing, drug dealing, selling car parts, whatever they could. By this time the mood on the streets was changing profoundly, mostly the result of incarcerations. Guys who went into juvenile hall with long hair came out bald, speaking spanglish ("Orale, homes"). MS was being assimilated into a prison version of the American melting pot. The new look was from jail: clean shirts, Dockers, "creased up." There was even a different stroll, slouching back. They wanted to grow the goatee, cut the hair short, slicked back with Tres Flores hair grease, no more petroleum jelly. Tres Flores with a palm comb—that's what they wanted. The system was shaping the homie style.

In 1985, Alex the Rebel saw real violence for the first time. Before that, any fights were either getting down one on one, or gangbanging limited to chains or knives. Then it all changed out of nowhere. One of Alex's homeboys, known as Rocky, was killed with a gun, set up by girls from a rival gang at Fourth and Normandy, right after school let out. The bullets were from a .38 to the back of the head and the face. Rocky was older, an original gangbanger, while Alex's circle were still the younger homies. But "after the first murder, you know, it wasn't about fun and games anymore." Everybody started muttering that "we gotta put in work." At about the same time, Alex was sent to juvenile hall and began bouncing through the state's juvenile camps. At eighteen, in 1990, he was in Camp Gonzales, then began stints in state prison. The crimes were classic ones: driving under the influence, possession of weapons, car theft. He was in jail on the day everyone else in his family became legalized U.S. citizens.

Inside and outside, the streets of Pico-Union reflected the civil strife bleeding El Salvador. Salvadoran death squads hunted refugees in Los Angeles, kidnapping, raping, and torturing one victim in July 1987, and threatening activists, sympathetic priests, even Silvia Beltran's mother. The immigrant community, already traumatized, feared going to the police for assistance because the majority was undocumented, a fear that intensified when an INS spokesman ridiculed the reports as "orchestrated PR."[23] Making matters more eerie, nativist vigilantes and private security squads were freelancing against the perceived gang threat. (In 1995, a vigilante would kill one and wound another "skinhead Mexican" under an overpass in the San Fernando Valley; the assailant was not indicted, but the wounded youth was charged for graffiti.[24]) If there was a difference between the two battlefields, perhaps it was the lack of any larger purpose to the L.A. street war. Or perhaps the common purpose of all wars, once they are under way, is the same: to ensure that the soldiers do not die in vain. Or perhaps both wars were about inclusion in Salvadoran national aspirations being long denied to the poor. Whatever the causes, Alex's gang went to war with the Crazy Riders, whose turf was a few blocks away, at Third and Normandy. It was never about "business" (the narcotics trade), Alex said. It was about "vengeance for the dead homie." But would they ever get revenge? Did it ever even out? Who was to say? The killing was happening because the killing was happening. Soon the wars expanded to a bloodier conflict between MS and 18th Street, one of the worst in history.

Until 1992, MS and 18th Street had a loose alliance. Salvadorans were welcomed into 18th street, making it the first multicultural super-gang. No one is sure where the spark was ignited. Perhaps both sides had gotten too big, too powerful. Alex himself is unsure, only saying "I think it was behind a girl." 18th Street came looking for someone from MS over a fight that somebody had lost. A homie named Shaggy was killed. Talks to prevent a war collapsed. Many families had children in both gangs. Yet if you were raised in a certain neighborhood, you had no choice. It wasn't like a central committee was ordering you to fight. But Shaggy's clique knew they *had* to do it, as soldiers everywhere know these things, and everyone else in MS decided the hell with 18th Street, too. After a while, as the death toll surpassed 100, Alex lost count. This is why the wars were called the madness.

Then came the 1992 riots, widely interpreted to the outside world as a *black* insurrection. At the time, Latinos in general (and immigrants in particular) had languished invisibly in politics and culture, and the week of rioting was little different. For example, the Christopher and Webster commission reports noted little about the Latino presence. Lou Cannon's authoritative history *Official Negligence* devoted only a few paragraphs on just two of 695 pages to Latino participation.[25] Cannon, reinforcing the stereotype of Latinos as hard-working and law-abiding, exonerated the county's 3 million Latinos for *not* participating. Instead, he utilized a *Los Angeles Times* analysis of court records to show that 80 percent of Latinos arrested during the week were foreign-born.[26] But Mike Davis pointed out that 17,000 alleged Latino looters and arsonists were detained, and that uncounted hundreds of undocumented ones were deported "before the ACLU or immigrant rights groups had even realized that they had been arrested."[27] Fifty-two percent of those arrested had Spanish surnames, 36 percent were African American, and 10 percent were white. The largest number of arrests took place in the LAPD's Rampart territory, all facts that would grow in significance. For many angry immigrants, the time was known as *quemazones* (great burning). Hector Tobar, a Central American immigrant and *Times* reporter, wrote a novel describing the events as a moment when housekeepers, garment workers, bus boys, and others could enjoy "a day without submissiveness, a day without coffee to pour or strangers' babies to feed or the whine of sewing machines in a factory."[28]

The Webster Commission found no hard evidence to confirm "persistent rumors" by some police and worried white citizens that gang members were mobilized to carry out a "pre-conceived plan."[29] Alex certainly didn't know of any plan. He was in county jail when the streets exploded, and watched it all on television. A lot of the homies joined the looting of places they felt had disrespected them, which is why Alex received a package in jail containing new shoes from Big 5. But if there was a "municipal day of vendettas," as one of Hector Tobar's fictional characters claimed, no one in the neighborhood knew about it. In fact, MS homies carried shotguns to defend a friendly liquor store owner who once had taken Alex to the doctor for some stitches. Another liquor store and Los Comales restaurant on Eighth and Irolo were guarded by MS homies as well. Loyalties mattered.

Alex earned respect in the jails and prisons as a "clean" warrior. The "dirty" ones included informers, backstabbers, rapists, and child molesters, or simply those who failed to put in work when obliged to. A "clean" person maintained respect, put in work, acted righteously, kept their word. Lists of the dirty and clean were carefully kept. In 1993, just after being released from another confinement, Alex and other homies found themselves in the middle of peace negotiations and truces, which lasted nearly three years. MS wanted La Eme to take off the "green light" that was causing so much destruction. La Eme wanted to cut out the plague of drive-by shootings. It was not easy, since the prisons were filled with guys doing life terms for murdering other gang members "for the neighborhood." Any cease-fire

meant enemies would have to turn into friends. Were the life sentences of all
those incarcerated "big brothers" for nothing? For any peace to hold, approval was
needed from those behind bars. But the Crips and Bloods were doing it; they were
a model. Alex didn't quite know why, but he knew one thing: the blacks weren't
killing each other, but the Latinos were. Maybe it could stop.

Alex, at twenty-one, a man with respect, was among those representing MS in
the truce summit. At the time, Alex trusted no one but his homies, but was willing to take a risk for peace, to end the green light, even (some were assuming) if
it might mean paying some rent. He talked to others, like Luis "Blinky" Rodriguez in the San Fernando Valley, who were trying to broker the truce. There
were no assurances, his contacts said. If they went to the meeting called in
Elysian Park, they might get the green light taken off or they might not come out
alive. Whatever. Alex took fifteen homies into a mass meeting with 1,000 Mexican gang members. They left their weapons in the car, knowing they might die.
"It took a lot of guts, it was like a sea parting when MS came to talk," said Silvia.
Out of those encounters came an immediate reduction in overall drive-by
killings, as much as 25 percent in gang neighborhoods.[30] While media and police
attention focused on whether La Eme was consolidating its control of the drug
business, those on the street like Luis Rodriguez remember that gang members
"were feeling a heavy weight lifted off them . . . for the first time a semblance of
calm and even hope visited these streets."[31] A Latino peace process was being
launched that would continue, with many ups and downs, and little or no official
support, into the new millennium. If only a dozen lives were spared as a result of
these efforts each year—the rate estimated for the first five months of 1993[32]—that
would mean *120* persons saved in the nineties.

Life was changing for Alex Sanchez. Back in prison for auto theft in 1994,
he became the father of Alex Jr., with his homegirl back in Pico-Union. These
were often the children of fatalism. "Even when they know they are not going to
take care of the child," Silvia said, "they pressure the girl not to have an abortion,
they won't stand for it, they beat them up." Such homeboys want a child because
they expect to die. Alex, on the other hand, was among those who, at the birth of
a child, decide to live. But there were worse trials ahead. One month after the

birth of his child, Alex was released from prison and transferred to the INS for deportation. Soon he was back in a homeland he hadn't seen in fifteen years.

Deported gang members were truly strangers in a strange land. Wearing L.A. tattoos, speaking an unfamiliar Spanish, unemployed, and often homeless, they tended to band together on the streets, commit crimes for survival, experience threats from the police, new rivals, and revived death squads. Above all, they conspired among themselves to make it back to their new homeland in Los Angeles. The overall U.S. policy, intended to reduce crime in the states, had the immediate effect of globalizing the gang subculture. These "deadly exports," as they were described by a *New York Times* headline,[33] were destabilizing to a society emerging from a decade of war. Alex Sanchez was one of 4,000 young Salvadorans forcibly deported between 1993 and 1997.[34] For Mexico and Central America, the annual numbers averaged over 40,000 by the late nineties.[35] "Five years after a peace accord ended El Salvador's long and brutal civil war, gang warfare transplanted from the United States has emerged as a new threat to security," lamented the *New York Times*'s Latin American expert, Larry Rohter.[36] Death squads with names like Black Shadow began assassinating gang members with public approval.[37]

On a macro global level, the deportations were not unlike the domestic police practice of sweeping homies out of one jurisdiction into another, then declaring victory without any consideration of the impacts of the displacement. The result in El Salvador, and throughout Central America, is a mushrooming gang violence problem that simply didn't exist before. American complicity was evident, to those who cared to look, at every stage of the cycle: from colonizing and impoverishing Central America, then fueling its wars in the seventies, then arresting and returning the immigrants who had fled the poverty and violence.

Like many others, Alex Sanchez had only one priority: to escape the violent atmosphere of El Salvador and reunite with his son, who now was being raised by his mother in Los Angeles. So he took the risk of returning illegally in 1995, entering the U.S. at the Brownsville, Texas, border and slipping into the shadows of L.A.'s vast underground immigrant economy. On the run, with tattoos marking his body, it was difficult to make a living, but he cobbled together some odd jobs and settled down. His crazy days seemed to be ending. He stayed out of sight of the police and the INS.

Back in El Salvador, Homies Unidos was being formed. The deported home-boys were realizing they had to cooperate and stop the madness, just as the MS, 18th Street, the Mexican gangs, and the Crips and Bloods were trying to do in L.A. They found a mentor and friend in Magdaleno Rose-Avila, a burly Mexican-American with painful knees and a big heart developed in the farmworker and Chicano movements in the United States. Magdaleno happened to be living in San Salvador with his wife, Carolina, an international children's advocate, when he started coming across these lost homeboys from L.A. Using his community organizing skills and fund-raising contacts, Magdaleno made his living room the birthplace of Homies Unidos. "The key to organizing," he later said, "was that we listened to them, to their pain. We offered 'comprehension.' It was dangerous for them, because once they were involved in Homies, as opposed to their old gangs, they became open targets with no one to turn to for protection and safety. But the alternative, they knew, was more dying."[38] Magdaleno likened the listen-ing to the therapy sessions among torture victims he previously had done for Amnesty International. "Just the ability to talk was healing, freeing them from their monsters. Also to talk about your dead homeboys was to honor them, so the gatherings were like funerals."

Magdaleno listened to Hector Pineda, El Negro, a young man who as a child went with his father to the morgues filled with dead bodies from the Salvadoran war. Sent by his parents to the U.S. to avoid the killing, Hector there joined a street gang and met Alex Sanchez, whom Magdaleno later described as "a gang member of major stature and a wise street general." A bond was formed between El Negro and El Rebelde that would eventually bring fruits of peace. First, however, Hector returned to El Salvador to create a new gang in the image of what he'd seen in L.A. When Magdaleno first met Hector, he seemed quiet and unassuming, and showed no interest in talking with this older Chicano from the U.S. Behind the scenes, Hector disapproved of Magdaleno's work and told his homeboys to stay away. After a heated argument, the pair began to talk constructively. Magdaleno learned once again to listen instead of preach. He began to know when it was appropriate to speak and how to say things with respect. He realized that Hector simply couldn't understand why an outsider was interested in Salvadoran gangs. Was Magdaleno an undercover cop, an enemy? What could explain his interest?

It was a question many gang researchers or interested parties, myself included, have faced. Magdaleno honestly didn't know why he was so attracted to them. He wasn't being paid for his interest. He wasn't a former gang member, although he had been violent sometimes in his younger days. But for one thing, he found that people like Hector did not fit the stereotypes that justified their persecution. For instance, Hector kept coming over to explore and use Magdaleno's advanced new Acer computer. Gradually, Hector became Magdaleno's tutor in street life. Magdaleno even found himself spending more time with Hector than with his own family those first months. "I learned to listen to him and trust him with my life. I trusted him with the life of my spouse, and with that of my 13-year-old daughter, Aviva. Once a gang member takes you on as his 'dog' or soul/spiritual brother, you can count on their word and their honor, and that is more than you can get from many people in today's society."

Hector was strong-willed and autocratic, problems that would surface later, but qualities necessary to pull others out of their powerless drifting. Magdaleno, always the organizer, began a discussion of gang members creating their own organization for peace. El Negro gradually agreed, and led Magdaleno into many dangerous streets and parks for conversations with key individuals. One of them was known as El Pajaro, another was a fearless woman named Claudia Linares, or La Huera (the fair-skinned one). Hector's politically active parents offered their garage in the barrio of El Modelo as a meeting place. On November 2, 1996, Homeboys Unidos was launched, its name changing soon after to *Homies Unidos*, a gesture to the locas. The vision of the new organization was to end the set tripping and ego rivalries that led to so many funerals, specifically to initiate nonviolent dialogues between members of MS and 18th Street. The immediate program was to find alternatives to the crisis of the thousands of deportees coming out of California streets and prisons.

I first heard of these deported homies through an article by Luis Rodriguez in *The Nation* in 1994,[39] where he proposed an "urban peace process." That led me to visit Luis in Chicago to learn of his programs with at-risk youth that had drawn him to El Salvador. Father Greg Boyle returned from a visit to El Salvador very supportive of the deportees as well. In 1996, two representatives of Homies Unidos (who lacked criminal records barring them from travel) came to California, where they addressed a statewide meeting of some 1,000 youth from different gang backgrounds. Alex showed up, leaving the shadows where he was avoiding the INS. By now I had hired Silvia as a field representative, and she arranged meetings for me with Magdaleno, Alex, and my chief of staff, Rocky Rushing, at my house. Over a long dinner, they explained their plan.

One of Homies Unidos' first projects was a survey, undertaken by university researchers, of the attitudes of gang members in El Salvador. The survey, supported by both MS and 18th Street, enabled Homies to train teams of interviewers to listen to the voices of different neighborhoods. It was Magdaleno's technique on a larger scale: listen to all the voices before deciding on a course of action. Done in 1996, the survey findings were revealing: 85 percent of those interviewed hoped for *calmado,* a calmer life. The specific findings were encouraging and instructive:

Factual findings:

1. average age of entry into a gang: 14.5 years
2. percentage who can read and write: 96.3%
3. percentage no longer in school: 75.9%
4. percentage who do not work: 74.5%
5. percentage who live with their mother and father: 24.8%
6. percentage who have children: 32.2%

Motivations:

1. reasons for entering a gang: to hang out, 46%; family problems, 21.6%; for friends, 10.3%; for protection, 2.9%; for women, 2.8%
2. what they got out of gang membership: friends, 24.4%; community, 21.1%, tattoos, 16.8%, nothing, 6.5%, hanging out, 6.5%, memories, 5.9%, everything, 5.3%, respect, 4.6%, women, 1.6%
3. why some left gangs: drugs, 46.8%; violence, 13.7%; no reason, 11.4%; hanging out, 8.8%; all reasons, 6.8%; problems, 2%

Experiences as gang members:

1. ended up in the hospital due to gang violence: yes, 51.3%; no, 44.5%
2. suffered the killing of a loved one: yes, 69.3%, no, 24.4%
3. who has beaten on you in the last months: rival gang member, 48.3%; the police and a rival gang member, 26.9%; the police, 10.8%; a particular person (perhaps a family member), 4.6%
4. (female respondents) have you gotten pregnant while in a gang: yes, 55.7%, no, 40.3%

Opinions of gang members:

1. what do you want for your future: a job, 30.6%, a stable family, 25.5%, an education, 16.7%; to be somebody, 7.6%; calmness, 5%; self-improvement, 4.8%; finding God, 2%
2. what are the real problems for today's youth: drugs, 26.6%, lack of jobs, 12.7%; do not discriminate, 18%; understand, 11.5%; provide a helping hand, 11.4%; provide greater safety, 8.9%; do not fear them, 6.8%; give them a chance, 6%; give them respect, 5.2%; give them an education, 4.7%[40]

While opinions were scattered, certain findings glared from the tables of statistics. These were very young people being socialized (hanging out) in the streets. They were drenched in violence, including domestic violence. They had little expectation for the future, but their number one desire was for work. The deportees had a more specific subset of needs, which the Homies summarized in a platform:

Platform

1. *Visas*—that the authorities allow Homies Unidos organizers on the streets of L.A. without fear of deportation or arrests. From the INS, this would mean granting a special visa waiver for undocumented organizers from El Salvador working on violence prevention. Consent would be required as well from the police and sheriffs. On their part, Homies Unidos would avoid deploying people with major warrants.
2. *Notice of deportations from L.A.*—Homies wanted deportees provided with organizational literature and phone numbers when being deported, and a kiosk for Homies representatives at the airport in El Salvador to meet them. Otherwise, the deportees would go back to the streets or return to the U.S.

3. *Micro-loans* to start little businesses run by ex-deportees.
4. An immediate need for *computers* and a doctor skilled in *tattoo removal*.

I thought these demands were well-conceived, small steps that could lead to breaking the global cycle of violence. I agreed to organize a delegation to visit Homies Unidos in El Salvador. It was an unusual venture in peace diplomacy, to say the least. Alex, still living underground, wasn't available to go, but Silvia, Rocky, a leader of Barrios Unidos, two Salvadorans from Father Boyle's network and, for balance, Dewayne Holmes and John Heyman were included. It was the peace process in action. We spent a week meeting and listening to homeboys at Hector's parents' garage, where they hung out, learned computers, worked on silk-screens and glass carving. We ventured into urban parks crowded with gang members and remote villages where L.A. graffiti marked bathroom walls. We met unforgettable characters. There was Huera, the big girl from 18th Street, who was living with a homeboy named Moreno, who was on crack. There was Deborah, a tiny homegirl with a background of all the worst addictions, who eventually would become a social worker. There was Panza Loca, whose stomach could gyrate like the "belly dancer" of his street name. He was becoming their computer graphics expert. Sometimes as they narrated their stories, it was impossible to remember what country I was in.

I was greatly interested in two charismatic individuals named Gato ("the cat") and Bullet. Gato, who took his name because of his feline eyes and agility, saw his father shot in the head by a death squad when he was a little boy. The shooters came to his Modelo neighborhood in a car with tinted windows, and said nothing after the killing. Gato kept a chain of Our Lady from his father, however, which became his link to his childhood when he fled to Pico-Union with his mother in the eighties. As an L.A. schoolboy, Gato at first took a distaste to the *cholos* on the corner. He held the classic immigrant aspiration of making it in America. It was not to be. One day a gang member called Gato a *chuntero,* an almost untranslatable put-down, and ripped the chain of Our Lady off his neck. Infuriated, Gato wanted to fight for the chain on his own, but his new friends convinced him that he needed backup, protection, that he needed to belong to the neighborhood.

Thus Gato was jumped into 18th Street, which then was mostly Mexican, so he tattooed a big "El Salvador" in block letters on his chest.

With his new friends, Gato soon found the homeboy who ripped off his father's chain of Our Lady. "Remember the *chuntero?*" he asked him, then wounded him with a knife. It was first blood. Not long after, the Crazy Riders drove into Gato's neighborhood, shooting and killing one of his homeboys. Gato shot back, hitting the Crazy Riders in their car. Acting on an impulse, he pulled the wounded assailants from the vehicle, told them to call 911, and took off running. He was stopped by unsuspecting police and told them to go help the injured. But his luck ran out. Gato was identified by a neighborhood resident who had seen the shoot-out and was arrested when he returned to Pico-Union a few weeks later. Convicted of attempted murder, he was sentenced to one of California's high-security prisons, where life could be just as dangerous as on the street. One day Gato came upon a cell mate masturbating on a photo of his girlfriend, an insult that could not go unpunished. To do nothing would reveal weakness, which could lead to sexual assault. So Gato stabbed him. To avoid further time in the California penal colony, Gato took the legal option of "voluntary departure" and was deported back to El Salvador in 1997, which is where I heard his story as he leaned against a barrio wall overlooking a little creek where neighborhood women dumped their plastic garbage bags.

Reflecting on his experiences, Gato said that in El Salvador "the people were terrorized by war, then there was peace, and now there is MS and 18th Street killing each other. You never know when you're going to be dead." His mother had pushed him to the Homies' garage, where he participated in workshops on nonviolence. One day during our week's stay, Gato's prediction almost came true. While riding the bus to our meeting place, he was stabbed by a rival MS member. But Gato seemed strangely composed when he showed up hours later in bandages. "I told the guy, 'Man, I don't bang no more. You don't know why you're into all that.' And then he told me, 'Fuck you, *puta*,' and claimed his MS 'hood." I couldn't quite understand Gato's new willingness to accept insult and stabbing. "It's hard to forgive somebody when they do bad to you," he replied, as if the answer was obvious. That's why the wars went on.

Within the next year, Gato moved with his girlfriend, Spanky, and their new baby, into his family's old house in Modelo. By now, however, the neighborhood was MS territory. Not only was Gato covered with 18th Street tattoos but, even worse, Spanky was an *MS* homegirl. Magdaleno knew at once it was an absolute no-no. This was a homie version of Romeo and Juliet, like an interracial couple moving into a segregationist neighborhood in the fifties. But Gato, now liberated from the gang wars, wanted to go all the way. "A lot of the MS homeboys don't like me 'cuz I'm with my lady, but I don't think anyone should choose for me the woman I'm going to be with the rest of my life." The fates were too strong. In November 1999, Gato would be shot six times and killed in front of his father's former home, before the eyes of Spanky and their small son, Vladimir, in a full repeat of the horror he had experienced as a child in that very yard. The killers were presumably from MS, but who really knew?

The other homeboy who fascinated me was nineteen-year-old Marvin Novoa Escobar, or Bullet, the composer of "The Fruits of War." Like his street name, Bullet came straight at you. The numbers 1 and 8, for 18th Street, were tattooed on his earlobes. A hand was missing, blown away by a molotov cocktail he once planned to use against a former girlfriend in a jealous frenzy. His head, throat, and back were disfigured by machete and knife wounds inflicted by gang rivals. He definitely had attitude. Once, Bullet strode into enemy territory yelling, "18th Street Rules!" and calling out for MS to shoot him. They didn't—not that time.

Mangled as he was, Bullet had charisma, intensity, spark. You had to like him. When we met in 1997, he was twenty-one. It was Thanksgiving night at an open-air restaurant, Casa de Piedra, on a lovely hill above the capital. Homies Unidos was enjoying the momentary relief of a dinner party, under the friendly protection of San Salvador's new police chief, a wiry former revolutionary commander in the civil war, Eduardo Linares, who had taken a liking to Homies, and was deeply concerned that El Salvador's right-wing government and postwar dependence on neo-liberal economics would spawn an even greater lost generation. Linares was appointed chief as part of the 1992 Salvadoran peace agreement, and ironically was attending seminars with the U.S. FBI and an obscure U.S. agency called the International Criminal Investigative Training Assistance Program (ICITAP). Asked what he thought of American-style policing, he laughingly said that "everything they failed there, they are implementing here."

While we enjoyed the pleasant evening, Bullet had everyone's attention with "The Fruits of War." He seemed fully transformed from his fanatic 18th Street period. Once, during our visit, while we strolled unsuspectingly through a public square, Bullet had protected Dewayne and John, two African Americans, from a clique of homeboys planning to seize their jewelry and provoke a fight. Bullet also was known to take risks in particular for his former rivals in MS. But he was becoming best known for his Cypress Hill–style rapping.[41] He was a street poet with an audience and a future.

Bullet had been moved to the U.S. to flee the war as a child, which is where he became immersed in la vida loca. His worried mother moved Bullet (and his brother, Bandit) to Maryland, where his gangbanging continued. In anger, she finally sent the brothers back to El Salvador, where, in the course of things, Bullet transitioned from 18th Street to Homies. In the process, he picked up many scars and fell in and out of serious drug addiction. It was while Bullet was on crack that he ventured into MS territory, screaming, "18th Street Rules." Maybe he wanted to die, but Bullet seemed immortal.

I still have a letter from Bullet that I now deeply regret failing to answer, written after his release from a rehab center where Silvia and my son Troy had found him. Bullet had discovered Jesus and was selling "Have a Nice Day" stickers, jumping on and off sixty buses a day, where he testified to his recovery. He started rapping again, even performing at a theater. "I'm back on track now and this time's for sure," he wrote me. "Know why? 'Cause nobody told me to change. It came straight from my heart, the need of a change. Well, I really don't want to bore you with too much writing. Take care and really hope that you write back 'soon' to counsel me a little, it'll help on my everyday living."

I kept the letter, meant to write back, never did, became too busy to answer. I would get to it someday. I was comforted that Bullet was doing fine. But that's not the way it goes. Bullet was so cleaned up that perhaps he became careless, which can happen when you are no longer in the gang. So, on New Year's Day, 2002, Bullet was shot to death in broad daylight near San Salvador's main cathedral.

He was waiting for his brother, Bandit, simply to wish him Happy New Year, when he was shot in the head and spine at 11 A.M. His little brother found him lying by the bus stop.

There were many tears for Bullet. "He's the one who paid for everything," was all Silvia could say. Bullet had been most ashamed of stealing oranges from an old lady when he was on crack. He had a plan to make amends for everything. He even had removed the part of his earlobe that bore a gang tattoo, then took an aspirin as painkiller. He left behind some tapes of his music, little else. His mother, who sent him back down from Maryland because he was messing up, who didn't believe that he was "doing good" in Homies, came to the funeral in San Salvador to ask for forgiveness. The Homies got up and left. Slowly, however, the healing started, and the mother would eventually find herself accepting peace plaques in Bullet's name from the Homies in Los Angeles.

There were other Homies who paid the price for changing. There was the charismatic Ringo (Mario Sigredo Rivera), who helped arrange our peace delegation's visit. A deportee who was married three times, Ringo was killed by the owner of a restaurant in 1999, in unknown circumstances. There was Boobee (Amilcar Rodriguez), whose poem on loneliness is printed in this book. After deportation from L.A. and seven years in a Salvadoran prison, he was in charge of security at Save the Children, the nonprofit directed by Magdaleno's wife, Carolina. Boobee was stabbed while getting off a bus. At the hospital, doctors refused to treat him because of his tattoos. Boobee had four heart attacks before he bled to death and died. Finally, there was the leader, Hector/El Negro himself. During his work at Homies Unidos, Hector was shot in the head by a rival faction. After some time, he disappeared back into the streets. Magdaleno summarized the story best:

> Negro could not remove both feet from the quicksand of la vida loca . . . Negro's addictions if he had any were about power and women. He knew how to use power on the streets. He used those skills and natural talents to benefit Homies Unidos. Sometimes he would forget how to work within a democracy and would fall back on the authoritarian top-down management system of many gangs. Sometimes late at night I blame myself for not being creative or consistent enough

to give Negro the proper coaching that would take him on a new orbit to farther and safer stars. So he left the organization and moved back into the comfortable role of a gang leader, a much more experienced person but still back on the streets, and now a well-known and visible target.

Spanky, Gato's wife, lived, though she never went back to the neighborhood after his death. She had two more children with an MS member, and began working on a women's cooperative. Deborah, the drug addict, became a political activist, then social worker among deportees in an immigrants' rights project in Phoenix, Arizona. Huera became the first tattooed gang member to become a registered nurse in El Salvador, or perhaps anywhere. She has "Ringo" tattooed on her heart. Many more would live than would die.

The official interest in our peace mission to El Salvador was significant, and we began to make progress on the Homies' demands. We met with U.S. Ambassador Ann Patterson, who arranged a reception at her residence with over fifty officials, including the CIA, USAID, Salvadoran police, and even former FMLN guerrilla commandantes. The mayor of San Salvador, Hector Silva, proved especially sympathetic to the violence prevention agenda. Through these contacts we opened a dialogue with INS officials in Washington, D.C., and met with the INS planning director, Robert Bach, at the Los Angeles airport on our return. Soon there were meetings in Washington with more bureaucrats than the Homies had seen in their lives. While there were skeptics, the central message from INS Commissioner Doris Meissner and Bach was a welcome one. They were very interested in a "pilot project" perhaps involving visas, literature for deportees, micro-loans, and a halfway house in San Salvador. They conveyed lofty hopes: "your activities in promoting an inner-city peace process sound extremely valuable for addressing the increasing transnationalization of gang activities," Bach wrote on August 18, 1997.[42]

But we learned there was a significant "If"—if there was signoff from the LAPD, and if there was signoff from the L.A. regional office of the INS. These were the agencies on the front line of the deportations, blessed by the Washington INS officials who were suggesting we meet with them. It sounded more like a handoff than a signoff, but with official support from the Clinton administration, it was worth a try.

And so it was that I first visited the LAPD CRASH headquarters, housed discreetly in a nondescript building in downtown L.A. Unmistakable undercover police strode back and forth among the immigrant shoppers and homeless people at the building's entrance. An unmarked elevator deposited me in a busy administrative office filled with street maps and charts laden with undecipherable pushpins. It was a war room. I sat down with the CRASH unit's commander, Dan Koenig, who entered the room wearing one-way, wraparound, silver shades.

Here I must detour to disclose my past association with the Rampart CRASH unit itself. It was in 1996 that I befriended an officer in the antidrug detail there, who invited me to a war-on-drugs operation, which happened to target the epicenter of Homies (and immigrant) territory, the corner of Bonnie Brae and Fourth Street. I went with my wife amidst a coordinated task force of local, state, and federal undercover agents who hid themselves on the second floor of an LAPD safe house of sorts, where they could monitor drug sales on the corner below. The transactions were between a handful of teenage homies—whether MS or 18th Street, I don't remember—and otherwise law-abiding motorists stopping by for this improvised narcotics take-out service. The officers were perpetually alert, often tense, as they tried to photograph and trap their prey below. After several hours they made three arrests, all several blocks away so as to not give away their stakeout. It didn't seem very cost-effective for a multi-agency unit funded on a special federal grant, but the cops seemed fully satisfied by the night's end. I found myself more interested in observing the homies going about their business, however. In the first place, they were very young; it seemed all under twenty. Second, their furtive patterns—darting from the shadows toward the customers, circling their cars, engaging in conversation, making the deal, handing off the cash—were choreographed with an electric energy. It was as if they knew that the cops were watching them from somewhere, either wired up as a buyer or hidden behind a window. Most impressive was the way they kept "the books," by adding up the night's totals with chalk marks on the street. There were numerous passers-by—local residents, women with shopping bags, elderly couples out on a stroll—all in polite silence. My deepest impression was the colossal waste of cops' time and the homies' buoyant energy.

Thus, I wasn't a newcomer to CRASH when I met Koenig. He seemed friendly, professional, wearing a creased white shirt and a tie that distinguished him from the informal street clothes of the agents. He readily admitted that Salvadoran police and intelligence agents were recent visitors to CRASH headquarters. During the same period as our meeting, a director of Salvador's department of criminal investigations had told the *New York Times* that "it is important for us to have an album of photos that we can show to people, to have fingerprints and a rap sheet of the crimes these people have committed in the United States, to know what tattoos or other identifying features they may have."[43] Koenig was ambiguous about the degree of intelligence-sharing, if any, that was taking place, since it was clearly unknown to, and unauthorized by, city officials. However, he was surprisingly interested in any peace efforts, acknowledging that the LAPD's tactics were failing to stem the violence. "After we go into a community and suppress the crime, there's no comprehensive violence prevention program to fill the vacuum. If someone could reproduce a 'Blinky' Rodriguez or a Father Boyle in every community we go into, that would be an important accomplishment." Given this expression of interest, I raised with hope the issue of providing a special visa waiver for Homies Unidos organizers in communities like Pico-Union. The police routinely support waivers for illegal aliens who snitch, don't they? Why not waivers for peacemakers? Koenig didn't respond to the question of snitches, but offered no resistance to the idea of a pilot project. But he was careful not to support the idea, either, instead passing the ball to the INS. "If it's okay with the INS, it would be okay with us."

At the time, I didn't know with certainty of the ongoing collusion between the CRASH units and the regional INS, and the FBI (both the latter agencies under the U.S. Department of Justice). These previously mentoned links, later documented by the *Los Angeles Times*'s Ann Marie O'Connor, were cemented through antigang and antidrug task forces hidden from any oversight.[44] Unknown to the public, the civil rights division of the U.S. Justice Department had been monitoring the LAPD since the 1994 O.J. Simpson trial, but apparently it was not monitoring its own Los Angeles agents in the INS and FBI.[45] Or perhaps not listening to their complaints, since an INS task force coordinator raised "moral objections" to the operations because, he said, "only a very small portion of those arrested were actually hard-core gang members," which also was my impression after participating in the CRASH stakeout. The INS coordinator reported that "there was a gang out there, consisting of mostly juveniles, who were involved with extortion-type things, but this did not constitute an OCDETF-type case," referring to the Organized Crime Drug Enforcement Task Force.[46] When the *Times* went public with the allegations, they were visited by the FBI's regional director who accused them of being unduly harsh—until he was shown the pile of secret documents.

Another explosive document, cited earlier, quoted Special Agent Danny Hudson as saying "this was a political move" that came from Mayor Riordan's office.[47] This was a key insight since Riordan, like Giuliani, was elected mayor in 1993 and 1997 on promises to unleash the LAPD to fight the war on gangs. The special agent's political charge, which appeared in the twenty-second paragraph of a twenty-eight-paragraph story on February 29, 2000, just faded away. A Riordan spokesperson told *Los Angeles Times* reporter Jim Newton that she was "unaware" of any involvement by her boss. "This never happened that I knew of. I think sometimes people wrongly attribute motives to the Mayor's office."[48] It was a non-denial of the possible role of the mayor who, in addition to urging a tougher crackdown on gangs, appointed both the police chief and the police commission. Certainly Mayor Riordan (along with Chief Parks) was unrelenting in waging constant warfare against the *Times*'s Rampart coverage and reports.[49] Looking back, a top *Times* editor said that "the political part didn't seem that important compared to the consuming job of uncovering the facts of the story."[50] In May 2000, the *Chicago Tribune* bought the *Times,* dissolved its city-county bureau shortly thereafter, and sent the savvy editor in charge of Rampart, Tim Rutten, to the features section. While lead reporters Matt Lait and Scott Glover remained on the Rampart story, it would never be the same.

It was no wonder that the cops at Rampart CRASH weren't buying any notion of going easy on the homies they were conspiring to suppress or deport. According to officer Rafael Perez's deposition, the unit especially looked for homies who were witnesses to police misconduct, turning them over the INS for deportation, or beating them up to turn them into informants.[51] The idea of a gang peace process was totally alien to the Rampart creed. LAPD office Robert Hansohn, a veteran of the 1992 riots and future captain at Rampart, said he'd "never seen one of these [truces] work in 29 years."[52] The 1992 uprising of the Pico-Union immigrants and widespread property destruction only reinforced the siege mentality at Rampart. The ease of the April 1992 sweeps and deportations, in violation of city policy restricting collaboration with the INS, was noticed by the Rampart officers as well. Their heavy-handed tactics against the immigrants and homies seemed to work with little or no concern from the higher-ups. In the 1988 beating inflicted on Luis Murrales, for example, described as "lynch mob" by one commanding officer, the case was settled behind closed doors for $177,000 with no allegations upheld against the officers who had clubbed him blind in his right eye.[53] Then there was the case of CRASH officer John Shafia in 1996. A civil jury had found Shafia guilty of pulling a motorist over on suspicion, dragging him onto the pavement, beating him with a baton, then leaving without charging the victim with a crime. Shafia's disciplinary record already included over 150 days of suspensions. Nevertheless, in a closed-door meeting, city officials agreed to pay Shafia's punitive damages. However, at one point Councilman Mike Hernandez, a street savvy representative of Pico-Union battling his own problems of addiction, asked a question which, if pursued, might have prevented the Rampart scandal: prior to coming into office, Hernandez had heard of Rampart's reputation for "problem officers," known as "Rampart Reapers"—was there an indication that Shafia was one of these "Reapers"? The LAPD official present "shrugged off Hernandez' alarm," saying "I'm not familiar with that term."[54]

This singular moment aside, the overall truth was that few if any civic leaders, not the Christopher Commission or the Webster Commission or even the African American and Latino leadership, were raising many questions about the paramilitary culture of the war on gangs. The calls for police reform centered on respecting the constitutional rights of *law-abiding* minorities, curbing old-fashioned racism, racial profiling, and the like. Gang members? They were an embarrassment to most of the minority leadership, dangerous scum to the general public. The notion was so internalized, there was no need to ruffle anything by expressing it publicly: the police had a green light on this menace to society. That was the loophole, the omission, that the Christopher Commission and others permitted consciously or otherwise. The unspoken double standard was that constitutional protections could be relaxed so the CRASH units could do their messy work. That was the very idea of "total suppression," the stated CRASH mission, was it not? The mission certainly wasn't to "protect and serve" the homeboys, or honor their rights to hang out on street corners. No, total suppression meant taking them off the streets by any means necessary. The mission was approved, at least tacitly, by the mayor and city council, the newspaper editorialists, and the public they had succeeded in panicking. The CRASH budget was a secret. So were the CRASH lines of command and accountability. A brave *Los Angeles Times* columnist, Shawn Hubler, went into the Short Stop Bar near Dodger Stadium, where CRASH officers regularly partied after shootings, and interviewed the bartender, who said, "I don't care if they have to hit some 'Chuy' upside the head to stop crime in this city, and the public doesn't either. You think LAPD is the only department with the little secret tattoos? What's going on here is no mystery. We've always stepped one toe over the line to put assholes in jail." Hubler wrote that the public was "reaping what we sowed."[55]

This CRASH immunity rested on more tangled webs of the internal LAPD culture than anyone could unravel. First, there were related "antiterrorist" commands such as the Office of Strategic Services (OSS), the Public Disorder and Intelligence Division (PDID), the SWAT teams, and the Special Investigations Squad (SIS). At the time of the 1992 riots and truce efforts, the "first among equals" of the assistant chiefs, responsible for overseeing 85 percent of the sworn personnel,[56] was Robert Vernon, who maintained thousands of secret files on civilians, including city council members and social justice activists.[57] Vernon was a Christian fundamentalist who recruited and organized a "God squad" subculture throughout the department. He was featured in audio tapes on "the True Masculine Role," which described police as "ministers of God" whose manly duty was to discipline others, starting with their wives and children.[58] Though Vernon was eased into retirement after the Rodney King riots, the subculture he cultivated would continue to exist in submerged ways, not only within the LAPD, but beyond. One could volunteer to "fight crime in L.A.," for example, through a Web site associated with the "Disabled American Veterans" group that announced that the LAPD "needs you *now* as an active civilian partner in the war against crime." With a click or a phone call to Officer Ron Stilz, one could join "our select group of surveillance team volunteers" and work "onsite and directly" with LAPD officers in the conservative San Fernando Valley.[59] In due time, the official war on terrorism would supply new tools and resources for gang suppression.[60]

Then there was the L.A. sheriff's department with antigang units of its own and in the nineties, another "tattooed subculture" of deputies with names like the Grim Reapers, Pirates, Vikings, Rattlesnakes, and Cavemen, "in some cases, an inside track to acceptance in the ranks."[61] A federal judge pronounced the most well-known of these deputy gangs, the Lynwood Vikings, a "neo-Nazi, white supremacist gang," forcing county taxpayers to pay $9 million in penalties and training costs in 1996.[62] Then there was the whole legal system headed by District Atttorney Gil Garcetti, who could remember only one prosecution for police perjury.[63] There was a judiciary stacked by Governors Pete Wilson and George Deukmejian, with a majority of former prosecutors and only 7 percent of appointees with backgrounds as public defenders.[64] There were state laws and a judicial culture that promoted plea-bargaining, which meant in case after case that homies were pressured to plead guilty and express remorse for crimes they may not have committed in order to avoid even harsher punishment. This was the case with Javier Francisco Ovando, the homie who was shot in the head during the incident that triggered the Rampart scandal. Ovando was offered thirteen years for pleading guilty to carrying out an armed hit on Officers Perez and Nino Durden. Ovando, who was innocent, refused the deal, went to trial, and was given a twenty-three-year sentence instead.[65] Much the same dilemma faced Alex Sanchez, the Rampart case would eventually show. In an exceptionally hard-hitting analysis, the *Times* concluded in 1999 that "courts regularly allow people to plead guilty while claiming they are innocent. It keeps the system moving."[66] The writer even admitted that the Rampart scandal "came to light not because of checks and balances in the criminal justice system . . . but only because [Officer] Perez was himself caught stealing cocaine from a police locker and confessed to win himself a deal."[67]

Beyond this inscrutable web of police, sheriffs, prosecutors, judges, and customs, beyond the networks of Christian fundamentalists and citizen surveillance volunteers, was a broader paramilitary culture across America who saw in the LAPD the front line in a war against gangs, drug dealers, subversives, terrorists, and the rest. In their recreational time, they could join SWAT in video games designed by Darryl Gates himself, complete with interactive segments in which "you get to unload a few rounds."[68] Or they could review a military analysis of what went wrong in the Los Angeles riots by William Mendel of Fort Leavenworth, Kansas (who noted that his Foreign Military Studies Office views did not "necessarily" represent the official policies of the Pentagon).[69] In Mendel's view, cities like L.A. and Rio are the battlefields of the future, "the post-modern equivalent of jungles and mountains, citadels of the dispossessed and irreconcilable."[70] Based on "police intelligence," he claimed that Bloods and Crips had met a few days before the Los Angeles riots "to establish a truce so that they could devote their efforts towards killing Los Angeles police." According to this analysis, the uprising was "inter-ethnic" in its dynamic, and emphasized a core demand to invest in the inner city in exchange for the end of "targeting of police officers." The fact that there was no evidence of the gang pre-meeting, that no police were killed during the riots, and that the truce continued after the disorder didn't affect Mendel's paramilitary analysis. Instead, he favorably commended the 1994 Operation Rio, which involved an invasion of Rio de Janiero by land, sea, and air with brigade-sized troop formations by the Brazilian armed forces to quell gangs. He offered no analysis of why Rio's gangs continued to thrive almost a decade later.

All these forces—not so much a conspiracy as a loose culture of active and passive support for the war on gangs—were bearing down on the unfunded, unorganized peacemakers of Homies Unidos. No one in authority seemed quite willing to break the pattern, take a risk, approve the unconventional. After my in-conclusive meeting with Koenig, Rocky Rushing went to see the regional direc-tors of INS. He came back with a gloomy report. They seemed "decidedly inhospitable." In December 1997, I returned to Washington for meetings with INS, federal prison officials, and congressional staff, sponsored by Robert Bach. Although there was no overt opposition from these permanent power-wielders, there were no promises beyond further study. Bach candidly told me that the concern was "the Hill," where the Newt Gingrich/Republican revolution was in full throttle, with immigrant-bashing, law-and-order politics the order of the day. No one in the Clinton administration or among congressional Democrats was going to seem "soft on gang members" unless Republicans signed off on a bipar-tisan approach. That was not likely politically, as I discovered shortly afterward when a local headline announced, "Hayden Seeks Return for Deported Gang Members." Not an attractive profile for an elected official. I began to wonder if *anyone* could be elected as a critic of this war. And if that was impossible, how could it ever end?

By now, Alex Sanchez was creating a Los Angeles office of Homies Unidos. He obtained the blessing and shelter of the Reverend Frank Alton, pastor of the Immanuel Presbyterian Church on Wilshire near Normandy. Homies Unidos started holding weekly meetings, poetry classes, and outreach to street youth—even to parents. Slowly some homies came around, totalling about forty. Sym-pathetic volunteers helped out with tutoring and legal defense. Father Boyle was a mentor and friend; Luis Rodriguez, too. Alex and Silvia gave presentations to the ACLU, the president of the police commission, legislators, and govern-ment staff in Sacramento. Cross-town dialogues blossomed with Manny Lares in Santa Monica, "Bo" Taylor at Unity One, Dewayne Holmes and John Hey-man in Watts, and various professionals interested in violence prevention.

But relentless CRASH harassment continued on the streets, as if the existence of Homies Unidos was an insult to everything the LAPD believed. There could be nothing positive in gang members—ex-criminals, current criminals, future criminals—coming together. Homies Unidos was a front for criminal gangs, Rampart cops told the Police Commission.[71]

What subsequently happened is still unclear, but we can begin with an INS agent named Hung Nguyen, whose name would turn up in files later divulged at the trial of Alex Sanchez. A complaint to the Los Angeles INS bureaucracy, by an unknown source, led Nguyen on October 6, 1998, to search the files for the name Alex Sanchez.[72] Given the Rampart-LAPD-INS level of coordination, it perhaps was a Rampart officer seeking to remove Alex from the streets. As already noted, there was a collaborative effort between CRASH, INS, and the FBI to deport immigrant gangbangers. Then the question is why they would single out a gang *peacemaker*, which the long hostility of the CRASH units to gang truces might explain. In any event, Nguyen obligingly searched his database and discovered that this Alex Sanchez had been deported on October 31, 1994, with no record of an application to return following his convictions. Nguyen further snooped in State Department of Motor Vehicle records and found that Alex Sanchez recently had applied for a driver's license. The photos matched.

According to later accounts by the LAPD, the INS was "actively looking" for Alex.[73] But the federal authorities publicly denied the LAPD's account.[74] The secretive collaboration between INS and police units was the probable explanation. In any event, the LAPD now had a closely held warrant for Alex's arrest on immigration violations anytime they wished to pick him up. As if in a parallel universe, our peace process initiative went forward with calls for investigations of police harassment of gang peacemakers. Little did we know what was unfolding around us. Officers Rafael Perez and Nino Durden shot Ovando in 1996, while Perez also confessed to fatally shooting another homeboy, Juan Saldana, and wounding a fifty-one-year-old man and his eighteen-year-old son in the same year, without raising questions from LAPD investigators.[75] With another partner, David Mack, Perez partied in Las Vegas after Mack had robbed a Bank of America outlet of $700,000.[76] Then, on March 2, 1998, Perez checked out the fateful cocaine from the LAPD's downtown locker room under another officer's name.[77] Perez's luck finally ran out, and the internal LAPD investigation into his cocaine theft widened into the fuller Rampart probe by late August 1998.[78]

On September 30, 1999, as the Rampart scandal hit the headlines, I convened a state Senate task force at Immanuel Presbyterian Church in Pico-Union. The location and agenda could not have been more timely: a review of police harassment cases throughout the city. Present for the unique testimony was a distinguished panel of civil rights advocates, clergy, attorneys, and immigrant rights experts. Alex, as the star witness, recounted an LAPD raid on a restaurant where he was giving a Homies Unidos talk. He was handcuffed and placed in a squad car, and accused of being a "shot caller" before being released. On another occasion, he was interrogated at the Wilshire substation by CRASH officers who then took him in a squad car to a rival neighborhood to create the impression he was cooperating with the police. Another time, police raided a surprise birthday party Alex was throwing for a young woman who had just ended a period of drug addiction. As Alex quietly recounted these stories and answered questions, there came a surreal commotion in the hearing room. Standing in the back was a tall CRASH officer, Jesus Amezcua, who had been accused by church personnel of seeking to spy on the Homies Unidos meetings.[79] At one time or another, he had arrested some, if not most, of the two dozen Homies members sitting in the audience along with others. More oddly, there were several other LAPD officers in doorways, the hall, and the bathrooms. They were listening, which was their perfect right, but more than listening, they were surveilling the place, muttering threats to homies as they went to the bathroom, warning that they would be arrested. As they themselves had said, their mission was not to listen to homeboys complain, much less *testify*, but to stop and frisk them, to put them out of business. Suppression was the order, not comprehension. "If you talk to a gang member, any time they are stopped by the police, it's harassment," said a Rampart commander, but "we have a *duty to talk to them and gather intelligence*"[80] even if they are hanging out and minding their own business. They cited legal prohibitions on "association" between gang members while on parole, a ban that could apply even to a parolee talking about peace with his former homeboys. So the very *existence* of Homies Unidos as such an "association" was a total challenge to the CRASH way of seeing the world. What this could mean when implemented was explained more candidly by Rafael Perez to investigators:

Uh, There's so many incidents. I couldn't possibly go into every one of them. What I'm saying is, specialized units need to be looked at. Believe me when I tell you, if there were 15 officers in CRASH, 13 of them were putting cases on people.

Q: When you say "putting cases on people," do you mean manufacturing probable cause, or do you mean actually, in essence, framing somebody who did not do something, for a crime?

A: Both. Both.[81]

No sooner had the church hearing ended than Rampart officers, including Amezcua, began pushing the departing homies up against the walls of the church, not caring that they were carrying out the very behavior of which they were accused. On Wilshire, traffic slowed as the flashing red lights of the LAPD vehicles reflected off the church walls. We couldn't let Alex be arrested, so Rocky and I hustled with him out a side door into a car and sped away.

The complete testimony from the hearing played over and over for weeks on the Adelphia cable channel. For the first time, the general public was seeing and listening to the grievances of gang members in the context of a respectful public hearing. The secrets of CRASH were out of the closet and into the living rooms of Brentwood and Westwood. As the LAPD's Rampart misdeeds kept being reported, the homies' claims became more credible. For a brief moment, at least, the public climate was changing. Alex and other peacemakers began receiving invitations to speak from audiences that previously would have assumed there was nothing worth knowing from gang members.

What anger and resentment was building up within the inner sanctums of CRASH after that September night is unknown. But an example of the seething discontent was revealed in a 2000 survey of internal department attitudes for the U.S. Justice Department by UCLA's Wellford Wilms and two colleagues. Between 1996–97 and 1999–2000, the percentage of LAPD officers who agreed with the statement "Compared to a year ago, the Department receives more support from the community" had fallen from 57 percent to 34 percent. Especially irritating was the belief that members of the public or juries might believe the testimony of a gang member.[82]

The hammer fell on January 21, 2000, when Amezcua pounced on Alex while he was entering a car on Normandy and Eighth. According to Alex, Amezcua said, "It's over. You can take Homies Unidos and shove it. I'm going to take Homies down one by one."[83] It was a Friday night, so it was likely that Alex would remain in jail without bail over the weekend. Within minutes, I was on the phone with the LAPD's Internal Affairs unit with a Lieutenant Gus Martinez. The urgency felt like the old days in the Deep South. I told Martinez that I had reason to believe Alex was targeted for harm. He left for the Rampart station to interview Alex and promised to call me back. When he called, I learned for the first time that Alex was arrested on the INS warrant that was fourteen months old.

We immediately launched a campaign to "Free Alex," with Silvia, Rocky, Alex's brother Oscar, and other activists all joining in. Posters and petitions calling for Alex's freedom were produced. Clergy, civil rights, and immigrant advocates, frustrated with the Rampart scandal, seemed eager to help. Latino politicians signed letters of support, most notably Congresspersons Lucille Roybal and Sam Farr, and legislative leaders Antonio Villaraigosa, Richard Polanco, Liz Figueroa, and Hilda Solis. A personal plea was sent from Ethel Kennedy, an old friend with a deep interest in gang intervention programs, to Doris Meissner at INS. I sent a letter to Meissner as well, indicating for the first time that Alex Sanchez was the individual I had hoped would receive a visa waiver to stay in the United States. With Meissner's facilitation, I organized a meeting of Alex's family with U.S. Attorney Alejandro Mayorkas.[84] L.A.'s Spanish-language daily, *La Opinion,* put Alex on the front page consistently. Several of us went downtown to brief Bill Boyarsky, the veteran city editor the *Times.* As he and a couple of editors sat sphinxlike listening to our tale, I wondered if we were becoming too emotional, too conspiratorial. Finally, however, Boyarsky thanked us, then said, "this sounds like a—police state," and ordered an investigative story on the Sanchez case. The investigation would find that the INS was "blindsided" by the arrest, and that Amezcua's possible motive was to deport Alex before he could serve as an alibi witness for a teenage homie the police had arrested mistakenly on murder charges.[85] I personally continued to believe that Alex was being railroaded by CRASH officers who detested the peace process.

On January 25, four days after Alex's arrest, we organized perhaps the first picket line at the front door of the Rampart station. About 100 people showed up, including homies belonging to the peace network from around the city. The crowd was angry but disciplined, lining up on the steps to individually file complaints against Amezcua. When the commanding officer tried to break things up, he was informed that he could arrest us or allow us to exercise our right to fill out an employee misconduct form. Since each complaint had to be filled out individually, it promised to be a lengthy public intervention into the department's own turf. You can imagine what the CRASH officers thought of homies filing reports on police misconduct. When Clever, who would become the Homies Unidos leader in Alex's absence, strode into the CRASH reception room, several officers cursed him and threw gang signs of their own. What was happening was unusual, even historic. Immigrant gang members were exercising their citizenship rights, perhaps for the very first time, in a system that had long kept them at bay. No one in that line believed the police would actually investigate themselves, but that was not going to stop the Homies from "representing" their constitutional rights, either. Even the television coverage was respectful that day.

We showed up in the U.S. federal courthouse in downtown Los Angeles on February 16, 2000, not knowing what to expect. Alex's mother was glad to see her son, even handcuffed and wearing orange prison garb, but otherwise she was silent, trying her best to understand the complicated proceedings encircling him. Alex had been transferred by the LAPD to the Feds for illegal reentry to the United States, a violation of federal law. Needing more time to research his possible defense on those charges, we relied on the political argument that Alex was being scapegoated by the LAPD because of his peace work, that the LAPD was being investigated and exposed for widespread corruption and fabrication of evidence, and that Alex faced great danger in either the prison system or El Salvador. Alex's court-appointed attorney was Evan Janess, from the U.S. public defenders office, a sharp, experienced practitioner by now used to seeing hundreds of immigrant gang members deported with dispatch.

But this day was different. To our pleasant surprise, Mayorkas's office, represented by U.S. Attorney Shannon Wright, announced that they would not prosecute

Alex Sanchez for illegally reentering the U.S., "based on equity considerations and all of the information he learned in the past few days about Mr. Sanchez."[86] Evidently, our pleas and presentations to Washington, INS, and Mayorkas had been heard sympathetically. Perhaps, more importantly, no one wanted to be associated with the CRASH units during the Rampart scandal.

Laugh now, cry later. As Alex was freed of the federal charges, he was transferred at the same moment to the INS for a determination of whether he would be deported. He was *not* being held for illegally returning to the country, but he was *on hold* as a man who was illegally here. With a brief good-bye to his family and friends, off he went to the federal detention center in San Pedro, a remote gulag filled with hundreds of immigrants whose fates were "pending," too.

Even before September 11, 2001, the INS hearing system was far more restricted than the judicial system. Nearly everything is up to the appointed judge. There is no jury, no open courtroom, no media access, and, technically, no bail, though there are provisions for parole. Because Alex's deportation order of 1994 was "reinstated" by the INS after his January arrest by Amezcua, the question of parole was not up to an immigration judge but to Thomas Schiltgen, the INS's district director in Los Angeles, whose very office we suspected of harboring the rogue conspirators with the CRASH units.

Alex was becoming what the papers called a "cause celebre," largely because of our Free Alex campaign. He was interviewed by the *Los Angeles Times*, CNN, and Spanish-language media outlets from Terminal Island. His captors were not happy with the attention lavished on an inhabitant of their normally closed world. Neither were some of the inmates. While most of them respected and identified themselves with Alex's cause, there were a few who wondered why he was so special. In such a claustrophobic setting, Alex thought some were informants. It seemed dangerous to sleep. Someone prescribed Prozac, which helped him with anxiety but left him defenseless, listless for days at a time. On the outside, we wondered sometimes if he would go crazy. Alex never was one of those larger-than-life heroes standing against an oppressive world. He never was the poster child for human rights that we had been forced to make him. He was really a regular person, who missed his little son while he was still growing up himself.

History had defined his role, and Alex had stepped up. Now as his public persona was growing, and with it his obligations as a symbol, he sometimes felt isolated as never before. On the outside, his girlfriend, Christina, who was working on his legal case, felt the pressure, too. She had married Alex, which would allow him to adjust his immigration status upon release. But the relationship wasn't stable, and soon it was in tatters. Meanwhile, little Alex stayed with Alex's steadfast mom. A note from Alex hinted at his anguish at that time:

THE PAST HAS COME TO HAUNT YOU

What the hell happened?

I thought I was doing good,
Going to school, trying to help somebody do good
But how can I do good when I don't see nothing
Good around me?

How can I help someone when I can't even help myself?

"The past has come to haunt him," they say.
Can I change the future by the failure of my past?
Has the past become the failure of my future?
Or will my future always be haunted by my past?

How can I become a righteous man?
How can I define a righteous man
When the righteous men around me are rotten and corrupted?
Tell me what did I do wrong?
Was it me trying to help the young do good
Instead of wrong?
Was it me trying to help them not have as many
Failures in life as I did?
Or, was it me standing up for their rights?
They!!! Only know the answer
For they are the ones who have judged me today
For my past.

As the months dragged on, I too felt a terrible responsibility. Would Alex pay the price for sticking his neck out? Would the story end with his deportation once again? Was I responsible for exposing him to this danger? Could one accept that without helping build an underground railroad to help bring him back? How could the cycle of fate be challenged? The impact of Alex's detention on Homies Unidos was serious, too. Magdaleno Rose-Avila was in El Salvador or elsewhere in Latin America, in touch only by cell phone or e-mail. Clever had taken Alex's place in the organization, but he was constantly risking his parole status by his "association" with gang members. We opened a dialogue through the state attorney general's office, seeking to soften the definition of "association," and I introduced a bill to the same effect. "What the heck," Clever complained, "if I can't 'associate,' I can't even live in or walk through my neighborhood 'cuz it's a gang neighborhood." Worse, Clever seemed to be a continuous target, either for rival gang members or provocateurs. Once while he was in a phone booth, he was assaulted with a baseball bat by several attackers who broke his arm and split his scalp. When attending meetings with public officials in his bandages, he used the lame excuse that he "fell down." He was in a double bind: if he admitted defending himself in the assault, it was a parole violation; if he was caught lying, it was a violation as well. So like many homies, he was forced to tell the lesser lie. Clever was brilliant, a rapid-fire speaker, strong and tall, but only twenty-one years old. The strains of leadership, including personal struggles with his girlfriend, gradually wore him out. He eventually turned to crack, and we lost him to the streets for a time.

Meanwhile, the Alex Sanchez case revolved around some maddeningly complicated and slow-moving legal processes. Put simply, we needed someone to clear Alex of his prior felonies in order to make him eligible for release and to improve his chances at fighting deportation. Onto the team came Mark Geragos, a seasoned, well-connected criminal defense attorney, already well-known for his defense of Clinton aide Susan McDougal, who later became famous in the Beverly Hills cases of Wynona Rider, Scott Peterson (husband of the murdered Laci Peterson), and Michael Jackson. Once again, connections not available to imprisoned gang members made it possible to enlist Geragos. The link was Shepard

Kopp, a neophyte at the Geragos firm, whose father Quentin was a Senate colleague of mine. Shep Kopp, an idealist, suggested that the Geragos firm take the Alex Sanchez case pro bono, and we were in business. It helped that Geragos came from a deep heritage of Armenian human rights struggles, too.

Geragos performed some legal magic in the Superior Court of Judge Larry Fidler, known as a serious jurist with an obsessive interest in the fine points of law. While there was no minimizing the political nature of the case, the judge made it clear that we would need to reopen complex issues going back ten years. The core of the case was similar to that experienced by literally thousands of deportees. Were they fairly treated by the criminal justice system in the events leading to their deportation? Or were they being railroaded by overzealous police and prosecutors who took advantage of their limited English skills, immigrant status, and vulnerability to plea bargaining? In Alex's case, he was prevented from seeking a stay on deportation because of two prior felonies. The first was a 1990 plea of guilty to auto theft, when he was nineteen years old, for which Alex had served two years in state prison. Was he properly advised by his court-appointed lawyer at the time that a guilty plea would bar him from seeking to legalize his status and join his family in the United States? The second felony, for possession of a weapon, automatically arose from the first one, so if the first felony conviction was voided, the second could be as well. Geragos's research revealed that Alex was not properly informed that he was waiving his rights by pleading guilty. Anyone who knew Alex would realize he would not have agreed to permanent exclusion from the U.S. as the price of a plea-bargain since his motive for illegally returning was to reunite with his son. A review of the docket sheet for August 7, 1990, the date of Alex's guilty plea, showed no advisement of his Sixth Amendment right to call witnesses in his favor, nor any evidence that Alex understood and agreed to the effect of his plea on his immigration status. Geragos argued that Alex thought he would be deported and could try to adjust his status later, because his father had followed the same path to legal status. He would not have pled guilty if instructed that he would be excluded for life and left in El Salvador.

Prosecutor Norman Montrose, representing District Attorney Gil Garcetti, countered that Geragos's argument to change Alex's 1990 plea wasn't "season-ably made," that there had been a "monumental delay."[87] They further claimed that the exact language of an advisement to a defendant was unimportant. The 1990 transcript showed that Alex was advised that he might be "denied re-entry," which of course he mistakenly understood could be appealed as his father had. Garcetti's lawyers nonetheless asserted that the vague language was the "func-tional equivalent of exclusion," as if an immigrant defendant should have under-stood the full consequences of his plea without having them spelled out. "It is immaterial whether the defendant was actually aware of the degree of risk of de-portation he faced by pleading guilty, but what is of actual paramount impor-tance is whether the defendant was properly advised," the prosecutors wrote. The issue was not whether justice was done, but whether the judicial formalities were observed, not whether Alex was "actually aware," but only whether he was "properly advised." Listening, I cringed at how many immigrants had been de-ceived and deported in this way. Perhaps most insulting was the prosecutor's im-possible claim that this was "just a case" and he'd "never heard" of Alex Sanchez. The climate in Los Angeles was changing because of Rampart. On June 3, Homies Unidos responded by suing the LAPD, a rare step for previously margin-alized gang members who claimed they were stopped, detained, and questioned without justification.[88]

While the courts took these matters under advisement and Alex was returned to Terminal Island, other tensions were dominating the climate of Los Angeles, namely the 2000 Democratic National Convention. The mayor and business elite were excited at the chance to gloss L.A.'s image as a tourism and investment mecca after the 1992 riots and more recent Rampart scandal. The threat they feared was a huge confrontation modeled after the historic "battle of Seattle" the year before, and indeed, thousands of protestors were making plans to converge on the down-town L.A. convention. It also represented a massive opportunity to break the iso-lated invisibility of Pico-Union, call for Rampart reforms, and let the world know about Alex Sanchez. There was a danger, too, that any police-related riots could lead to sweeps, arrests, and deportations in the immigrant community once again. The LAPD was preparing a massive pre-emptive build-up based on wildly inflated

FBI estimates that tens of thousands of "anarchists" would descend on the city, some carrying explosives and weapons of biological terrorism.[89] No evidence of these claims was presented. Taking charge of apportioning the First Amendment, the police and mayor at first offered the organizers only a fenced-off "protest zone" far from the convention center. After the ACLU took the city to court, they offered to move what became known as "the First Amendment cage" closer to the convention center, but still delayed in granting permits for marches. It appeared that a confrontation like Chicago 1968 was in the making.

A unit of the peace process network—including Dewayne, Manny, and Silvia—began pursuing a two-track strategy. On the one hand, we opened up a channel of communication with Sherriff Lee Baca, who was in the thick of law enforcement coordination. Since relations with the Rampart-stricken LAPD were chilly at best, Baca was our best chance at rational negotiations with law enforcement. We essentially needed to convince him that riots and property destruction could be prevented or minimized, but only if the police allowed the demonstrators to march and technically break the law (from our point of view, civil disobedience) short of committing violence. We also wanted to probe Baca's perception of the Rampart scandal and the struggle to save Alex.

Second, we needed to engage the incoming protestors directly and creatively. I myself had participated in the "battle of Seattle" for a week, as an elected official outraged by the World Trade Organization's usurpation of state and local democratic decision making, and found myself gassed and driven off the streets. It was an exhilarating occasion, certainly the most powerful manifestation of a social movement I'd experienced since the sixties. As chance would have it, I also met Alex Sanchez's brother Oscar one night in the midst of the Seattle confrontation. His own rebelliousness, I guessed, had led him to the antiglobalization movement instead of the crazy life that Alex dove into. The encounter also helped me realize how close up and personal was the new issue of globalization, though it was defined by many as being distant and legalistic. If you looked at globalization from the inside out and bottom up, the case of Alex Sanchez was a perfect symbol. War, oppression, deindustrialization, immigrant flight—all were underlying reasons for Alex's plight. Homies Unidos itself was a globalized response to a globalized crisis.

There were serious issues of strategy and tactics to sort out, however. This new wave of revolutionaries favored direct action in the streets, and was decidedly opposed to any reformist electoral politics. After all, they had shut down the Seattle WTO ministerial meeting, a secretive gathering of trade ministers from all over the world. They also refused to bow to outside criticisms of the trashing by some protestors of Starbucks and other branded commercial outlets that exploited the youth culture as consumers and workers in sweatshops. Although carried out by a small minority, the images of black-clad, gas-masked "anarchists" defined "Seattle" for the world. For most of the 50,000 who came to Seattle to "shut it down," the issue of property damage was simply a tactical one. Was it counterproductive to reaching an American majority, or was it like Lexington and Concord, a millennial shot heard round the world?

Good questions, I agree, but the movement seemed to ignore one central fact in the equation: the impact of mass confrontations on organizers in local communities. In the case of the coming L.A. Democratic convention, they had opened their "convergence center"—a vast clearinghouse for nonviolence training, making of street puppets, and nightly planning of the next day's actions—right in the center of Pico-Union, and specifically in the jurisdiction of the Rampart CRASH units. Since the FBI and/or the police could be expected to raid the convergence center, the protests would be bringing down heat on a community that was virtually 100 percent immigrant. They were little aware of the possible response of numerous local gangs to the invasion of thousands of mostly white outsiders labeled as hippies or anarchists. We had to open a dialogue with the most influential people in the center of this new anarchist tendency, thought to be clustered in Eugene, Oregon. We knew that a conversation with them would reverberate by word-of-mouth and Internet through the vast decentralized movement. People could decide their own course of action based on greater sensitivity to local conditions.

The track-one meetings with Sheriff Baca began awkwardly at first. Baca is a Latino in his early sixties, a thirty-five-year man in the department, a Republican, a highly disciplined, zero-body-fat individual who frequently runs five miles at five in the morning. He was elected sheriff in an odd election in which he defeated a dead man, an incumbent who had suddenly collapsed shortly after the candidates' filing period had closed. Perhaps because of the opinions he encountered on the campaign trail, Baca instinctively realized one thing: that the tradition-bound sherriff's department had to catch up with the times to avoid a Rampart scandal of its own. That was the good news. On the other hand, it was unprecedented in the sherriff's subculture to break bread with the homies. "Homeboys, are you kidding? What kind of name is that?" Baca asked at first. "There's nothing cute about these guys! Do you understand what the public thinks of you? You're violent criminals! Get a new name." Still, Baca took us out to lunch at his favorite Mexican restaurant and engaged in a spirited discussion with Dewayne and Manny that lasted more than an hour. Baca was listening, I could tell, and as the minutes passed, I could detect subtle shifts in the discussion. It was a dream come true. They were talking with each other, not past each other, trading jokes more than barbs. A tour of the county jail followed, and several more discussions to which Baca's trusted lieutenants were invited.

The sheriff sized up his convention dilemma rather quickly. He could try persuading law enforcement to ease up, but how could we guarantee that there weren't 50,000 raving anarchists coming to town? Did we know something the FBI and police intelligence didn't? Yes, we responded, it was all an exaggerated myth to scare the public and allow the police to purchase some advanced weaponry and pepper gas. In any event, police bluster and a denial of permits would not deter a confrontation, but only fuel the fire. We suspected that the police didn't want mass demonstrations in front of the Rampart division telling the world about officer misconduct and calling for the release of Alex Sanchez, but that's what we were determined to do. Baca listened, and said he'd get back to us.

Then six of us—Dewayne, Manny, Silvia, John, Alex's brother Oscar, and myself—boarded a night plane for Eugene, considered by the media and intelligence agencies to be the very center of "the Great Seattle Conspiracy." In reality, it was small university town with a significant counterculture community that included a network of people who took their anarchism very seriously. In rescuing a nineteenth-century ideology from the graveyard of labels and dismissals, they faced an overwhelming challenge. For the average American, the term "anarchist" translated into violent disorder for its own sake, an ideology of riot. For these

Eugene anarchists, however, the term was a link back to a revolutionary movement that once competed with Communism and therefore might return again in
the Cold War's wake. For them, anarchism meant direct action, direct democracy, popular control of neighborhoods, schools, and factories, the maximum
feasible decentralization of power, a reaction to movements top-heavy with leaders and central committees. The destruction of property in Seattle was, frankly,
what property deserved, they believed, especially the properties of corporations
pretending to be hip to consumers while sweatshop workers slaved away on coffee plantations or garment *maquiladoras*.

Sitting across a round table in a cloistered meeting place, the homies listened respectfully but felt the discussion was much too abstract. They had seen *real* riots in
1992, they pointed out, much more devastating than broken windows at a Starbucks. They had witnessed, participated in, and been on the receiving end of gang
violence and police violence, too. They had lived under occupation by the *LAPD*,
not the polite police officers of Seattle and Eugene. They lived in communities that
were not white, that were mostly inhabited by immigrants or people with police
records, the very people that the antiglobalization movement wanted to reach.
They advised that it was dangerous to plop down in the shadows of the Rampart
division without knowing where you were. There was no criticism of anarchism or
violence: "Hell, you can do whatever you're gonna do 'cuz we probably done it already," Dewayne laughed, "but we want a greater understanding, and greater organizing around Rampart and police brutality to come out of this."

What came through most of all in the dialogue was that the homies were offering *respect*, which is what they were denied in most discourse and, in a different
way, was denied the anarchists as well in the endless media diatribes against them
as spoiled children of privilege. There was no "tripping" in the encounter, the
cause of the defensiveness that so often polarizes. As a veteran of too many faction fights and ego rivalries, I was learning something from the homies. There
was a single exception, from a respected anarchist theorist in the room, who
questioned our motives, claiming that we were counterinsurgency "agents" representing electoral reform. He made the interesting point that anarchists were
being demonized and targeted in the same manner as gang members, but his

accusations broke the growing harmony of the discussion, and he became isolated. The long meeting ended in a constructive spirit, and we returned to L.A. feeling the message was communicated. The homies, ever conscious of an impeccable style, joked that the white anarchists could "take some lessons in body hygiene." But they felt pleased that they had gained support for Alex, and learned they could build political alliances.

Back home, it wasn't clear who was preparing to break the law. The convention was turning into a nightmare for downtown businessmen. First there was the June "Laker riot," when celebrating basketball fans, some of them described as gang members from South Central, started fires and attacked police cars while officers appeared to keep their distance. Next, the headlines repeatedly reported that officials were "bracing" for the coming convention protests in August.[90] The ACLU and LAPD were at loggerheads over permits to rally and march. The quiet conversations with Sheriff Baca were inconclusive. During budget hearings in Sacramento, I discovered once more the mysterious ways of law enforcement. Someone in the LAPD, in collaboration with someone in the mayor's office, talked to someone in the governor's office—the "someones" would never be revealed— about slipping $3.4 million into the state budget to secretly buy a paper shredder for the LAPD, not to mention $125,000 worth of pepper spray, forty semiautomatic launchers capable of shooting 20,000 pepper balls, twenty 40-millimeter gas guns, 1,400 "exact impact sponge rounds," $60,000 for surveillance cameras, and other devices for their law-and-order arsenal. I figured the LAPD was seeking the $2,400 paper shredder from state funds since it wouldn't help their image during the Rampart scandal to ask the city council.[91] Behind the scenes, representatives of the California Highway Patrol were annoyed that their budget request for securing state highways during the convention was being used to secretly expand the LAPD's capacity to fight riots and gangs.[92]

"Don't take away our less-than-lethals," Baca pleaded during one of our conversations. Pepper spray, it turned out, was promoted after the 1992 Los Angeles riots as a "safe" alternative to guns, batons, Tasers, and dogs. Police use of the spray jumped from thirty-five occasions in January 1993 to 5,000 sprayings by the year's end.[93] It was a favorite weapon of the state's attorney general, Dan Lungren.

It allegedly had worked to stop demonstrators in Seattle, though it mainly served to discredit the WTO. The problem was that questions surrounding its health effects had never been answered by state officials. A 1993 U.S. Army evaluation found that oleoresin capsicum (OC, a key ingredient in the pepper spray) is capable of "producing mutagenic and carcinogenic effects . . . cardiovascular and pulmonary toxicity, neurotoxicity, as well as possible human fatalities."[94] In 1996, an FBI agent pled guilty to taking over $57,000 from a maker of pepper spray in exchange for writing false reports used by his agency in purchasing the manufacturer's product.[95] Between 1993 and 1996, there were seventy reported deaths nationally of suspects in custody who were subdued with OC pepper spray by police, including twenty-six in California between January 1993 and June 1995. The ACLU expressed concern about police imposing "a painful chemical 'street justice' without resort to criminal charges or the courts."[96] In 1991, one state health researcher wrote in an e-mail:

> I am receiving phone calls and being pressured by California police departments in major cities (L.A. called me this morning) to reconsider our decision to disapprove the use of oleoresin capsicum tear gas in California . . . It is clear to me we should sit on this. The major problem is that toxicology studies do not exist. The second problem is we have limited resources to conduct a risk assessment.[97]

The "anarchist threat" was the immediate pretext for the LAPD buildup, but homeboys and inmates were the main long-term target of this controversial acquisition of chemical weapons. How, then, would we succeed in marching through a heavily undocumented immigrant community to the doors of Rampart? The first night of the Democratic convention did not bode well. A concert by Rage Against the Machine! was permitted in a fenced-off parking lot near the Staples Center. Thousands attended, and began leaving in droves as the concert ended at the negotiated time. Then a small handful of black-flag-waving activists clung and climbed to the top of the fence. It was not certain who gave the order, but the police overreacted, surging toward the crowd, spraying gas, and shooting a form of rubber bullet. A National Lawyers Guild observer was shot in the face;

my son Troy was shot in the wrist; a homeless activist was hit point-blank, collapsed, and was hospitalized—to name a few casualties. Inside the Staples Center, where I was a delegate, many straw-hatted, flag-waving Democrats applauded the party's retreat from liberalism.

Tensions were very high when about 1,000 protestors gathered in Macarthur Park for the march to Rampart two days later. The interim nights had been edgy but peaceful, and as small groups of tired activists arrived in the park, the feeling was that the day was going to be dangerous. Only one prominent individual took the risk of showing up at the rally—the former Republican-turned-independent Arianna Huffington, who was coordinating an alternative "shadow" convention concerned with issues like the drug war and campaign finance.[98] Meanwhile, Alex sent a message that he and his fellow inmates at Terminal Island were going on a hunger strike in solidarity with the demonstrations.

The march to Rampart was an hour long, with police phalanxes in front and behind. It wound through immigrant neighborhoods that had been "imported" to Los Angeles by globalization and war. Occasionally a lonely hand waived a peace sign from a second-story window. Otherwise, the streets were quiet and people stayed indoors. When at last we arrived at the Rampart headquarters, the precinct looked something like the Winter Palace being defended against the Russian peasants. Columns of police stood stiffly on the surrounding street corners, weapons at the ready. On the roof stood the chief, Bernard Parks, along with his top command, peering through binoculars, protected by what appeared to be sniper units. In contrast, the demonstration was led by a huge puppet representing the head of Alex Sanchez, followed by marchers with "Free Alex" posters, banners, and drums. We had chosen a daylight hour, deliberately.

If these were "anarchists," they were disciplined, unprovocable, and nonviolent. Maybe the message from the Eugene discussions had filtered down, or maybe there was simply a collective sense of what was appropriate. The CRASH units who thought they could remove Alex from the streets like garbage were now staring at his wide, brown face on the Free Alex posters. The cops were, as usual, wound too tightly, which meant they could go wild if confronted, even if eyeballed. This was the turf of their "gang." Earlier in the week, I had been saved and bundled away by the CHP while trying to cross through an LAPD line. Now I was stopped and physically threatened by ramrod officers for trying to speak to their commander a few feet away about whether soft drinks could be brought from a nearby truck to quench the crowd's thirst. No way, I finally was told by an officer dressed like Darth Vader, because the cans could become weapons. Better to dehydrate the demonstrators as a crowd control technique, apparently. But no one in the march was planning to divert the focus from the steps of Rampart where, one after one, community representatives started articulating complaints about police misconduct in front of the shielded centurions. After an hour, about twenty-five persons sat down nonviolently and were carried off, one by one, to waiting patrol wagons. It was over. Rampart, and what it had done to Alex Sanchez, had been confronted and exposed by the largest demonstration in its history.

A short time later, in September, Alex was determined a "low-risk of flight," and quietly released from detention where he'd spent nine months. The campaign for his freedom had succeeded. A rare jubilation burst out among the peace process network, immigrant rights and civil liberties groups. The lobbying in Washington, where Latino congresspeople and Central American refugee groups had met with Doris Meissner, was effective. The top INS decision makers seemed sympathetic to the pressure they were receiving. The stigma surrounding Rampart drew sympathy to Alex.

Now came the last stage of the bureaucratic process, before INS hearing judge Rose Peters. Terminal Island is a remote port facility where inmates can easily sense their "termination" from American society. Hundreds of immigrants are detained in cells within a prison-style facility, which includes administrative offices and sparsely furnished hearing rooms. The historic issue was whether to grant asylum to a former gang member who was an illegal resident of the U.S. There were two options besides immediate deportation: first, a suspension, or withholding, of deportation, which would mean a sort of supervised parole and would prevent Alex from becoming a U.S. citizen; second, the outcome we desired would be granting political asylum on the grounds that Alex would be in mortal danger if forced to return to El Salvador. But under the complicated laws, political asylum was possible only if all of Alex's previous felonies were cleared. Then there were more hurdles, beginning with having to prove that gangs were a "social group" protected from harassment and torture under the law. Ultimately, the issue was proving that a deported gang member like Alex would be marked for torture or death in his homeland.

There never has been an INS case like that mounted for Alex by immigration attorney Alan Diamante, whom we first met at the September 1999 Senate hearing at Immanuel Presbyterian Church. Diamante called three anthropologists to testify that street gangs were "social groups" under the terms of the asylum law. The police chief of San Salvador, Eduardo Linares, flew up to testify that he was powerless to prevent street-level killings of deportees from Los Angeles. A Salvadoran jurist concurred in this gloomy analysis, as did a whistle-blowing member of the national police. Magdaleno Rose-Avila testified about his history with Alex, with Homies Unidos, and recounted the recent killings of Homies leaders in El Salvador. Clergy, family, and friends testified that Alex's work resulted in "community benefits," another finding required by immigration law. While the evidence certainly indicated that Alex would be endangered by deportation, there was ample room for the judge to deport him, anyway. After all, if El Salvador was an uncontrolled killing ground, how could the U.S. government justify sending 4,000 deportees there yearly? Would the case of Alex Sanchez be a precedent for those other deportees? It was a good question, we knew, but the narrow answer was that Alex's notoriety would increase his vulnerability like no other deportee. One ex-gang member whom Alex knew, Marvin Rodriguez, who didn't have the resources to fight his case in the same court, chose deportation back to El Salvador, and was killed two months later.[99]

Months went by. Media interest waned. George Bush was elected president. John Ashcroft replaced Doris Meissner. The attacks on September 11, 2001, radically hardened the climate against immigrants. Judge Peters still hadn't ruled. Would she ever? There was no obligatory time line, so Alex could remain in the legal twilight zone for years. As the time dragged on in the Bush era, the goal of asylum seemed more dreamlike. Perhaps orders to deport Alex were being crafted in Ashcroft's office, who knew? Most likely, we feared, Judge Peters would follow the least controversial path and choose suspension, leaving Alex in permanent limbo.

It wasn't simply Alex, but the Homies Unidos project as a whole that remained under layers of harassment despite the Rampart revelations. A typical obstacle was doing outreach work in neighborhoods under a gang injunction. For example, one former gang member, Mirna Solorzano, handed out bags with candies, condoms, and "Know Your Rights" brochures to young girls in the area defined as a "safety zone" under the injunction. But gang members were technically barred from "associating" even in groups of two, even at a church, "for any reason other than religious worship." The Homies office was in the middle of the safety zone, which meant gang members were taking a risk entering the office even to ask about a tattoo removal program.[100]

Perhaps the most curious campaign by the LAPD to eliminate the gang subculture was that against the homie dolls, which started in late 1999, when one-inch plastic homeboy figures started appearing on the shelves of barrio supermarkets. With names like Droopy, Smiley, Sapo, Mr. Raza, Big Loco, and Eight Ball, draped in *cholo* outfits, the tiny figures were lovable caricatures of "young lowrider Chicano kids," according to their designer.[101] The craze spread throughout the country by way of Urban Outfitters and Tower Records, with tens of millions of homie dolls being sold.[102] It was too much for the LAPD. Starting in 1999, they waged a pressure campaign to rid the city of the figurines, which they declared to be soft on the gang lifestyle. One Latino supermarket chain succumbed to the police pressure and eliminated the homie dolls from their gumball machine. Another vending machine company fell in line. There was no similar police outcry, incidentally, against the countless toy figures carrying bazookas and automatic weapons in every American toy store. Not long after, as the Rampart scandal peaked and Alex awaited his verdict, the LAPD officers' union began marketing dolls of its own.[103] The *Los Angeles Times* described the one-inch cop replicas as "handsomely chiseled," and armed with pepper spray, a gun, handcuffs, and other paraphernalia. The first of the LAPD dolls was named "Officer West" in order to remain "ethnically bland." Along came a female LAPD doll, a SWAT doll, and an air-support doll, all with "enough attitude to keep the peace from Rampart to West L.A."

Just as it appeared that the culture of limbo would continue indefinitely, Alex received notice to appear for a verdict on July 10, 2002. We shuddered and prepared. Alex chose to hold a press conference in Los Angeles before taking perhaps his last ride to San Pedro and Terminal Island. I was too worried to be much help. Heart surgery had reduced my energy and schedule. A few friends and cameras showed up at Immanuel Presbyterian, in the same room where it had all begun nearly three years before. Alex came in wearing a white shirt with a yellow tie, the first he'd ever bought. He had a sore throat, seemed nervous, overweight, perhaps near exhaustion. He spoke solemnly, however, saying he felt good about the legal arguments, appreciated all the support, and expressed confidence that the work would go on, whatever the outcome of the case. I felt he'd truly matured, and I was proud to know him.

Meanwhile, lawyer Alan Diamante was even more worn out. He'd taken on the immigration case after Geragos had finished the arguments in Judge Fidler's court over Alex's past felonies. From there, Geragos dropped out, concluding that he'd used up his ammunition and contacts. Diamante threw himself into the thicket of immigration issues, making Alex his cause. In the process, Diamante, who was only in his thirties, wound up having a stroke from the pressures of the case, and now was making his rounds on a cane. Yet he would not stop. The previous day he appeared in Judge Fidler's Superior Court pleading that Alex's remaining felony charge be dropped. It made no sense, he pointed out, if the earlier car theft felony had been reduced by the judge to a misdemeanor. If the first felony was dropped, then Alex could no longer have been a felon in possession of a weapon, which was the second charge. So the final felony disappeared, the prosecution consenting with the arrangement. Judge Fidler and the D.A. wished Alex well, joking that he would never be able to afford Mark Geragos again.

The importance of this maneuver was that it cleared the way for the INS judge Rose Peters, to consider granting political asylum, an impossibility in cases with a prior felony. The disabled Diamante rushed into INS with the news. Presumably, Judge Peters already had labored to prepare a written decision before being faced with this radically new development. Perhaps it was my Irish personality, but I found this new ray of hope almost unbearable. Regrettably, I chose not to go to

Terminal Island for the verdict, but instead waited in my office, expecting bad news and more interminable appeals. My experience in fighting for underdogs had not prepared me for victories.

A few hours later, Silvia called in tears. "He got asylum! . . . It's the first time . . ." She was sobbing and couldn't talk. Alex was bundled in a car, and went home to dinner with his family, free at last.

As this is written, over one year has passed since Alex's release. He now has a second child, a little girl, a new lady, and loving support from his family. Alex still works at the Homies Unidos office next to Silvia every day. He takes classes in empowerment and economic development at Los Angeles Trade Tech. He has been presented a peace prize by Harry Belafonte, and honored by the Southern Christian Leadership Conference, the ACLU, and the Agape Church. But Alex hasn't received a call from the "reformed" Rampart Division commanding officer, nor from the new police chief, and probably never will.

On the day the *Los Angeles Times* carried word of Alex's victory—"Ex-Gang Member Gets Political Asylum," said the headline—the paper printed an immediately adjacent photo, apparently for balance, perhaps as a warning, titled "Crackdown in Pacoima," showing an LAPD officer aggressively searching for tattoos on the shoulder of a silent homeboy, one of 300 who received traffic citations and 48 arrested for warrants on a single-day sweep by 100 cops on Van Nuys Boulevard.[104] It was a message from law enforcement that Alex Sanchez was the exception. The war was still on.

Until the handshake occurs, all talk of police reform is simply that. When and if Hollywood does the Alex Sanchez story, it will likely end with the feel-good celebration of his release, leaving unexplored the legacy of the Rampart scandal that nearly took his life.

The fundamental issue in the Rampart scandal was the dirty war against gang members who were judged by police to be incorrigible, and therefore outside the scope of constitutional protection. When the reformers reacted to the scandal, they tended to skirt this central issue. Instead, perhaps by a habit going back to the civil rights movement, they reacted by imposing a 1960s paradigm on the police crisis. In that paradigm, police were a *racist* force harassing and brutalizing *innocent* African American, Latino, and Asian citizens. The solution, then, was to increase racial and gender diversity in police departments, improve training in the academies, send the officers off to places like the Simon Wiesenthal Museum, where the state paid for a one-day immersion in the Holocaust, and ponder new mechanisms of accountability like police commissions, inspector generals, or citizen review boards. These reforms, it was believed, would change the organizational culture of us versus them and the notorious code of silence.

As a result of these reforms, there *were* changes; for example, by the nineties, more than 40 percent of uniformed LAPD officers were persons of color. Two chiefs in the decade were African American, while the sheriff of L.A. County was Latino. A similar pattern of reform spread across the country, particularly in the south as official segregation was dismantled. This certainly was a historic triumph over white supremacy.

But the officer at the center of the Rampart scandal, Rafael Perez, was himself a mixture of Latino and African American. The police chief responsible was African American. The "thin blue line" was drawn not in the name of white male supremacy but in the name of the respectable society to which they at last belonged themselves. The "enemy" was nonwhite, but the stigma, the crime, was *associating with a gang subculture, which meant by definition that they had no civil rights, or extremely abridged ones.*

That's why the paramilitary units ran wild without oversight, why the STEP Act was passed, why the gang database was carefully maintained, why the injunctions were imposed on neighborhood after neighborhood, why the cycle of violence from street to prison kept revolving. That's why once you were listed in the gang database, there was no appeal, no due process, not even a phone number to call. While *racial* profiling was no longer politically correct or legally defensible, *gang* profiling was seen as a matter of justified security.

That's why the Rampart scandal broke: not because the civil rights safeguards installed by previous reforms worked, but because a single cop, caught blatantly dealing cocaine out of his locker, unexpectedly snitched on his fellow officers to save his own skin. The system, in fact, was working *properly* until Perez began describing how he shot, planted drugs on people, and framed them.

On November 2, 2000, the mayor and city council of Los Angeles approved a consent decree settling the Rampart scandal as an alternative to going before a jury. U.S. District Court Judge Gary Feess formally entered the decree into law on June 15, 2001, requiring the implementation of numerous reforms over a five-year period.[105] Many of the reforms were echoes of the Christopher Commission proposals of 1992: making the inspector general a more effective watchdog, setting better protocols regarding the use of force, stops and searches, improper racial profiling, tracking "problem officers," and strengthening Internal Affairs inspectors. Squads of lawyers drafted some 100 detailed reforms with time lines for compliance.

Civil rights advocates soon learned the bureaucratic bunker was not broken, however. The history of the scandal had been sanitized. It was not clear if CRASH units had fabricated evidence in other divisions besides Rampart, nor was any higher level of complicity revealed or explained. In particular, the code of silence still prevented some officers from blowing the whistle. It was claimed that one, Armando Coronado, was destroyed by the command staff because he had reported on Rafael Perez and Nino Durden several years before the Rampart scandal became public.[106] In the two-year period 2001 to 2003, ninety-six LAPD officers accused of crimes avoided possible prosecution because the LAPD delayed its probes until after the statute of limitations was passed.[107] By 2002, even Chief William Bratton supported reopening the investigation of Rampart, as it appeared that foot-dragging might jeopardize his goal of lifting federal oversight by 2006.[108]

Meanwhile, as noted before, Bratton launched his new antigang offensive as if there were no contradiction with achieving the Rampart reforms. Repackaging the former CRASH units as Community Impact Action Teams, composed of detectives, narcotics officers, special enforcement units, parole and probation officers, and prosecutors, Bratton deployed them at all eighteen divisions. Additionally, he asked for changes in the carefully negotiated consent decree to permit officers to work in local gang units for up to five years instead of three. The focus would be on obtaining intelligence, then planning stakeouts and sting operations.[109] While this loosening of the consent decree was being approved, auditors were still finding "substantial concern" with the antigang units, including bookings being approved by precinct supervisors who printed their names, strangely identical signatures from supervisors and arresting officers, and familiar failures to articulate a legal basis for warrants.[110] It seemed reminiscent of the former CRASH units, warmed over and served again.

Lacking in the consent decree was any new *mission* for police regarding gangs. The decree could have included an explicit statement that Los Angeles police officers treat suspected gang members with dignity and respect their constitutional rights. It could stress the need to target police resources on crimes actually committed, not crimes of identity. It could enjoin division commanders to meet frequently with the experienced gang peace workers in every neighborhood they patrol. It could order the gang database to be turned over to an independent authority for public hearings into due process and accountability. It could have terminated the gang injunctions as too draconian. After all, if injunctions were necessary to the new urban order, why not issue an *anti-sweatshop injunction* in downtown Los Angeles to restrain the *illegal* behavior of owners of America's largest sweatshop district (known in polite society as the Fashion District), where far too many parents of gang members, many of them living in Pico-Union, work in conditions where wage and health and safety laws are systemically violated?[111]

Luis Rodriguez once said that the war on gangs has tried everything during thirty years except bring gang members to the table. That certainly was the case with the LAPD and Homies Unidos. But what if the madness, the crazy life, could only be ended by somehow including those who had started it? That was the question posed by the very existence of an Alex Sanchez and others like him. If Alex Sanchez could change his life *in spite of law enforcement,* wasn't that an alternative model worth exploring? The mind-set that had made Alex Sanchez a gang member had to change before Alex could become a peacemaker. In the law enforcement worldview, that principle wasn't trusted. Once a gang member, always a gang member. They continue to believe Alex is a menace deserving deportation. They wait for him to slip again, and who knows, maybe he will. But what if the reverse is true? What if the mind-set that created the Rampart scandal was a mind-set so resistant to change that it was doomed to crash over and over again? What if the need for scapegoats like Alex Sanchez is greater than the desire to face and finally address the structural exclusion and festering resentment that spawned the gang life as the "fruit of war"?

8

Restoring Community Action

Father Gregory Boyle's approach to inner-city youth represents a living alternative to the war on gangs. As pastor at Dolores Mission Church in Boyle Heights on L.A.'s east side, he chose in 1986 to engage the neighborhood gang crisis rather than stay aloof and let the CRASH units do their job. Perhaps it was an Irish instinct (he has family in Belfast), perhaps it was his roots in liberation theology (he served a year in Bolivia), or perhaps it was his decision to take Jesuit doctrine seriously. Perhaps the homies touched a place in his heart that no one else had. But he perfected his Spanish, rode a bicycle around the Pico-Aliso housing projects, opened the church doors, and became a good listener who offered unconditional love and job placements. The practice became the nation's first gang ministry.

He wrote me on January 20, 2003:

> I am on my way to Javier Castaneda's house—he was gunned down on Sat. evening in front of his house. He was from Breed St. gang and the word is that Cuatro Flats did it. He will be the 114th kid I will have had to bury because of gang violence.

Greg worked tirelessly for peace, which meant much more than gang truces. He believed that gangs had no obvious right, and no capacity, to carve up territory.

This wasn't Northern Ireland. The Cuatro Flats killer was not in search of a homeland, where you could put entities at a table to work out peace accords. I argued with him that truces were life-saving pauses, moments when wiser heads might intervene with jobs and hope. While we enjoyed an intense dialogue, Greg never faltered in his love for the same homeboys who were acting out their insanity. He gave me a powerful insight that "gang violence is always about something else. The one who happened to kill Javier surely *wants to die more than he wants to kill*."

> Who is shooting? I can only speak for Boyle Heights. Only homies who want to die are shooting. Only homies who find themselves in the darkest place of their lives walk into an enemy territory hoping to get killed (not intending to get killed, but dying to catch a bullet). How do you mediate that?[1]

Over time, Greg built a network in Boyle Heights that functioned as a *rehab center* for gang members, including alternative schools, tattoo removal services, and jobs for rival gang members who agreed to work in a community bakery and silk-screening centers collectively known as Homeboy Industries. Parents and community members were organized in a committee for *paz en la barrio* (peace in the barrio), holding peace marches and dialogues with police at the local Hollenbeck Division. He personally intervened numerous times in dangerous situations, saving lives and proving his word. Greg is a realist who believes that the police have a role to play, to provide sensible "heat" on the 5 percent of the homies who he thinks need to be arrested for "time-outs." He has hoped to foster that kind of police approach in the barrio. But he gave 100 percent to the notion that 95 percent of the effort had to be "manufacturing wholesale, huge hope in this community, to which almost all gang members would gravitate towards if it existed."[2] The motto of Homeboys Industries, appropriately, was "nothing stops a bullet like a job." I thought Greg represented an ideal, community-based counter-approach to the prevailing punishment paradigm, one that had a long and distinguished history going back to the settlement houses of the early twentieth century through liberation theology movements in the late sixties.

Then, in March 2000, at age forty-nine, Greg was diagnosed with chronic lymphocytic leukemia and given six months to live. When I talked to him not long after, he was complaining only about the swelling and itching caused by his chemotherapy, nothing more. He was more obsessed with an upcoming fund-raiser than his possible death. A few weeks later I attended the fund-raiser at the downtown Los Angeles Cathedral. It was sold out, the banquet room filled with hundreds of prosperous civic leaders, served by courteous homies dressed for the night in waiters' garb. The *Los Angeles Times* had promoted the event with a respectful front-page story that morning. Longtime supporters like Angelica Huston and Robert Graham hosted the ceremonies. Cardinal Roger Mahoney was present front and center. The mood was one of intense concern for Greg, who spoke briefly and emotionally of his vision.

First, he tried to put the crowd at ease by joking about his condition. Homies, he said, came flocking to his office after hearing the news. He was supposed to bury them, not the other way around. One of them asked, what do I have that you need?, to which Greg replied, "organs." Another said, "Hey, Father G, heard you had leukemia," adding after a moment, "My cat had leukemia. She died." "Nice to hear that," Greg told him.

He related an experience at a May 23 homeboy baseball tournament while going through chemotherapy, where he witnessed former enemies playing together. Two who used to stab each other were high-fiving. One in a wheelchair had been shot by another player. For some people it was a baseball game, he said, but for Greg it was a deeply religious experience, "exactly what God had in mind, that enemies will be friends, and heaven will not be different than this." The audience was profoundly moved.

Perhaps a turning point had been reached. Chief Bratton came by the cocktail hour to extend his concern, publicly ending a historically cool relationship between Greg and LAPD officers who had felt he "pampered" gang members. (A cop had once shouted in his face, "I just want to know why you glorify gangs by having these funerals! I want to know, man to man, how you can live with yourself?"[3]) Cardinal Mahoney was graciously participating in the dinner although the Church's previous efforts to marginalize Greg were well known.[4] Attempts by the Jesuit order a few years earlier to remove Greg permanently from East L.A. for the "greater good" were fought off by the parishioners and community.[5] In eighteen years, the *Times* had featured Greg on the front page only once before, when he had faced the ban by the Jesuits.[6] Now his cancer had generated a public solidarity that the 114 homie funerals never had.

The longtime isolation of Greg Boyle is rooted in the established view of gang experts and law enforcement. Expressed most succinctly by Malcolm Klein at the University of Southern California, perhaps the leading gang research authority of the past generation, *"to recognize is to legitimize."*[7] Street gangs should be quarantined and left to wither, in this orthodoxy. Since gangs seek status and dignity, supportive programs only inflate their self-importance. "To program [with gang members] is to solidify," Klein has written, advocating the avoidance of meetings, sports activities, truce efforts, and other formal outreach. Though praising Father Boyle as "the most *emotionally* dedicated gang intervenor I've come across in many years" (whatever that means), Klein argues that Greg Boyle "epitomizes the kind of *ill-conceptualized reinforcement of gang life and cohesiveness* that I have found to exist in almost every traditional gang city."[8]

This is the same line drawn by law enforcement against any community-based alternatives to the gang problem. LAPD Captain Bob Medina told the *Times* that because of Greg's pampering approach to gang members, "the way some of these people have been brought up, that would make it easier for them to go out and break the law. These people understand only one thing, and that's force."[9]

For Malcolm Klein, whose research and writings are more complex than the orthodox suppression view, the alternative to "recognizing and legitimizing" is a programmatic approach aimed at breaking up gang cohesion through such methods as sanctions, punishment, and successful law enforcement. He apparently bases this conclusion on a singular field study he directed in the late sixties on the Clover gang in Los Angeles (which, for confidentiality reasons, he calls "Ladino Hills"). The approach avoided any group meetings with homies, instead focusing on *individual* tutoring, counseling, and job placement in order to cause withdrawals from the gang. Klein claimed a reduction of gang cohesiveness and delinquency, especially in the first six months.[10] The findings were contested by other researchers,[11] and Klein himself acknowledged that "several years later, the [Clover] gang regenerated themselves, and [Clover] reassumed its pre-project gang-ridden character."[12] He blamed the community for a lack of sustained effort to change its structures. His view had hardened that any form of outreach that "recognized" gang membership was bound to intensify gang cohesion.

This debate was not limited to Los Angeles-based gang experts, but was rooted in conflicting views going back at least a century, when Jacob Riis wrote that gangs were "a distemper of the slums, a friend come to tell us that something has gone amiss in our social life."[13] Instead of defining the gang problem as primarily a criminal one, many early sociologists tried to analyze what had "gone amiss" that fostered slums. This notion was embraced in the 1920s by a so-called "Chicago school" of sociologists, most notably symbolized by Frederic Thrasher, author of a 1927 classic, *The Gang: A Study of 1,313 Gangs in Chicago*.[14] The Thrasher tradition would be eclipsed eventually by the criminalized definition of the gang problem, but it would strongly influence later authors I have mentioned, including James Diego Vigil, Joan Moore, and David Brotherton.

To search for the roots and results of the Thrasher tradition, I decided to visit Chicago neighborhoods in 2002, one of the nation's three largest centers of gang organization and violence. Was the Thrasher tradition alive or smothered? What had come of it? Was someone like Greg Boyle the descendant of a lost tradition, or a one-of-a-kind, uniquely committed aberration? As an additional agenda, I was interested in studying a model "community policing" project in Chicago's Little Village immigrant barrio, which was being recommended by gang experts as a solution for Greg Boyle's still-violent Boyle Heights community.

Frederic Thrasher and Chicago: www.gangstertour.com

Shortly after arriving in Chicago, I was startled to see a tourist bus rolling down the street, filled with white tourists listening to a guide dressed as a gangster from the twenties. The tour company was called "Untouchable Tours," www.gangstertour.com, and promised visits to "the old gangster hot spots," with stories of "the exploits of Capone, Moran, Dillinger and the rest of the boys," an experience

of "excitement" as "we cruise the city in search of the old hoodlum haunts, broth-
els, gambling dens and sites of gangland shootouts." This was "the city Capone
made famous," as the tour brochure promised, the city that Frederic Thrasher studied, but it had changed profoundly. Thrasher's 1927 work contained thousands of
interviews with white ethnics—Irish, German, Polish, Jewish, and Italian—while
also noting Negro gangs that were forming after the 1919 race riots in which thirty-
eight people were killed. These modern tourists I was watching were buying tickets to revel in past white ethnic nostalgia, while the current gangs existing outside
the bus windows were African American and Latino, including thousands of new
immigrants. There was a clue here to the unique gang nature of Chicago. From the
era of Al Capone forward there existed an uninterrupted urban culture of organized criminal gangs that left a deep footprint on the city's politics, construction con-
tracting, policing, and social image that marked Chicago different from any other
city. The hierarchal black and brown gang structures that arose from the 1960s
through the 1990s were modeled after what came before.

First of all, where did the white ethnic gangs of Thrasher's era go? Some disappeared into America's violent Western frontier, with outlaw heroes like Billy the
Kid (1859–1881), Butch Cassidy (1866–1908), John Wesley Hardin (1853–1895),
and Jesse James (1847–1882).[15] The white ethnic gangs took root in New York City,
Chicago, and other urban areas in the mid-nineteenth century, lasting into the
twentieth century. Like those who would follow, they arose from ethnic oppression, brutality, and chaotic immigrant upheavals. They inhabited swarming tenements and back alleys, filled the jails and mental hospitals, were characterized as
"armies of the street" and many, as in the scenario recommended today by many
neoconservatives, were shipped off to reformatories to be raised as Protestants.
What was achieved, according to one account, was "to breed successive generations of professional toughs."[16] As histories of the Jews, Irish, and Italians amply
reveal, these early white ethnic gangs were considered violent, remorseless, incorrigible, prone to alcoholism, prostitution, gambling, and countless other vices.[17]
Rich Cohen writes that "prosecutors did not even see the gangsters as men. They
saw them as strangers, a foreign presence, the cause of every social evil; it's the
way many white people now see black and Hispanic gangs."[18] A gang member in

those days was scorned by polite society as typically "a Catholic or Jewish immigrant who has broken from his slum to ravish a Protestant countryside."[19]

Not that they were misunderstood angels. One of my favorite Irish keepsakes is a T-shirt from a New York tenement museum showing a nineteenth-century Irishman with a bandaged nose and an itemized list of the rates charged for committing mayhem: from $10 for "nose and jaw broke" to "$100 and up" for "doing the big one" (a killing). In a book that fondly remembers "tough Jews" like the big-shot gambler, bootlegger, and Murder Inc., boss Arnold Rothstein, Cohen writes that "the boys" received $250 weekly retainers for gang-ordered killings.[20] So demonized were the Irish gangs that the "paddy wagon" was named after them. The Sicilians were described by Henner Hess in ways similar to the Crips and Bloods:

> The mass of Sicilians who have to suffer humiliations day after day without a chance of revenge see a Mafioso who has created for himself this chance of revenge or whom no one even dares offend any longer, as the male ideal . . . [21]

Modern media mythology romanticizes this white ethnic gangster tradition while largely ignoring the parallels with today's gang violence crisis. Many of the same Americans who enjoy watching *The Sopranos, The Godfather, Once Upon a Time in America, Bugsey,* or *The Gangs of New York* are likely to be the first to vote for politicians promising to suppress or deport Crips, Bloods, 18th Streeters, and Latin Kings. Many beneficiaries of yesteryear's bootlegger generation adamantly support the current war on drugs, blindly ignoring the parallels between the eras of booze and crack. The achievement of lace curtain, middle-class respectability seems to require a forgetful distancing from white ethnic gangster roots. As Cohen remarks, "the Jewish gangster has been forgotten because no one wants to remember him, because my grandmother won't talk about him, because he is someone to be ashamed of."[22] The disconnected amnesia is tragic, since a proper viewing of these romanticized gangster films might serve as the basis for increased understanding of the similarities of gangs across time and ethnicity. For example, Martin Scorcese's *The Gangs of New York* was described as presenting a "fairly radical notion" of

American history by the *New York Times* reviewer.[23] Instead of the neoconservatives' "usual triumphal story of moral progress and enlightenment," he wrote, the
film suggests that a vulgar urban working class battled its way into respectability
and power. They were not invited to the table by the powers that be.

That is exactly right, though little acknowledged in conventional history. The
nineteenth-century white ethnic underclass eventually became middle class by
acquiring tools of power ranging from community activism to labor organizing,
electoral politics, *and criminal activity*. The forces and coalitions leading to the
New Deal lifted the immigrant tide. To take the Irish as an example, by the time
of World War I, most male Irish-American workers were skilled workers "disproportionately concentrated in the best-paid, most highly unionized trades," a
huge shift from 1850, when the vast majority were locked in unemployment or
unskilled and semi-skilled jobs.[24] Eventually, they could leave the gangster past
behind as they became blue-collar managers, plumbers, steamfitters, and boilers.
In Thrasher's phrase, the old gangs "succumbed, for the most part, to the Industrial Revolution."[25] Herbert Asbury wrote in the twenties of "the passing of the
gangster," since "improved social, economic and educational conditions have
lessened the number of recruits, and the organized gangs have been clubbed out
of existence by the police."[26] By the era of the New Deal, the majority of white
ethnic immigrants were assimilated or forced themselves into the economy and
civic life in sufficient numbers to drain the mass basis of the gang appeal, leaving
a smaller number who were permanently enmeshed in professional, vertically organized criminal syndicates. In Cohen's words,

> As Europe ran out of Jews to send across the ocean, as the ghettos dried up, as the
> universities and medical schools and law firms filled with Jews, as the Jewish people
> prospered in America, the gangsters would fade even from memory . . .
> The ghettos broke up and the Jews left, so who was there left to recruit?[27]

The significant difference between the white ethnic gang era and the present
one of Crips, Bloods, Latin Kings, Blackstone Rangers, etc., is that *there is no sign
of a New Deal for this generation's alienated young people of color*. There is no industrial

revolution for today's homeboys to "succumb to," in Thrasher's terms. The gang cycle thus repeats itself without the exit once provided by expanded economic and political opportunity.

In New York, and especially in Chicago, the organized syndicates became entrenched in government and the economy until they declined with age, racketeering indictments, and prison sentences. In Chicago, as we shall see, the culture of the Capone era lasted through the mayoral regime of Richard J. Daley, who began his own career as an Irish gangster.[28] Daley, who dominated the Democratic machine and the city from 1955 until his death in 1976, was the president of an Irish gang known as "the Hamburg Athletic Association," which "reportedly played a large role in a four-day race riot in 1919," according to a *Chicago Sun-Times* report.[29] At the time, Chicago's black population had doubled in only five years with migrants from the South. In July 1919, white gangs lynched two black men as they left work, and signs urging "get all the niggers" were posted widely. During the subsequent rioting, of thirty-eight people killed, twenty-three were black and, of those, twenty-one were lynched and one was stoned to death while a white photographer recorded the scene.[30] Testifying about the role of white gangs to an investigative commission, a municipal judge said "they seemed to think that they had a sort of protection which entitled them to go out and assault anybody. When the race riots occurred it gave them something to satiate the desire to inflict their evil propensities on others."[31] In that sobering context, Richard Daley's role could not be explained simply as youthful exuberance, but it was officially ignored in Chicago's subsequent history.

Those 1920s gangs, according to Thrasher's firsthand interviews, supplied political muscle for their ward bosses, corrupting the city's political structure during Prohibition when beer-running, gun-toting gangs were distributing $1 million yearly to "fix the law" with immunity.[32] Between November 1924 and October 1926 (the dates of two sensational gangland assassinations), 115 died in Chicago's gang wars.

These criminal rings continue to exist today either in the burgeoning underground drug economy or indirectly, having laundered their ill-gotten riches into more ambiguous but respectable white-collar niches in business, politics, labor, and entertainment. Their roots in, and appeal to, their original underlying ethnic culture has waned severely. Even old-line Mafia members decry the "lack of values of today's more modern criminals" in such businesses as the international drug trade.[33] They are properly seen as criminal organizations rather than ethnic street gangs rooted in poverty, discrimination, and immigrant identity problems.[34] This phenomenon of organized crime was strangely ignored by FBI director J. Edgar Hoover, who regularly claimed "there is no Mafia in America," until 1957, when two rural cops in upstate New York happened upon a clandestine gathering of sixty dons from across the country.[35] Then, busting organized crime became a formative crusade for Rudolph Giuliani, first as a U.S. attorney in New York (1983–89), and again as mayor of the city in the nineties. Like other prosecutors, Giuliani defined the mafia as a hierarchal "racketeering enterprise," and utilized the RICO laws to take down several organized crime families.[36] But the grave mistake made by those in Giuliani's mode was to assume—even insist—that African American and Latino street gangs in the nineties were of the same mold as the bureaucratic dons of an earlier age. As Greg Boyle frequently pointed out to Chief Bratton, Los Angeles street gangs are "*dis*organized crime." While some blacks, Latinos, and Asians have made sporadic attempts to form modern mafia-style hierarchies, they have mostly failed to transcend the inherent localism, set-tripping, and fragmentation of homeboy culture. A recent authoritative police survey showed that the most common gangs reported were composed of delinquents engaged in vandalism, and that even more serious gangs most often lack clear, hierarchal structures.[37] Most are organic rather than bureaucratic organizations, adapting to community processes. Typically, the organic-adaptive model allows for individual as well as group goals, exhibits a diffuse leadership, a variety of subgroups, and a "continuity despite the absence of hierarchy."[38]

If there is an exception where the bureaucratic model superceded the more organic one, it arose most notably in Chicago, where many street gangs followed the organized mob model glamorized and inherited through the local civic culture.

When Thrasher was writing in the twenties, he was unaware that the patterns he described would be repeated far into the future in the Blackstone Nation, the

Gangster Disciples, and the Conservative Vice Lords, and among new Latino gangs like the Latin Kings and the Latin Disciples. But Thrasher's interviews and analyses laid the predictive foundations for a permanent gang subculture across lines of race and ethnicity.

While his book is brimming with examples of gang mayhem, Thrasher rejected the circular argument that criminal subcultures themselves breed crime and violence. While the gang for Thrasher was an important contributing agency in the *spread* of crime, it was not the *cause*. Wiping out gangs, even if it was possible, would not "remove the unwholesome influences with which the boy in gangland is surrounded."[39] The cause of crime for Thrasher lay in quite specific socioeconomic conditions of poor neighborhoods. Gangs arose in what he called the "interstices" of society, gaps where the fabric of order was weakest (like the interstitial tissues between our ribs). Such an interstitial area in Chicago was the "belt of poverty" consisting of dilapidated housing, junkyards, railroad tracks, and back alleys, running as a broken border between orderly residential neighborhoods and the guarded downtown Loop. Immigrant communities, too, were interstitial in their very nature, constantly changing inhabitants and cultural patterns. Thrasher also understood youth as experiencing an internal crisis during the interstitial period called adolescence: "The gang appears to be an interstitial group, a manifestation of the period of readjustment between childhood and maturity."[40] The gang "is a spontaneous attempt on the part of boys to create a society of their own where none adequate to their needs exists."[41] His interviews showed then (as now) that marriage and family are among the "most potent causes for the disintegration" of gangs.[42] In these writings, he focused on the Chicago *street gang*, distinguishing it from *organized crime*, which was more structured and without the spirit of the younger gangs.

Where today's neoconservative orthodoxy cannot admit the positive appeal of gangs to youth, preferring instead to stress the attraction of immoral addictions or pathologies, Thrasher recognized a romantic dimension that continues today. He wrote that in the "dreary and repellent" environment of the slum, there was a "vivid and fascinating" dimension, a self-made world that was distinctly their own—far removed from the humdrum existence of the average citizen . . . Here are comedy and tragedy. Here is melodrama which excels the recurrent "thrillers" at the downtown theaters. Here are unvarnished emotions. Here also is a primitive democracy . . . The gang, in short, is *life*, often rough and untamed, yet rich in elemental social processes significant to the student of society and human nature.

What boys get out of the association that they do not get otherwise under the conditions that adult society imposes is the thrill and zest of participation . . . in hunting, capture, conflict, flight and escape.[43]

Internally, Thrasher described the gang culture as a struggle for recognition, which offered "the underprivileged boy probably his best opportunity to acquire status and hence it plays an essential part in the development of his personality."[44] The gang offers a "substitute for what society fails to give . . . it fills a gap and affords an escape."

In the last few pages of his work, Thrasher proposed a blueprint for preventing gang violence. Like Vigil among others in later decades, he began by cataloging the failure of those institutions most responsible for the socializing of youth. The "freedom that leads to ganging" is born in the matrix of "inadequate family life; poverty; deteriorating neighborhoods; and ineffective religion, education and recreation."[45] He includes "any condition in *family* life which promotes neglect or repression of any of its boy members"; "the failure of present-day *religion* to penetrate in any real and vital way"; the type of *schooling* which does not interest the boy or provide for a satisfying organization of his lively energies." On the role of policing in the formation of gang identity, Thrasher sounded entirely up to date:

As a rule, policemen assume that the gang must be suppressed—must be broken up. They fail to understand that boyish energies, like tics, suppressed at one place are sure to break out at some other. And when the breaking up of the gang has been accomplished, there is usually no attempt to provide substitute activities for the boys. Under ordinary circumstances, then, the "cop" becomes the natural enemy of the gang.[46]

Placing boys in penal institutions, he believed, resulted in deterrence in some cases, but was "evading the real problem."[47] "If acquiring a court record, or being 'put away' in an institution, gives him prestige in the gang, society is simply promoting his rise to power."[48] His critique of social agencies extended from juvenile halls to do-good organizations like boys' clubs that enrolled at-risk boys but "never had a conscious attempt to enlist the potential [hardcore] delinquent as such."[49]

He also lamented the cost-effectiveness of policing and prison strategies, which then was estimated at $5 billion, "a staggering load for any country when we reflect that the direct cost of education is only about one billion dollars a year."[50]

In the earliest reference to a gang peace process I have found in the literature, Thrasher proposed that "were I to think only of the boys and their welfare, *I would spend a large part of the money expended on institutions in hiring 'Boy Men' to cover the city and spend their entire time with the gangs.*"[51] His interview notes describe an effort to "negotiate a treaty of peace," actually signed by two leaders, after which "the warfare was ended and gradually the boys learned to mingle and even to fraternize with their former enemies."[52]

Thrasher's program for preventing gang crime needs updating and expansion, but the core principles are sound and remain the road not followed. *"The problem of redirecting the gang turns out to be one of giving life meaning for the boy,"*[53] primarily by offering a role in the wider scheme of things from which they are excluded. Thrasher stood for a "radical departure" from traditional social work, advocating the reorganization of the slum community itself rather than trying to adjust individuals to their oppressive surroundings. The public school system, he believed, was strategically located to perform a coordination function. Next, he insisted on a social science research approach based on careful interviews with hardcore youth themselves, because "it is just the child who is missed by the methods of the ordinary leisure-time [after school] program, or who drops out of the wholesome group or institution, or who is shunted from one agency to another without any consistent plan for his adjustment or attempt at follow up, who so often is the pre-delinquent or the candidate for a criminal career."[54] He suggested that new social agencies would need to be created beyond "the community chest and the status quo." Finally, Thrasher thought it crucial that the public be informed and mobilized in support of such a violence prevention emphasis. But it was much easier to excite the public about catching notorious "public enemies" than preventing crime in the first place with programs based on a public health model of preventing disease.

One can quarrel with certain of Thrasher's methodologies or observations. Modern social science is far more "scientific" in approach. Certain lessons may be out of date; for example, transforming a gang with a name like the "Holy Terrors" into a Boy Scout troop seems farfetched today, but it actually happened in Thrasher's time. The crucial point for Thrasher was that breaking up gangs shattered the social world of the gang member and required an immediate substitute, "not of the artificial type found in an institution, but one which will provide for a redirection of his energies in the habitat in which he must live."[55] It was precisely this strategy that Greg Boyle was trying to implement seventy-five years later in Los Angeles.

Power to the People: Community-Based Antipoverty Movements

Thrasher's vision, and that of the Chicago school of sociology, was manifested, at least indirectly, in a subsequent range of violence-prevention movements that I characterize as *community based* to distinguish them from the law enforcement model. The spectrum of these approaches included social work by "detached workers" (jargon for working in the streets instead of offices), antipoverty programs, and more radical attempts to empower and transform ghettos and barrios symbolized by the Panthers, Lords, and Kings.

The Newark Community Union Project (NCUP), where I worked in the mid-sixties, was initiated by student organizers who lived in the ghetto, knocked on doors, recruited from street corners and pool halls, and organized local people to fight for a controlling voice in programs affecting their community. Shortly after our work began, the federal government's war-on-poverty organization, the Office of Economic Opportunity (OEO), installed offices and service programs in the very precincts where NCUP was alive.

In retrospect, the early Kennedy administration acted on an important insight into what then was called "juvenile delinquency," gleaned from the research of Lloyd Ohlin and Richard Cloward, sociologists in the Thrasher tradition. Their 1960 *Delinquency and Opportunity* argued that delinquency arose from blocked opportunities for the poor to achieve middle-class security. Robert Kennedy believed that "delinquency" described a misguided response to poverty and discrimination. Ohlin went to work at the New Frontier's Office of Juvenile Delinquency, which spawned many of the antipoverty programs initiatives,[56] often derived from the Chicago school tradition.

There was some overlap among young, idealistic, officially sponsored Volunteers in Service to America (VISTA) volunteers and the occasional community leader who was hired or appointed to the official agency, but a tension existed from the beginning. The official poverty program supported only the "maximum *feasible* participation of the poor," meaning an advisory role that we felt was tokenism. NCUP, like other activist groups around the country, tried to elect genuine grassroots leaders to the poverty program's community advisory boards, believing their voices at least might become heard in the citywide process. We especially favored bringing street-corner hustlers, ex-cons, and school dropouts—the hardcore of the time—into the process. They were articulate and knowledgeable in the way of the streets. This made public officials—from politicians to the white-collar professionals of the antipoverty agency—distinctly uncomfortable, and apparently wasn't "feasible." Despite our best efforts, the contradictions between the two approaches proved irreconcilable. At bottom, the street and community activists wanted to change power arrangements—over control of services, levels of rents, policing standards, and so forth—while the official poverty program served more like a buffer between the restive community and the civic elites who ultimately kept control of things. It became clear that the "detached workers" in the official war on poverty actually were "attached"—to the local power centers. There were exceptions, for example, among the OEO-funded attorneys who engaged in courtroom battles with landlords, police, and welfare offices. But these disputes nearly always involved individual grievances rather than class actions affecting thousands and textured lawyers as surrogates for the poor instead of mobilization. We viewed the antipoverty programs as selecting, managing, and co-opting those "respectable" leaders of the poor, while at the same time undermining any basis for independent efforts, especially by more militant or nationalist community groups.

While we were trying to push the antipoverty program to have a real impact, there were stronger forces who felt it went too far. Even in its mild form, the war on poverty legitimized the idea that the status quo was unacceptable, that issues of poverty and powerlessness needed to be addressed, that even militant voices deserved a hearing. In places like Chicago, New York, and Los Angeles, public funds were occasionally expended on gang members, or former gang members, claiming a desire to "represent" within the system. Those experiments were squelched, and followed by a retrenchment that began in the seventies and has continued ever since. The trajectory of policy analysis moved away from Thrasher and toward defining gang membership as *solely* and *exclusively* evidence of sociopathic and criminal behavior. This approach downplayed the significance of any differences among gang members, assuming the peewee and the shot-caller shared the same propensities. It also discredited the argument for community approaches that might steer gang members, or a faction of them, in safer and ultimately non-criminal directions. Not that Thrasher had ignored the criminal dimension to his street gangs, but he viewed the gang in a socioeconomic context. The new, harder emphasis was that the underlying cause of gang formation was not to cope with inner-city pressures but to create criminal conspiracies. The corollary of this view was a disparagement of anyone like Greg Boyle who reached out to those tainted by their association with the streets. The gang member became a leper, an untouchable.

Gangs are contradictory and complicated, I am arguing—not one-dimensional, as in the super-predator model. Over time, some elements in a gang will conclude that their energies are mischanneled, and they will move in the direction of militant politics, to demand a share of whatever resources the system provides. At the other extreme, a few will seek to emulate the legend of La Cosa Nostra, and try to form a super-gang organized on the lines of a crime syndicate. In between are those who think they can have it both ways who are transitioning from the criminal to the political, or who simply want to focus on work and family beyond the gang.

There is a further complexity that needs to be acknowledged here. In his *American Project,* based on a decade's research in Chicago's Robert Taylor Homes, Sudhir Alladi Venkatesh describes an almost hopeless effort by public housing tenants to navigate between drug-dealing gangs and overzealous police. Venkatesh's tenants sometimes reported a feeling that the local gang was not "a foreign invader but a distortion of collective youth energies that carried the potential for social change."[57] Later in the nineties, he said, the public housing residents "witnessed the metamorphosis of the gang from a grass-roots youth organization that had always been delinquent but on the precipice of being a potential resource base, to an organized criminal enterprise with diminishing signs of promise."[58] These fluid attitudes exactly reflected the ambiguous nature of gang involvement. But Venkatesh disparages the efforts of key organizers in the projects to work with gangs on truces and community projects, because the trade-off allowed the gang members to maintain their drugs business. On the other hand, Venkatesh recognizes that Operation Clean Sweep and other draconian police measures were "terribly ineffective" in deterring gangs or drugs. My own sense is blame lay in the failure to intervene with jobs at the earlier stage, and that the author may underestimate the value of lives saved because of his frustration with the persistence of the drug economy.

Obviously, law enforcement, government agencies, and the business sector exercise enormous influence over these choices and directions homies may take. By shutting all doors for gang members to legitimate opportunity until they effectively renounce their affiliations, the administrators of the system make a transition to politics harder. In this view, law and order must be established first, and then and only then should jobs and opportunity be offered.[59] If I had not been hearing this promise for forty years, I might have more patience with it. But the promise was broken long ago, and the crisis only worsens.

The real alternative would be to target law enforcement strategies more narrowly on the most dangerous crimes committed by a tiny fraction of gang members, and flood the inner city with jobs and social programs like community-based mental health centers instead of with CRASH units. To be serious, such an effort would have to provide economic opportunities comparable or better than the wages available in the underground economy.

A more radical option, thus far politically unacceptable, would be to largely decriminalize and rechannel the drug economy into a public health approach because of the violence-prevention benefits. There is no question that white ethnic gang violence in Thrasher's time was directly related to Prohibition, and the evidence points to sharp reductions in violence when alcohol was legalized in the thirties. Drugs could be similarly decriminalized and taxed, with revenues going into treatment programs instead of promotional advertising. The future of the underground economy is a matter of government policy, not a reflection of the human condition. With or without the illegal drug economy, government must ensure that jobs with meaningful wages are available in the inner city, to those seeking a transition from the economic opportunities now available through the gang culture. Current policies offer too few opportunities comparable to those in the drug economy, and the moralized crusade against gangs and drugs has proven useless.

A good example of these dynamics in action is found in the history of gangs and politics in Chicago that evolved after the Thrasher era. The street gangs he described in the twenties faded away after Prohibition and the Great Depression. But the organized gangsters who defined their subculture as a business were assimilated into the Democratic political machine, where they became unintended role models for gangs like the Blackstone Rangers, the Gangster Disciples, and the Conservative Vice Lords in the sixties. One such example was the evolution of Chicago's Second Ward Democratic machine, associated for thirty years (1942–71) with the leadership of the late U.S. congressman William Dawson.[60] Dawson and his brother Julian grew up under Jim Crow, and served during World War I in segregated African American units under French command. The atmosphere of the time was summed up in a pamphlet authored by U.S. military officials and passed to the French, under the title *Secret Information Concerning Negro Troops*. The U.S. military was concerned that the African American troops would not only learn the skills of warfare but would experience sexual freedom with French (white) women. The *Secret Information* document advised the French that black men were "inferior" despite being American citizens, and that "the vices of the Negro are a constant menace to the American who has to repress them sternly."[61]

This brutal worldview was reinforced when the brothers returned to a Chicago that exploded in race riots and lynchings. While Julian went on to a medical career, William was drawn to politics, which in those days for African Americans meant the Republican Party. He finally became a Democrat in the New Deal, and headed the organization in the Second Ward. Chicago was always a more highly organized city than most, with a tightly woven political culture. The Democratic machine soon cemented a mutually beneficial deal protecting the (Italian) mafia, which controlled numbers, jitney cabs, and rackets generally on Chicago's South Side. The arrangement remained in place through Dawson's rise to the House of Representatives, where he chaired the powerful Government Operations committee for decades. When he died in 1971, the franchise for the Second Ward political machine was sold to his successor for $10,000 and a white woman.[62]

This was the world in which the African American gangs of the sixties grew up. Ethnic politics and crime, gangsters and politicians—all fused in a monolithic web. Any reformist models based on clean, progressive politics were crushed or marginalized. The lessons were not lost on ambitious, frustrated youth growing up in the ghetto. "The black gangs [of the sixties] had all sorts of models" to draw on, says the late congressman's nephew, Michael Dawson, now a Harvard professor specializing in the history of African American politics.[63]

The Black P. Stone Nation

Named after Blackstone Street on the South Side, but also recalling a holy black stone in Mecca,[64] they grew into a powerful gang by every definition of the word, on the South Side of Chicago. There they found constructive engagement from the Reverend John Fry, of the very white middle-class First Presbyterian Church, who later told the story in his 1973 memoir, *Locked Out Americans*.[65] Like Greg

Boyle, or Luis Barrios in New York City, Fry became immersed in the gang world unexpectedly, simply by implementing his religious beliefs in the ghetto outside the church's walls.

Born in the streets and juvenile halls, the Blackstones grew phenomenally between 1965 and 1967, reaching an estimated level of 3,000. Fry viewed them as modern Stagolees, "locked out" from the gains and promises of the civil rights movement:

> Ordinary analysis makes no provision for the lower-than-poor, lumping poor and lower-than-poor together in the sloppy category "black poor." The lower-than-poor know there is a great difference. They suffer more than the regular black poor and they are defiant, too. They resist the authorities—*"give 'em fits."* As though in prison they struggle against their guards. They are alien-natives whose resistance spooks regular Americans and their police.[66]

Reverend Fry recognized that the Blackstones were a kind of "nation" precisely because of their consciousness of being permanently locked out. In the wake of the civil rights movement, the white authorities opened the doors to icons like the Student Nonviolent Coordinating Committee's (SNCC) Julian Bond—light-skinned, handsome, educated, aristocratic—which only widened the gap for those left behind in the "jungles." This was no fault of Julian Bond, whose eloquence and activism over four decades has been extraordinary, but evidence for those like the Blackstones that "the system" would never change. What was progress for the Julian Bonds meant that the Stones were left further behind. Fry also realized that resistance by the Blackstones would have a *physical and psychic* dimension because their *bodies* were the constant target of harassment, beatings, and lock-downs by authorities activated by fear. The Blackstones could (and would) pass out leaflets, sign petitions, offer testimony, and register voters, but their presence would never be the same as conventional protest. Their unbowed existence, their power chants, salutes, cadence, and style said it all. They were modern runaways, and they expressed the needs of other young men like themselves. The slogan STONE RUN IT in huge block letters on hundreds of ghetto walls was more than unnerving to police and properly elected representatives. If they couldn't "run it," they would "give 'em fits."

The Nation had a positive program, however, the kind of program that always confounded the authorities. They wanted to build power from the streets to access the system for jobs and police reform. They frequently took direct action, most notably shutting down white-dominated construction sites until the trades agreed to enroll more black people. They tried to open a restaurant but were closed down by city inspectors. They organized thousands of gang members to march for peace after the assassination of Martin Luther King. They carried out a successful "no vote" campaign in the 1968 elections, denying the Democratic machine some 30,000 votes from its customary totals in black precincts. But their most important breakthrough, abetted by Reverend Fry and the white liberals at First Church, was to obtain federal funding directly for job-training programs through The Woodlawn Organization (TWO), one of the foremost antipoverty projects in the country. The sum—nearly $1 million—was huge for the time, scandalous and visible.

The job-training program was based on the strategy of using Blackstones and Disciples in a three-stage process of creating legal employment opportunities for hardcore youth. Enrollees were paid $45 per week. In stage one, they received an individually tailored upgrade of math and literacy skills. Second, they would enter a subsidized on-site training program. Finally, the trainee would move into the actual job. At all stages the supervisors would be Rangers and Disciples, the only ones able to make trainees show up at seven every morning, rule out lollygagging, and protect the trainees against disrespect by bosses and administrators. The city establishment was opposed, however, because of the status that inevitably would accrue to the gangs. The program was funded, then attacked and finally shelved. The police gang units accused the Rangers of arranging kickbacks with public funds, eventually bringing 132 indictments against twenty-four Stones. What actually happened, Reverend Fry explained, was that the Stones often would sign one another's names to their paychecks—"not an uncommon occurrence among people without identification (or verifiable names presently being used), hence without means to get checks cashed."[67] The case finally ended with three convictions of "conspiring" to defraud. The long-term impact of the police campaign against the federal funding, Reverend Fry pointed out, was to push the Stones back into the criminal economy of the street.

> A crime-fighting policy which drives people to criminal work seems at best ill-thought out and perhaps demonic.[68]

On May 9, 1969, Mayor Richard Daley and State's Attorney Edward Hanrahan declared "war on criminal gangs in Chicago," especially targeting the Blackstone Nation.[69] From that point forward in the public mind, writes Reverend Fry, the Blackstones were no longer symbolic of a crisis of the outcasts, but reframed exclusively as an organized criminal syndicate. Police charts announced that between 1965 and 1969, there were 290 gang-related deaths, 150 in 1967 alone. U.S. Senate hearings chaired by Senator John McClellan commenced in the same period.[70] But Reverend Fry was having none of it. He knew more than most civic leaders about the suicidal and self-destructive violence outside the privileged sanctuary of his church. But he noted the difference between the city's official "war" and other criminal justice processes. The Blackstones and other street gangs were accused and convicted through a press conference. None of the crimes announced at the press conference were "alleged." They already were accepted as matters of fact, the police version morphed into guilty verdicts. There was no recognition of due process, defendant's rights, the need to take further testimony, or permit cross-examination. In the course of time, dozens of Rangers would be taken down. Their charismatic and/or megalomaniac leader, Jeff Fort, would eventually be charged with attempted murder, murder, kidnapping, aggravated assault, contempt of Congress, fraud, conspiracy to commit fraud, mob action, and disorderly conduct, a chain of events Reverend Fry said had begun in 1968 with a crime that the antigang units knew was committed by someone else.[71] Fort skipped bail, became a fugitive, was arrested again, and was put away for life.

As seen in the career of Jeff Fort, the Blackstones were afflicted deeply by the passionate personal ambitions and set rivalries that characterize the gang life, particularly against enemies known as the Disciples. Even as the Blackstones grew to unprecedented numbers, the war with the Disciples would rage, die down, and flare up again. In addition, the Blackstones remained anchored to the street culture, where illegalities were a way of life. However, there was no doubt of the aspiration *on the part of some* to ascend to a purely political level, though always on *their* terms, not those of the power structure. Some members of the so-called Main 21, the Stones' central committee, were talking politics with Fred Hampton and the Black Panther Party, while others were discussing a truce with the Gangster Disciples.[72] While the dynamics were fluid, Jeff Fort apparently remained on the antipolitical side of the split.[73]

No one in the Chicago power structure was encouraging the evolution of the more political and truce-oriented factions. On the contrary, federal OEO officials were sharply criticized for opening a channel to the Rangers. Chicago's respected journalist-historian, Mike Royko, touched on the real reason for the rigid and absolute exclusion of the Stones:

> The Black P. Stone Nation had grown to a looseknit membership of several thousand and was beginning to show signs of political and economic awareness and the use of such power. Black politicians were currying its favor, and private social agencies were making efforts to channel it into legitimate business activities.[74]

One of the more amazing chapters of this history came in 1966, when First Church hosted talks between the Blackstones, the police, and federal agents over disarmament of the gang itself. The Rangers were facing endless indictments and prison terms on weapons-related charges, while the official agencies had failed to actually seize and eliminate stashes of prohibited Ranger guns. The terms of the unusual agreement were these: the police would lift charges in cases against several Rangers, and deploy additional units to protect the disarmed Rangers against the nearby Disciples. The Rangers would turn in some 100 weapons. The federal agents would confiscate those required by federal law. The remaining weapons would be inventoried, and the Church would act as mediator and storehouse for

those weapons until the police promises were kept. The deal shortly unraveled
on the police side, ending in a raid by thirty police officers on the Church itself,
where they destroyed property and held over 100 people at gun point for two
hours. The firearm "arsenal" taken from the Church's safe turned out to be inop-
erable junk, since the feds already had confiscated the operable weapons. The
rest included knives, machetes, and a golf club. Forever after, however, the First
Presbyterian Church building would be known as "the arsenal for the Blackstone
Rangers."[75]

The final chapter for Jeff Fort was a shocking one. He traveled to Africa in 1987,
at a time of confrontation between the U.S. government and Muammar al-Qaddafi.
The Libyan leader nursed a grievance against the Reagan administration for its
bombing of Tripoli in April 1986 in which some forty Libyans were killed, including Qaddafi's infant adopted daughter in his home. Qaddafi already had embraced
Muhammad Ali, Elijah Muhammad, and the Chicago-based Nation of Islam (NOI)
with millions in donations to a Chicago mosque.[76] Louis Farrakhan was the person
who introduced Jeff Fort to the Libyans, according to one former Stone who is now
a PhD in Chicago. "It was really scandalous how the thing happened," according to
the source.[77] At the NOI's Savior's Day that year, Farrakhan arranged for Qaddafi to
speak via satellite. He brought several El Rukns onstage, calling them "my angels of
death." Farrakhan "was afraid that the government was about to get him like they
got Malcolm, and so he used the Blackstone Rangers as a shield. But they didn't
know what they were getting into," the former gang member believed.

It was also Farrakhan who connected Jeff Fort with Qaddafi. During a visit to
Libya, a heady experience for a Chicago street-gang leader, the Libyans presented
the Blackstones with a ground-to-air rocket launcher. Was this preparation for
terrorism or an unfocused ego trip? Did Jeff Fort plan to attack a target with the
single device or use it as threat in negotiations, say for the release of inmates? No
one has divulged the answer. The CIA followed the plot, intercepted the launcher
and installed a tracking device in place of the trigger. The Blackstones took it to
their headquarters on College Grove and Thirty-ninth, where federal agents arrested everyone and tore the place down.

Fort soon was indicted for making a $3 million arrangement with the Libyans that included the missile deal. It was the first case of "a curious and disturbing link between such gangs and terrorism," the London *Economist* worried.[78] If true, Fort's actions were indefensible, but one could also detect a misguided quest for power for the "locked out" ones to the very end. The crime was political, not just gangster thievery, but the authorities had no interest in nursing such interests by Fort or any other Blackstones. In the end they took their enemy down. Other indictments, exorbitant bail, incarceration, and the weight of internal strife fueled by informants weakened the Blackstone organization terminally.

When the Soviet Union collapsed not long after, the White House announced it would reassign 100 top FBI agents to the war against these Libyan-connected street gangs, apparently the closest substitute for the Communist Menace at hand.[79] According to Chicago's leading gang researcher, Irving Spergel, at the University of Chicago, it was an 18.5 percent jump in FBI manpower targeted at gangs, perhaps the largest re-allocation in FBI history.[80] This led to "the application of cartel thinking to street gangs," in the analysis of Klein, which defined street-gang networks as vertically organized, sophisticated conspiracies.[81] No longer were street gangs "a distemper of the slums, a friend come to tell us something has gone amiss in our social life," but now they were mafias to be destroyed at the top. Even where centralized networks existed, however, the prosecutors ignored that new ones would fill the vacuum left by the Jeff Forts. Toppling the gang leadership was a politician's desired victory but it did nothing to create alternatives to the thousands of homeboys selling drugs in a deindustrialized inner-city economy.

The Gangster Disciples

The vacuum created by the Blackstone prosecutions in the eighties was soon filled by the Blackstone's rivals, the Gangster Disciples. It led to the bloodiest gang war in the city's history, another cycle of violence ending in suppression. The Disciples emerged in the same era as the Blackstone Rangers, in the mid-sixties. One of its founders was Larry Hoover, a young man from small-town Mississippi with a speech defect. Despite imprisonment for murdering a drug dealer, Hoover managed to build a relatively organized structure with thousands of followers, which evolved from drugs and gangbanging toward political objectives by the early eighties. At that point, according to federal investigators, they were the nation's largest gang, with a drug network police claimed to be worth $100 million.[82] That was enough money to "go legit," apparently a frightening challenge to the power structure of the time.

A fascinating window into the Disciples is preserved in hundreds of letters written by Hoover while he was in prison.[83] In a familiar pattern, he came to understand the significance of education, business, and politics in making a transition from violent crime to the pacified mainstream. It was a story copied from the pages of white ethnic gang history. By 1982, the Disciples were registering Chicago voters while Hoover was denouncing rape and violence against women, promoting black heritage, and a style he called the "art of debate." The authorities became concerned by what they called Hoover's "cunning and guile" in attempting to introduce a "New Concept" that *they are not a gang.*[84] Rather than welcoming and testing the possible reform, investigators found "cult-like" communications from Hoover urging Disciples to show young people how they might "fall into this pit" (of gang violence) unless they took the vote seriously.

Hoover's personal agenda was to gain parole and return to the streets, a possibility thoroughly alarming to his jailers. In 1989, the U.S. Attorney's office initiated a racketeering investigation of the Gangster Disciples. The federal drug laws simplified the task. First, the prosecutors well knew, anyone convicted as the "leader" of a "continuing criminal enterprise" would be imprisoned for life, despite any evidence of personal maturing or change. Even better, a leader like Larry Hoover could be held responsible for any deeds of his most remote and lowly co-conspirators.[85] By 1992, the Disciples had formed what prosecutors called a "front group," known as United for Peace, that worked to end shootings in the Cabrini-Green housing projects. This, too, was a sinister sign of Hoover's alleged evolution. Even worse apparently, 5,000 Chicagoans signed petitions to free Larry Hoover, among them several aldermen, assistant school principals, and NAACP leaders. More shocking, the Disciples held a "Gala Illinois Family Day Voters' Picnic" in Kankakee County, Illinois, at which 10,000 people showed up. According to gang investigators, it was more subversion:

Think of it as a "Woodstock" for GD's [Gangster Disciples] . . . They partied, ate, listened to music, got high, milled with the throngs of GDs, took pictures of each other in their finest gang clothing, and made quite a picture as a massive gang gathering, perhaps the largest ever recorded in U.S. history.[86]

Next came what investigators labeled a major "coup" in the fall of 1993, an organization of a "peace treaty summit meeting" in Chicago involving Crips from all over the country. The investigators reported that it "was not a hard alliance to make [since] both Crips and GDs wear 'blue' colors."

Obviously, the ability of the GD gang to hold this conference and stage other *ludicrous* events in Chicago during the Fall of 1993 made them formidable.[87]

In August 1993, Hoover went before the parole board, which voted 8 to 0 against him. About the same time, the Feds moved their behind-the-scenes intelligence probe of the Disciples, code named Operation Headache, into high gear. Security badges worn by prison visitors to Larry Hoover were wired to eavesdrop some 8,000 private conversations. As the criminal hunt intensified, so did the Disciples' evolution into politics. In 1994 and 1995, they "fronted" candidates for city council, losing yet breaking out of isolation in the process. One of them, Wallace "Gator" Bradley, an alleged Disciples "enforcer" and leader of the "front group" "21st Century Vote," met with President Bill Clinton at a White House summit on gang violence. Rappers came to Larry Hoover's defense as Disciples marketed a popular "Ghetto Prisoner" jersey for $45 each. In March 1995, two university researchers testified at Larry Hoover's next parole hearing, particularly emphasizing a "gang *deactivation* program" the Disciples initiated at Englewood High School. Faced with this testimony, the board voted 10 to 0 against Hoover's parole. At that point, Larry Hoover issued a letter to his followers:

I learned this week, for the 13th time, that I have once again been denied parole. My thoughts, as they have been for years now, are of my family and of you. My sons, who have grown from infants to men during my imprisonment, and their mother, whose commitment has been unwavering, all continue to pay with me, the price for the terrible crime I committed, for which I am solely and fully responsible. They have been strong, as the families of tens of thousands of other black prisoners have been and must be strong every day of their lives.

But, brothers and sisters, we must have more than strength. We must have vision, too. We must see that we, ourselves, are the victims of the crimes that ignorance, poverty, hopelessness and drugs lead us to commit. We must see that, just as no man is an island, we all wear the shackles of the ghetto. We are all Ghetto Prisoners.

Our only hope for release is to use our strength and vision in the cause of change. Ignorance is our enemy; we must honor learning and those who learn. Poverty is our enemy; we must gather our pennies and dollars and use them in our own communities. Hopelessness is our enemy; we must organize and vote by the hundreds of thousands, to give voice to the voiceless. Drugs are our enemy, destroying many of us with the lure of profit, more of us with addiction, and still more with the crime that results; we must join our voices with those across the land, of whites and blacks, churchgoers and convicts, gays and straights—all who share the purpose of taking the profit out of drugs and ending the slaughter made easy by guns. Whether and when I will be released is beyond my control. Whatever my personal destiny may be, I will fight to strike the shackles that imprison us all.[88]

How could anyone not be convinced that this letter reflected an evolution of thinking, one that should be encouraged? For the investigators, the fact that it was "well-crafted" only meant that it "probably actually was written by one of his aides or attorneys," a surmise for which they offered no evidence. The "Ghetto Prisoner" store was only a "gimmick." The peace award ceremonies at the high school were "infamous." Apparently it was time to destroy the Disciples before they made any further claims of repentence and reform. On April 10, 1995, the IRS raided and destroyed the Ghetto Prisoner company, netting the headline "Cops Raid Businesses, Seek Gang Ties."[89] Six months later, on August 31, they indicted Hoover and thirty-eight other Disciples on charges of conspiring to operate a drug-dealing criminal enterprise for twenty-five years. Most, including Larry Hoover, were convicted and are serving life terms, Hoover in a "no human contact" supermax federal prison in Colorado.

The prosecution of the Disciples was seen as an overwhelming triumph by law enforcement officials. In particular, they cited a political victory in eliminating "the large-scale gang picnics of the GDs and their massive protests in Chicago's Loop." The Disciples' purported media credibility was eliminated as well: "We still see some of them craning their heads and necks toward the cameras at police brutality or excessive force social protests, but their ability to draw a 'news conference' is gone today."[90]

But while the Disciples were destabilized by the suppression of their leadership, the triumphant investigators acknowledged that "no programs of prevention and intervention were basically put into place in areas of buildings controlled by GDs at the time of the indictments."[91] As a matter of fact, in the years 1991–95, city officials slashed 30 percent of positions in health, human services, and housing.[92] In the law enforcement terminology of the time, it was all "weeding" and no "seeding." It didn't seem to matter. They admitted that the same cycle had occurred before, when the dismantling of Jeff Fort's Blackstone Rangers/El Rukn structure by federal prosecutors in the eighties "allowed the GDs to take control of the turf previously held by the El Rukns."[93] The prosecutors were concentrating on proving that the Jeff Forts and Larry Hoovers were not invincible, but in ways that made the continuing cycle inevitable.

So it was no surprise in 2002 that the *Chicago Sun-Times* reported once again on "powerful gang empires" in Chicago still making a minimum of hundreds of millions in the drug trade.[94] In that year alone, 249 deaths were linked to gang activity, up from 212 in 1995.[95] The Gangster Disciples' membership was estimated at 30,000, the same figure as 1996.[96] The press reported that gang members, in response to the prosecutions that took down their hierarchies, were engaged in even more bloody shoot-outs over power and turf, and no longer displayed the outward trappings of gang membership that attracted police patrols. Many former gang members were pushing for peaceful alternatives, saying that greed and guns (to protect the proceeds of greed) had become too dominant in the subculture in the eighties. Police and prosecutors condemned these gang peace activists as "strictly dirt."[97] And, no surprise to veteran observers of these wars that, in 1997, the Chicago Police Department's antigang unit was shut down in a scandal. One officer ran cocaine to Nashville, another operated a drug ring from Miami to

Chicago. Another dated one of Larry Hoover's closest operators. Another was a ranking member of the Conservative Vice Lords.[98]

The Conservative Vice Lords

In 2002, the History Channel produced a documentary on the history of street gangs, narrated by Roger Mudd, including an in-depth report on the Conservative Vice Lords, one of the oldest of Chicago's current generation of gangs, identified as having 20,000 members overall.[99] The Vice Lords arose in the late fifties in Lawndale and the West Side, where their membership was gauged at 8,000. Like the Blackstones, they, too, were born and molded in an instititution for delinquent boys, the Illinois State Training Center for Boys at St. Charles. Bonding there, they decided they should get their share of the American pie. As one told the History Channel, "The white man was normally the lord of all vice. We just took the title. We wanted to be the vice lords." After several years of experiencing violent rampages, however, the Vice Lords began to change in the late sixties. One of their leaders, Bobby Gore, then thirty-one, described the effort as entering the system to "see what we could do through political endeavors." They were joined by other supporters, including whites like David Dawley, a Dartmouth graduate who settled in Lawndale as a community organizer. Dawley told the History Channel, "We wanted community action, respecting the leadership of the Vice Lords, but changing the values." They soon obtained a $30,000 government grant, opened an ice-cream parlor, a boutique, an art studio, and a management-training program. The new Vice Lords suddenly were seen out cleaning up the broken glass and trash. They painted African heritage murals and opened a "hang in" storefront called the House of Lords for after-school programs. Crime soon declined in the Vice Lords' territory while it rose in other neighborhoods.

"It was working too good," Bobby Gore recalled. "We were making asses out of people who said we were no good and would never be nothing but gangbangers." Another Vice Lord said of the Chicago power structure, "They see us as a threat to *their* gang. It's like they'd rather have it be the haves and have-nots, because that's the only way their structure can continue." Then the roof fell in.

Part of the problem was that other gangs continued to cause chaos for the Vice Lords. The Vice Lords had difficulty themselves keeping their members—now over 10,000—under a common discipline. No one knew who the informants were (although law enforcement sources maintain that one-third of gang members can be turned into snitches or informants).[100] Bobby Gore spoke honestly and emotionally of the conflicts in meetings with other gang members: "What I'm saying, man, . . . the things we doin' to each other . . . we can't have it no more, you see, 'cuz our problem is not among ourselves." Later he would blame the Vice Lords for falling into a trap: "We screwed ourselves somewhat because if it hadn't been for guys doing dumb shit, excuse the expression, they wouldn't have the excuse to pounce on us like that."

Still, his pleas for peace, according to the History Channel, met with "some success" in 1969 when the Vice Lords and rival gangs "joined forces in a demonstration of unprecedented unity." But in November of that year, Gore himself was arrested for a murder he denied committing. "A fight broke out one night, they found I was in the area, and when they finished I was the one that committed the murder, 25 to 40 for something I didn't do." Gore made parole in 1979, ten years after he was locked up. But his incarceration caused a crumbling of the Vice Lords' attempted transformation. Dawley recalled those early years as "a spring blossoming, energetic, passionate." The History Channel concluded that the Vice Lords' campaign was "at least a partial success" because it "showed the city of Chicago that street gangs, if given resources and trust, could forge a positive life in an impoverished community." The effort, while strangled, never flickered out completely. In 1992, Sharif Willis, Minister for Justice of the Vice Lords, began to urge "that we had to be the ones to stop the violence because we are the ones governing these gangs."[101] For the time, the Vice Lords and other gangs came together in United for Peace. But a resumption of violence, by individual gang members unconnected to United for Peace, undermined the effort again. The process was up and down. As late as 2003, Willie Lloyd, another longtime Vice Lord leader (a chief of the Unknown Vice Lords), was drawing attention for his street work against drugs and for peace. When he spoke to students at DePaul University, a police official called it a "joke" and "obscene."[102] On the History Channel tape, an older Bobby Gore seemed to sum it up, lamenting that "the sad part about it is nobody believed us. We thought the Mayor would grab us and kiss us, you know what I mean, do everything in his power [because] we tried to work within that system."

But that was a profound misunderstanding of Mayor Richard J. Daley Sr. On the History Channel tape, the mayor is heard at a press conference decrying "the glorification of the gang structure" and declaring that "we want to set it back and reverse that kind of trend." The city's establishment, and much of the general public, seemed to have little interest in exploring the mayor's own history in this regard. But Mike Royko alluded in his 1972 book, *Boss*, to the fact that

> Daley had seen the same thing happen before. He recalled Regan's Colts, the Irish thieves and street fighters who became the most potent political force in neighboring Canaryville, and his own neighborhood's Hamburgs, who got their start in the same brawling way before turning to politics and eventually *launching his career*.[103]

Launching his career? Wasn't that worth some elaboration—or was it as far as a journalist could go in Daley's Chicago? I had heard these stories during the periods I spent in Chicago in the midst of the 1968 protests at the Democratic National Convention and the later trial of the "Chicago Conspiracy," which lasted from September 1969 through February 1970. The mayor's geographic roots were in what Thrasher called a "vast cultural frontier of Irish cliques" engaged in bitter territorial feuds around railroad tracks, el stations, canals, and alleys.[104] Modeled after New York's Tammany era, and unlike the later gangs of Los Angeles, in Chicago, alliances between gangs and political machines became commonplace during the political emergence of the Daley family. The Blackstone Rangers, the Gangster Disciples, and the Conservative Vice Lords were only continuing a local tradition, springing up in the permanent interstices of the city.

In 2003, University of Illinois researcher John Hagedorn wrote that Daley was a member of the Hamburgs as a seventeen-year-old teenager when the race riots broke out in 1919,[105] which left thirty-eight dead, and set in motion Chicago's first black gangs in self-defense. Daley became the president of the Hamburgs for fifteen years "and never commented on what he did during the 1919 race riots," Hagedorn wrote.

Later histories tended to rationalize gangs like the Hamburgs as mere "social clubs" vastly different from contemporary gangs. They just "smoked cigarettes and played cards," never engaging in criminal enterprises says one revisionist expert.[106] Nevertheless, the Hamburgs "reportedly" played a major role in the 1919 race riots, according to *Sun-Times* reporters and gang researcher Hagedorn.[107] In addition, there is the 1927 description of the Hamburgs by Thrasher, written long before the need for political sanitizing arose. According to Thrasher, the Hamburgs were involved in gang wars, not simply smoking and playing cards. As one of his informants said,

> Hamburg ran from Thirty-first to Fortieth. And south of Fortieth was Canaryville. The deadline was the old street-car tracks. No Hamburg lad, unless he thirsted for a fight, crossed the dead line. Vice versa for the Canaryvillians. But sometimes—on Saturday nights—there was mutual thirst. And the broken noses and black eyes that were seen the following Sunday were too numerous to count.[108]

Some of those Irish gang members grew up to be Chicago cops. One of them apparently grew up to be mayor. The office of the Hamburg Club remains at Thirty-fourth and Emerald, in Bridgeport, seven blocks from the old mayor's family home. It is a nondescript building with an American flag in the window. There is no sign on the door, but the trash cans are painted with the letters "HSC," for Hamburg Social Club. From those roots, the Daley machine grew into a permanent political machine, and as Hagedorn has written,

> It was the political threat posed by black gangs in the 1960s that led . . . Richard J. Daley to declare war on them in 1969.[109]

When Daley was elected mayor in 1955, the city's conservative establishment hinted at his shady past. The *Tribune* opined that "the political and social morals of the badlands are going, if not to dominate, then surely to have a powerful influence on [his] decisions."[110] Shortly after taking office, Daley took steps that the Blackstone Rangers, the Disciples, and Vice Lords could only dream about: he appointed a reputed gang chieftain as captain of the police precinct in the City's First Ward; removed the antimob head of the civil service commission; and disbanded the police intelligence unit then known as Scotland Yard.[111] He also took "vast sums of money from the hoodlum element," according to FBI files. He defended handing out jobs and contracts to mob-connected individuals, stating publicly that:

> I've been criticized for doing this, but I'll make no apologies. I'll always stand alongside the man with a criminal record when I think he deserves another chance.[112]

Needless to say, Daley never showed the same forgiving, kindly attitude when it came to funding of the Blackstone Rangers' job-training program, or the Vice Lords' drop-in centers. A charitable interpretation of Daley's attitude by journalist Gus Russo concluded that "Daley understood better than most that the sooner the 'hoods were promoted up the social ladder, the sooner they would disappear into the landscape" through a "process of ethnic succession."[113] But he held out no such ladder of opportunity for the city's black and Latino gangs. The Irish gangsters "matured out of their gangs into city jobs," Hagedorn believes, but Daley used his political power to design and build a "wall of highways and public housing to concentrate, segregate, and isolate African Americans."[114] These became the new "interstices" where black and Latino gangs were formed amidst a vast and excluded underground economy. The doors to upward mobility were closed because of racism and disenfranchisement. There was to be no "process of ethnic succession" for them. Instead, there was deindustrialization: Chicago lost over 400,000 manufacturing jobs in three decades, developments that "contributed to the surge in youth gangs and crime," according to *Scientific American*.[115]

Building a Contemporary Peace Process in Chicago

In the summer of 2002, I visited the offices of BUILD, a community group working on violence prevention in the west town barrio of Chicago. BUILD grew out of the "detached worker" programs in the late sixties. But when the federal government cut back funding, the BUILD activists turned to whatever meager private funding they could scavenge. The executive director now was Freddy Calixto, a Puerto Rican in his early forties, who started community organizing in 1976. Freddy's father had come to the States to work as a contract laborer on a Connecticut farm, then had journeyed back to Puerto Rico bringing word that he could only afford to take one son back to America. It was Freddy who migrated, leaving a brother behind. After moving to Chicago when he was very young, Freddy hung around a gang in Lincoln Park until the life became so crazy that his homeboys started talking about retaliating by shooting. That caused Freddy to start thinking, and ask basic questions like, "Didn't that brother grow up with us? Why should we shoot him?" He soon decided to leave the gang. "I got my violation. They formed a line and I got punched out. Two more guys left after me. Finally, the shooting didn't happen anyway."

Before becoming a community organizer himself, Freddy noticed some detached workers in his barrio. "What's he up to? I was always asking. I was curious. They didn't tell you that they were trying to change your life, 'cuz that just wouldn't work. They didn't say they were intentionally bringing in guys from different neighborhoods either. I grew up in Lincoln Park, where you had Cabrini Green, Latin Saints, Vice Lords, Kings, Young Lords, Gangster Disciples, you name it. The detached workers didn't say it, but they were trying to build relationships."

When he understood my questions, Freddy went to the bookshelf in his second-story office and pulled down a worn copy of Frederick Thrasher's 1927 book. He was a follower. (I had seen copies on Nane Alejandres's shelf in Santa Cruz before as well.) "The critics [of detached worker programs], you know, always refer here to the Blackstone Rangers and the reverend [Fry] in the 60s who set up an agency, got federal grants but it turned out they were scamming the money. Who knows, there were no indictments,[116] but it created a permanent impression that 'stolen money runs gangs' or 'you can't trust the gangs with the money', ever since then you hear that."

Freddy lamented, however, the decline of the community-based or detached worker programs. "You can't just tell guys to get out of gangs, which is what the funders and officials want; you have to offer services too." He remembered how the YMCA once made connections with local colleges to offer scholarships, "and then the workers went out on corners to the older guys and enrolled them. Then those guys would become street workers and go right back to their street corners, working with young kids on things like camping trips on the weekends."

The YMCA program shut down in 1968. The results from the detached worker programs were too hard to measure for results-oriented officials, Freddy said. Of course, he could measure the improved course of his own life, but that was being "subjective." "We would say we *see* the results, guys becoming productive, starting families, but that wasn't enough, so you'd get academics coming out to evaluate us. They would demand quick results, like how many did you get out of the gangs this month."

He admitted there were mistakes in implementing the outreach programs. Turning over a teen post to a single gang to have its meetings wasn't the way. "Our philosophy is that if you do outreach, you have to work with all the gangs, not become the agency for just one gang." If the homeboys see your agency van driving members of only one clique around, "you start getting the rocks and bottles thrown at you." For Freddy, the bottom line was the "relationship building" he'd observed the first detached workers doing, keeping the homeboys busy so they wouldn't be thinking about a drive-by. Building cross-gang relationships through sports competitions, for example, might ultimately save lives. "Say if you got caught in an enemy neighborhood, the guys might know you from sports. Instead of a tragedy, they give you a pass and say 'hey, don't worry about it.' "

Freddy supported helping homies get out of gangs when they wanted to, when they were married, had babies, found jobs, and finally felt they didn't have time for hanging out. "If you are a young kid in a gang and want to get out," he said, "around here, that's when you need the detached worker, for instance, to negotiate a kid out." While the gang codes were not always "blood in, blood out," members couldn't simply walk away from their obligations to the collective. To leave a Chicago gang it was necessary to be "violated out." One could be beaten on a gauntlet for five or ten minutes, Freddy said, or "you can negotiate it down, or you can pay your way out," for as much at $500.

Freddy also had worked in the past with Luis Rodriguez (who lived for fifteen years in Chicago and has a son, Ramiro, in the Illinois state penitentiary) and YMCA officials on "collaborative intervention" in order to "remediate" gang behavior (which was where he became immersed in professional social work jargon). The problem, he said, was that Mayor Daley (Junior), "didn't believe in the intervention work, but only was interested in suppression." Under the earlier African American mayor, the late Harold Washington, Freddy noted, intervention programs were officially supported, if not flourishing. The major difficulty now was funding for such intervention under any political regime. "Reaganomics killed it all," he complained. In the seventies and eighties, BUILD had significant staffing because of subsidies from work-study money. Now the organization had only two and one-half street workers, five "prevention specialists," six staff in the county's juvenile detention centers, and a total budget of $1.2 million. The problem with the discrediting of street workers, he said, was that cutbacks in funding destroyed the stable, patient relationship-building that was the heart of the effort.

From Freddy's vantage point, while it was necessary and occasionally fruitful to work with the Chicago police department, the underlying police-gang relationship never changed. The traditional police street sweeps remained as prevalent as garbage collection, with BUILD workers sometimes being rounded up and forced to watch their identification cards torn up. "Get the fuck outta the car" remained a customary police greeting to approaching homies.

He warned that the drugs crisis in the eighties and nineties had underscored the urgent need for treatment options. At first the new self-appointed drug dealers tried to negotiate with gang leaders for their old spots, which led to the gangs pushing the dealers out. "Now they will kill for corners. Three thousand parolees will be released here in this neighborhood this summer," he said gazing out the window to Ashland and Milwaukee, "all of them saying, 'I want my corner back.' And now we have heroin from Afghanistan landing in the streets of Chicago." From Freddy's street vantage point, it was a vicious circle, with the mighty U.S. government either failing to prevent, or allowing, the import of drugs from Afghanistan and Colombia while spending excessive time planting drugs—and criminal charges—on too many homeboys at the lowest level of the drug chain.

After I met Freddy, I caught a ride through several neighborhoods with an animated threesome of young street organizers. Hekter Gonzales, twenty-one, identified himself on his business card as the "ambassador of educational joy" at the so-called University of Hip-Hop founded around Hubbard High School on the South Side several years before. Hekter, a Mexican whose name was spelled in hip-hop style, teaches mc'ing, breakdancing, and graffiti art at the "university," which he calls "a kind of refuge for shorties," meaning young gang members or wannabees. Jasson Perez, a Puerto Rican and also twenty-one, organized against the gentrification of urban neighborhoods. An African American girl named Charity, twenty, sat quietly in the back as we took off in an old Chevy four-door.

It appeared as we drove that the city authorities everywhere named buildings after dead legends whom they would have marginalized when they were living. There were Harold Washington community centers, a Malcolm X college, Harriet Tubman housing, a library branch named for Rodolfo (Rudy) Lozano, a councilman who helped Harold Washington get elected mayor and then was assassinated in the late seventies. "That stopped the movement in these neighborhoods, just like the killing of [Black Panther] Fred Hampton before that," Hekter commented, "and the effect on our generation is that we have to attempt to keep the history alive."

Faded murals tell stories. Off Halstead near Ashland, we stopped to inspect a once-bright, now peeling, panorama of unofficial history. Two Indian faces with the inscription in Spanish, "our voice will never be silenced." A Mayan codex. Skulls. The Chicano black eagle. A Puerto Rican flag. Speedy Gonzales next to Benito Juarez. Che alongside Moctezuma. Fat politicians, generals, and bankers stuffing themselves on turkey with naked women draped over them while starving masses suffered below. Peace on Earth. Stop World War 3. All painted before my three narrators were born. But they admired the legacy. "You can teach through hip-hop," Hekter said proudly, "we say it stands for healthy independent people helping other people. There's no way around here to express your *anti*-feelings. The city programs teach what they call proper European training in the arts. Hip-hop, though, began in the inner city, and we are claiming it, want to take it back. A kid will come in the office wanting to learn how to tag. We tell them it's not about gangbanging, that graffiti is an old art that goes back to the cave men. We also teach them the Constitution for their survival, cause they gotta pass tests in eighth and twelfth grades to survive. And if they want to know about Che Guevara"—he smiled—"we teach that, too."

Hekter wears lots of facial hair and a rasta hat. As he drives he talks a little about himself. To Hekter, hip-hop is "everything." Originally from uptown, he was arrested in school for vandalizing, painting his name and "things like 'teachers suck' "on bathroom walls. Hekter traced his alienation to the fact that his mother was deported back to Mexico after he was born. After getting in trouble enough times, he was sent to a detached worker program, Youth Outreach Services, where they told him to go paint a mural. "That was great!" The graffiti gave him the freedom to let off his frustrations "instead of growing up having a gun in my hand." As a result of being channeled into hip-hop, his criminal record was limited to misdemeanors like loitering and "waking up neighborhoods in the early morning, what do they call it? . . ." At this point, Charity, whom I thought was dozing, looks up to say "disturbing" (disturbing the peace), then sinks back down in the seat next to me. I ask about her background. Her roots are in the Mississippi Delta, where her mom grew up in a shack with some twenty people and had to leave school in the eighth grade to take care of her sisters and brothers. Of fifteen relatives on both sides of her family, three are doing life sentences, and seven of her aunts have been incarcerated. "My mom's a pretty down person, she's never been arrested," she notes.

It was almost impossible to avoid arrest when Hekter, Jasson, and Charity were growing up. The Chicago police, using injunctions and sweeps, arrested some 45,000 young people in the early nineties.[117]

We drive through the Cabrini Green public housing projects, segregated by a train line from the Loop and Gold Coast, where average family incomes are $8,600 a year. Some of the main buildings have been razed as part of Chicago's drive to push 60,000 people out of the forty-year-old "bullet-scarred projects," leaving a huge green field, now called Seward Park. But there still remained five of the ominously tall buildings, with their thick wired cages over the windows and elevators. I stare at a basketball court with a rim bent completely out of shape. There is a field dedicated to Sammy Sosa, a Sojourner Truth elementary school, a faded mural to the Last Ghetto Poets, and suddenly, as we swing toward downtown, a new condominium development with a sign proclaiming, "Extraordinary Riverfront Community!" "They hire homeboys for security," Jasson remarks. The city claims to be desegregating and dispersing the poor, but for my three guides it is more of the same gentrification. Indeed, a *Time* magazine report provided evidence for such fears. During the nineties, Chicago lost 52,000 net rental units, pushing up rents on the remainder. In 2001, the average rent, according to experts, was beyond the budget of families earning less than $28,000, three times the income of Cabrini tenants. To tighten the squeeze, 7,300 units were demolished by the time I visited, while only 699 had been built by the city's housing authority. The vast majority of the families relocated in the previous three years found themselves back in all-black neighborhoods where household incomes averaged $15,000 or less.[118]

John Hagedorn's research indicates that the massive displacement caused by such gentrification contributes to gang violence by disrupting neighborhoods and the lives of young people. The disruption, for example, pushes gangs inevitably into new feuds over turf. The uprooting in Chicago in the nineties, Hagedorn reported, was far greater than it was in New York City, where $1 billion was invested in housing in the South Bronx, where murder rates plummeted. The new affordable housing, Hagedorn wrote, fixed the actual "broken windows" problem the neoconservatives complained about. He therefore proposed that the city saturate the Chicago ghettos "not with police patrols, but with affordable housing."[119]

I ask the trio about community organizing in the face of such massive gentrification. Jasson recently had a plan. A Youth Congress for which he worked organized 1,000 kids to draft a "Bill of Rights for Youth." But then the funding was dropped, he said, "when they gave some serious ultimatums to the city." So it was important to understand that official funding would dry up when youth became provocative on their own behalf. The organizing, therefore, had to occur at the grass-roots level until their movement grew stronger. Jasson said,

> Once grassroots people see real options, the context of an actual gang will change. Killing and drugs will go down because the new politics will be going towards the real enemy. Once you hit a certain pinnacle though, the money always seems to get cut off. A friend of mine had had three gangs chilling until his youth opportunity funding was slashed. When the money gets cut off, you can't go back to them.

In the traditionally Puerto Rican Humboldt Park, at a gentrifying intersection renamed Wicker Park, we came upon another mural from the seventies era, portraying the evolution from gang violence to social justice that is the dream of these young organizers. From right to left, the mural begins with skulls, a police gun, people in tears, a gang knife fight, a dead boy, grieving parents; then, in the center panels, black and brown hands clasped in unity and coming together; then, on the left, a funeral procession, a march with fists in the air, Puerto Rican flags, placards demanding "decent housing," "*justicia*," ending in the proclamation UNIDOS PARA TRIUNFAR. On Division Street, by the mural, Jasson comments on the fresh grass and newly paved sidewalk. "It was never this nice before we were displaced," he says. A yuppie wearing a Body Masters T-shirt and shorts, in from a jog, walks by the mural, oblivious. Across the street from the seventies mural is the new face of the neighborhood, the chic Settimana Café with outdoor tables for patrons of the affluent street life.

Hekter, Jasson, and Charity make virtually no money for their organizing. But they seemed rich in optimism, at least for the moment, and conveyed a spontaneous, almost casual, example of possibilities between Mexicans, Puerto Ricans, and African Americans of their generation. And they were already wise.

During a discussion of why so many young people kill each other, Jasson says it's about money and media glory, but is also due to the psychology of oppression.

They are oppressed, and they take it out on each other. They're not like a corporation that has all kinds of mechanisms for controlling its world, they have to kill
each other physically. It's like what Frantz Fanon wrote about the colonized mind.
They have self-hate. There's self-hate in whites too, because of guilt, but the white
middle class has more outlets, they have quieter houses, more money, they can go
to a therapist, buy a hip-hop tape and be cool. In communities of color, you have
more self-hate with fewer outlets.

Listening until now with her eyes closed, Charity suddenly sits up and says of
gang suppression efforts that

You can kill a weed but not the roots—poverty, government taking money from the
community, that sort of thing. But our government will never address the roots because then they would have to change the whole basis of American society.

We drove around Little Village, the mainly Mexican barrio that was touted by
law enforcement as a model for Greg Boyle in East Los Angeles and for police departments thoughout the nation.[120] It seemed to be a thriving immigrant barrio
with great possibilities for community organization and social services. But it was
not until I returned home to Los Angeles that I received a confidential report on
Little Village from well-respected gang researchers at the University of Chicago
that revealed a different story of gang violence prevention there.[121] The documents confirmed Freddy Calixto's concern about the ability of detached community workers to perform their necessary work when the police insisted on a
dominant role. Funded by the U.S. Department of Justice, the report analyzed a
five-year gang reduction project from 1992 to 1997 in Little Village based on collaboration between community activists, social agencies, and law enforcement.
Youth outreach workers formerly with the Spanish Cobras and Latin Kings were
among those employed.

The project appeared to be successful in terms of reducing gang violence. A
mostly voluntary coalition had been built, Neighborhoods Against Gang Violence (NAGV), involving hundreds of people in meetings, marches, graffiti

paint-outs, and the like. There was one catastrophe recorded, during a poorly planned graffiti paint-out, when two Latin Kings broke away and later committed a drive-by shooting. Despite this, the social scientist evaluators, using techniques of self-reporting, found statistically significant drops over the five years in the frequency of violent crime, including aggravated assault, aggravated battery, armed robbery, drive-by shootings, and homicides, though drug selling was not reduced. The largest reduction in lawbreaking occurred among those youth who were identified as the most violent offenders. The declines were significant compared to adjacent or similar neighborhoods. In several specific instances, the workers who were ex-gang members were credited with moderating intergang hostility and conflict. But, according to the report's authors, the crime reduction statistics

> . . . appeared not to be sufficient to convince the Chicago Police Department (CPD) that the project was effective and feasible. . . . The CPD was not prepared to manage an approach to the gang problem that required significant modification of its suppression philosophy . . . The CPD was clearly not interested in the use of community youth workers.[122]

The Chicago police, according to the report, insisted on defining "community policing" as "enlisting local neighborhood groups to support and enhance the police suppression function." The police saw benefits in a partnership with parole officers because they could quickly obtain information on a gang member's status, "a very powerful tool for monitoring gang members." Professor Spergel, on the other hand, tried to show that a fully collaborative model involving community youth workers as well as police and probation officers was more successful than a narrower one between only police and probation. Frustrated community leaders supported the deployment of the youth workers because their street savvy helped in the successful provision of services and reduction of violence.

It was more of the same, this time documented with interviews and crime data analysis. The punish-and-control model was dominant not because it necessarily worked, but because it reflected the interests of the police as the final arbiter. Community-based approaches were secondary, legitimate only under the eyes of law enforcement. The real alternative was a revival of the independent community sector represented by Freddy, Charity, Jasson, Hekter, and countless others at the grass-roots level. But how could they compete? Their budgets were minimal. But they were rooted in a long tradition of democratic opportunity that continues to offer a flicker of hope.

Street Workers in History

By the 1930s, the settlement house tradition and Thrasher's pioneering sociology led to the Chicago Area Project (CAP), established by Thrasher's colleague at the University of Chicago, Clifford Shaw. By the late 1940s, New York City had established a Youth Board along the same lines. Intervention programs, sometimes known as "curbside counseling," helped promote occasional gang truces in Central Harlem, the South Bronx, and Tompkins Park. According to Eric Schneider's account, "in retrospect, it seems suprising that the street workers accomplished as much as they did," having few resources beyond advice.[123] The street workers seemed to be most effective on individual levels, or during a crisis, but lacked the resources to remain organizing in neighborhoods once gang conflicts settled down. Thus was born the strategy of institutional intervention by community organizations modeled after the Chicago CAP. Schneider's history shows that "some of the more successful intervention projects in New York were those that ceded significant control to youths themselves and involved them in their own reform."[124] For example, in East Harlem, a council of rival gangs was established to meet weekly on neutral turf to sort out their differences. In 1954, the Lower East Side Neighborhood Association (LENA) was created by social workers and visionary activists for community empowerment. LENA also promoted gang truces in its heavily divided neighborhood, with truce violations reported to local clergy. The police commissioner, however, immediately blasted the Youth Board and LENA for "coddling criminals" and denounced the truce for ceding "sovereign powers" to gangs.[125] The issue apparently was whether gang members should be encouraged to settle their differences internally where possible, instead of reporting each other to the police. Lacking official support, berated by a sensationalist media, the community-based gang peace work foundered. Sometimes lives were saved; at other times, the efforts collapsed in a hail of bullets. The difficulty was not only from the police, but at times from gang members who resented being treated as servile clients of social workers.

However, in 1962 the LENA project evolved into the Mobilization for Youth (MFY), which was based on the Chicago CAP model, funded by the Ford Foundation, supported by President Kennedy's Committee on Juvenile Delinquency and Youth Crime, and resting on the research of Ohlin and Cloward. The hope was to go beyond gang intervention, which was only stopgap, into community and economic development. In theory, gangs would be less likely to form if services, job training, and economic opportunities were created through a complete revitalization of the communities that had given rise to them.[126] Eventually the MFY emphasis turned away from gang intervention toward the underlying issues of community self-determination. The MFY organizers, listening at the doorstep and trying to empower individuals seeking change, sent delegations to the 1963 March on Washington, became involved in school reform, advocated a civilian review board, and pushed tenant rights initiatives, including picketing landlords during a Harlem rent strike in early 1964. I remember those of us preparing to settle into ghetto organizing projects were extremely encouraged by the role of MFY in the Harlem rent strike. It seemed to show that if poor people were organized they could expect some resources and tacit official approval by the incipient war on poverty. However, it quickly became clear that MFY was "alienating local political and economic powers within the first few months of its operation."[127]

The dilemma of the federal government was this: it wanted, if only moderately, to take the side of angry blacks, Puerto Ricans, and poor people in the South and North before they spilled into "the fire next time." But Northern politicians—most of them considered liberal Democrats and allies of the president on national issues—wanted no part of government-subsidized community organizers talking about renters' rights or "power to the people" on front porches in their local jurisdictions. The New York Daily News reported that the MFY staff included Communists and had fomented the 1964 rioting in Harlem. Using wiretaps and paid informants, government officials began investigations of the agency. The moment of promise was over, though I didn't realize it at the time. Between go-slow segregationist Democrats in the South and go-slow urban Democrats in the North, there was no room politically for a real war on poverty.

So, "with its radical potential squelched, MFY settled back into a service provider role,"[128] and federal antipoverty funds henceforth would be safely channeled through the local mayor's offices and patronage subcultures that were responsible for neglecting and exploiting the poor in the first place. The same scenario played out in Newark, where I was living. At first, the Newark antipoverty program was modeled after Mobilization for Youth; in fact, its director, Cyril Tyson, came from the New York MFY offices. But despite an initial idealism, the concept of empowerment was soon shelved and funding channeled to those in the community willing to play the game. By 1966, MFY closed down its detached worker program altogether, replacing it with counseling centers for adolescents. What was lost was significant. I agree with Schneider that "MFY in its original conception may have offered the best opportunity to 'reform' gangs."[129] One purpose of the empowerment programs, for example, was to link an individual to a larger purpose, while at the same time linking the transformation of the slum into a wider community. As Schneider says, "masculinity could be defined through resisting foes far more powerful than another neighborhood gang of adolescents."[130] Alienation from the marketplace could have been combated collectively, through forming community-based unions, instead of being reduced to counseling for low-wage jobs that shamed the applicants. The job training and placement programs were premised on making young people adjust to the low expectations of working-class life at just the moment that the civil rights movement was calling for "freedom now." Defining the gangs as the problem and low-wage, low-skill jobs as the solution was the flaw built into the community action model.

The tragic result was a sudden abyss, in northern cities, when anger had to be channeled quickly and productively. As Martin Luther King said after the Watts uprising, "We as Negro leaders—and I include myself—have failed to take the civil rights movement to the masses of the people."[131]

Officially they were classified as "urban disorders" or "riots"—terms meant to mask their meaning, since the authorities apparently were wary of recognizing rebellions on American soil. In plain language, however, they *were* rebellions, even if they lacked a coherent, lasting, organized program. They also set the stage for America's next generation of gangs. The black scholar Kenneth Clark put the rebellions in perspective this way: "I read that [commission] report of the 1919 riot in Chicago, and it is as if I were reading the report of the investigating committee on the Harlem riot of '43, the report of the McCone Commission on the Watts riot. I must say in candor to you members of this commission—it is a kind of Alice in Wonderland—with the same moving picture re-shown over and over again, the same analysis, the same recommendations, and the same inaction."[132]

In the 600-page Kerner Commission Report ("Official Report of the President's National Advisory Commission on Civil Disorders," 1968), the index shows no reference to the words "gang" or "delinquency." There is an interesting analysis, however, of the extent of the crisis of at-risk (gang age) youth. The commission's data collected in twenty cities hit by rioting showed that "Negro males between the ages of 15 and 25 predominated among the rioters: that more than 20 percent of the rioters were unemployed, and that when they were employed, they tended to be underemployed . . ."[133] The Commission staff estimated there were 500,000 hard-core unemployed persons who needed immediate literacy programs, education, training, and jobs.[134] The Commission's goal was to create 2 million new jobs for the hard-core unemployed in three years, half in the public sector and half in the private sector. (In today's dollars, the single-year cost of 1 million new public service jobs in day care, transit services, school support personnel, nonprofit centers, and the like would be $20 billion, or one-twentieth of the current Pentagon budget and $10 billion less than the amount of uncollected federal taxes lost through tax evasion in a single year.[135] (A three-year phase-in, as suggested by the Kerner Commission, would reduce the annual cost to just under $7 billion.)

The Commission placed a principal emphasis as well on reducing powerlessness, by proposing "neighborhood action task forces," sort of community cabinets to advise big-city mayors, involving "comprehensive grievance-response mechanisms," and more opportunity "for ghetto residents to participate in the formulation of public policy and the implementation of programs affecting them."[136] If followed, such proposals would have given representatives of at-risk youth a place at the table by creating youth councils

> . . . which would employ young street leaders (*regardless of previous police records*) to develop programs for "alienated youth" such as operating remedial libraries, neighborhood clean up campaigns, sports competitions and "police-community dialogues."[137]

The authors hoped that the Action Task Forces would make proposals for "an appropriate *non*-police response"[138] to police-related misconduct incidents and rumors. Such proposals for a community-based peace process were central to the Kerner Report's reexamination of the war on poverty's confusing policy of "maximum feasible participation" of the poor. The Commission came down on the side of more participation rather than token measures.

> Yet, the demand for a community voice represents a marked and desirable gain over the apathy that existed before. Despite its problems, we believe that meaningful community participation and a substantial measure of involvement in program development is an essential strategy for city government.[139]

Recall that these were consensus proposals by a commission composed of mainstream leaders that excluded more radical voices at the time.[140] Nevertheless, the Kerner Commission was influenced by the optimistic climate of the era, which included widespread support for demands like community control, one person–one vote, and participatory democracy. If the Kerner proposals had been fully implemented, I believe, the next decades would have been better for millions of young people, and the rise of serious gang violence may have been prevented. These were sensible starting points for dealing with both joblessness and alienation among young street leaders. In today's climate, they even appear bold and prophetic. The Kerner Commission recommendations, however, were never carried out. It is not even clear if they were intended to be. Instead, they disappeared under the weight of Vietnam spending. And instead of a meaningful war on poverty, involving young street leaders "regardless of police records," the nation's leadership soon embarked on the war on gangs.

COINTELPRO

Whereas the government was reluctant to intervene in the economy with jobs, there was little hesitation about intervening with SWAT teams, lethal force, and FBI task forces. While the Office of Economic Opportunity was drying up, the FBI's counterintelligence program (COINTELPRO) was gearing up. According to COINTELPRO documents directed toward the nonviolent Dr. King, "no holds were barred," so one can only imagine the nature of efforts to disrupt the fledgling militants growing out of street organizations. According to internal FBI memos, 43 percent of blacks under the age of twenty-one, the age cohort most likely to be in street gangs, had "great respect" for the Black Panthers.[141] Hoover declared the Panthers—not, say, urban poverty—to be "the greatest threat to the internal security of the country."[142] One hundred million dollars was spent on COINTELPRO, including $7 million in 1976 alone for informants and agents provocateurs, which amounted to twice the budget for informants in the world of organized crime.[143] According to congressional investigations, the FBI payroll of "racial ghetto-type informants" grew from 3,300 in 1968 to 7,500 by 1971. Over sixty were actively spying on the Panthers in 1969.[144] FBI and local police departments made countless arrests (111 episodes in Chicago alone during the summer of 1969[145]), instigated lethal rumors and divisions, and even targeted the Panthers' free "breakfast for children" programs for closure.[146] At their brief peak, the Panthers were estimated to have served 50,000 kids in forty-five communities, and distributed 100,000 copies of their weekly paper. They definitely were reaching those they called "the brothers on the block." But the toll was heavy: 29 Panthers died in raids or shootouts; over 100 were imprisoned for lengthy terms; and an additional 150 were driven underground or into exile.[147] The party withered from external pressure and internal stress by 1971.

In Chicago, the FBI and the police actively conspired to prevent any transformation of the Blackstone Rangers into Black Panthers.[148] When Fred Hampton, the charismatic young leader of the Chicago Panthers chapter began to discuss merging the organization with the Blackstone Rangers,[149] the FBI sent fake letters to the Rangers, warning that the Panthers were invading their turf. An FBI memorandum stated that: "consideration has been given to a similar letter to the BPP, alleging a Ranger plot against the BPP leadership: however, it is not felt this would be productive, principally since *the BPP at present is not believed as violence-prone as the Rangers,* to whom violent-type activity—shooting and the like—is second nature." The FBI apparently was not interested in lessening homicidal violence if the alternative was greater political militancy by blacks.

Fred Hampton not only tried to draw the Rangers into the Panthers, but also had a major influence from prison on the formation of the Puerto Rican Young Lords, a development that might have channeled young Puerto Ricans into political organizing instead of the gang life. Hampton befriended and counseled "Cha Cha" Jimenez, who helped found the Young Lords while in an Illinois prison, according to Juan Gonzáles, who at the time was a member of the Lords national central committee. All factions were united by Puerto Rican nationalism, and "the paramilitary nature of the group sort of provided a channel for the energy for people who would otherwise have fallen into gangs." But the Lords were divided between criminal factions and more political ones, with the fissures being manipulated by the FBI and police. "As I recall, the FBI and police agents went pretty high up into the organization, not within the top five leaders but certainly the top ten or fifteen," Gonzáles says. As a result of the inner and outer strife, "we lost touch with the base in our communities." The NYPD's antigang units, which attempted to disrupt the Lords, included a young sergeant named Ray Kelly, today the police commissioner of New York City. Occasionally, Juan and Ray Kelly have lunch and trade war stories from the old days when Kelly says he "was chasing you guys around East Harlem."

The tragedy is that Fred Hampton is not around as well. Court documents show FBI complicity with the Chicago police antigang units who assassinated Hampton and another Panther, Mark Clark, on December 4, 1969. In an early dawn raid, ninety bullets were fired during the ten-minute assault, including thirty-one into the bedroom where Fred lay sleeping. According to a subsequent federal grand jury report, all but one of the bullets were traced to the police. Fred lay dead on his own bloody sheets, with two bullets in his head. The FBI agent who was Fred's personal bodyguard received a special bonus "for uniquely valuable services" from the FBI a week later.[150]

I knew Fred Hampton well. I heard of his murder early that morning, and visited the site of his death amidst long lines of Chicagoans on a freezing day. Fred often appeared at the courthouse and led rallies during the Chicago Conspiracy trial, in which I was a defendant with Black Panther leader Bobby Seale. I always found him to be disciplined, passionate, and, at the same time, cheerful. From my experience, I can say with certainty that, at age twenty-one, he was a hugely positive force in an ugly time. There are those to this day who cannot understand or sympathize with the fact that the Black Panthers were armed and dangerous. Sometimes they were crazy, too. But they carried guns for self-defense and for symbolic reasons, the same reasons why the Blackstone Rangers shouted, "Stone Rule," why the Young Lords wore Che-style berets, and why the Latin Kings marched in military formation. Something had to be done when the civil rights movement failed and the antipoverty bureaucrats folded their show. "Give 'em fits!" The defiance of the locked-out drove their oppressors wild and continued to ignite the dying pride of millions of young people.

Perhaps the authorities desired passive zombies instead of those angry youth. But their real choice, in retrospect, was either to create space in society for minority rage to be channeled in militant but political directions or to foster an economic alternative to the drug economy, or to repress and twist youthful hope until only the nihilistic stance of the gang member remained. If the price to pay for crushing groups like the Panthers was to guarantee that gangs would fill the vacuum, that was a price the authorities would pay.[151] There is even consensus among many gang researchers on what happened next. According to professor Louis Yablonsky, there was

. . . a hiatus in gangs, gang violence and warfare during the late 1960s through the early 1980s, partly as a consequence of various quasi-political groups like the Black Panthers and the Brown Berets. These groups and others channeled many black and Chicano youths who might have participated in gangbanging violence into relatively positive efforts for social change through political activities.[152]

Professor James Diego Vigil similarly has concluded that

. . . following the Watts revolt of August 1965, rival gang hostilities were put aside to some degree for a period of three to four years. . . . *the abrupt destruction of the Panthers and the cutbacks in War on Poverty programs probably contributed to the acceleration of street gangs in the early 1970s.*[153]

Former gangbanger-turned-writer Luis Rodriguez remembered that

In the 1960s a lull in gang activity coincided with the apogee of the civil rights struggles and the advent of groups such as the Black Panthers, the Brown Berets, and the Young Lords.[154]

Even an official law enforcement gang background manual has acknowledged "there was a drop in gang membership during the civil rights movement of the 1960s when black pride was at its height."[155] In a 1997 discussion I had with L.A. Sheriff's Deputy Wesley McBride, known as the dean of America's antigang units, he too reflected on the path not taken:

If we'd got on this in the Sixties . . . I can't prove it, but my theory is that when the militant movements like the Panthers died down, these kids didn't have anywhere to go. They wanted to improve themselves, they wanted money, and we should have gotten in with heavy remedial programs then.[156]

In summary, the entire range of community-based gang violence prevention programs—from the detached workers, to the work of Father Boyle, to the official community action programs, to community organizers, and to radical alternatives like the Panthers—have been rejected for many decades in favor of the crime-fighting priorities of conservatives and law enforcement. No force yet has been great enough to make the richest country in the world do something about the perpetual cycle of the criminal justice system that Luis Rodriguez likens to a "giant breeder reactor" that produces its own fuel.[157]

Yet history also suggests that the war on gangs will never be won.

The history of gangs in Los Angeles, Chicago, and New York reveals a continuous effort to rechannel instincts like vengeance into creative alternatives built around empowerment of individuals and communities.

The aspiration for peace and dignity will not surrender. It seems to be an integral part of the human condition.

Whatever the failings of these community peace efforts, two important things are beyond dispute. The first is that countless *lives have been saved*. Each time a gang member is transformed, each time gangs resolve their feuds at the table, each time a street counselor has an effect, violence is avoided and lives are spared. The second is that *no human being can be judged incorrigible with certainty*, and therefore *no situation is beyond hope or possibility*. The lives recorded in these pages are only a representative few among the many who keep growing like flowers through cement.

Ask a simple question: if every homeboy and homegirl removed their tattoos, stripped off their jewelry, apologized to police and parents, made reparations to their victims, and showed up for work, would this country be ready to hire them at decent wages, accept them as equals, and include them as citizens with full rights to vote, run for office, and serve on juries?

Or does the perpetual war on gangs reflect what we really want?

9

Education, Politics, and the Future

School reform has received too little attention in the debate over preventing gang violence. Significant attention instead goes to identifying and removing suspected gang members from school campuses and placing them in the equivalent of reform schools with euphemisms like "opportunity schools." Too often they spend their time there adrift until the criminal justice system finally draws them in. The drop-out rates in our urban public schools are hard to estimate, often for public relations reasons, but it is probable that percentages are up to 50 percent in many poor areas. James Diego Vigil cites a rate of 30 to 50 percent in such schools in Los Angeles, including some that are perilously higher.[1] At Fremont High, for example, where 80 percent of the student body comes from economically disadvantaged black and Latino families, every year, two-thirds of the ninth graders leave before high school graduation.[2] California leads the nation in numbers of children living in households headed by a high school dropout. According to UCLA's Jeannie Oakes, "poverty is most predictive of educational achievement, and poverty is concentrated in particular neighborhoods." In other words, zip code is the best predictor of school outcomes despite fifty years of "equal opportunity."[3]

Nationally, the drop-out rate among immigrant Latinos between ages sixteen and nineteen was 34 percent.[4] A Johns Hopkins study described 300 high schools as "drop-out factories," while Presidents Clinton and Bush rattled on about "leaving no child behind."[5] In 2003, the gross failure to report accurate drop-out rates mushroomed into a scandal at the Houston school district once celebrated by President George Bush as "the Texas miracle."[6] Instead of meeting the president's pledge of leaving no child behind, the Houston district was disguising the attrition of thousands of at-risk students through "Enron accounting" techniques, according to a district staff member.[7] The dirty secrets were revealed also in a *New York Times* report that accused the school district of creating thousands of "pushouts" in order to raise academic standards. One advocate described frightened guidance counselors "calling on their cell phones from bathrooms saying they've been told to get rid of kids."[8]

Ominously for the future, census data showed the number of children living in poverty during the gilded nineties remained "virtually unchanged."[9] The largest immigration wave in American history is doubling the number of students with limited English skills, and straining states like North Carolina, Nebraska, Tennessee, and Georgia without an existing capacity for bilingual or English-as-a-second-language classes.[10]

The drop-out rate in inner-city schools is both a measurement and a major cause of the persistence of the gang subculture. As Vigil's work concludes, "What is important to note is that school problems generally precede and contribute to involvement in the gang. Thus, if only we could find effective ways to turn students on to the benefits and values of an education, the educational system could be a powerful factor in preventing students from joining gangs."[11] Of course, numerous gang members attend and even complete school, but in general the gang subculture is a drop-out subculture. Abandoning or being driven out of school is a definitive moment after which a gang identity becomes more important. Already plagued by feelings of inferiority, these dropouts are bombarded with the message that a college education is necessary to a middle-class life. They don't need math to know from an early age that the goal of a college education has become less affordable as they grow up, even if they beat the odds and succeed in school.[12] And the failure of the civil rights movement is apparent in the resegregation of the nation's schools which has worsened in their lifetimes.[13]

Jonathan Kozol has chronicled the agony of inner-city school children for three decades. Through the sixties, he notes, spending levels in New York City public schools stayed level with surrounding suburban counties because white children still attended those schools in large numbers. By 2002, however, as the white student percentage dropped to 14.5 percent, public school spending sank comparably. The median teachers' salary in a 99 percent black and Latino school in New York City was $42,000 in 2002 compared to $82,000 in suburbs like Great Neck and Manhasset.[14] New York City in a recent year spent $8,000 per child in its public schools contrasted with $93,000 per child per year in its new South Bronx juvenile detention center.[15] In addition to rampant inequalities in the public education budget, middle- and upper-middle-class parents routinely raise thousands of dollars for classroom amenities that are beyond the pocketbooks of inner-city parents. The result is a *three-tier public school system* for the middle class, the poor, and the pushed out. As Kozol laments, "The nation's largest and now uncontested bastion of apartheid education does not even seem prepared to live up to the tarnished promises of *Plessy v. Ferguson.*" In 2002, a New York appeals court seemed to affirm this gloomy assessment. In the previous year, a state Supreme Court judge, Leland De-Grasse, ruled that a "sound, basic" education meant preparation for "competitive employment," something more than "low-level jobs paying the minimum wage."[16] He went on: "the majority of the city's public school students leave high school unprepared for more than low-paying work, unprepared for college and unprepared for the duties placed upon them by a democratic society." Before reformers could capitalize on the ruling, Governor George Pataki appealed the decision to an appellate court where it was overturned. The higher court concluded that a student need only be provided "the ability to get a job, and support oneself, and therefore not be a charge on the public" dole. Ironically, while the court was setting this minimal aspiration for learning, the state was implementing tougher graduation requirements in five subject areas with no plans for adding more funding to the schools. "So we're left with a system that is fine for turning out bicycle messengers, and absolutely terrific for preparing kids for Rikers Island," wryly noted *New York Times* columnist Bob Herbert.[17]

I visited Rikers Island that year on a cold and windy day in the company of

Clinton Lacey, a dedicated youth counselor for the Island Academy, which educates youthful inmates passing through. With federal funds, the academy has grown to thirty-five staff from just two in a decade. We parked on a vast lot under a billboard that proclaimed, "Rikers Island. The Boldest Corrections Officers in the World," and made our way through several checkpoints to the school entrance. Once you passed the watchtowers and concertina wire, I marveled at how interchangeable the academy facility was with an inner-city school in appearance—the crowded hallways, frantic staff, warning notices interspersed with student drawings on the walls. It was an extreme version of what exists in the outside world. In this place, my guide told me, "if you are not affiliated [with a gang], you are food." The biggest source of power and violence, he said, was control of the phones. "Kids run them like little fiefdoms." Many of these juvenile Kings, Nietas, Bloods, and Muslims were purged from the New York schools during a nineties panic that gangs were achieving too great a foothold, the assumption being that gang members by nature were impossible to educate. Roseann DiAngelo, a former elementary school teacher, chose to work at Rikers Academy in 1986. She used to pick up kids coming out of Rikers and encourage them to warn their peers about the realities of confinement. "The right of passage for young men is to come to jail, just like getting pregnant is for the girls. We tried to show them the dead end, the strip search, the crying, how horrible it was." Whether it worked, she couldn't say. Or perhaps couldn't think about it. Instead, she focused on the everyday work at hand.

Down the hall I visited a culinary class, a barbershop, a drivers education room, and a computer graphics class where the kids were making Mother's Day cards on thirty computers. The teachers were worrying about the state's tougher new standards, which would be implemented on new software. "We are trying to get as many of our kids to take the GED before the change," one said.

Mike Pines, the principal of the academy, was a three-decade veteran of New York's education struggles. A white man with a gray beard, yellow tie, and green shirt filled with fountain pens, sitting in a small cubicle overflowing with paperwork, he seemed used to looking for the narrowest ray of light in the heart of darkness. For example, only two years before, an inmate on Rikers Island achieved the highest GED score in the city, he said, out of some 50,000 who took the test. On any day, between 100 and 130 student inmates are enrolled in academy literacy and education programs. About 40 percent pass a fifth-grade literacy test and, of those, about two-thirds go on to pass the GED, or about 12 percent of the academy's total enrollees. His students are in classes five hours per day, plus study time in their cells. The alternative to the academy, he noted critically, was the military-style shock program that required inmates to start at 4 A.M. with 100 pushups; "the politicians like it, and it's good for inmate safety and cleanliness, but it has no impact on the post-release situation they face, which is being homeless and jobless."

America's retreat from equal educational opportunities means that more and more youngsters are schooled in the streets or in places like Rikers Island. In fact, inner-city schools, instead of being pathways of hope, are acquiring the characteristics of the slums themselves. So argued the Southern California ACLU and education reformers in a 1999 state Superior Court case that still remains in litigation. The background is a story of America's abandonment of the equal educational opportunity promised by seventies court cases like *Serrano v. Priest*. Not so long ago the notion was presumed and implemented through public policy that education was a fundamental right accorded every student equally regardless of his or her family income or place of residence. That principle foundered as middle- and upper-class parents left urban schools behind. The education debate shifted, too, toward the premise that students needed to work harder and be tested more frequently, and their schools held "accountable," the bipartisan buzz word of the nineties. Defenders of public education for the poor, like the NAACP Legal Defense Fund, Inc., were put on the defensive. They questioned how disadvantaged students could take more tests and still be accorded equal opportunity with less resources per capita flowing to their schools. But the Clinton administration and Democratic governors were embracing the new paradigm launched by neoconservatives like Education Secretary William Bennett in the Reagan era. The public schools were failing in comparison with America's "rivals," it was said, and would have to become "competitive." It was a strange argument on its face, since the United States already was the world's superpower, which meant that becoming more competitive would only increase the global inequality gap. The concept of competition also meant competition between students at home, which meant more "losers" than "winners," which is exactly what occurred. By 2003, however, many large school districts were retreating from solutions like exit examinations that lay at the cold heart of the new competitiveness. In California, high failure rates prevented thousands of students from graduating and caused the state board to postpone the exit exams for two years. In New York state, something was radically wrong: 70 percent failed the state's new math test in 2003.[18]

Yet there was bipartisan agreement that "throwing money" at failing public schools was a bad idea, as if *less* money was an answer. Bennett's thesis of "moral poverty" rationalized the new policy of raising expectations amidst diminishing resources. All students, regardless of neighborhood, were exhorted to go "back to the basics," even as technology was changing the world, and meet higher standards in competition to the "foreign threat." The new conservatism positioned itself as "concerned," rather than hard-hearted, about the floundering schools of the inner cities. The conservative solution wasn't more public investment—not even with greater accountability. The solution to the education crisis was to be found in the marketplace, starting with vouchers for poor families. They simply would shop around for better schools in which to enroll their children, apparently leaving the rest to the famous creative destruction powers of capitalism.

Fearing the combined momentum of the voucher and accountability movements, many civil rights advocates developed a new strategy in the early nineties that sought to link school achievement (results) with funding (resources). Many dropped their longstanding opposition to achievement tests and exit exams, which they previously had feared only would escalate the drop-out rate, and instead agreed that students could take up the challenge—but only if the government and educational establishment would provide the resources necessary to even the competitive playing field. The implicit retreat was from guarantees of equal educational *funding* to a new contract for equal opportunity to *succeed academically*. By agreeing to the new accountability and testing guidelines, the civil rights advocates hoped eventually to build a case for more resources.

For example, South Carolina governor Richard Riley, who became Clinton's education secretary, opposed new testing requirements in his state as long as he could while staying viable politically, then he switched to supporting the new requirements in exchange for his legislature adding a one-cent sales tax for the public schools. But the inequalities built into the educational institutions were deeper than any sales tax hike could cure. As in the New York court case, the definition of the state's obligation to provide resources was lowered even as performance obligations on students were being toughened. It seemed perfectly designed to sweep the gang problem out of inner-city schools and into the Rikers Islands of the nation.

Two *Los Angeles Times* reporters investigated ten L.A. schools near the Watts housing projects that had been chosen for special attention starting in the eighties. What they found was tragic. Even after an additional $1 million per year per campus, the schools utterly failed in meeting the original objective of reaching average scores on reading, math, and language up to the national median. The schools near Jordan Downs and the Nickerson Gardens performed the most poorly. Credentialed teachers were difficult to recruit and retain. Twenty percent of the kids who started at a specific school left before the year ended. As the *Times* writers described it, the ten schools were places where first graders, when asked to use the word "which" in a sentence, offered, "Which boy got killed?", and where special bells ordered a lock-down because of violence on the street. They quoted a fifth grader named Consuela:

> I am a strong black child.
> I wonder if I'll make it through life.
> I hear the sound of gunshots and curse words.
> I see homeless families and drug addicts.
> I want a better life.[19]

Smaller classes and personal attention seem to have helped, the reporters concluded, at least in the elementary years. Then students' performance slipped as they became older, raising the question for the reporters: "Are the schools doing something wrong? Or does the drop simply reflect the influence of the inner city over time?"

The neoconservatives had succeeded in disconnecting poverty from educational achievement, claiming that somehow underfunded schools could produce graduates from inner-city zip codes able to compete with the privileged from Beverly Hills and Pasadena. It was a preposterous notion, reinforced by the deepening cynicism of middle-class taxpayers deluged with reports of violence and failure in inner-city schools, and renewed claims of innate cognitive deficiencies among African Americans in neoconservative best sellers like *The Bell Curve*,[20] which won wide visceral public support because of "endless accounts of crime."

In 1999, with a team of civil rights advocates and UCLA educational reformers, I tried to legislate disclosure of resource inequalities in schools across the state, with the goal of establishing basic standards assuring all students the equal "opportunity to learn," which by then was the modified goal of the equal opportunity movement. The Gray Davis administration, like many in the national education establishment, was threatened by the prospect of information about school disparities becoming public, and vetoed the bill. But the lawsuits by the ACLU went forward, with findings that were shocking. Often, students in inner-city schools lacked desks at which to sit, and instead perched on counters in their classes. Some classes lacked any teachers at all, but instead were void for weeks at a time or were filled by permanent substitutes. Without classes to attend, students were channeled into "service" classes two periods each day, where they were allowed to run errands or sit on the floor. Most students had no books to take home. In one math class, students waited an entire semester before receiving books. Students were forced to pay for their own education materials, including test primers. The multitrack system meant that students received twenty fewer days of instruction yearly than students in schools without multitrack years. At one school with more than 3,500 students in Los Angeles, there were only two functioning bathrooms each for boys and girls, with stall doors broken open and missing soap and toilet paper. There was just one college counselor for the same school's student body. As the lawsuit charged, "experts have found that student achievement falls as many as 11 percentile points in schools with substandard building conditions . . . [and] the difference between an effective and an ineffective teacher can be a full grade level of student achievement in a year . . . *repeated deprivation of basic learning tools continues to create learning deficits from which chil-dren can never recover.*"[21] Only 3 percent of students at some of these "educational slums" were proficient readers, while the statewide achievement gap between poor and affluent schools in reading and math widened in every grade between 1997 and 2002.[22]

A Harris poll uncovered a further pattern of hidden socioeconomic disparity in California. Comparing schools with high concentrations of disadvantaged students to more affluent schools, the Harris survey concluded that the disadvantaged were twelve times more likely to be in a school with untrained, uncredentialed teachers; twice as likely to lack adequate textbooks; and twice as likely to have nonfunctional bathrooms.[23] Racial stereotypes lingered in the classroom too. For example, a language reader sanctioned for use in 2002 in the Los Angeles Unified School District (LAUSD), a district that was 85 percent Latino, included a section called "The Hat." It featured a drawing of a boy with distinctly Anglo features wearing a large sombrero. The accompanying story describes how boys fan themselves with the sombrero and fall asleep under it until a man steals it. One education reformer dubbed the section "Teaching Cultural Insensitivity."[24]

Instead of settling the ACLU suit, Governor Davis fought back with high-priced attorneys who browbeat thirteen young people who submitted affidavits regarding inequalities they had experienced. One of them was eleven-year-old Carlos Ramirez, from the Bay Area, who asked to be excused because his mother had been murdered recently in a drive-by shooting. Instead, the state's lawyers interrogated him for four days, including twenty straight questions about the quality of cafeteria milk.[25]

In summary, despite thirty years of desegregation and equal opportunity efforts, schools in California and nationwide reflect sharp disparities based on the race, class, and zip code of the students. Given this entrenched inequality among students who *attend* these schools, the drop-out rate reflects an even deeper line between the mainstream and the marginalized.

I remember the story told to me by a community worker named George Sarabia about going to school in the Hazard housing projects in East L.A. A kid's first days in school are almost always difficult. (I still remember, fifty-plus years later, crying when I was deposited in my first-grade class and saw my mother wave and walk away.) On the first day George walked to his new school, he discovered that the houses in the next neighborhood had grass on the lawns. He began to feel out of place, like the dirt yard he came from. The students with grass yards started to pick on him, and that's when George first felt the need to protect himself. He soon dropped out of school and went loco. It would take years before he straightened out. A recent academic study by Maria Eugenia Matute-Bianchi has "highlighted the *oppositional* stance toward school authorities of second- and third-generation Chicanos and cholos and their low levels of academic achievement."[26] The anthropologists Marcelo and Carola Suarez-Orozco call the process *"learning not to learn."*[27] The assimilationist perspectives of school professionals, backed by a public majority, put young people like George in an impossible situation: they're supposed to abruptly abandon the forces shaping their identity in their own neighborhoods to become obedient models of middle-class behavior, virtually on their own. This is the Puritan model advocated by the Bennetts and Olaskys, and it does not work for millions like George. It is a Darwinian sink-or-swim experience that guarantees a wake of dropouts and gang members. Joan Moore and James Diego Vigil (with concurrence from Malcolm Klein) have argued that the inherent nature of gangs is to *"maintain an oppositional, rather than a deviant subculture,"* representing "an institutionalized rejection of the values of adult authority—especially as exhibited in the Anglo-dominated schools . . ."[28]

In middle-class life, to be oppositional when young is considered a phase of life, but when it emerges from nonwhite children it is seen as a permanent pathology, a condition. Vigil interviewed a Salvadoran gang member who recalled that he "would just go sit on a bus bench and collect a bunch of bottles. I'd just sit there and wait for cars to drive by, especially if it was a fool who was trying to act cool. Then I'd just throw the bottles at the car. I'm not sure why I did it."[29] I did the same thing when I was fourteen years old. If I had been apprehended, I would have been counseled as a maladjusted youth, not criminalized and jailed. The delinquent, nonconforming impulses of adolescence remain universal. Meanwhile, many teachers in the overburdened inner-city school system are unable to teach in the midst of the implicit resistance to authority that boils up in so many of their students, and the primary function of the school becomes control. Teachers and administrators need to be more prepared for alienated students in their classroom. But there is a segment of at-risk students, already frustrated by problems with authorities or the job market, who will act out their anger in ways that seem impossible for the average teacher or counselor to turn around. The increased drop-out rate becomes a convenient way to restore classroom order while also indirectly raising test scores by eliminating low-achieving students. The pool of future gang members rises in the tide.

The crucial aim of the system is obedience to a range of middle-class (which ultimately are associated with white) norms of behavior, including dress codes, orderly classroom demeanor, the use of proper English, rote learning, acceptance of dominant cultural icons, regimented study habits, timeliness, silence, and submissiveness to authority, norms that place many schools on a collision course with most of the oppositional instincts that inner-city life fosters in its youth. The moral function of the school, according to James Q. Wilson and most neo-Puritans, is to "insist on the habitual performance of duties" and to teach how to "defer the satisfaction of immediate and base motives in favor of more distant and nobler ones."[30] Under this philosophy, what hope is there for the education and transformation of a gang member?

In her 2001 study *Bad Boys: Public Schools in the Making of Black Masculinity*, Smith College professor Ann Arnett Ferguson has demonstrated how at-risk African American students, classified as "unsalvageable troublemakers" in their school setting, "recoup a sense of self as competent and worthy under extremely discouraging work conditions. Sadly, they do this by getting in trouble."[31] These young men respond with "attitude" when expected to perform with the "absolute docility that goes against the grain of masculinity," Ferguson found.[32] They identify with blackness (or, for Latino boys, chicanismo) in the face of a school system that denies the existence of racism. In doing so, they refashion themselves to "recoup personal esteem" in a manner that subverts white authority, if only unconsciously. They fight both ritually, for respect, and to avoid being picked on later, in a middle-class, *kumbaya* setting where disputes are supposed to be "talked out." They become involved in what Herbert Kohl describes as "active not-learning," expending their intelligence and energy in distancing themselves from their schoolwork because, as he describes it,

> To agree to learn from a stranger who does not respect your integrity causes a major loss of self. The only alternative is to not-learn and reject the stranger's world.[33]

Another insightful researcher, L. Jannelle Dance, has described how this oppositional behavior is seen by those in authority as dangerously gang-related. Like most careful observers, Dance knows that "only a small minority of urban youths are actually involved in hardcore criminal activities."[34] But they adopt a "tough front" in the form of "gangsterlike mannerisms, language and dispositions," most often temporarily as a strategy for navigating and surviving the streets. Such youth are classified as troublemakers for behavior that might be tolerated among white youth, but is unacceptably threatening when coming from youth of color. Ferguson notes studies that have shown minority youth to be at higher risk of punishment than whites who have committed the same delinquent behavior.[35] When disciplined, the youth she observed were sent to an isolated room, which, significantly, they called "the dungeon" or "the prison," where their newly born "bad" reputations were further reinforced. The alternative, that *schools might be designed to lessen alienation or shame,* is beyond the imagination of many administrators, teachers, parents, and public officials who are more likely to support even sterner academic "boot camps." In 2002, the Philadelphia school district suspended thirty-three *kindergartners* for punching teachers and stabbing one another with pencils.[36]

Certain of these forms of disobedient student behavior are classified as "mental illness" by the American Psychiatric Association (APA), under the label "Oppositional Defiant Disorder," or ODD, under code 313.81 of the APA's official *Diagnostic Manual.*[37] Such a classification permits the disobedience to be seen as individual pathology rather than a predictable, if misguided, response to the hierarchies of authority, thus justifying expulsion of the disobedient rather than reform of the institution. The APA definition is broad and ambiguous, with symptoms defined as "arguing with adults" and "deliberate or persistent testing of limits." The U.S. Surgeon General describes ODD as related to "conduct disorder," which is defined as fighting, vandalism, truancy, and the like. The government agency recommends parent education and lithium or methylphenidate as possible remedies, but makes no reference to educational or social reform.[38]

No tinkering will be sufficient to turn this crisis around. But a more conscious approach to educating at-risk youth is needed before the tide takes more youngsters away. In fact, the relative lack of any such approach is evidence that much of the public has given in to "compassion fatigue," or that powerful forces have concluded that the urban underclass is uneducable, redundant, and fated for life behind bars.

Teacher preparation programs are problematic because of the perverse, seniority-driven incentives that channel experienced teachers to more affluent suburban schoolrooms while inexperienced newcomers are assigned to what is often labeled "combat duty" in the inner city. As a result, up to half of those new teachers give up and leave in the first three years of their careers. Those who stay face the challenge of teaching at-risk youth while lacking the resources such as new textbooks, computers, and after-school programs that are vitally needed. More important, they are forced to teach in a school environment that inevitably marginalizes and punishes the students who need the greatest attention. Can schools raise the spirit and the skills of at-risk students, or are they simply holding centers until those students drop out or end up incarcerated?

There is a powerful "pedagogy of the oppressed," associated with the late Brazilian educator and government minister Paulo Freire, which represents proven hope, but its very premise runs counter to most mainstream educational theory and practice.[39] In Freire's pedagogy, students need to participate directly in the learning process instead of being treated as objects who consume information or orders dictated by their teachers. *Education is a process of experiencing freedom,* in this view, which inevitably pushes the student to question and resist oppressive stereotypes of race and gender and the classroom power relations with authority figures that reinforce their feelings of inferiority. The writer bell hooks, a follower of

Freire at City College in New York, has written similarly of "teaching to transgress."[40] At UCLA, the researcher and former teacher Jeannie Oakes has called for "teaching to change the world," the title of a book with Martin Lipton.[41] Citing the research of Henry Giroux that many students act up in resistance to an arbitrary power that limits their life chances, Oakes and Lipton support "new, more emancipatory classroom norms" about teacher-student relationships and goals, including the involvement of students "in a constant dialogue with their teachers examining experiences that allow students to plan and act on the conditions of their lives, in school and out. Inevitably this means probing, rearranging, and at times even undermining the unspoken power and authority of the teacher so the students can experience a partnership in the quest for knowledge." At UCLA's innovative Center X, funded with $800,000 annually from the legislature, Oakes is fostering a network of young, sophisticated teachers committed to educating at-risk youth. These graduate students and teacher trainees are organized collectively to combat the wear-and-tear of the traditional educational culture.

Glaring examples of the dominant culture are police-based classroom programs such as Drug Abuse Resistance Education (DARE) and the federally supported Gang Resistance Education and Training Program (GREAT). Though little evidence exists that DARE accomplishes its purported goals, the program is widely entrenched nationally.[42] In 2000, the California legislature succeeded in preventing a subsidy of $1 million in public funds annually for DARE. GREAT is a newer program, taught by police with little involvement of teachers, whose stated goals are to reduce gang membership, prevent crime and violence, and develop positive attitudes toward law enforcement. Since the youth drawn toward gangs carry more antisocial beliefs than mainstream students, a police officer forcefully demanding respect is likely to have little impact. Studies showed a relatively unfavorable effect among students two years after attending the classes, followed by modest success four years later as many students matured. GREAT had virtually no effect on the cohort of students who dropped out or were highly marginal. Concentrating on the Puritanical notion that students join gangs out of character weakness, GREAT is utterly unable to address such basic issues as police-community relations.[43]

Dewayne Holmes, Manny Lares, and I once visited Indian Springs, one of fifty "opportunity schools" operated by the L.A. school system for students considered too troublesome to teach but not yet lawbreakers who could be simply swept off to jail. In short, it was an experiment in teaching dropouts. Set in a middle-class west L.A. neighborhood, the place had a pleasant small-scale feel to it. The seventy or so students were African American and Latino in the main, with a handful of whites who had been expelled for drugs. In this place, at-risk students were the norm. The rationale was that they needed special attention, but the reality was that they were stigmatized troublemakers. If they succeeded here, theoretically they were eligible to return to the mainstream schools. If not, they could drop out and land on a still lower rung of life's ladder. But how to succeed in a room full of kids like themselves? The teaching staff, no doubt underpaid and overworked, seemed to have short fuses against the spectre of bedlam. Dewayne and Manny, on the other hand, were in their element. They could see themselves in the kids before them, and the kids could see themselves in Dewayne and Manny.

The school hoped that Dewayne and Manny would be constructive role models who could "reach" these supposedly hopeless charges with messages that gangs, violence, and drugs were bad, that prison was brutal, that they could pull themselves up like, well, like Dewayne and Manny. But Dewayne and Manny made it clear that they were not there to urge obedience on anyone. They were diplomatic, however, not wanting to provoke a quarrel with the teachers. Their energy crackled through body language, hand gestures, and smiles. They could "relate," they said, and were "just coming by to hear what you guys think is going on, you know what I mean, and the alternatives out there." Manny started by identifying himself as a fourth-generation Santa Monica gang member, and Dewayne described his life as a Crip and long-time inmate in youth facilities and state prisons. They said they were "representing" young people, gang members, and ex-gang members who had no voice in government.

They were critical of society, the schools, and the prison system, and spoke with passion of the need for young people to have some power, and especially the importance of finding ways to work out conflicts while avoiding bloodshed. The cold stiffness in the room began to melt as kids started telling stories and asking questions. Suddenly, however, a teacher peered over the shoulder of a young man who was writing on paper in the back row, and interrupted the flow of discussion. "Look what he's writing," the teacher exclaimed, "and you'll see the problem." The young man complained that he wasn't doing anything, but the teacher strode up the aisle, asking, "Look at this, what do you think of this?"

The young man had been quietly practicing drawing block letters in the Gothic style popular with gang members and graffiti muralists. The teacher continued berating the young man as he sat quietly in his seat. I opined that I didn't see anything wrong with the lettering, and wanted to continue the class discussion, which frustrated the teacher more. Dewayne and Manny said they weren't bothered, and asked the class what they thought. The response was instant and engaged. Some kids raised their hands, while others simply blurted out their objections to the interruption. Soon things settled down, but we had witnessed a small example of how power worked every day in that school. When the hour ended, all the students had one remaining question: When were Dewayne and Manny coming back? Clearly our presence had allowed them to act more freely than normal, and they wanted more. Sadly, it wasn't going to happen. There were hugs, handshakes, and photos, then the doors would close on them again. It was an exceptional moment. Under existing law, people like Dewayne, Manny, or Alex Sanchez would normally be fingerprinted and severely limited in access to students under new laws regulating associations with past gang members.

School systems across the country, their funding linked to tougher standards, are in danger of pushing out greater numbers of at-risk students into misnamed dumping grounds like these "opportunity schools." In New York City, for example, many high schools simply will not accept young people older than seventeen with backgrounds of trouble or language deficiencies, even though they are entitled by law to remain in school until age twenty-one.[44] These students desperately need "last chance educational" opportunities, like those provided for 800 young people at Manhattan Comprehensive Night and Day High School, privately funded and located in a schoolhouse built for nineteenth-century immigrants. Underfunded and overwhelmed, such schools often have one asset: the devotion of teachers to their disadvantaged students, many of whom dwell in the gang subculture. (One American-born student from Washington Heights lied about his ethnicity to gain entry, claiming he was Dominican.) In small pockets of hope around the country, various alternative schools are attracting committed teachers devoted to the education of the homeboy and homegirl.

Looking for such a spark of hope, I turned to Rachel Greenwald, a teacher at the Youth Opportunities Unlimited Alternative High School in South Central L.A. Rachel, twenty-eight, had worked actively with Homies Unidos, visited El Salvador and Nicaragua, spoke Spanish. The daughter of the film director Robert Greenwald, she was a university graduate, an active rock-climbing athlete, a curly haired dynamo. There were thousands of young social activists like Rachel coming out of the universities in the nineties. Could they survive and make a difference in institutions like these? I found that liberatory change might start as simply as giving your students your phone number.

When we met in Venice, Rachel was wearing a sweatshirt with "South Central" written in huge block letters, and preparing for her fall classes. Her spirit was high, though she was troubled by the challenges. The Alternative High School enrolled over 100 students, and Rachel's classroom usually held fifteen to twenty. She taught something called intercoordinated science, which seemed to mean basic biology, with a total of only twenty textbooks for the sixty or seventy students she taught daily. Most of her students struggled to complete a single class in a year at very low reading levels. "They just can't decipher what the book is saying," she said. "But the main problem is behavior. They know they're not going to be kicked out of here, so they'll take advantage of one or two teachers. Unfortunately, some maybe should be kicked out. But first the teachers need to collaborate and figure out better ways to handle the problem ones."

Having said this, Rachel reconsidered. "The weird thing is, I believe in them, that in their own way every single one is extremely smart. But we need another way to deal with the behavior."

"The way it's set up now, the teacher is supposed to know everything, be the boss. It's not set up for students and teachers to be amicable in their relationships. I'm honest, I say I don't know everything, I am not the boss. It's true, they can walk out, no one can stop them. Here's an interesting thing: all my students have my phone number. Some say that's a boundary issue. But I choose to answer the phone, pick them up and take them places. It helps me as a teacher if I know if something's going on. They are not used to having teachers who listen, take it in and not tell them it's wrong. I try to ask them questions, like what about their dreams and what needs to happen."

Do your students really have dreams, goals for the future? I asked. Maybe half of them do, she replied, while the rest expect to live a gangster life or think that nothing will change. None think they will make big money, enjoy a big house, or even move away from their 'hood. Of those who dream, she added, the dreams are not of being athletes but of being rappers and poets. "None of them likes life the way it is but they don't know how to change it. They don't like killing each other. Three have died in the six months I have been here. They come to school and someone's gone. They might reference it, joke about it, but they will not open up and talk about what's going on."

Clearly, students cannot concentrate on biology if their feelings are bottled up about a dead classmate. Education as usual is fruitless. Rachel spoke of simple alternatives. "First, try to get them out of their environment, out to the mountains or desert, anything to expose them to other things. Second, let them get to know you as a person." Thinking abstractly of how to transform schools in those directions, I asked her how to get there. Thinking concretely, she answered, "In vans." Phone numbers and vans. Could it be that simple? I asked how she would have handled the incident at Indian Springs when the homie was humiliated for scribbling graffiti on paper.

Rachel became red-faced. "I don't *care* if they are writing on my blackboard!" Instead of putting the students back in their seats, she recommends letting them take over the blackboard, then asking them questions about their work. "I ask— why are you crossing that letter out? I have one guy who writes his 'hood over and over again—HOOVER, in block type—and I asked him why, and he says because he loves writing it. What I think is, it's to show loyalty because he's new in school and wants to prove himself. Then he X's out almost every letter because each letter represents an enemy neighborhood. I asked him what does it mean? Why do you hate them? If I can't understand that, and he can't open up about it, how can I teach anything? I had one kid in class with his enemies, and I asked him how he avoided problems. He says, "Dunno, I got respect." He would sit talking and laughing together with his rivals. They worked it out somehow, and I need to understand how they do that as a teacher. I turn it into my class on ecosystems and talk about predators and prey and symbiosis and balance."

The students hate politics, the law, and schools, she said. "But I say to them gangs have politics and laws, too, and I ask them what they like about their 'hood and representing and what they'd like to see changed. I tell them if you could ever band together and stop killing each other you could have power. Most say 'huh.' Sometimes they say 'yeeah,' they like it. But you know what's interesting, most say they never heard of the idea."

People on the west side of town often ask if she's afraid of driving to the 'hood and working there. She says she isn't. "My students sometimes will curse me and walk out of the classroom, and I let them. But nothing else happens. One said to me, 'We might be angry at you, Miss Greenwald, but you real, you care, you never have to worry 'bout us." From the depths of their alternative universe, the students had given her a pass. Rachel is what Jannelle Dance perceptively calls a "down teacher,"[45] which she defines as:

1. Understanding the code of the streets enough to provide advice on safe passage. Puritan advice such as "Just Say No" and "Just Walk Away" reflects a complete "lack of understanding of the code of the streets or the realities of survival on the streets."[46]
2. The ability to deconstruct stereotypes of inferiority and villainy, and communicate on the deepest level that blacks and Latinos are not "suspension, expulsion, and drop-out accidents waiting to happen."[47]
3. Providing access to male role models able to redefine masculinity and call the bluff on hardcore behavior.
4. Making real and vivid links to economic alternatives to dependency on the underground economy.

Rachel was carrying out Freire's "pedagogy of the oppressed" on the basis of her own experience. So are countless others on the margins of school systems and in community centers around the world. In Los Angeles during the past few years, independent publicly funded charter schools targeting at-risk youth have been created in Inglewood, Lennox, Boyle Heights, and Pico-Union by experienced organizers with community service backgrounds who have chosen to work in the inner city.[48] Though the methods do not narrowly target gang members per se—the 400-page Oakes-Lipton work indexes no reference to "gangs"— the approach is a starting point for what might be called a *pedagogy for homies*.

Another example of making a difference on the margins is the Pico Youth and Family Center established in the Santa Monica barrio as a follow-up to the truce of 1998, directed by Oscar de la Torre, a Santa Monica High School leader who graduated from college, then returned to his neighborhood. Central to the program is hip-hop culture. The walls are covered with graffiti in an effort to decriminalize and claim the art form. A music production room includes microphones, synthesizers, and keyboards. Computers are available for teaching Web page design. A film library featuring African American and Latino history is being built. The entrance features huge paintings of César Chávez, Malcolm X, and Rigoberta Menchu. A central space includes a round table for tutoring by UCLA students, most of them students of color. This is not a traditional "teen post," the post-riot centers often established to give students safe outlets for their teen energy. Underlying the center is an ideology and educational vision that blends liberatory teaching methods that start from the assumption that young people are smart on levels that the system doesn't recognize. There is an elaborate intelligence in graffiti, for example, behind rap lyrics, or in the uncanny agility of young people who master video games or computer graphics. The faces looking down from the wall send a message of heritage, too, that counters the feelings of nothingness that so many youngsters carry. The point is to draw on this innate, community-based intelligence as a building block to wider learning. The Pico Youth and Family Center can be seen as a supplement to the public schools and as an alternative at the same time. Neither a traditional community center nor a school, the Pico center is a creative transformation of the destructive energy that ripped the community apart only four years earlier. Oscar was elected to the Santa Monica–Malibu school board in 2002.[49]

It is important to support these efforts toward reform at the margins, until a critical mass can develop to change the larger institutions. In Sacramento, I found support for two other initiatives that will help these street-savvy youth learn. First, parent empowerment in the schools, which has been defined mostly as the right of middle-class parents to watchdog the public schools. But the idea can be extended to parents at the lower end of the socioeconomic spectrum, particularly immigrant parents whose children are most in danger of failing. The legislature and the governor were willing in 2000 to spend $2.5 million annually in grants for a San Diego–based parent-training institute that ran nine-week-long workshops for immigrant parents to understand everything from how to help their kids with homework to the right to protest and organize. From these workshops came grass-roots support for new candidates for school boards from powerless communities.

There also was reform of the inequities in Scholastic Aptitude Test (SAT) preparation. One of the class advantages of middle-class students is the relative ability of their parents to afford thousands of dollars for private tutors for the SAT. In most inner-city public schools, SAT preparation wasn't provided at all, and where it existed, the tests were rarely taken. The state supported my legislation channeling $5 million annually in federal funds for SAT preparation classes in public schools. The legislation even was worded to allow homies in juvenile probation camps to take the tests. In a pilot project, all the incarcerated homies received calculators, which "they begged to take back to their dorms" and sat studiously through three-hour classes. The program offered by the Princeton Review improved the practice test scores of these "unsalvageables" by a surprising average of 122 points. One student, named Jason, who was locked up for attempted burglary, scored an increase of 200 points.[50] Now, Jason said he wanted to attend Howard University to study anthropology.[51] Educational reformers like Paul Cummins, who in the eighties started prestigious private schools like Crossroads and New Roads, now are beginning to extend their efforts to Los Angeles County's Camp Gonzales with surprisingly positive results. "The whole culture of punishment only makes things worse, but a lot of these kids have terrific potential that we ought not to waste," says Cummins.[52] (Meanwhile, the California prison guards' union is lobbying to de-fund a unique community college program for inmates at a state prison, despite evidence that "it breaks down racial barriers that dominate all aspects of prison life."[53])

However helpful, these alternatives being constructed in the cracks and cata-combs will only be successful if they eventually transform the culture and priori-ties of urban schools and prisons. Reform has to move from the margins to the mainstream. Failure simply means more young people abandoning education in the bedlam of jails or prisons; more illiteracy; more uneducated, unskilled, un-employables. The schools and community colleges can abet this cycle of violence or choose to intervene with a different ethic of education.

Innovative research on the potential of successfully educating gang members has been done by researchers like David Brotherton at the John Jay College of Criminal Justice in Manhattan, whose team has been doing innovative street re-search with the Latin Kings for several years. Brotherton points out that most gang research assumes that gang members reject schooling or are flatly unedu-cable, instead of asking whether schools as institutions are designed to reject gang members. In interviews with the Latin Kings and the Asociación Neta from 1997 to 2000, however, Brotherton found a strong belief in the empower-ing function of education. These gang members felt that knowledge was a mys-tical sacrament they had been denied. Knowledge, Brotherton heard over and over, was the key to self-improvement, cultural identity, and overcoming barri-ers. Internally, education—learning Puerto Rican history, studying King mani-festos, teachings, and by-laws—was a means of advancing within the organization. Externally, education meant advancing the next generation of "little homies" and being able to relate to the mass media, politicians, and potential allies. Brotherton found that many local Kings placed a priority on checking school at-tendance records of the peewees, enforced their own 10 P.M. curfews on youths under sixteen, engaged in counseling those in trouble, and tried to steer younger members out of needless conflicts. "Our goal is to strive for more knowledge, more kids, more of our brothers goin' into schools without being kicked out for being a King. Becoming lawyers, doctors, cops, becoming all these things we're striving for . . ."[54]

In notes on "a pedagogy of possibility," Brotherton stressed the critical role of schools in the inner city. Based on his interviews and experiences, he summarized the following:

- Gang students want to be mentored. They want attention, and crave to be valued other than in street guises.
- Gang students have hope. Many see their gang experience as transitional; all spoke of wanting to leave at some point.
- Gang members are expressive, with a flair for artistic imagery and poetry.
- Gang students are very interested in their ethnic culture.
- Gang students are communal and collective; they hate the competition and favoritism in typical school culture but are open to learning together.[55]

I would argue that homies exhibit a *mischanneled* intelligence, not a hopeless deficiency. Like people who know baseball averages but can't understand mathematics, homies are frequently brilliant in video arcades but can't function in a classroom. They invent complicated hand signs, tattoos, and graffiti symbols but often read at third-grade levels. It is not creativity that is lacking so much as a setting for intelligence to flourish.[56] As Brotherton puts it, "In a more humane and reasonable world, we would have an enormous amount to learn from these groups' efforts to organize the disenfranchised and underserved populations," citing three specific possibilities: first, public schools could learn how groups such as the Kings build self-esteem; second, the schools could study the ways the Kings develop leadership skills and bonds of loyalty among youth who drop out of conventional structures; and third, schools could learn from the curriculum that such groups develop, inevitably stressing new interpretations of colonial history, the dynamics of oppression, and the role of spiritual and intellectual resistance to assaults on identity.

Schools remain contestable sites in the struggle to ensure a better future for gang members and all at-risk youth. But will policymakers and teachers be committed to the challenge? As long as the war on gangs continues, how many Americans will support increased resources to educating those who are demonized as an incorrigible enemy?

The Politics of Gang Violence

I recall walking to work one morning across the Capitol lawn, a magnificent landscape of stately California trees, shocked to come upon hundreds of wooden coffins brightly painted white, laid out in front of the Capitol steps. There was to be a rally for Governor Pete Wilson's 1996 reelection proposal for the three-strikes initiative. The coffins were the visual props for the television cameras. I asked one of the Capitol sergeants where the coffins had come from and who had paid for them. It was taken care of by the prison guards, he said quietly, at a cost of $50,000. Pete Wilson won his election that year by declaring war on youth crime and immigrants.

Four years later, on the November night when Gray Davis was elected governor, I sat in a hotel victory suite next to Don Novey, the president of the prison guards' union. Though Davis was a Democrat running against a hard-line law-and-order Republican attorney general, Dan Lungren, Novey had understood long before most insiders which way the wind was blowing. The union spent $2 million on Davis's election that year, and would add another $662,000 in direct and indirect contributions in the next two years.[57] I was glad Davis was victorious over the Republican alternative, but sitting there watching Novey, surrounded by aides busy with cell phones taking in early poll returns from around the state, I knew that the election also signaled the triumph of a self-perpetuating party of law and order capable of driving the larger two-party system. It meant that politicians of both parties, dependent on endorsements and contributions, were fundamentally compromised in their independent ability to perform oversight, investigate scandal, and check the intimidating power of the law enforcement establishment. It meant that the scapegoating of gang members in the revolving culture of punishment from the streets to courts would continue without independent review. I knew what unchecked power led to.

Those were the years when the shooting of inmates by guards at Corcoran state penitentiary numbered more than the cumulative total in the whole country, when the "Friday Night Fights" and the rumored sadism of the "Booty Bandit" finally drew the attention of Mike Wallace, when internal investigations were exposed as a whitewash, when Rampart-style policing remained unchecked. The secret horrors behind the walls had leaked out with the blood of inmates, and something had to be done to restore the semblance of accountability. Senate hearings were finally scheduled on these festering problems, and the governor and legislative leadership agreed that a watchdog office was needed for a system swollen with over 150,000 inmates.

But it was only a Band-aid, not a cure for the disease. In fact, it was widely denied there even was a disease, only the usual handful of bad apples. I remember the day Novey testified in the Senate hearings, smoothly agreeing with the need for greater oversight while denying there were cover-ups that justified the oversight, which was when I suspected the fix was in.[58] The guards' union was held blameless for the culture of violence and corruption, and soon secured yet another major increase in wages and benefits. In 2002, Governor Davis signed a pact promising a 34 percent pay hike over five years, costing $680 million.[59] Included was a more lenient work rules' provision that increased sick leave by 20 percent in a single year. As guards predictably called in with "illnesses," overtime shot up 20 percent as well.

When success-oriented politicians gauge the alignment of interests, near the top in contributions and desirable endorsements is the law enforcement lobby, topped by the prison guards' union. While our national armed forces are forbidden to give campaign contributions, endorse candidates, and walk precincts as military personnel, the California prison (and police) lobby can and does. The conflict of interest is evident but overlooked. It was no surprise that the California prison guards were the fasting-growing public sector lobby in the nineties. Their union contributed nearly $1 million to Governor Pete Wilson in his 1996 reelection campaign, as well as tens of thousands to many other candidates. That million dollars came from union dues automatically deducted from the guards' paychecks for their political action fund. The same union sat down with the otherwise anti-labor Republican governor to negotiate more lucrative contracts than other public employees' unions. According to little examined state budget formulas, every addition of approximately six inmates to the prison system automatically adds another employee to the guards' payroll. The more inmates, the bigger the union. The bigger the union, the more contributions. The more contributions, the better the union contracts. In 2003, California prison officials flagrantly reclassified thousands of low-risk prisoners as "high-risk" to justify a $700 million maximum-security prison.[60]

Brave was the soul of an incumbent who would stand up to the union during reelection, when mailboxes would fill up with scary multicolored 8-by-11-inch postcards complete with a simulated law enforcement badge and implications that a candidate wanted to leave violent criminals on the street. Few stood up. One exception was my Senate seatmate, John Vasconcellos, a four-decade veteran of Sacramento's political wars, and at one time the chairman of the assembly budget committee. During one year of severe budget cuts, John had to deny the prison guards the funding they believed themselves entitled to. In addition, John sat on the public safety committee as a traditional liberal who refused to vote automatically for every sentence-enhancement bill put forward by legislators trying to look tough on crime. So one day a virulent mailer showed up in the voters' mailboxes in John's Santa Clara County district suggesting that he was the criminal's best friend. The union had spent $75,000 on the mailing as a warning shot. John was slumped over in unhappiness as he read it, though as a longtime incumbent he knew he could survive and be reelected. But what about a candidate locked in a close race, or a Democrat in a so-called "swing" district evenly divided between the two parties? They were trapped by the pressure of the prison guards and other law enforcement lobbies. It didn't matter what they might think on a given issue, because their survival instincts dictated that they win, or at the very least neutralize, the law enforcement endorsements in their district.

The same patterns of police hegemony are pervasive in municipal politics, where city councils are notoriously unable to reform the police, depending instead on citizens' lawsuits, or investigations triggered by outsiders, particularly the federal government. Locally, the good-old-boy infrastructure of police and prosecutors, combined with public opinion, makes it impossible for city councils to appear to take the side of gang members whose constitutional rights are violated. Shauna Clark is a former city manager of San Bernadino, California, and a research consultant on crime issues to many city governments. From her insider experience, "It's the budget that drives everything. Prevention doesn't bring in dollars. When gang members shoot each other, privately officers will tell you 'that's a good kill.' If a politician raises questions, police tell them if that's the way you want it, we just won't respond in your ward. Any city manager who's candid will tell you that."[61]

What was being created was by no means a police state. That would cause a public outcry to which politicians would have to respond, as when the LAPD was exposed as having collected private information for years on members of the Los Angeles City Council. But it surely was a self-perpetuating "state" of its own within the state government, a secretive, well-financed group with lethal powers over the lives of a scapegoated, voteless, voiceless population of inmates. Governors Wilson and Davis both vetoed legislation that would have allowed reporters to interview inmates, claiming it was a security risk and that criminals didn't deserve publicity, anyway. If this was beginning to sound like the gulags of the former Soviet Union, how many politicians would support an inmate's claims against those of a guard? It was an almost perfect authoritarian system, American-style, hollowing out the democratic process rather than blatantly overthrowing it.

Fear of being soft on crime was the driving force in American politics during the thirty-year gang war. Perhaps it crystallized nationally in 1988 when George Bush ran television ads accusing Michael Dukakis of being lenient toward black predators like Willie Horton. The issues of the death penalty and membership in the ACLU also played into the character assault on Dukakis. Before the Horton attack ads played, Dukakis was leading Bush by double digits. I was supporting the Massachusetts governor at the time, and saw the oxygen depletion created by these law-and-order attacks. Certainly the policy-driven Dukakis might have responded more aggressively to Bush, but it didn't matter in the end. In the voting electorate of the time, the fear of crime had trumped the Democratic Party's traditional stances on poverty and racism. After that election, the party chose to follow the voter focus groups rather than fight back. Four years later, Bill Clinton was emphasizing his willingness to execute even a mentally retarded Arkansas prisoner and push for longer prison sentences to stop the coming "super-predator" wave. After Dukakis's failure and Clinton's triumphs, there wasn't much public stir at all at George Bush's record-setting number of Texas death-house executions.

It is too simple to blame law-and-order conspiracies for the pervasiveness of the wars on crime, gangs, and drugs. The voting public itself buys the argument because it accords with their experience and what they see on television. In past years they may have supported civil rights reforms and billions in tax dollars for antipoverty programs, and so feel they shouldn't be accused of being uncaring racists. Second, they kept hearing that the problems were continuing to worsen, anyway, which suggested that there was something wrong, something dysfunctional, about those at the bottom of the ladder. Third, burglaries, drug dealing, and violent crimes kept occurring despite the end of official segregation, which meant it was time to send in the police—with regret, perhaps, but with good conscience, too. In a phrase of the time, conservatives were no longer heartless bastards, just liberals who had been mugged. The New Deal and Great Society platforms seemed exhausted.

In short, liberals collaborated with conservatives in separating the issue of violent crime (gangs, super-predators, Willie Hortons) from its previous anchorage in socioeconomic conditions. The political exhaustion of the liberal message meant that the relevance of its content went ignored in the circles where political power was being exercised. It was true, as Klein noted, that the Reagan era shredded social programs like job training and housing. It was true, as many authors and headlines pointed out, that corporate globalization stripped the ghettos of jobs and downsized the ability of most Americans to be generous.[62] It was still true, as a 1997 California study revealed, that the strongest correlates explaining 1,702 gang-related homicides from 1988 to 1992 were employment and income levels.[63] But most of those in power, and the majority of the minority of the population that constituted the voting electorate, were driven by the politics of fear, which triumphed over fact. The only emotions that could rival fear were hope and compassion. But who could feel either sentiment toward gangs and convicts?

To make matters more complicated, the gang violence issue was fused with the great scare over narco-trafficking in the early nineties, then finally with the fear—and subsequent war against—terrorism after September 11, 2001. Police chiefs like William Bratton even interchanged the 18th Street gang with al-Qaeda in public speeches. Jose Padilla, a thirty-one-year-old Latin Disciple (and converted Muslim) from Chicago was accused by the FBI of plans to detonate a "dirty" radioactive bomb in the United States. It was never clarified how Padilla planned to obtain and assemble the components, nor how the weapon would be exploded. It wasn't necessary, since he was imprisoned as an enemy combatant without charges or access to an attorney. All that was necessary, apparently, was the FBI's word and a media profile that "read like the depressingly typical early trajectory of an inner-city street thug."[64] Padilla, according to one U.S. official, was a "unique mixture of a Chicago hardened ex-con street gang member, mixed with the single-mindedness of an Al Qaeda member."[65] An image now was planted in the fearful public mind: from Willie Horton in 1988 to Osama bin Ladin and the likes of Jose Padilla, Americans were threatened by a fearful, shadowy, dark-skinned menace that the authorities claimed could only be met by strong measures and the partial suspension of the Constitution. Who would ever know that three-fourths of the convictions the Justice Department classified as "international terrorism" after September 11, 2001, were "wrongly labeled," according to a report two years later by a congressional watchdog agency?[66]

With these hardening public perceptions, panic, and pervasive political expediency, how could there be a turnaround on the issue of gang violence?

The crucial point is that while the public may be diverted by law-and-order politics, there is no escaping the real issues. Sometimes liberal, progressive social activists and caring citizens understandably try to distance themselves from the gang problem. They find the gang subculture politically indefensible and morally discomforting. They harbor a sense that the problem is truly insoluble, and that tough law enforcement and long prison terms, while unfortunate, are necessary to quell the mayhem. Their sense of pragmatism tells them that appearing "soft" on gangs will set back progress on other issues they care deeply about. Perhaps they have trimmed back their early idealism. All these instincts are entirely understandable, but self-defeating.

Gang members are modern scapegoats, as Riis phrased it a century ago, a "distemper of the slum," come to tell us something is "amiss in our social life." By definition, persons with distemper are not rational social-change organizers with platforms and clipboards. If the public is not ready to see them as human beings capable of changing, they at least should be seen as signifiers instead of scapegoats. As signifiers, they direct us to what is "amiss in our social life," while as scapegoats they serve to deflect our attention away from deeper issues of social injustice and spending priorities. The war on gangs serves the political purpose of framing public dialogue around a law-and-order agenda, which leads to expanding police and prison budgets at the expense of everything else. As the war on gangs continues, there are fewer budget resources to invest in public housing, job training, and employment, parks and recreation, health care for the poor. An excuse for disengagement is provided to those in the corporate sector who may wish to divest from the inner city, anyway. The politics of the war on gangs results in a judiciary dominated by prosecutors, in banks and corporations that refuse to invest in urban areas unless the natives first are pacified or removed, and a caste of politicians fearful of questioning the police or ever siding with tattooed youth. The underclass is quietly pronounced redundant, ready for prison or the scrapheap of the new economy, even doomed.

That the scapegoating is out of proportion only proves its nature and utility. By comparison, the current crimes of corporate raiders, the sensationalized violence of modern entertainment, and the spiral of Ponzi schemes and tax evasion have never stimulated the public anger that street gangs do. Nor do assassins of abortion doctors like Eric Rudolph or armed white militias and prison gangs like the Aryan Brotherhood.

A new paradigm is needed, one that disallows scapegoating altogether. For the conservatives, as I have tried to argue, this would mean a major overhauling of their barely concealed defense of power and privilege in the name of "free markets" (except for defense contractors) and "individualism" (except for those favored by birth). It seems an unlikely possibility, unless conservatives draw radical lessons from Christian forgiveness and inner-city ministries, or decide that the sheer cost of prisons and policing requires a pragmatic alternative. For the liberals, it may seem that the challenge is more political than ideological, that is, to reassert that there are indeed root causes of crime in the face of conservative pressure. But liberal advocates face an ideological challenge rooted deep in their heritage. Like the conservative Victorians, the Marxist traditions share a disdain for the lumpenproletariat as a class of hopeless incorrigibles. *The Communist Manifesto* declared that while the lumpen "may, here and there, be swept into the movement by a proletarian revolution," it was much more likely that the conditions of life had prepared them for "the part of a bribed tool of reactionary intrigue." This disdain continues to color the analysis of countless progressive thinkers, researchers, and political activists.

In the *Eighteenth Brumaire of Louis Napolean,* Marx was puzzling over a problem with a familiar contemporary ring: how did a lazy, incompetent like Bonaparte become president of France? The answer partly lay in his lumpen support. Similarly, Marxists in the twentieth century would explain the rise of Hitler and Mussolini by their ability to militarize the lumpen as hooligans and strikebreakers. This analysis deeply impacted all sectors of the political left for over a century.

The Marxist theory was flawed, however. In the first place, the category of the lumpen was a catch-all, including "vagabonds," "pickpockets," "discharged soldiers," "beggars,"—all seen as the common detritis of society. In the Marxist division of the world between capitalist and proletarian, the lumpen were at most a secondary social formation. Outcasts on the streetcorners were incapable of becoming a class-conscious proletariet.

There was a minority in the Marxist tradition that felt otherwise, and their insights are worth remembering.[67] In the period between World War I and World War II, elements of what became the German Communist Party thought of themselves as a "party of outlaws," not simply a party of class-conscious workers. The tenements of Berlin teemed with unskilled, unemployed manual laborers whose children formed youth gangs, variously known as *klicken* (cliques), *verwahrlosing* (the wayward), or *wanderkrahen* (wild ones), similar in many respects to those appearing in American cities. They adopted names like Red Apaches, Bloody Bone, and Sing Sing. According to one study, 71 percent were apolitical, but a majority of the rest were sympathetic to the Communists in their neighborhoods. Efforts to organize them included a 1923 meeting of 700 *klicken* from 74 separate gangs. About 10 percent were considered hopelessly criminal; the rest simply antisocial. They represented a colorful, antiauthoritarian response to the experience of long years of dangerous labor for little if any compensation.

Those who wanted to work with them adopted a community-organizer stance, rooted in what they called "the politics of everyday life." This view recognized that factory-based proletarian organizing was too narrow to encompass the broader expressions of restiveness in culture or neighborhood life. It was true, as Marx had predicted, that the atomized condition of life on the streets made it difficult to organize collective, class-conscious struggles out of individual deviance. Nevertheless, the *klicken* were organized spontaneously and informally against the miseries of slum life. They rebelled both morally *and criminally,* in this perspective, against the police and the capitalist social order, and could be potential allies in the struggle against impending Fascism. Those who professed the politics of everyday life sought to identify the proletarian qualities in street culture and infuse a Socialist, instead of individualist, content. From this standpoint, the *klicken* were fighting the wrong enemy, usually others like themselves. Indeed, some were turned around and fought the Nazis in the streets and underground before the Third Reich crushed all forms of German resistance.

Many years later Huey P. Newton and the Black Panthers announced themselves as a party of the *lumpenproletariat,* partly because of their base in the criminal element ("the brothers on the block") and partly in response to the failure of any other ideology to address the chronic issues of the underclass. Their rivals in the US organization, as noted earlier, offered their own analysis of how to reach the lumpen. There was even an implied modification of *The Communist Manifesto* in the original manifesto of the Latin Kings. Where Marx and Engels had proclaimed that *"the history of all hitherto existing society is the history of class struggles,"* the anonymous Kings' manifesto proclaimed that *"the history of all hitherto existing gang feuds is the history of label struggles for the sake of clique recognition."* The assertion of identity by the left-outs, or lumpen, was plain to see. Street gangs remain mischanneled members of a potentially progressive alternative to Victorian neoconservatism.

This obscure detour through early Marxism is relevent today because categories like class and historical materialism still influence non-Marxist liberal social thought. If the broad political left has a firm disinterest in trying to salvage street gangs from incarceration, who in the mainstream will raise the issue in the broader public discourse?

The tradition of organizing around the politics of everyday life has continuing relevance today. The neoconservatives have succeeded in transforming the daily American experience of crime into a successful politics that scapegoats virtually all at-risk youth. On the other hand, the daily atomizing pressures on the underclass and the destructive addictions of everyday life, continue to undermine the ability of inner-city youth to galvanize by themselves into a collective voice for ending the conditions of their suffering.

It might seem politically suicidal to recommend that progressives break this impasse by taking up the issue of gang violence more seriously. But running from the issue has only meant victory for conservatives, chronic disaster for the inner cities, and a skewing of American priorities. The issue of gang violence has to be decriminalized and reframed, not avoided.

During my time in the California legislature, caravans of homies drove by bus or car on several occasions to lobby for bills, their first time in the halls of power. They did so for several reasons. First, to overcome their own feelings of isolation and inferiority. Second, to provide themselves with a learning experience in testifying and lobbying within the system. Third, to humanize them in the eyes of decision-makers. Fourth, to demand that street voices be included in debates about public policy. Finally, to build a broad, community-based network of gang violence prevention advocates.

One day we found ourselves in a discussion with Governor Davis's top press aides on the subject of the gang image and what might be done to change it. For the governor's seasoned aides, Philip Trounstein and Michael Bustamante, it was a strange "spin" session indeed. They were used to promoting semi-mindless tough-on-crime slogans, not defending the voteless victims of those same policies. Dewayne Holmes and Manny Lares made a presentation about their backgrounds, their run-ins with the law, the poverty sinking their communities. After about two minutes—a long attention span for a press secretary—Trounstein and Bustamante cut them off impatiently. "Look, you're sounding like victims here," Trounstein told them. "People don't want to listen to victims. The question is how you are going to reach the average voter in Van Nuys." It was a cynical assessment, but not wrong. Dewayne and Manny were getting a free lesson in politics, and they were listening. With the decline of inner-city voting, the locus of politics had shifted to wooing the conservative swing-voters in places like Van Nuys. That was the practical reality we all were forced to face. Then Trounstein had an idea. "Maybe you should say to the Van Nuys voter that you have a *solution* to the problem of gang violence. That's something they'll want to listen to, something positive."

It was good advice, and we shaped a legislative approach around it. Barrios Unidos had influenced their assemblyman, Fred Keeley, to carry successful legislation providing $3 million in annual grants for community-based groups engaged in violence prevention. We amended the law to include outreach work in juvenile halls and prisons. As a result, many local gang peace groups received grants in the $100–$250,000 range, enough to keep their doors open, the fax and phones working, and an organizer or two on the streets.

Another small step was grants for tattoo removals. Greg Boyle was the first to call my attention to the need for gang members to remove their tattoos when seeking employment. What merchant was going to hire a homie to work the cash register with "f.u.c.k.y.o.u." tattooed on his knuckles? Greg had recruited volunteer doctors for several hours of tattoo removal a week, but 700 homies were lined up waiting on the only morning they were available. A single laser machine cost $65,000, and the treatments were not painless, usually requiring several visits. We crafted legislation providing $750,000 and requiring 250 treatments per year for two years. Law enforcement was suspicious that dangerous criminals were seeking to remove the telltale tattoos that police had photographed and filed in the database. It wasn't so, but we included an amendment requiring community selection panels and screenings to show that applicants were indeed seeking jobs. I would have preferred $10 million, which would have enabled the governor to announce that he was removing tattoos from 10,000 gang members. It seemed to be a win-win solution, for the homies, the voters in Van Nuys, and the politicians. But only the smaller pilot project received bipartisan support.

The lesson of such endeavors was that untapped political support was possible for positive measures, like counseling, tattoo removal, after-school programs that helped individuals avoid or escape the gang life. It was possible, too, for networks of gang peace activists to win at least a public hearing where formerly they were out in the cold. These were important steps in breaking a monotonously one-sided debate. On the other hand, we were frustrated by Governor Wilson's and Governor Davis's unwillingness to formalize the peace process. On two occasions, the legislature passed bills establishing the Gang Violence Prevention Task Force. The legislation would have created a "round table" involving gang peace activists, business, clergy, government agencies, and law enforcement. In addition, former gang members would have been used as analysts and mediators in selected neighborhoods torn by violence. The task force would have reported back to the state on a larger violence prevention strategy for neighborhoods and prisons.

It was a novel idea and opened many doors for unprecedented discussions. It received support from the governor's own law enforcement adviser. In the end it was vetoed, however, because it broke the taboo against "legitimizing" gang members. To win legislative approval, we were willing to specify that task force members had to be "ex"-gang members. After passage of the amended bill, the homies around the state were excited at the feeling that their lobbying had mattered. Some were competing half-jokingly over who might be appointed, and whether they would get official jobs or certificates as state appointees, when the veto message was slipped under my door. When it happened under Wilson, it was a setback. The second time, under Davis, was devastating. The homies concluded that, at the end of the day, they would always face "the same bullshit." It was essential to those in power that gang members remain scapegoats, castaways. No exceptions.

When "Blinky" Rodriguez was in a meeting with Chief William Bratton two years later, he brought up the same issues. Blinky was riding the success of a San Fernando Valley truce at the same time, which made him valuable to police officers on the ground. But how can you ask for cooperation from those you proceed to stigmatize? Blinky asked Bratton. He proposed three steps to the chief: "Don't ask for help if you are gonna demonize us later. Stop the types of police suppression, like injunctions, that lead young men to rebellion. Do something about jobs." The chief listened, but no formal action resulted.

Over the years I have worked with or personally known about fifty of these gang peacemakers, all of them human beings in spite of the rap sheets that stalk their reputations. Only one has returned to jail. The others have worked for a decade, a few for longer, at the challenge of learning how to stem the addiction of violence. They should by now be considered a source of raw wisdom from which our society can learn. They have had an impact, both in saving lives (including their own) and giving voice to the voiceless. Through hip-hop artists such as Tupac Shakur and entrepreneurs like Russell Simmons, that same voice has touched tens of millions beyond the gang subculture. The music's offensive mysogeny and commercialism cannot erase its message from the streets and prisons. Many Americans seem to want to listen to the music, even co-opt its beat, but continue to ignore the diagnosis of the "distemper" it contains.[68]

But gang peacemakers and their friends can't transform our politics and priorities on their own. Just as it is impossible to imagine solving the gang violence crisis without their involvement, it is clear that the peacemaker circle needs the second circle of public advocates to protect their backs and ripple outward into a transformation of the larger society toward jobs and justice.

That means a new and reconstituted social justice movement with a central commitment to addressing the needs of at-risk youth, a new peace movement on the home front. It means making the case that the war on gangs (and the war on drugs) has led to a quagmire of failure, not hope for the future. That means ensuring that a growing percentage of public budgets go for inner-city education, gang intervention programs, housing and parks, and living wages for the working poor, that a percentage of developer profits go to hiring inner-city youth, and it means more arts classes, remedial education, and job training in the juvenile halls and prisons. According to most surveys, majority support for such goals already is there. Americans favor not only legitimate deterrence but also stronger prevention programs, not pre-emptive law-and-order alone. Much of the country—by no means all—seems ready for a return to the idealistic days of the early sixties, when it seemed possible to confront poverty and discrimination through a social move-ment and responsive national officials. But instead, our government is dominated by neoconservatives whose war on gangs has left an explosive quagmire in our in-ner cities, and whose foreign policy seems headed in the same direction, imposing a militarized U.S. empire on millions of uprooted, angry, at-risk youth, with Special Forces, bases, and embassies looking like fortified extensions of the CRASH units and the Rampart Division headquarters back home. In comparison with the overemphasis on expensive military solutions to social and economic problems, antipoverty efforts have been slashed to levels below that of the New Frontier.[69]

What blocks a transformation of our priorities is not so much the power of the conservative coalition over politics as the persistent appeal of scapegoating in political culture. The existence of a frightening "other" always reminds people of their relative good fortune and the need to unify against the barbarians. And when middle-class incomes remain flat, our frustrations are safely chan-neled against teen-age criminals instead of the white-collar thieves of this new Gilded Age.[70]

"Small wonder the fruit is bitter," wrote Jacob Riis after surveying the nineteenth-century tenements, adding that

> The remedy that shall be an effective answer to the coming appeal for justice must proceed from the public conscience.
>
>   Neither legislation nor charity can cover the ground. The greed of capital that wrought the evil must itself undo it, as far as it now can be done.[71]

Without knowing it, Riis was anticipating the New Deal, the era that enabled millions to leave the gangster life. If we are to avoid the globalization of gang vi-olence, the time has come for a new New Deal for those who were left behind.

Afterword: Looking for Miracles

I composed these final thoughts while a visiting fellow at Harvard University's Institute of Politics, located in the Kennedy School of Government. Here in the nineties a Harvard brain trust conceived a national solution to the gang violence crisis, heralded as "the Boston Miracle" by U.S. Attorney General Janet Reno.[1] My experience with the gangs crisis had left me in search of a miracle, so I decided to explore the Boston experience more closely. Was it a miracle or ultimately only a mirage?

In comparison with Los Angeles, Chicago, and New York, Boston barely comes to mind as a center of gang violence, though it has a long history of racial division over issues ranging from school busing to police brutality. In fact the official Boston policy was to deny the existence of an inner-city gang problem until the end of the eighties.[2] The 1988 drive-by shooting of a young girl, a 1990 Halloween gang rape and murder, and a 1992 knife attack by gang members during the funeral of a deceased homie at the Morning Star Baptist Church in Mattapan shocked the city into an awakening. By 1990 the city's murder rate reached an all-time high of 152, half of them said to be gang-related.

There had been deep divisions between the police and African American leadership at the time, arising from heavy-handed "search on sight" tactics, known as "tipping kids upside down," used indiscriminately against young black males. Then in 1989 the city was shaken by the bizarre Carol Stuart murder case that altered the racial climate and prompted reform. Stuart was a pregnant white woman killed in Mission Hill. Her lawyer husband, Charles Stuart, identified a black male suspect for the killing, a false claim that led to a police manhunt among black youth. The truth was that the husband himself killed Carol Stuart, and ultimately jumped off a bridge rather than submitting to arrest.[3] At that nadir of police-community relations, the police leadership realized they could no longer continue with their daily patterns of extraconstitutional behavior in the black community. Civic leaders seeking solutions were at their wit's end.

William Bratton, whose career looms large in this book, was Boston's chief at the time and helped launch the subsequent policy of "problem-solving policing." One prong of the offensive was a renewed crackdown on allegedly hard-core gangbangers after a police scandal had forced the dissolution of the older "search on sight" units. An aggressive Operation Clean Sweep was conducted in ghetto housing projects with little or no observable protest from the black community. At the same time, black ministers, rocked by the increase in gang violence, launched a community intervention through a new Ten Point Coalition. Street workers were deployed. Friday night street ministries were initiated. Peace leagues sponsored basketball games between gang rivals. A "freedom summer" featured voter registration, and math and science tutorials. The coalition made the cover of *Newsweek*. The police and the preachers, longtime adversaries, discovered a common interest. The cops needed partners to overcome their isolation from the black community. The Ten Point Coalition created an "umbrella of legitimacy" for the policing but could formally withhold that legitimacy by going public when officers resorted to abusive tactics.

I met one of the ministers, Reverend Ray Hammond, on a winter day in late 2003. "Reverend Ray" grew up in Philadelphia at the height of the gang wars there, went to Harvard and became an emergency room physician before choosing to devote himself fully to the ministry. Working to end gang violence, he felt, was "the natural extension of a faith commitment." He and his wife Gloria, also a church worker, lived in the center of Mattapan, known at the time as "Murderpan." "The kids are broken and bleeding, how do you step over them on the way to Church?" he asked himself and others. Through Ten Points, they joined with other clergy, notably another Harvard graduate, Reverend Eugene Rivers, in the discovery that many young people were redeemable. One of the homies he met a decade before, Dexter Sandiford from Trinidad, became an activist and is finishing his degree at the University of Massachusetts. Through people like Dexter, Reverend Ray learned the value of intervention programs. "It's intensive, but it's possible. We learned that the line between intervention and prevention is more mirage than reality. You impact one Dexter, you impact his daughter and his friends."

Harvard researchers were deeply engaged in these "problem solving" efforts, particularly David Kennedy from the Kennedy School of Government and his associates Anne Piehl and Anthony Braga. With federal funds, they became the research arm of the ad hoc new partnership. The Harvard team conceived the Boston Gun Project and Operation Cease-fire, both efforts to shut down the estimated 1 percent of gang members using the weapons, by targeted zero-tolerance techniques. The strategy, called "pulling every lever," utilized pending warrants or petty offenses of any nature—jaywalking, unregistered cars, probation violations, etc.—to drive gangbangers off the streets while also holding open meetings with gang members to offer job training, summer employment, or other rewards. It was a combination of two strategies—selective enforcement and a community peace process—that were rarely integrated in other urban settings. Getting the Harvard team and especially the African American ministers to the table with Boston police commanders was described as "miraculous" in its own right. But the official "Boston miracle" was the sudden drop in youth homicides after Operation Cease-fire began. "Serious gang violence has almost stopped," concluded Harvard's lead expert. Indeed, for twenty-nine months, there were no teenage homicides in Boston at all. That was the miracle that caught Janet Reno's attention. The federal government announced plans to replicate the miracle nationwide.

The miracle was somewhat exaggerated, however. In 2000, two years after the *Newsweek* cover story, Boston experienced forty homicides, in 2001 another sixty-six, though not all were gang-related. "Boston's violent crime remission was over. After years of decreases, the number of gun incidents in the gang strongholds of

Roxbury and Dorchester started to creep up again," announced the public policy journal *Governing*.[4] Harvard's research team struggled with variables too complex to describe (negative binomial regressions) to conclude that Operation Cease-fire had in all probability caused the violence reduction, but could not determine the reasons for the violence resumption. New York's combative conservative mayor Rudolph Giuliani couldn't help suggesting that Boston, unlike New York, wasn't tough enough.

The fact remains that Boston gang homicides have lessened sharply from a decade ago. For Reverend Ray, the change is "audible—you don't hear gunfire all the time," and "palpable—when you see a corner you don't think of somebody who was just killed there."

While Boston was avoiding notorious police shooting incidents like that of Amadou Diallo, the police department maintained a tough philosophy at the core. By 2003, they were being trained not to target people on "subjective things," which would be racial profiling, but to view as suspicious "their reaction to law enforcement" whenever young people's eyes darted away upon seeing a policeman.[5]

Still, Boston's model was better than New York City's because of the formal, active inclusion of the black clergy, with their civil rights backgrounds and community ties, in the process. The clergy-based coalition monitored, educated, and trained the police to become more sensitive. Boston never adopted the "broken windows" philosophy of Giuliani and the neoconservatives, although the "pulling all levers" approach bore similarities to it. The partnership left the clergy open to the concern that they were collaborating with law enforcement; indeed, the ministers created an informal system of "remote surveillance" for the police.[6] As Reverend Ray explained it, "after you offer alternatives to the high-impact player, you have to warn him that the alternative is becoming a candidate for high-level surveillance." He would rather provide a prison ministry than a funeral. Nevertheless, he acknowledged that other homies would fill the places of the incarcerated ones, and that a humane, rehabilitation-oriented prison setting was a distant hope.

But, according to one Harvard study, "the coalition's primary contribution to Boston's success most likely has not been a result of its street ministry, that is, its attempt to turn kids around through one-on-one counseling, but rather stems from its role in both controlling and legitimizing police activity."[7] As one participant stated more bluntly, Operation Cease-fire "was really about enforcement and not about religion."[8]

But the "partnership," while highly progressive by law enforcement standards, remained a voluntary informal arrangement based on a fundamental imbalance. It was not a structural reform or an institutional shift of power, like a civilian police review board with storefront offices or attorneys to challenge police misconduct. The police retained ultimate control of policy, operations, and, of course, budget. The ministers represented a moral authority, a citizen base, and an ability to generate headlines. But the fundamental difference was that the police could deliver swift and certain punishment while the coalition couldn't deliver swift and certain jobs. Those depended on "the economy" or the goodwill of Boston's business leadership to generate more summer jobs than a market philosophy could justify. Dorchester and Roxbury remained ghettos throughout greater Boston's other "miracle" of the eighties, the transformation to a glittering high-tech new economy. By 2003, the last of Boston's locally owned economic institutions, the Fleet Bank, had passed into absentee ownership.

The Boston miracle was limited as well by its focus on the jurisdiction of Boston proper, and specifically on the African American ghettos like Roxbury and Dorchester rather than the wider metropolitan region or the prison system that manufactured hardened criminals. The Boston region has increasingly generated the "rainbow of gangs" described by James Diego Vigil. In Lynn, on the rim of the Boston metropolis, there are black youth today in the Marion Garden Millionaires, but also Salvadorans, Dominicans, and Puerto Ricans in the various Vatos Locos, and Crips and Bloods dominated by southeast Asian kids descended from the refugee camps of Vietnam and Cambodia. According to police, there were 1,000 to 1,600 teenage gang members in thirty-eight distinct gangs in Lynn alone this year, with 500 more in next-door Lowell,[9] springing up from global socioeconomic conditions faster than they could be put away. "This is only going to get worse," said a frustrated member of Lynn's antigang police unit.

As for the de facto gang incubator known as the Massachusetts state prison system, nearly half the inmates were functionally illiterate at the time of the Boston miracle. State funds for prisoner education were being cut in half, leaving only 1 percent of the state correctional budget for addressing illiteracy and skills deficits.[10] By 2003, Massachusetts was spending more on jails and prisons than on public higher education.[11] After indefinite solitary confinement for being identified as gang members, many inmates reported such mental health problems as "insomnia, depression, nightmares, violent mood swings, anxiety attacks, claustrophobia, paranoia, hallucinations and generalized feelings of nervousness, irritability and anger" according to an expert's opinion. There were 148 inmates released from such harsh confinement back onto the streets of Boston and other Massachusetts cities between April 1995 and January 1997, more than the total arrested in those two years by prosecutors and police "pulling levers" to send them away.[12]

Federal funding for the Harvard researchers ran out after three years, in 1999. The original professors stopped participating in the interagency partnership, according to one I interviewed, although Harvard itself supports the continued work of Braga with the police. As it existed in 1996–97, Operation Cease-fire was "entirely gone," said one. When I asked why this had happened, there was a long silence. "I don't think we thought about it," the researcher then replied. "Attention went elsewhere. As there were fewer homicides, it became harder to maintain resources. The [partnership] decayed." A "falling out" among the parties was cited as well. Apparently while too many sought credit for the miracle, no one wanted blame for its problems.

Still, the claim is that the Harvard group were "the key players in the development and propagation nationwide of the theory of community policing during the late 1980s and 1990s."[13] As this book has tried to argue, however, community policing itself is problematic. It sounds progressive: who could object to a community dimension? Who favors *non*-community policing by an occupying army anymore? Certain aspects of community policing, like neighborhood patrols, are positive. But the problem is the chasm that grows between an academic idea and its implementation in reality. Under community policing, the police have the power to define who the "community" shall be and, not surprisingly, it turns out to be those community elements who positively support the police rather than those who worry about police overreaction, profiling, and brutality. As someone who legislated California's "neighborhood watch" programs in the eighties, I observed a process in which a handpicked few from the "community" simply became extensions of the police departments. There was no requirement that the "community" include civil rights advocates, clergy, or, God forbid, former gang members. What seems unique about Boston as a city is the liberal consensus that expects the police to be answerable, if only informally, to the clergy in the Ten Point Coalition.

If Harvard University—with its intellectual talent, its massive endowment, and its extensive property holdings—could not deliver a policy solution in its backyard, that was a disturbing commentary on the entire nation's capacity to think its way out of the urban quagmire. It was also a small reminder of an earlier generation of Harvard's "best and brightest," whose Vietnam folly was chronicled by David Halberstam. Despite the stark differences between the Vietnam War and this chronic skirmishing in our cities, there are similarities to take to heart. America's Vietnam strategy was twofold: first, to deploy special units (the Green Berets) to crush the enemy Vietcong while, secondly, "winning hearts and minds" by building hospitals, schools, and the like. Policy intellectuals, many from Harvard, affirmed the soundness of the policy. President Lyndon Johnson promised that American taxpayers could afford both "guns" and "butter." What actually happened, however, was disastrously different than the intellectual blueprint. The "enemy" proved hard to pinpoint, and kept reproducing their numbers even after countless thousands were killed or "neutralized." The military tactics alienated significant numbers of the civilian population instead of winning them over. The budgetary cost of supporting suppression overwhelmed any resources left over for hearts and minds. The secret culture of the military fraternity led to cover-ups of brutality and a damaging credibility gap. In the end, there proved to be no military solution to a problem that was racial, social, economic, and political in nature.

Obviously, modern street gangs are hardly the North Vietnamese Army. But in one sense the quagmire of gang violence is perhaps more serious than Vietnam. America can't withdraw and go home. We are home. The violence is not 13,000 miles away but down the street. Failure will mean more guns and less butter for the inner cities, and a crippling gap in American life between the comfortably affluent and criminalized youth of color.

Word

The two main stories recounted in this book—of local police using excessive force to suppress gangs, and of local communities inventing peace processes to reduce the madness—are likely to go on indefinitely unless Americans become willing to grapple more deeply with what we have become. We incarcerate more of our people per capita than any comparable developed country (perhaps more than any nation on earth). We create the greatest gap between wealth and poverty, too, of any comparable nation (European welfare spending is twice the percentage of their gross domestic product as ours). We celebrate annual salaries like $70 million for Michael Jordan and $31 million for David Letterman while we shred the social safety net. We insist that the solution to our permanent racial gap is that every black and brown child adapt to the individualistic, punitive, sink-or-swim capitalist model. Until they obey, we will punish them psychologically and economically, then punish them again in jails and prisons, as the scapegoats on which our civilization seems to depend.

Of many factors that keep this cycle repeating, the one most under our control is the "word," or "story," the underlying American mythic narrative that blinds us to our real history. Americans go to extreme lengths to distance ourselves from our own roots in crime, violence, and gangs. For example, the state of Georgia, now a bastion of hard-line, punitive law-and-order politics, was first created as a colony of deported criminals—"thugs" as defined under British rule. Today's respectable life grew from thug life. But to project an ethos of superiority, respectability, and success, this untidy white ethnic history is air-brushed, forgotten, stored in amnesia, and often projected by transference onto today's at-risk youth. The war on gangs becomes a purgative expulsion of our own sordid history, establishing our virtue, superiority, and innocence. Until America's white ethnics get their true story straight, they will be unable to understand, face, and help in healing the wounds of today's inner-city youth. America's universities bear a special responsibility in this regard because, like Harvard, they train the "best and brightest," and serve as custodians and perpetrators of the mainstream "word," or culture, not to mention being agents of gentrification and displacement of the inner-city poor.

Fundamental to this distancing process is our moral and religious heritage. The Puritan conception of sinners in the hands of an angry God deeply affects this country's notions of punishment. As Gilligan writes, the emphasis on punishment as a cure for violence has continued for thousands of years in spite of every rational effort to question whether it might be the cause.[14]

But there is another religious tradition, that of compassion, which has been distorted, maligned, and marginalized in the modern discussion of crime. The restoration of compassion in public policy is a key prerequisite, however, to solving the problem of gang violence.

Homies are not demons, but complex human beings capable of changing for the better. When they commit serious crimes, they need to be arrested. But that does not mean being "tossed," intimidated, disrespected, or punished with further punishment. Homies themselves cite a new compassion or spirituality, more than punishment, as crucial to their changing. In addition, those most likely to reach out to them are not politicians, businessmen, or journalists, but people of faith, from Father Boyle in East Los Angeles, to Father Barrios in Spanish Harlem, to Reverend Frank Alton in Pico-Union, to Reverend Jesse Jackson in Chicago, to Boston ministers like Ray Hammond, to the Quakers, Christian pacifists, to Malcolm X and the Nation of Islam, to the late Rasta man Bob Marley, all of whom made personal commitments to stop the violence while leaders from other sectors of society held back.

Whatever our faith tradition (if any), Americans generally are in thrall to the conventional story of Jesus of Nazareth. In that story, he is the "Christ" who, through his resurrection, promises redemption. But there is also the story of the *historical* Jesus, often reduced by orthodox religion to a catechism of sayings and parables divorced from the historical context of Galilee. The historical narrative has always been a powerful tool for religious advocates of civil rights and social justice. My chords of memory were moved, for example, when I heard Father

Luis Barrios tell the Latin Kings that the historical Jesus was left alone by the authorities until "he went downtown" to challenge the temple elite in Jerusalem.

Was the historical Jesus himself a homeboy? The child of a dysfunctional but loving family, lost somewhere during adolescence and young adulthood, we know that he bonded with local communities at the edge of a cruel and punitive empire. Among his friends, or homies, were a variety of maladjusted souls. He felt forsaken by his father. He was demonized and criminalized for his identity and finally crucified alongside thieves. Only in death did he transcend life.

I wrote Greg Boyle to ask his opinion. Though hooked up intravenously to cancer medication, he e-mailed me back:

> This much was certain—Jesus made a beeline (always) to stand with those on the margins, those whose dignity had been denied, the poor and the excluded, the easily despised, the demonized, and those whose burdens were more than they could bear. He chose to stand precisely with them. And they killed him for it. . . .
>
> In the Beatitudes, it says, "Blessed are the single-hearted, Blessed are those who show mercy, Blessed are the peacemakers." The original language ought to be translated more accurately and precisely: "you're in the right place if . . . you're a peacemaker."
>
> It is, in the end, about location. Where have we chosen to stand.
>
> This is how I feel about Homeboy Industries. Sure, it's about jobs and concrete help. But it is a symbol as well, a choosing to "be in the right place," to stand with the homies. And so I get thousands of letters from prisons, from guys I don't know, wanting something to happen in their lives after release.
>
> Jesus stood with everybody who was nobody. And they killed him for it.[15]

Tupac Shakur's last works, *Crucifixion* and *Resurrection*, suggest a deep identification with the original Jesus movement. For Tupac, the criminals on their crosses were *thugs*, crucified for the *thug life*, for hanging out with "all the people you threw away." The "thugs" were not criminals ("robbers" in Matthew, "criminals" in Luke) but the underdogs of their time, threats to the empire defamed by officials as nothing but petty hustlers.[16] Tupac made a "prophecy" of his coming

death. As for death and resurrection, he like other "hopeless" homeboys antici-
pated this inevitability with a kind of relief.

Jesus' crew included a snitch (Judas), a power-tripper (Peter), and other fallible
human beings. In time the movement became a church and finally the state religion of the very Roman Empire that crucified their founder, turning the revolutionary Jesus story upside down. Today Jesus Christ is invoked by Rush
Limbaugh, William Bennett, the Christian Coalition, Christian police commanders, and countless crusaders for greater punishment of the very kinds of people
the historical Jesus tried to heal. A strain of the same punitive orthodoxy can be
seen in the nation's official war on terror, with its raging fear against new barbarians at the gates.

But the demons that Americans most need to exorcize, I believe, are more
within our souls and repressed memories than lurking outside our barricaded
walls. Dewayne, Manny, Sylvia, Aqeela, Daude, Luis, Nane, Alex, John, and so
many others chronicled in these pages are prophets representing the signs of the
times. Their examples call for forgiveness, healing, bread, and justice. Their destiny may hang between miracles and martyrdom.

Blessed are the peacemakers.

Notes

Preface to the Paperback Edition

1. *Atlantic Monthly*, July–Aug. 2005, p. 118.
2. "Honduras Condemned Over Child Killings," BBC News, Aug. 11, 2001, citing the report of Asma Jahangir, UN special rapporteur on extra-judicial, summary, or arbitrary executions.
3. Hearings, ad hoc committee of the Los Angeles City Council, April 2005, Councilman Martin Ludlow, chair.
4. Ana Arana, "Supergangs in Central America," *Foreign Affairs*, May/June 2005.
5. Tim Weiner, "At Least 100 Are Killed in Prison Fire in Honduras," *New York Times*, May 17, 2004, describes the 2003 and 2004 fires. While reporting that no evidence of foul play was available, Weiner quoted Bishop Romulo Emiliani of San Pedro Sula saying that "there are people who think they should all be exterminated," and cited U.S. State Department reports of vigilante death squads.
6. U.S. State Department, "Country Reports on Human Rights Practices: Honduras," Feb. 25, 2004, p. 22.
7. T. Christian Miller, "Dying Young in Honduras," *Los Angeles Times*, Nov. 25, 2002.
8. Reports cited in the 2004 U.S. State Department "Country Reports on Human Rights Practices: Honduras" estimated that while no perpetrator could be identified in most of the killings, 15–20 percent were blamed on police, private guards, or neighborhood vigilantes, mostly in "shootings usually involving a truck, often without license plates" (p. 2).

9. See Associated Press, "Novice Follows Giuliani Example," *Holland Sentinel Online*, Nov. 25, 2001.

10. *Miami Herald* (Cancun edition), Sept. 8, 2003.

11. Ibid.

12. "Honduras Condemned Over Child Killings."

13. U.S. State Department, "Country Reports on Human Rights Practices: Honduras," p. 8.

14. The accusations of torture appear in ibid. Further from the report: "Prisoners suffered from severe overcrowding, malnutrition, and a lack of adequate sanitation, and allegedly were subject to various other abuses, including rape by other prisoners. Pretrial detainees generally were not separated from convicted prisoners. The 24 penal centers held over 12,500 prisoners in 2002, more than twice their intended capacity; *more than 88 percent of all prisoners in 2002 were pre-trial detainees. . . . About 3 percent of prisoners were thought to be gang members in 2002*" (p. 8).

15. Dr. Jose Acevedo and Dr. Mario Posas, "Investigacion Sobre Pandillas Y Violencia Juvenil," Asociacion Cristiana De Jovenes (AJC) y Save the Children—Reino Unido, 2004.

16. Ginger Thompson, "Shuttling Between Nations, Latino Gangs Confound the Law," *New York Times*, Sept. 26, 2004.

17. *Los Angeles Times*, May 15, 2005.

18. *Time* reported on March 15, 2004, that marines headed for Iraq "have been studying how the Los Angeles police department patrols gangland neighborhoods." On March 25, an LAPD spokesman responded to my inquiry about marines visiting the LAPD by saying, "I have spent time with General Mattis at Camp Pendleton and have visited with members of his staff here at Parker Center to discuss policing methods, strategies, and tactics. We also discussed community involvement in targeting gangs and narcotics enforcement. Also, two marine captains attended the LAPD/FBI Gang Symposium in January 2004 prior to their departure for Baghdad." Communication courtesy of Rabbi Allen Freehling, director of Los Angeles's Human Relations Commission.

19. John F. Burns, "The Conflict in Iraq: Night Patrols; Marines' Raids Underline Push in Crucial Area," *New York Times*, Dec. 6, 2004.

20. Damien Cave, "Army Recruiters Say They Feel Pressure to Bend Rules," *New York Times*, May 3, 2005; Eric Schmitt, "Army Recruiting More High School Dropouts to Meet Goals," *New York Times*, June 11, 2005.

21. Evan Wright, *Generation Kill: Devil Dogs, Iceman, Captain America, and the New Face of American War* (New York: G.P. Putnam's Sons, 2004), p. 24.

Foreword: *Adelante*

1. *New York Times* "Week in Review," Aug. 24, 2003.

2. James Alan Fox, "Ganging Up," *Boston Globe*, Dec. 1, 2003. Fox, a criminologist at Northeastern University and consultant for the Bureau of Justice Statistics, has been chal-

lenged by Mike Males in *Framing Youth, 10 Myths about the Next Generation*, Common Courage Press, 1999, and Franklin E. Zimring, *American Youth Violence*, Oxford, 1998.

3. Gregory Boyle, op-ed article, *Los Angeles Times*, Dec. 18, 2003.

Chapter 1: These Dead Don't Count

1. Winifred Reed, Scott Decker, eds. *Responding to Gangs: Evaluation and Research*, National Institute of Justice, 2002, p. 47.

2. I am indebted to Cheryl Maxson of the University of California, Riverside, for these observations. See also Mark Fleisher, *Dead End Kids*, University of Wisconsin, 1998.

3. Elijah Anderson, *Code of the Street, Decency, Violence, and the Moral Life of the Inner City*, Norton, 1999, p. 34. See also James Diego Vigil's observations on "street socialization" in *A Rainbow of Gangs*, University of Texas, 2002.

4. Statewide Organized Gang Database Act, Illinois Criminal Justice Information Authority, Nov. 1998.

5. Reed and Decker, p. 116.

6. California Penal Code, Sections 186.20–186.28.

7. Opening remarks for J. Robert Flores, National Youth Gang Symposium, June 11, 2002, Orlando, Florida, Office of Juvenile Justice and Delinquency Prevention.

8. Communication with author, 2003.

9. Maxson, Curry, and Howell, in Reed and Decker, p. 112.

10. Communication from Marianne W. Zawitz, Bureau of Justice Statistics, U.S. Dept. of Justice, May 7, 2003.

11. U.S. Department of Justice, Bureau of Justice Statistics, *Homicide Trends in the United States*, Nov. 21, 2002.

12. Miller cited in Maxson et al., p. 113.

13. NYGS data supplied by Arlen Egley, NYGS researcher, 2003; FBI data through 2000 from Bureau of Justice Statistics, Nov. 21, 2002.

14. Interview with Egley, 2003.

15. Communication with author, 2003.

16. Los Angeles County Sheriffs' Department, Jan. 2003, Violence Prevention Coalition of Greater Los Angeles.

17. Violence Prevention Coalition of Greater Los Angeles, based on LASD data, revised Sept. 13, 1996.

18. According to FBI data, 643 law enforcement officers were "feloniously killed" from 1992 to 2001. No data is published for gang killings of officers. The data shows that no officers were killed in "civil disorders," thirty-eight were killed in "drug-related matters," and seven were killed while alone on foot patrol. FBI National Press Office, Dec. 2, 2002.

19. LAPD monthly gang unit reports, Dec. 1993–Dec. 2002.

20. Carolyn Block and Richard Block, *Trends, Risks and Interventions in Lethal Violence*, Proceedings of the Third Annual Spring Symposium of the Homicide Research Working Group, July 1995.
21. Chicago police numbers are available from annual reports online at the Municipal Reference Library of the Harold Washington Library, Chicago.
22. *Chicago Tribune*, Jan. 16, 2003.
23. For perspective, here are the official 2002 overall homicide numbers for major cities with more than 100 homicides from all causes:

City	2002 Homicides
Los Angeles	658
Chicago	647
New York	584
Detroit	402
Philadelphia	288
Washington	262
Houston	259
Baltimore	253
Phoenix	183
Memphis	162
Las Vegas	145
Columbus	129
Milwaukee	108
San Antonio	100
TOTAL	4,180

24. Data supplied here from NYGS to author, 2003.

25. Interview with author, 2003.

26. One official I interviewed told me, "This isn't LA. We're not overrun by kids with AK-47s." An NYPD insider wrote that "Gang violence has not been as big a problem in New York as it has been in other cities. Consequently, we don't have a lot of historical data." Some variation on this theme seems to precede all analysis of gang crime in New York City.

As recently as 2003, top NYPD officials were maintaining that gang wars were long over, if they had ever existed. From January to June 2003, they said, there were only eight gang-motivated homicides, compared to fourteen in the same period the previous year. There had been only one grand larceny involving gangs. (Source: Paul Browne, NYPD)

There was one suspicious exemption during this period, however, in 1999. It was the time following the killing of the unarmed immigrant named Amadou Diallo, shot with a volley of forty-one bullets by a special police unit, leading to an upsurge of civil rights marches, arrests, and a protest song by Bruce Springsteen. Police officials attacked the news media for criticizing the Diallo shooting, saying that the criticism caused many officers to become demoralized and therefore less aggressive. (See criticism by Deputy Commissioner Edward T. Norris, *New York Times*, Nov. 5, 1999.) Mayor Rudolph Giuliani, famous for his gruff war-on-gangs rhetoric, was gearing up for a U.S. Senate race. For whatever reason, police experts suddenly produced inflated numbers for gang homicides: Forty-two for 1998, and eighty-seven through November 1999. These numbers were higher than the recorded totals for the previous years going back to 1976.

27. New York Police Department data, analyzed in Andrew Karmen, *New York Murder Mystery: The True Story Behind the Crime Crash of the 1990s*, NYU Press, 2000, p. 39.

28. Ibid.

29. Correspondence with the author, May 12, 2003; see also Karmen, p. 76.

30. *New York Times*, June 20, 2003.

31. *Christian Science Monitor*, Dec. 28, 1998.

32. This reclassification was acknowledged in the Philadelphia police department's UCR for 2003.

33. *Women's News*, Detroit, June 25, 2003; see also David Ashenfelter, "Detroit's Crime Data Wrong," *Detroit Free Press*, April 14, 2001.

34. Attorney General's Office, State of Texas, *Gangs in Texas 2001: An Overview*.

35. *Chicago Tribune*, Jan. 16, 2003. Data for 2002.

36. Interview with Timothy Bray, School of Social Sciences, University of Texas, Dallas.

37. Walter Miller, Office of Juvenile Justice and Delinquency Prevention, *The Growth of Youth Gang Problems in the United States, 1970–98*, April 2001, p. 4.

38. Arlen Egley Jr., *National Youth Gang Survey Trends*, Office of Juvenile Justice and Delinquency Prevention, Feb. 2002, #03.

39. Miller, p. iii.

40. "Analysis Shows Blacks Are Bulk of Toronto's Gunshot Dead," *National Post*, Nov. 8, 2002.

41. Communication to author, 2003.

42. Miller.

43. Ibid., pp. 42–47.

44. Ibid., p. 43.

45. Ibid., p. 44.

46. Regrettably, this book does not focus on Asian street gangs like the Vietnamese, the Cam-

bodians, the Chinese tongs, or such groups as the Korean Crazies in Los Angeles. In certain ways, they parallel and model themselves after the larger Latino and African American gangs. But others are vertically organized like traditional syndicates. Their rates of homicide are tragic, but statistically small compared to those of blacks and Latinos. For more information, see Vigil, *A Rainbow of Gangs*.

47. The estimate comes from Professor Tony Platt, longtime criminologist at the University of California, Berkeley.

Chapter 2: Roses in Concrete

1. Tupac Shakur, *The Rose that Grew from Concrete*, Pocket, 1999, p. 3.
2. *West Side Story*, produced by Robert Wise, screenplay by Ernest Lehman, music by Leonard Bernstein, 1956.
3. Luis J. Rodriguez, *Always Running: La Vida Loca, Grang Days in L.A.*, Simon & Schuster/Touchstone, 1993. The book had sold 175,000 copies by 2003.
4. Sanyika Shakur, aka Monster Kody Scott, *Monster: The Autobiography of an L.A. Gang Member*, Penguin, 1993.
5. Alex Haley, *The Autobiography of Malcolm X*, Ballantine, 1964.
6. Tupac had an ambiguous definition of "thug life" as an outlaw lifestyle that reflected his own contradictions, as discussed in chapter six.
7. The term echoes President Dwight Eisenhower's 1959 warning about a military-industrial complex as a self-perpetuating interest group.
8. A California Field Poll in 2002 showed that four times as many people would cut prison spending before cutting education. Forceful special interest groups clearly counted for more than an inactive preference of the public.
9. See Richard Jacoby's *Conversations with the Capeman: The Untold Story of Salvador Agron*, Painted Leaf Press, 2000, which tells the story of a sixteen-year-old Puerto Rican who killed two white teenagers in a gang fight in Hell's Kitchen, the former Irish neighborhood that spawned the gangs of the nineteenth century. Labelled "the Capeman" because he wore a black cape, his case shocked the city at the time. Agron was sentenced to death, then commuted to a life term after civil rights protests. His gang was the Vampires on the Westside. They had a distinctive diddy-bopper strut, wore stylish jackets, drank cheap wine, hung out on street corners, engaged in rumbles and petty theft (Agron first went to the reformatory for stealing $7 and a flashlight from someone). In their violent rumbles over turf, the weapons were usually home-made zip guns, bats, sticks, and knives. By his account, "usually when a gang member became eighteen or twenty-one, he or she would quit the gang and become a 'coolie,' meaning that he was in no gang or had stopped bopping or gang fighting," p. 148.
10. Robin D.G. Kelley, *Race Rebels: Culture, Politics and the Black Working Class*, The Free Press, 1994, 1996, p. 167.

11. Luis Valdez, *Zoot Suit and Other Plays*, Arte Publico Press, 1992, p. 180.

12. Haley, p. 43.

13. Ibid., p. 44.

14. Taylor Branch, *Pillar of Fire: America in the King Years, 1963–65*, Simon & Schuster, 1998, p. 296.

15. Ibid., pp. 418, 423.

16. Ibid., p. 296.

17. Johnson's war on poverty was established officially on the night of the Tonkin Gulf Resolution. Branch, pp. 445, 455.

18. James Baldwin, *The Fire Next Time*, Vintage, 1962.

19. The estimates are by Bob Moses in Branch, p. 454, and from logs in Doug McAdam, *Freedom Summer*, Oxford University Press, 1988, pp. 257–82.

20. Michael R. Beschloss, *Taking Charge: The Johnson White House Tapes, 1963–64*, Simon & Schuster, 1997, p. 508.

21. Ibid., p. 455.

22. For the White House transcripts during the convention crisis, see ibid. LBJ acknowledges that "the Northern states will probably prevail" if there is a roll call on the seating of the MFDP, and that "I don't have as much control or influence with these people as I would like" (p. 516). According to Taylor Branch, Johnson also told labor leader Walter Reuther that the convention would prefer the MFDP (Branch, p. 449).

23. Interview with Moctezuma Esparza, 2003.

24. Interview with Marshall Ganz, former UFW organizer, Harvard University, 2003. Ganz added, "my impression of the Sixties chicano gangs, is first of all, that they were the kids of the immigrants of the 1940s and 1950s, reinventing the pachuco thing, in the context of an emerging chicano movement, marked by the LA school walkouts in 1968, the formation of Mecha, the model of the civil rights movement, the Brown Berets, etc. I don't see this as due to blocks to racial political movements, though. I see the gangs as a time-honored way one group after another has had to struggle to make their way in this country, sometimes with more politics than others, sometimes with more crime than others."

25. Interview with Marshall Ganz, former United Farm Workers leader, at Harvard University, 2003.

26. See Henry W. Berger, editor, *A William Appleman Williams Reader*, Ivan R. Dee, 1992. Paul Buhle and Edward Rice-Maximin, *William Appleman Williams: The Tragedy of Empire*, Routledge, 1995; William Appleman Williams, *The Tragedy of American Diplomacy*, Dell, 1959, 1962.

27. Anna Deavere Smith, *Twilight*, performed at the Mark Taper Forum, Los Angeles, 1994.

28. Tom Hayden, *Rebellion in Newark: Official Violence and Ghetto Response*, Random House, 1967, p. 43.

29. Claude Brown, *Manchild in the Promised Land*, Simon & Schuster/Touchstone, 1965, 1999, p. 7.

30. Ibid., p. 8.
31. Glen C. Curry, *Sunshine Patriots: Punishment and the Vietnam Offender*, Notre Dame University Press, 1985. Curry estimates 113,055 military bad conduct and dishonorable discharges, and 503,977 undesirable discharges, for a total of 617,032 less-than-honorable, excluding "general," discharges.
32. James Baldwin, *No Name in the Street*, Bantam Doubleday Dell, 1972, p. 55.
33. Jim Wallis, "A Time to Heal, A Time to Build," in *Sojourners*, Aug. 1993.
34. John Brown Childs, "Street Wars and the New Peace Movement," *Social Justice*, spring 1997.
35. Los Angeles County Inter-Agency Gang Task Force Report on the State of Los Angeles Street Gangs, 1995–96, p. 17.
36. Ibid. p. 17.
37. *New York Times*, June 8, 1997.
38. Cited in Barbara H. Chasin, *Inequality and Violence in the United States*, Humanities Press, 1997, who references William Chambliss, "Policing the Ghetto Underclass: the Politics of Law and Law Enforcement," in *Social Problems* 41, no. 2 (May 1994), p. 179.

Chapter 3: The Peace Process

1. Poetry by inner-city youth written for DreamYard/L.A., August 2002. www.Dreamyardla.org.
2. Ibid.
3. A fifteen-year-old friend from San Diego, L.A., and Harlem, August 2002.
4. James Gilligan, *Violence: Our Deadly Epidemic and Its Causes*, Grosset/Putnam, 1996.
5. Franklin Zimring, *American Youth Violence*, Oxford, 1998, p. 80.
6. Orlando Patterson, *Rituals of Blood: Consequences of Slavery in Two American Centuries*, Basic Civitas, 1999, p. 184.
7. Richard Rhodes, *Why They Kill*, Vintage, 1999, p. 134.
8. David Macey, *Frantz Fanon: A Biography*, Picador USA, 2000, p. 144.
9. Ibid., p. 167.
10. Ibid., p. 473.
11. "From birth on it is clear to [the native] that this narrow world strewn with prohibitions, can only be called in question by absolute violence," Frantz Fanon, *The Wretched of the Earth*, Grove Press, 1968, p. 37.
12. Luis J. Rodriguez, *Always Running: La Vida Loca, Gang Days in L.A.*, Simon & Schuster/Touchstone, 1993, p. 9.
13. Sanyika Shakur, aka Monster Kody Scott, *Monster: The Autobiography of an L.A. Gang Member*, Penguin, 1993, p. 14.
14. Ibid., p. 102.
15. Gilligan, p. 134.

16. *Los Angeles Times*, Nov. 19, 1996.

17. *Los Angeles Times*, Sept. 26, 1999.

18. *Los Angeles Times*, Oct. 18, 1998.

19. Ibid. During the same period, only six inmates were fatally shot by guards in the entire U.S., all while trying to escape.

20. Ibid.

21. Fox Butterfield, "Freed from Prison, But Still Paying a Penalty," *New York Times*, Dec. 29, 2002.

22. *New York Times*, Sept. 28, 2003.

23. Gilligan, p. 175.

24. *Los Angeles Times*, Oct. 29, 1999.

25. Mark Arax and Mark Gladstone, *Los Angeles Times*, Oct. 9, 1998. See also summary of the *Times*'s series in *Sacramento Bee*, July 13, 1998.

26. *Los Angeles Times*, Oct. 9, 1998.

27. Ibid. See also Christian Parenti in *Salon*, Aug. 23, 1999.

28. Shakur, p. 104.

29. Rodriguez, p. 251.

30. Tim O'Brien, *The Things They Carried*, Houghton Mifflin, 1990, p. 21.

31. Interview with Tony Perry, 2003.

32. Julia Sitko, Occidental College, *Dying and Living in South Central L.A.*, Dec. 10, 2002, documentary.

33. In Jervey Trevalon, ed., *Geography of Rage*, Really Great Books, 2002, p. 37.

34. Jose M. Lopez, *Gangs, Casualties in an Undeclared War*, Kendall/Hunt, 2002.

35. Lopez, p. 108.

36. James Gilligan, *Violence in California Prisons*, testimony, March 2000, California State Senate.

37. Gilligan, testimony cited.

38. For a thoughtful discussion of "slave jobs" and the underground economy, based on several years of interviews in New York City, see Philippe Bourgois, *In Search of Respect*, Cambridge, 1996.

39. William Julius Williams, *When Work Disappears*, pp. 210, 232.

40. Conversation with the author, 1995; see Wilson, "'There Goes the Neighborhood,'" in *New York Times*, June 16, 2003.

41. *Los Angeles Times*, Feb. 12, 2003.

42. See Ric Curtis, "The Negligible Role of Gangs in Drug Distribution in New York City in the 1990s," paper, John Jay School of Criminal Justice. Curtis cites J.H. Mollenkopf and M. Castells, *Dual City: Restructuring New York*, Russell Sage Foundation, 1991.

43. *Los Angeles Times*, April 23, 2002, also Steve Lopez column, citing an Economic Round-table source, Feb. 6, 2003.

44. See *Atlanta Journal-Constitution*, April 9, 2000, on job losses, and *Atlanta Journal-Constitution*, April 29, 1991, for crime ranking in 1990. Cited in Elaine Brown, *The Condemnation of Little B*, Beacon, 2002.

45. John Hagedorn, "Gangs, Neighborhoods and Public Policy," in *Social Problems*, 38:4, (Nov. 1991), pp. 529–42.

46. Joan Moore, *Homeboys, Gangs, Drugs and Prison in the Barrios of Los Angeles*, Temple University Press, 1978.

47. Hagedorn.

48. Ibid.

49. Bob Herbert, *New York Times*, Sept. 3, 2001, citing Andrew Sum, Center for Labor Market Studies, Northeastern University, Boston.

50. "On the Road to Nowhere," *New York Times*, Sept. 3, 2001.

51. *Los Angeles Times*, April 25, 1997. There are an estimated 800,000 to 1 million heroin addicts nationwide, but only 180,000 spaces for methadone treatment; *New York Times*, Aug. 11, 2003.

52. *New York Times*, Aug. 11, 2003.

53. *Los Angeles Times*, April 25, 1997.

54. A conviction for 5 grams of crack cocaine ends in roughly the same sentence as a conviction for 500 grams of powder cocaine, approximately 70 months. *New York Times*, Mar. 20, 2002.

55. *Los Angeles Times*, Dec. 1–3, 1993. Gary Webb, *Dark Alliance*, Seven Stories Press, 1998, p. 370.

56. *Los Angeles Times*, Aug. 28, 1997.

57. *Los Angeles Times*, Sept. 13, 2002. The deputy chief, Maurice Moore, was a close ally of Chief Bernard Parks. Shortly after retiring in 2002, he was charged by LAPD investigators with laundering funds for his son Keven, who was serving a thirteen-year federal sentence for cocaine trafficking. The lead investigator was Thomas Lorenzen, a former CRASH head who left the department to become police chief in Taos, New Mexico. The relationship continued for seven years. The FBI's information on Moore's role in drug laundering was sent to Chief Parks in December 1999, who nonetheless appointed Moore to a central role in the Rampart investigation.

58. See Edward Behr, *Prohibition: Thirteen Years That Changed America*, Arcade, 1996.

59. RAND's George Tita studied patterns in the LAPD Hollenbeck Division, adjacent to Fr. Greg Boyle's office, in 1999, finding that only 10 percent of gang-motivated homicides involved drugs. "There's no evidence that the fighting in these communities is over drug-market share." RAND Corporation, Santa Monica, www.rand.org/publications/MR/MR1764. A John Jay College study of Brooklyn by Ric Curtis found that "gang involvement in drug distribution has been largely inconsequential with respect to the overall market. Despite exceptional cases that occasionally garner media headlines, gangs have not played major roles as distributors in New York City's drug markets."

60. U.S. Dept. of Justice, Bureau of Justice Statistics, Nov. 21, 2002.

61. Fox Butterfield series, in *New York Times*, Feb. 28, 1997.

62. Shakur, p. 365.

63. Webb, p. 186.

64. Ibid., p. 468.

65. Ibid.

66. Ibid., p. 113. See *Spy* magazine, April 1992, for Wackenhut quote.

67. Court records showed that Prohibition agents targeted the poor and recent immigrants, while the wealthy were virtually immune. Another similarity to today's drug war was the toll from poisoned black-market alcohol, estimated at 50,000 deaths by 1927, not counting non-lethal poisonings. Behr, pp. 221, 241.

68. In Chicago alone, there were 800 gang deaths attributed to Prohibition. Behr, p. 177.

69. See Mark Thornton, "Alcohol Prohibition Was a Failure," *Policy Analysis*, no. 157, July 17, 1991; Jeffrey Miron, "Violence and U.S. Prohibitions of Drugs and Alcohol," National Bureau of Economic Research, Feb. 1999.

70. See Milton Friedman, "The War We Are Losing," in Melvyn Krauss and Edward Lazear, *Searching for Alternatives: Drug Control Policy in the United States*, Hoover Institution Press, 1991, p. 55.

71. Bush's daughter Noelle was given a ten-day sentence for concealing crack cocaine in her shoe while undergoing rehabilitation, Associated Press/*USA Today*, Oct. 17, 2002; previously she had been charged with felony prescription fraud, which carries penalties of up to five years' imprisonment and $5,000, and sentenced to rehab, *USA Today*, Jan. 1, 2002. *USA Today* further reported that while she had "no known criminal record," she had been cited for a dozen traffic violations, including three car crashes since 1995. Bush, who favors harsh sentences for drug offenders, repeatedly stated that he was "praying" for his daughter.

Chapter 4: The 1998 Santa Monica–Culver City Gang Truce

1. James Diego Vigil, *From Indians to Chicanos*, Waveland Press, 1999, p. 188.

2. In 2003, several of the survivors sued the state of California, the L.A. Chamber of Commerce, and other entities for violating their constitutional rights. State Senate hearings commenced at the same time. Scholars estimate that 60 percent were U.S. citizens. *Los Angeles Times*, July 15–16, 2003.

3. Vigil, pp. 190–91.

4. All quotes from Manny Lares from an interview with the author, July 31, 2001.

5. This information is from an individual speaking on condition of anonymity.

6. *Los Angeles Times*, Sept. 28, 1993.

7. *Los Angeles Times*, Oct. 3, 1993.

8. *Los Angeles Times*, Sept. 21, 1997.

9. *Los Angeles Times*, Sept. 26, 1993.

10. Interview with "Blinky" Rodgriguez and "Big D" Garcia, 2003.

11. *Los Angeles Times*, Oct. 3, 1993.

12. Ibid.

13. *Los Angeles Times*, Sept. 21, 1997.

14. *Los Angeles Times*, Sept. 26, 1993.

15. *Los Angeles Times*, March 24, 1997.

16. *Los Angeles Times*, May 31, 1997.

17. Ibid.

18. Ibid.

19. *Los Angeles Times*, Sept. 21, 1997.

20. *Los Angeles Times*, March 24, 1997.

21. *Los Angeles Times*, Nov. 19, 1998.

22. *Los Angeles Times*, Nov. 3, 1998.

23. *Los Angeles Times*, Oct. 29, 1998.

24. Interview with author.

25. *Los Angeles Times*, Oct. 28, 1998.

26. *Los Angeles Times*, Nov. 19, 1998.

27. *Los Angeles Times*, Dec. 6, 2002.

28. Governor's Council on Physical Fitness and Sports report, spring 1998.

29. *Los Angeles Times*, Nov. 5, 1998.

30. According to the bail bondsman, Mark Herman, Nov. 7, 1998.

31. California Legislature Task Force on Preventing Gang Violence, hearing transcript, Nov. 20, 1998.

32. Analysis of Environmental Impact Report on Playa Vista, 1993.

33. Mayor Pam O'Connor set the official tone by testifying that "children make up a much smaller proportion of our population than in most communities, just 13.5 percent. But nonetheless, we value and we prioritize our kids because they are a precious resource, all our kids." The city budget included just $3 million annually to programs that targeted at-risk youth. Two of the victims, Juan Martin Campos and Jaime "Rebel" Cruz, were already in transitional programs when they were shot. A City Council member, Ruth Ebner, followed with a strong statement that she was "happy" with the police. Culver City administrators described an alphabet soup of programs: a Community Service Center, a Youth Economic Development Program, a Resident Safety Unit, a Youth Initiatives Unit, a Citywide Youth Council, and so on.

34. California Legislative Task Force on Preventing Gang Violence, Hearing transcript.

35. Senate hearings, ibid.

36. Eventually a coalition did sue the county, and reached a negotiated settlement five years later, in 2003.

37. The City of Santa Monica general fund for 1999–2000 was $154.8 million, and the bud-

get from all sources was $353.2 million. (City of Santa Monica official budget, from former mayor Mike Feinstein)

38. A city bond measure funded the expansion. The new facility opened in August 2003. The previous holding capacity was seventy-eight. *Santa Monica Observer*, Sept. 1, 2003. Also, from council member Mike Feinstein.

Chapter 5: The Demonization Crusade

1. Saul Bellow, *The Dean's December*, Harper and Row, 1982, pp. 228–29.
2. Bob Sipchen, *Baby Insane and the Buddha: How a Crip and a Cop Joined Forces to Shut Down a Street Gang*, Doubleday, 1993.
3. Ibid., p. 256.
4. *Los Angeles Times*, San Diego edition, March 12, 1992.
5. Sipchen, p. 336.
6. Ibid., p. 341.
7. Interview with producer Robert Greenwald, who optioned the book, 2003.
8. Sipchen, author's note.
9. *Los Angeles Times*, April 28, 1989.
10. *Los Angeles Times*, Aug. 31, 1990.
11. Ibid.
12. *Los Angeles Times*, San Diego edition, Dec. 25, 1990.
13. *Los Angeles Times*, Dec. 25, 2003.
14. *Los Angeles Times*, Aug. 31, 2003.
15. *Los Angeles Times*, San Diego edition, Dec. 13, 1990.
16. *Los Angeles Times*, June 9, 1991.
17. Interview with San Diego police public information officer, April 15, 2003.
18. Interview, March 13, 2003.
19. *Los Angeles Times* editorial, "Standing Up to Street Gangs," Feb. 18, 2003. *Times* editorials are published unsigned. According to Sipchen, he was not present at the USC conference but edited the editorial and "went back and forth" with the writer. "I will definitely take responsibility" for the editorial, he told me, and for the *Times*'s editorial series called "Standing Up to Street Gangs." Conversation with author, Aug. 11, 2003.
20. Ibid.
21. Ibid.
22. *Los Angeles Times*, Mar 17, 2002.
23. David Wyatt, *Five Fires: Race, Catastrophe and the Shaping of California*, Addison Wesley, 1997, p. 171.
24. James Q. Wilson, *Thinking About Crime*, Vintage, 1975, p. xv. "I have yet to see a 'root cause' or to encounter a government program that has successfully attacked it, at least with respect to those social problems that arise out of human volition rather than technological

malfunction. But more importantly, the demand for causal actions is, whether intended or not, a way of deferring any action or criticizing any policy." Wilson thus denies the possibility of working on short-term deterrence and long-term causes simultaneously.

25. See Marc Mauer, *Race to Incarcerate*, The New Press 1999; and Steven Donziger, *The Real War on Crime: The Report of the National Criminal Justice Commission*, HarperCollins, 1996.

26. L.A. Sheriff's Department records.

27. Philip Fradkin, *The Seven States of California*, University of California, 1995, pp. 388–89; see also Wyatt, pp. 170–71.

28. Joe Domanick, *To Protect and Serve*, Simon & Schuster, 1994, p. 207. For more weapons description, see "Felon Busters," in *Popular Mechanics*, May 1, 1997.

29. Kathleen Cleaver and George Katsiaficas, eds., *Liberation, Imagination and the Black Panther Party*, Routledge, 2001, p. 8. See Ward Churchill account in Cleaver and Katsiaficas, p. 99.

30. Jack Olsen, *Last Man Standing: The Tragedy and Triumph of Geronimo Pratt*, Anchor, 2000, pp. 359, 373. Julius Carl "Julio" Butler was a former Black Panther who became a leader of the First African Methodist Episcopal Church in Los Angeles. He was listed by the LAPD as a "confidential informant" in 1972, and provided misleading information about Pratt.

31. Domanick, pp. 294–95.

32. Interview with Ted Koppel, *Los Angeles Times*, May 23, 1991.

33. *Los Angeles Times*, Jan. 19, 1986.

34. Ibid.

35. *Los Angeles Times*, Dec. 4, 2002.

36. Report of the Special Advisor (Webster Commission), Oct. 21, 1992, p. 34.

37. Police transcriptions in *Report of the Independent Commission on the Los Angeles Police Department* (Christopher Commission), pp. 72–73.

38. *Los Angeles Times*, Dec. 1, 1993.

39. *Los Angeles Times*, Dec. 4, 2002.

40. Ibid.

41. Anne-Marie O'Connor and Tina Daunt, "The Secret Society Among Lawmen," *Los Angeles Times*, March 24, 1999.

42. Perez was a peculiar, idiosyncratic source in certain ways—for example, according to one of his interrogators at a hidden location, Perez continually picked real and imaginary lint off his prison outfit, perhaps indicating a need for order?—but the essentials of his story were accurate, which is why the city eventually agreed to a legal settlement. My sources include two attorneys who interviewed or took depositions from Perez.

43. *Los Angeles Times*, Feb. 29, 2000.

44. *Los Angeles Times*, Feb. 24, 2000.

45. *Los Angeles Times*, Feb. 29, 2000: "FBI Pressured INS to Aid L.A. Police Anti-Gang Effort."

46. *Los Angeles Times*, Feb. 24, 2000.

47. Ibid.

48. Ibid.

49. *Los Angeles Times*, Feb. 29, 2000.

50. *Los Angeles Times*, Sept. 17, 1999.

51. Interview with attorney Gregory Yates, 2003.

52. Correspondence, Sept. 21, 1999.

53. *Los Angeles Times*, Sept. 13, 1999.

54. Photo of Mack in red suit with Perez *in Rolling Stone*, June 7, 2001. See also Randall Sullivan, *Labyrinth: A Detective Investigates the Murders of Tupac Shakur and Biggie Smalls, the Implication of Death Row Records and the Origins of the Los Angeles Police Scandal*, Atlantic Monthly Press, 2002, and Ronin Ro, *Have Gun, Will Travel: The Spectacular Rise and Violent Fall of Death Row Records*, Broadway, 1998; "Who Killed Tupac Shakur?", *Los Angeles Times*, Sept. 6–7, 2002. The *Times* suggested that Crips, prodded by Notorious B.I.G. (Christopher Wallace), assassinated Tupac in retaliation for an earlier beating in a Las Vegas hotel after a Mike Tyson fight on Sept. 7, 1996. Las Vegas police were ill-equipped to understand or investigate L.A. gangs, the *Times* went on. The *Times* also revealed that Suge Knight's security head was a former Compton police officer whose father was in charge of the gang unit.

55. *Los Angeles Times*, Sept. 21, 1999.

56. *Los Angeles Times*, Dec. 15, 1999.

57. Interview with author, July 2003.

58. *Los Angeles Times*, Jan. 26, 2000.

59. *Los Angeles Times*, Sept. 23, 1999.

60. *Los Angeles Times*, Opinion, Sept. 26, 1999.

61. *Los Angeles Times*, May 16, 2003.

62. *Los Angeles Times*, May 11, 2003.

63. *Los Angeles Times*, May 19, 2003.

64. *Los Angeles Times*, Feb. 10, 2000.

65. Perez taped deposition with attorney Gregory Yates, 2003.

66. Interview with Wellford W. Wilms, UCLA; see Wilms, Schmidt, and Norman, "The Strain of Change: Voices of L.A. Police Officers," preliminary report, National Institute of Justice, U.S. Dept. of Justice, Oct. 23, 2000.

67. *Los Angeles Times*, Aug. 29, 2003.

68. The source is now a private investigator.

69. Interview with author, July 2003.

70. Robert Benson, "Changing Police Culture: The Sine Qua Non of Reform," *Loyola Law Review*, Jan. 2001, pp. 681–90.

71. Ibid. See also Christopher Commission Report, pp. 83–84. In the Christopher survey, there were no female officers among the 120 with the highest number of use-of-force reports.

72. Interview with author.

73. *Los Angeles Times*, Sept. 24, 1999.

74. Correspondence from William Lan Lee to Mayor James Hahn, May 8, 2000.

75. Interview with author, 2002.

76. *Los Angeles Times*, May 28, 2000.

77. *Los Angeles Times*, Dec. 16, 2001.

78. Ibid.

79. *Los Angeles Times*, Sept. 8, 2001; *New York Times*, April 10, 2001.

80. *Los Angeles Times*, March 20, 2002.

81. *Los Angeles Times*, Sept. 22, 2002.

82. *Los Angeles Times*, Dec. 3, 2001.

83. *Los Angeles Times*, *New York Times*, June 12, 2003.

84. *Los Angeles Times*, July 19, 2003.

85. Elaine Brown, *The Condemnation of Little B*, Beacon, 2002, p. 188.

86. Andrew Karmen, *New York Murder Mystery: The True Story Behind the Crime Crash of the 1990s*, NYU Press, 2000, p. 169. See also reference to Mollen in Amnesty International report on NYPD, www.amnestyusa.org/rightsforall/police/nypd-03.html.

87. Amnesty International report, ibid.

88. Michael Jacobson, "From the 'Back' to the 'Front,'" and J. Phillip Thompson, "Liberalism, Race, and Local Democracy," in John Mollkopf and Ken Emerson, eds., *Rethinking the Urban Agenda*, Century Foundation, 2001.

89. Jack Newfield, "The Man, the Mayor, the Myth," *The Nation*, June 17, 2002.

90. *Los Angeles Times*, June 5, 2000.

91. See U.S. District Court, Southern District of New York, *Memorandum Opinion and Order*, 99 Civ. 1695 (SAS), Dec. 13, 1999.

92. A *Los Angeles Times* poll published on April 9, 2000, showed a 51 percent unfavorable response to the LAPD Rampart scandal. Forty-four percent of whites approved of the police, against only 36 percent of Latinos and 18 percent of blacks. While 43 percent of whites said police brutality was common, 83 percent of blacks answered yes.

93. Troy Duster, "Pattern, Purpose and Race in the Drug War," in Craig Reinarman and Harry Levine, *Crack in America*, University of California, 1997, p. 262.

94. Ibid. p. 262.

95. Data provided by California Department of Corrections.

96. Duster, p. 262.

97. Ibid., p 263.

98. Anthony Platt, "Social Insecurity: The Transformation of American Criminal Justice, 1965–2000," in *Social Science Journal* 28, no. 1 (2001).

99. Ibid.

100. Ibid.

101. Ibid.

102. Liberty Hill Report, 2003.

103. *New York Times*, Sept. 28, 2003. At the time, over half of federal inmates were convicted of "relatively unspectacular drug-related crimes," the *Times* said.

104. Jerome G. Miller, *Search and Destroy: African-American Males in the Criminal Justice System*, Cambridge University Press, 1996, p. 6.

105. Ibid., p. 6.

106. My projection, based on Miller, p. 6.

107. Miller, p. 8.

108. Ibid., p. 7.

109. Ibid.

110. *New York Times*, Sept. 28, 2003.

111. Globalizing the Streets Conference, May 2–5, 2001, John Jay College of Criminal Justice, City University of New York, email: streetresearch@aol.com; Gangs in the Global City conference, May 16–17, Chicago, Ill., John M. Hagedorn, University of Illinois—Chicago.

112. James Diego Vigil, unpublished manuscript.

113. Ruben Martinez, "Mexico's Little Americas," *Los Angeles Times,* Aug. 17, 1997.

114. *Los Angeles Times*, Nov. 25, 2002.

115. *New York Times*, Oct. 20, 2002.

116. Laurie Gunst, *Born Fi' Dead*, Holt, 1995. See also Mark Kurlansky, *A Continent of Islands: Searching for the Caribbean Destiny*, Addison-Wesley, 1992, pp. 123–32.

117. *New York Times*, March 21, 2003.

118. About Paris, see the 1990s cult film *Hate*; about Poland, see the *New York Times*, April 5, 2002; for information on New Zealand's Maori, I am grateful for correspondence from Leah Greenwald.

119. Robert Kaplan, *Warrior Politics*, Random House, 2002, pp. 136, 119. See also his *The Coming Anarchy: Shattering the Dreams of the Post Cold War*, Random House, 2000.

120. From UNDP advertisement in *Financial Times*, Oct. 2, 2003. For details on the program, see www.TeamsToEndPoverty.org. The goal is to cut global poverty in half by 2015.

121. Kaplan, *Warrior Politics*, p. 119.

122. Ibid.

123. Michael Ignatieff, *Empire Lite: Nation-Building in Bosnia, Kosovo and Afghanistan*, Penguin, 2003, p. 124.

124. *Los Angeles Times*, June 11, 2002.

125. *Los Angeles Times*, Sept. 7, 2003. The evidence against Padilla may never be disclosed. However, a Pentagon document questions whether the sources who identified Padilla as a terrorist were "completely candid." One recanted parts of his affadavit, while another was on drug treatment at the time of the interviews.

126. *The Economist*, June 15, 2002.

127. Malcolm Klein, *The American Street Gang*, Oxford, 1995, p. 167. Klein writes that the FBI agents were "scoffed at by the Los Angeles Sheriff's Department, the county's central repository of gang intelligence. It's a long way from Al Capone and John Gotti to the Crips and Bloods and barrios of East Lost Angeles."

128. *Los Angeles Times*, Dec. 4, 2002.

129. Ibid.

130. Conversation with author, 2003.

131. Ibid.

132. Klein, p. 167.

133. Examples from interview with Sobel in 2002.

134. Confidential source.

135. Cited by Franklin Zimring, *American Youth Violence*, Oxford University Press, 1998.

136. William J. Bennett, John J. DiIulio Jr., and John P. Walters, *Body Count: Moral Poverty—and How to Win America's War Against Crime and Drugs*, Simon & Schuster, 1996, p. 26.

137. *The Weekly Standard*, Nov. 27, 1995.

138. Bennett et al., p. 194.

139. Ibid., jacket.

140. C. Horowitz, "The Suddenly Safer City: The End of Crime as We Know It," *New York*, Aug. 14, 1995, pp. 21–27; cited in Karmen, p. 194.

141. Karmen, pp. 194–95.

142. James Gilligan, *Preventing Violence*, Thames and Hudson, 2001, p. 24.

143. James Q. Wilson, *The Moral Sense*, The Free Press, 1993, p. 10.

144. Charles Murray, *Losing Ground: American Social Policy, 1950–1980*, Basic Books, 1984; Richard J. Herrnstein and Charles Murray, *The Bell Curve: Intelligence and Class Structure in American Life*, The Free Press, 1996.

145. Murray, *Losing Ground*, p. 21.

146. Herrnstein and Murray, p. 526.

147. Zimring, p. 5.

148. *Los Angeles Times*, July 23, 1996.

149. Zimring, pp. 8, 9, 13.

150. James Moore and Wayne Slater, *Bush's Brain: How Karl Rove Made George W. Bush Presidential*, John Wiley, 2003, p. 202.

151. Ibid., p. 205.

152. Ibid., p. 202.

153. Ibid., p. 206.

154. Zimring, p. 11.

155. "Head of Religion-Based Initiative Resigns," *New York Times*, Aug. 18, 2001.

156. Zimring, p. 63.

157. Ibid., p. 186.

158. Michael Males, *Framing Youth*, Common Courage Press, 1999.

159. Ibid., p 55.

160. According to official figures for Los Angeles County, the decline in teen homicides was as follows:

	Total	Latino	African American
1990	251	100	107
1991	220	146	70
1992	208	151	47
1993	164	91	68
1994	114	56	51
1995	148	88	42
1996	90	53	27
1997	75	46	17

(Source: Criminal Justice Statistics Center, California Department of Justice, 1998; in Males, p. 88.)

161. Bernard Harcourt, *The Illusion of Order: The False Promise of Broken Windows Policing,* Harvard University, 2001.

162. Bernard Harcourt, "The Broken Windows Myth," *New York Times,* Opinion, Sept. 11, 2001.

163. Harcourt, *The Illusion of Order,* p. 92.

164. Zimring, pp. 11, 64.

165. Ibid., p. 64.

166. Bob Herbert, *New York Times,* Sept. 3, 2001; data from Andrew Sum, Northeastern University.

167. Bennett et al., p. 22. To be exact, Bennett approvingly quotes the black neoconservative as saying crime is a problem of "sin, not skin."

168. Moore and Slater, p. 202.

169. *New York Times,* May 4, 2003.

170. William Bennett, *The Book of Virtues,* Simon & Schuster, 1993.

171. Reuters, May 5, 2003; see also *Los Angeles Times,* May 3, 2003.

172. Sally Denton and Roger Morris, *The Money and the Power: The Making of Las Vegas and Its Hold on America, 1947–2000,* Knopf, 2001.

173. Reuters, May 5, 2003.

174. *New York Times,* Oct. 11, 2003.

175. Rush Limbaugh, Oct. 5, 1995, cited in *Extra!,* Dec. 2003, p. 7.

176. New York *Daily News,* Oct. 11, 2003. The *New York Times* cited the *National Enquirer* for the maid's story of parking lot purchases.

177. Limbaugh, Oct. 5, 1995.

178. The theory was elaborated by Kelling and Catherine M. Coles in a 1996 book with an introduction by Wilson. George Kelling and Catherine M. Coles, *Fixing Broken Windows: Restoring Order and Reducing Crime in Our Cities,* Touchstone, 1996.

179. Harcourt, *The Illusion of Order,* p. 57.

180. *New York Post* editorial against Andrew Karmen, author of *New York Murder Mystery,* pp. xii, xiii.

181. Karmen, p. 261.

182. Ibid., p. 75; "The Commissioner vs. The Criminologists," *New York Times*, Nov. 19, 1995. (". . . Police Commissioner William J. Bratton will not be satisfied until every last criminologist surrenders.").

183. Kelling and Coles, p. 242.

184. Atwater, in panel discussion with author, Aspen Institute, 1994. Also see Sidney Blumenthal, "Crime Pays," *The New Yorker*, May 9, 1994.

185. Harcourt, *The Illusion of Order*, p. 10.

186. Ibid., p. 50. The reference to "hundreds of thousands" being searched and frisked in a given year is based on the fact that official numbers only include *reported* searches. Obviously, many persons stopped and frisked never filed official complaints to the very police agency that committed the search in the first place. Thus, it is fair to say that the actual numbers were much higher than the 45,000 reported in a given year like 1997.

187. Ibid., p. 186.

188. Kelling and Coles, p. 237.

189. Ibid. p. 115.

190. Ibid., p. 243.

191. Ibid., p. 245.

192. Ibid.

193. Ibid., pp. 246–47.

194. *Miranda* requires officers to inform arrestees that they have the rights to remain silent and have an attorney present. Failure to comply means prosecutors may not use confessions in court. But statements made without a Miranda warning can be used to generate information concerning other crimes. The LAPD and many other departments began training officers in the nineties to proceed with interrogations without advising arrestees of their Miranda rights. The LAPD only changed its policies after losing lawsuits, but other departments have continued the tactic. The California Supreme Court ruled unanimously in 2003 against the "widespread official encouragement" of such police practices. *Los Angeles Times*, July 15, 2003.

195. *New York Times*, May 13, 2002.

196. George Kelling, *New York Post*, Dec. 19, 2001.

197. *New York Times*, Mar. 7, 2002.

198. *New York Times*, Oct. 12, 1997.

199. Karmen, p. 157.

200. Ibid., p. 263.

201. Ibid., p. 264.

202. Ibid., p. 266.

203. Ibid.

204. *Village Voice*, Nov. 26–Dec. 2, 2003.

205. Ibid., p. 24.

206. Interview with Jack Newfield, *Tikkun*, vol. 15, no. 4.

207. Jacobson in Mollkopf and Emerson, p. 177.

208. Amy Wilentz, "The Price of Safety in a Police State," *Los Angeles Times*, Opinion, April 11, 1999.

209. Ibid.

210. *New York Times*, March 25, 2000.

211. Ibid.

212. Gilligan, p. 187.

213. Kelling and Coles, p. 237.

214. Diana R. Gordon, *The Return of the Dangerous Classes: Drug Prohibition and Policy Politics*, Norton, 1994, p. 26.

215. Ibid., pp. 18, 25, 26.

216. Ibid., p 18.

217. Ibid., p. 150.

218. *New York Times*, Dec. 22, 2003.

219. Interview with author, 2002.

220. David Brotherton, John Jay College of Criminal Justice, New York City, field notes, Jan. 18, 1998.

221. Brotherton et al., eds. *Between Black and Gold*, Columbia University, 2003. Most of the regular coverage in New York's City's media outlets sensationalized and distorted the Latin Kings. An HBO documentary in 2003, produced by Kathleen Kennedy, was particularly sensationalized and lacking in any historic context.

222. From Latin Kings archives at John Jay College of Criminal Justice, New York City.

223. Luis Barrios, manuscript to be published in *Black and Gold* (2004).

224. All references to Filthee from personal interview, 2003.

225. Brotherton interview with Tone.

226. Barry Bearak, "Man of Vision or of Violence?" *New York Times*, Nov. 20, 1997.

227. Ibid.

228. *Black and Gold* documentary by Big Noise Film, Rick Rowley and Jacquie Soohen.

229. Interview with author, 2002.

230. Bearak, "Man of Vision or of Violence?" Also see Andi Rierden, "Is It 60's Politics or Gang Warfare?" *New York Times*, May 2, 1993.

231. Instead, the *New York Times*'s subheadline on its King Tone story was "Where Gang Leader Talks Peace, Police See Just Talk." The head of the police department's crime intelligence section was quoted dismissively as saying "I still consider them a criminal gang, involved in narcotics, gun-dealing and robberies." He was right about the continuing involvement of many Kings in crime, but did those activities mean they were still a criminal gang, or a gang in metamorphosis? The *Times* at least interviewed Brotherton and Barrios to emphasize that some respectable opinion sided with Tone. Barrios said, "the police want to scoff at Tone, but I've seen him crying from all the pressure,

all those Kings who want to go on selling drugs and committing crimes. The police refuse to recognize the 1,000 good things he has done, but when he'll make a mistake—and he will because he's human—they'll come down on him and say, 'he's always been a criminal.' Why won't they see how far he has come?"

232. *New York Post*, June 19, 1999.

233. *Black and Gold* documentary tape.

234. *New York Times*, May 15, 1998.

235. Ibid.

236. Interview with author, 2001.

237. *Black and Gold* documentary tape.

238. Brotherton field notes, p. 3.

239. Ibid., p. 2.

240. *New York Post*, Dec. 19, 2001.

241. Wilentz, "The Price of Safety in a Police State."

242. *New York Times*, Nov. 11, 2002.

243. *Los Angeles Times*, Dec. 1, 2002.

244. Ibid.

245. *Los Angeles Times*, Dec. 4, 2002.

246. *Los Angeles Times Magazine*, Jan. 19, 2003.

247. *Los Angeles Times*, Dec. 4, 2002.

248. *Los Angeles Times Magazine*, Jan. 19, 2003.

249. *Time* magazine, March 6, 2002.

250. Ibid.

251. *Los Angeles Times*, Dec. 8, 2002.

252. *New York Times*, July 30, 2001.

253. *Los Angeles Times*, April 14, 2003.

254. Ibid.

255. Ibid.

256. *Los Angeles Times*, Oct. 25, 2002.

257. Ibid.

258. Ibid.

259. California Dept. of Corrections: Data Analysis Unit, "Second and Third Strikers in the Institution Population," Dec. 31, 2002; analysis by Mike Males and Dan Macallair, University of California—Santa Cruz, for state Senate hearings.

260. Conversation with the Peace Process Network.

261. Interview with author, 1999.

262. Donald Mace, California Dept. of Justice, "CAL/GANG, California's New Weapon in the War on Gangs," January, 1998; Raymond Dussault, "CAL/GANG Brings Dividends," *Justice & Technology, Government Technology*, Sacramento, Dec. 1998.

263. *Los Angeles Times*, July 14, 1997.

264. James Diego Vigil, *A Rainbow of Gangs: Street Cultures in the Mega-City*, University of Texas, 2002, p. 5.

265. *Los Angeles Times*, Jan. 24, 2003.

266. *Los Angeles Times*, editorial, Jan. 16, 2003.

267. *Los Angeles Times*, Jan. 24, 2003.

268. *Los Angeles Times*, April 25, 2003.

269. *Los Angeles Times*, Jan. 20, 2003.

270. Ibid.

271. Ibid.

272. *Los Angeles Times*, July 28, 2003.

273. According to the *Los Angeles Times* data, there were 44,960 false burglar alarms requiring police response in the San Fernando Valley in 2002 (or 39 percent of all police responses). At the same time there were 12,282 police responses to violent crime in the South Bureau. The mostly white Valley made 1,141 alarm calls in December 2002 while experiencing only 48 violent crimes. The Rampart Division showed 403 alarm calls and 245 violent crimes that month.

Chapter 6: Hidden Histories

1. *New York Times*, Aug. 25, 1991.

2. Claude Brown, *Manchild in the Promised Land*, Simon & Schuster, 1965, pp. 7–8.

3. David Wyatt, *Five Fires: Race, Catastrophe, and the Shaping of California*, Addison-Wesley, 1997, p. 210.

4. Eldridge Cleaver, *Soul on Ice*, Dell, 1968, p. 47.

5. Ibid., p. 46.

6. Gerald Horne, *Fire This Time: The Watts Uprising and the 1960s*, University Press of Virginia, 1995, p. 51.

7. Vigil, p. 68.

8. Ibid.

9. Ibid., p. 64.

10. The "residue" quote is from Nehemia Russell, a Chicago Gangster Disciple, cited by Diachara and Chabot, in Brotherton et al., pp. 78–79.

11. John Hope Franklin and Loren Schweninger, *Runaway Slaves: Rebels on the Plantation*, Oxford, 1999, pp. 77, 86.

12. Ibid., p. 86.

13. Ibid., p. 77.

14. Ibid.

15. Fox Butterfield, *All God's Children: The Bosket Family and the American Tradition of Violence*, Avon, 1995.

16. Ibid., pp. 32–34.

17. Cecil Brown, *Stagolee Shot Billy*, Harvard University, 2003, pp. 202–3.

18. Ibid., p. 202. The phrase to "jeer at life" came from Richard Wright, whom Brown quotes as follows: "they jeer at life; they leer at what is decent, holy, just, wise, straight, right and uplifting. I think that it is because from the Negro's point of view, it is the right, the holy, the just, that crush him in America." See Richard Wright, *White Man Listen!*, Doubleday, 1957, p. 92.

19. Cecil Brown, p. 24.

20. Butterfield, p. 64.

21. California Police Officers Standards and Training (POST) manual, March 24, 1994.

22. Butterfield, p. 119.

23. Ibid.

24. Miles Corwin, *The Killing Season: A Summer Inside an LAPD Homicide Division*, Ballantine, 1997, p. 83.

25. Wyatt, pp. 214–15.

26. Ibid., p. 215.

27. Horne, p. 204.

28. Ibid., p. 196.

29. See the citation of FBI documents by Ward Churchill, in *Liberation, Imagination and the Black Panther Party*, ed. Kathleen Cleaver and George Katsiaficas, Routledge, 2001, p. 93. In 1995, an FBI counterintelligence agent claimed that Carter and Huggins were shot by FBI informants (Churchill, p. 93). The claim is repeated in Jeff Donn, "FBI Recruits and Protects Violent Informants Nationwide, Ex-Agents Say," AP, Mar. 1, 2003. Donn cites former FBI agent Wesley Swearingen as his source. Whatever occurred at UCLA, two US members, George and Larry Stiner, were convicted of conspiracy to murder. With underground assistance, they escaped San Quentin in 1974, making their way to Surinam. Eventually, Larry Stiner, desiring to come home, negotiated a deal in the nineties with the FBI to turn himself in. The FBI ultimately reneged, and he remains in prison. His brother, George, still is out of the country. The US organization founder, Maulana Karenga, steadfastly denies that the Stiners were FBI informants, noting that US itself was a revolutionary organization targeted by the FBI (interview with author, 2003).

30. An example was Tony Jacquette's SLANT (Self-Leadership for all Nationalists Today) in Los Angeles.

31. Yusuf Jah and Sister Shah'Keyah, *Uprising: Crips and Bloods Tell the Story of America's Youth in the Crossfire*, Scribner, 1995, p. 123.

32. Donald Bakeer, *Inhale: Gasoline and Gunsmoke*, Precocious Publishing, 1994.

33. Sanyika Shakur, aka Monster Kody Scott, *Monster: The Autobiography of an L.A. Gang Member*, Penguin, 1994, p. 246.

34. Ibid. pp. 246–47.

35. For an account of the Crips and Bloods, see Leon Bing, *Do or Die*, HarperCollins, 1991, pp. 148–56; also Jah and Shah' Keyah; and Shakur.

36. *New York Times*, Dec. 6, 2000, "Anti-Gang 'Role Model' Is Up for a Nobel and Execution."

37. ACLU Foundation of Northern California, Alan Schlosser, Esq., brief of Amici Curie, before U.S. Ninth Circuit Court of Appeals, Nov. 5, 2002. Tookie's legal team noted that the prosecutor suggested that the jury think of the defendant as a "Bengal Tiger" in its "back-country" habitat, not as a "Bengal Tiger in a zoo" as he apparently appeared in court. The same prosecutor had been legally censured twice before for racially loaded tactics in death penalty cases.

38. *Newsday*, June 13, 2001.

39. ACLU Foundation of Northern California, brief of Amici Curie.

40. *New York Times*, Dec. 6, 2000.

41. *Los Angeles Times*, Sept. 11, 2001.

42. *Los Angeles Times*, Sept. 13, 2002.

43. *Los Angeles Times*, Sept. 19, 2002.

44. *San Jose Mercury News*, Nov. 8, 2002.

45. *Los Angeles Times*, Dec. 24, 1999.

46. Ibid.

47. Once during a gang fight, however, Dewayne forgot he was carrying the fake pharmaceutical. The Lynwood sheriffs charged him with possession of a controlled substance for sale. According to court records, "The defendant declares that he had some quick-start fluid and mixed it with butter. When you sniffed it, it smelled like phencyclidine but it was not. He had it for sale." The case eventually was dropped. Court records, 6-7-82, from probation officer's report, Superior Court, Sept. 24, 1992.

48. LAPD investigator's report, Officer G. Grant, #22444, Feb. 19, 1992.

49. See *Los Angeles Times*, Sept. 17, 2003, "The Healing of Scarface, Twenty Years Ago." Critics thrashed Brian Palma's immigrant saga. Now it's embraced by hip-hop fans.

50. From Bing's *Do or Die* (p. 205), a Crip named G-Roc describes a "mission":

> "We was on a straight mission, girl."
>
> I ask him what that means.
>
> "A *mission*. Like drivin' through an enemy 'hood, bein' in danger of yo' life." He looks out the window for a long moment; it is very quiet in the car.
>
> "Gangbangin' don't lie, girl. *It's real*. Niggers is out there to get you. Niggers is out there to *kill* you. It's fun in a way, but you got to look at it as a life-threatenin' situation, too. Every minute. And my homies and me, we be on the lookout, too. We be like—," he sighs, "whatever, Cuz. Whatever."

51. L.A. County Probation Records, Sept. 24, 2002.

52. *Los Angeles Times*, Dec. 6, 1992.

53. Ibid.

54. Ibid.

55. Bing, pp. 11–12.

56. Shakur, *Monster*, p. 277

57. James Baldwin, *The Evidence of Things Not Seen*, Henry Holt, 1995, p. xiv.

58. Interview with author, 2003.

59. *Report by the Special Advisor to the Board of Police Commissioners on the Civil Disorder in Los Angeles*, Oct. 21, 1992 (the "Webster Report"), p. 23.

60. Lou Cannon, *Official Negligence: How Rodney King and the Riots Changed Los Angeles and the LAPD*, Times Books, 1997, p. 282.

61. *Los Angeles Times*, May 18, 1997.

62. *Los Angeles Times*, April 23, 2002.

63. Ibid.

64. *Los Angeles Times*, Aug. 25, 2003.

65. Ibid.

66. *Los Angeles Times*, May 18, 1997. For example, a European-based shoe company named Eurostar unveiled a highly publicized plan for a multicolored "Truce" sneaker, to be sold at a community-based outlet in Watts. The truce shoe was never produced, however. A major homeboy named Gregory "High T" Hightower, from Jordan Downs, who was to sell the shoes was gunned down and killed during a breakdown of the truce. When informed of High-T's death, a Eurostar executive said he was very sorry but didn't remember anything about the promised shoe plan. "The bottom line is, it's a social situation. It's more of a job for the president of the United States than a shoe salesman."

67. *Los Angeles Times*, Jan. 5, 2001. The comparable top position in New York City paid $109,540.

68. Ibid.

69. Budget document, City of Los Angeles, 2000–2001.

70. Memo from Michael Gagan, Jan. 27, 2001.

71. Ibid.

72. Data from Robert Garcia, Center for Law in the Public Interest, 2001.

73. *Los Angeles Daily News*, April 9, 2001.

74. *Los Angeles Times*, Jan. 26, 1998.

75. *Los Angeles Times*, July 21, 2002.

76. *Los Angeles Times*, Dec. 6, 2002.

77. *Los Angeles Times*, April 23, 2002.

78. *Los Angeles Times*, Dec. 6, 1992.

79. Ibid.

80. Los Angeles County Probation Department, SB 1095 Report, 1999–2000.

81. Statement of Aqeela Sherrils, June 26, 2002.

82. The phrase "post-revolution" is from Michael Eric Dyson's insightful work, *Holler If You Hear Me: Searching for Tupac Shakur*, Basic Civitas Books, 2001.

83. Ward Churchill, "To Disrupt, Discredit and Destroy," in Cleaver and Katsiaficas, *Liberation, Imaginatoin and the Black Panther Party*, p. 102.

84. Ibid., p. 99.

85. Dyson, p. 67.

86. Ibid., p. 63.

87. Ibid., p. 150.

Chapter 7: Fruits of War: Homies Unidos and the Globalization of Gangs

1. Luis Valdez, *Zoot Suit and Other Plays*, Arte Publico Press, 1992. The acknowledgment of "secret vicarious revenge" is from General Andres Pico to the notorious bandit Tiburcio Vasquez in Valdez's play of the same name in *Zoot Suit*, p. 136. It is important to remember that California, Arizona, New Mexico, and Texas were historic Mexico. Thus Vasquez declares: "I didn't return to Mexico last winter to go back to stealing horses. If they intend to strangle California with railroads, fine. We'll rob the trains. If they insist on building in the wilderness, we'll sack their towns," p. 117. Pancho Villa, who was assassinated in 1923, was a general, horseman, bandit, womanizer, and celebrity. He became an outlaw when a farm overseer tried to rape his sister. Villa broke out of jail to join a gang in the mountains, then joined the Revolution, and fought nine years in a civil war. His legend continues in the *corridos* and folk tradition of revolutionaries, drug runners, and gang members today. See Elijah Wald, *Narcocorrido*, HarperCollins, 2001, p. 26. For the Mexican emigration, see for example, Lawrence Cardoso, *Mexican Emigration to the United States, 1897–1931*, University of Arizona, 1980.

2. Juan Gonzáles, *Harvest of Empire: A History of Latinos in America*, Viking, 2000.

3. *New York Times*, Aug. 10–11, 1997.

4. Interview with Silvia Beltran, 2000. El Salvador also memorialized the figure of "el Indio Aquino," a historic figure who rebelled against the Spanish and the Church.

5. Mario Lungo Ucles, *Salvador in the Eighties: Counter-Insurgency and Revolution*, Temple, 1996, p. 17.

6. Teresa Whitfield, *Paying the Price: Ignacio Ellacuria and the Murdered Jesuits of El Salvador*, Temple University Press, 1994, p. 404.

7. Ibid.

8. Ibid.

9. The quote is from Secretary of State Alexander Haig, in Whitfield, p. 146.

10. Ibid., p. 148.

11. Ibid.

12. Ucles, p. 12.

13. Ibid., pp. 12–13.

14. Ibid., p. 14.

15. Gonzáles, p. 129.

16. *New York Times*, Aug. 10, 1997.

17. Gonzáles, p. 138.

18. All quotations from interviewswith Alex Sanchez unless otherwise cited.

19. All quotations from interviews with Silvia Beltran unless otherwise cited.

20. U.S. Immigration and Naturalization Service (INS) record of sworn statement by Alex Sanchez, officer Brian Yamada, March 2, 2000.

21. James Diego Vigil, in *A Rainbow of Gangs*, University of Texas, 2002, p. 10. Vigil studied Salvadorans, Vietnamese, African Americans, and Mexicans in L.A., finding a common pattern of adolescent *street socialization* where families, schools, and law enforcement had failed.

22. Interview with author, 2003.

23. On the torture of Yanira Corea, see Paul Glickman, Inter Press Service, July 14, 1987. The INS accusation of "orchestrated PR" appeared in John Pine's article in Reuters, August 26, 1987. See also Jay Mathews, *Washington Post*, July 18, 1987, reference to threats against Rev. Luis Olivares of Our Lady Queen of Angels Church. See also the novel by *Los Angeles Times* correspondent Hector Tobar, *The Tattooed Soldier*, Delphinium Books, 1998; and my review, *Los Angeles Times*, Aug. 16, 1998.

24. Mike Davis, *Ecology of Fear*, Metropolitan, 1998, p. 391.

25. Lou Cannon, *Official Negligence: How Rodney King and the Riots Changed Los Angeles and the LAPD*, Random House/Times Books, 1997, pp. 337–38. Cannon cites a RAND researcher, Joan Petersilla, who later concluded that "this wasn't a black riot so much as a minority riot."

26. Ibid., pp. 337–38.

27. Davis, p. 369.

28. Tobar, pp. 274, 283.

29. Webster Commission report, p. 24.

30. Luis Rodriguez, *Hearts and Hands: Creating Community in Violent Times*, Seven Stories Press, 2001, p. 169.

31. Ibid., pp. 169–70.

32. The *Los Angeles Times* reported on May 26, 2003, the first anniversary of a peace dialogue between thirty-two Valley gangs that contributed to a decline in overall homicides from fifty to nineteen, and in gang-related homicides from twenty-seven to fifteen, in the period Jan. 1–May 15. Observers credited the guidance of "Blinky" Rodriguez.

33. *New York Times*, Aug. 10, 1997.

34. Ibid.

35. Ibid.

36. Ibid.

37. Ibid. Also see, "Alleged Delinquents Found Dead: Rebirth of Death Squads," in *La Prensa Grafica*, El Salvador, Feb. 1, 1999, which describes assassins wearing masks and driving vehicles with tinted windows shooting young men with tattoos in the head.

38. Interview with Magdaleno Rose-Avila, El Salvador, 1997, which appeared in *The Nation*, July 10, 2000.

39. Luis Rodriguez, "Throwaway Kids," *The Nation*, Nov. 21, 1994.

40. Summary done by Thaddeus Kouser, June 2, 1997.

41. I am indebted for this material to Gabrielle Banks, in "Eulogy for the Poet of the People," Homies Unidos 2001 *Annual Report*, p. 13.

42. Correspondence with myself, Aug. 18, 1997.

43. *New York Times*, Aug. 10, 1997, interview with Subcommissioner Carlos Ramirez Landaverde.

44. Anne Marie O'Connor articles, *Los Angeles Times*, Feb. 24–25, 2000.

45. My interview with Bill Lan Lee, former head of the civil rights division, U.S. Department of Justice, 2002.

46. INS task force coordinator John del George, quoted in *Los Angeles Times*, Feb. 29, 2000.

47. *Los Angeles Times*, Feb. 29, 2000.

48. Ibid.

49. The "constant warfare" quotation is from an authoritative source at the *Times*.

50. Confidential communication, 2003.

51. Perez deposition, July 15, 2003.

52. Interview in *L.A. Weekly*, March 24–30, 2000.

53. The Murrales case was described in the Christopher Commission report, p. 58.

54. *Los Angeles Times*, April 4, 2001.

55. Shaun Hubler, *Los Angeles Times*, Feb. 17, 2000.

56. Joe Domanick, *To Protect and Serve*, Simon & Schuster/Pocket Books, 1994, p. 325.

57. Ibid.

58. Robert Vernon, *L.A. Justice: Lessons from the Firestorm*, Focus on the Family Publishing, Colorado, 1993, p. 72. See also, *Los Angeles Times*, "Piety in LAPD's Ranks Raises Concern, 'Born-Again' Christians Occupy Key Positions." The Christopher Commission heard testimony critical of Vernon by deputy Chief Jesse Brewer, who said, "he's the head of the God Squad, as we refer to it. The way to get ahead, it's commonly known that the way you get ahead as far as Vernon is concerned is to become aligned either with his church or to profess that you are born again." (Included in Vernon, p. 124.)

59. "Fight Crime in LA . . . Volunteer," LAPD Volunteers—Partners Against Los Angeles Crime, May 20, 2001, © 1998–2001, The Webnut. http://www.2vc.com/lapdvolunteer.

60. The General Accounting Office, the investigating arm of Congress, found in January 2003 that 75 percent of those convictions classified by the Justice Department as "international terrorism" were inaccurately described, *New York Times*, Sept. 28, 2003. The LAPD, like other agencies, created its own antiterrorism unit with ambiguous functions.

61. *Los Angeles Times*, March 24, 1999. The new sheriff, Lee Baca, vowed to erase the deputy gangs, which were "enjoying renewed popularity among young deputies," according to the *Times* account.

62. Ibid.

63. *Los Angeles Times*, Dec. 31, 1999.

64. Ibid.

65. Ibid.

66. Ibid. An explanation is needed here for how guilty pleas are accepted from defendants who claim innocence. First, under plea bargaining, many prosecutors will pile up so many charges that the defendant's attorney will advise a guilty plea on one or two. Second, under a California Supreme Court ruling, *People v. West*, a defendant can testify that it is in their "interest" to plead guilty despite their avowed innocence. The attorneys must agree, and the judge must find "strong evidence" of their alleged guilt, which can be a secondhand account of a police report. In these cases, the judge asks the question of the attorney, "Is this a *People v. West* plea or is this a plea because the defendant is in truth and in fact is guilty?" See *Times* account for further detail.

67. Ibid.

68. Police Quest: SWAT, Sierra On-Line, http://www.sierra.com, March 1997.

69. William W. Mendel, "Combat in Cities: The LA Riots and Operation Rio," July 1996, Foreign Military Studies Office, 604 Lowe Drive, Fort Leavenworth, Kansas, 66027-23221, http://www.fas.org/man/dod-101/ops/docs/rio.htm.

70. The quote is from Ralph Peters, in Mendel, p. 1.

71. As reported by Jeff Eglash, then executive director of the Police Commission, 2002.

72. This account is from Evan Janess, attorney with the U.S. Public Defenders Office, Los Angeles District, Jan. 27, 2000. Janess defended Alex Sanchez in federal court against charges of illegal reentry, and prevailed.

73. *Los Angeles Times*, Sept. 20, 2000.

74. *Los Angeles Times*, Feb. 17, 2000.

75. *Los Angeles Times*, Feb. 10, 2000.

76. *Los Angeles Times*, Sept. 13, 1999. Mack was arrested on Dec. 16, 1997, for the heist, but the $700,000 was never located.

77. Ibid. The cocaine ripped off by Perez had been logged in by Detective Frank Lyga, a white officer who killed a black LAPD officer, Kevin Gaines, in an unexplained traffic dispute in the Valley. Gaines had been dating the estranged wife of gangsta rap mogul "Sug" Knight, owner of Death Row Records, where several off-duty LAPD officers worked security.

78. *Los Angeles Times*, Aug. 29, 1998.

79. Both Rev. Alton and church custodian Victor Cosme said the LAPD asked to hide in a room, perhaps a closet, where the meetings took place, and were refused. *Los Angeles Times*, Feb. 17, 2000.

80. Ibid.

81. *Los Angeles Times*, Feb. 10, 2000.

82. Wellford Wilms, Warren Schmidt, Alex Norman, *The Strain of Change: Voices of Los Angeles Police Officers*, preliminary report to the National Institute of Justice, U.S. Department of Justice, Oct. 23, 2000.

83. My statement to LAPD Internal Affairs, Serial Number 23892, Feb. 25, 2000.

84. In a Feb. 28, 2000, letter, Meissner's assistant Robert Bach not only agreed to facilitate a "conversation with the U.S. Attorney's office," but to launch "an internal investigation of its activities in Los Angeles," a virtual acknowledgment that the INS had permitted a rogue unit.

85. *Los Angeles Times*, Feb. 17, 2000.

86. Ibid.

87. Gil Garcetti, by Norman Montrose, Superior Court of the State of California, County of Los Angeles, *People vs. Alex Antonio Sanchez*, Case No. BA17138, Aug. 2, 2000.

88. Suit by Paul Hoffman, Mark Geragos, CNN.com, June 3, 2000; see also *Los Angeles Times*, same date.

89. *Los Angeles Times*, April 24, 2000.

90. See for example, "Bracing for Protests at the Democratic Convention," *Los Angeles Times*, April 24, 2000, and "L.A. Bracing for Convention Unrest," Los Angeles *Business Journal*, April 24–30, 2000.

91. Letter from myself to Sen. Steve Peace, Budget Conference Committee, June 1, 2000.

92. Based on conversations with CHP officials at the time.

93. ACLU of Southern California, June 1995, *Pepper Spray Update: More Fatalities, More Questions*, p. 7.

94. ACLU *Pepper Spray* report, p. 21. The U.S. Army study was by researchers at their Aberdeen Proving Ground.

95. CNN, Associated Press, Feb. 13, 1996.

96. ACLU *Pepper Spray* report, p. 1.

97. Ibid., pp. 10–11.

98. Arianna Huffington left before the march. Her "shadow convention," advertised as an educational alternative, was raided and shut down by the LAPD two nights later, claiming a mysterious bomb threat.

99. Information from Alan Diamante.

100. Declaration of Mirna Solorzano, Sept. 13, 2002.

101. *Los Angeles Times*, May 24, 26, 1999.

102. *New York Times*, May 1, 2001.

103. *Los Angeles Times*, Dec. 8, 2001.

104. *Los Angeles Times*, July 12, 2002.

105. *United States of America vs. City of Los Angeles, Police Commission of Los Angeles, and Los Angeles Police Department*, case 0011769 GAF (Rcx).

106. See Erwin Chemerinsky and Constance Rice, *Los Angeles Times* op-editorial, March 3, 2003.

107. *Los Angeles Times*, May 19, 2003.

108. See "Report Says LAPD May Miss Reforms Deadline," *Los Angeles Times*, May 16, 2003.

109. *Los Angeles Times*, April 8, 2003.

110. Consent Decree, Status Report, Feb. 3, 2003.

111. There are an estimated 130,000 sweatshop workers in California. In 2000, two-thirds of clothing companies in Los Angeles inspected by the U.S. Department of Labor were in violation of minimum wage and overtime laws. The state of California employed eighty field inspectors to monitor compliance with wage laws for 13.5 million workers statewide. *Sacramento Bee*, Jan. 28, 2001.

Chapter 8: Restoring Community Action

1. Correspondence, July 16, 2000.

2. Ibid., Jan. 20, 2003.

3. See the excellent biography by Celeste Fremon, *Father Greg and the Homeboys*, Hyperion, 1995, p. 4. For "pampering," see p. 33.

4. Ibid., p. 178–79.

5. Ibid., p. 23.

6. Of forty-eight *Los Angeles Times* articles referencing Greg on the *Times* database since January 1986, only one appeared on the first page (see Jesse Katz, "Praying for a Father's Return," Jan. 25, 1993). Another by the same writer appeared on June 24, 1993, on the front page of the *Times*'s Spanish-language edition, *Nuestro Tiempo*.

7. Malcolm Klein, *The American Street Gang: Its Nature, Prevalence and Control*, Oxford, 1995, p. 150.

8. Ibid., p. 158.

9. Fremon, p. 33.

10. Klein, pp. 49, 76.

11. See, for example, Joan Moore, *Homeboys, Gangs, Drugs and Prison in the Barrios of Los Angeles*, Temple University Press, 1978.

12. Klein, p. 146.

13. In Frederic Thrasher, *The Gang: A Study of 1,313 Gangs in Chicago*, University of Chicago Press, 1927, p. 342.

14. Ibid. Thrasher was linked with Herbert Asbury, author of *The Gangs of New York* (1927).

15. *Maxim* magazine, Dec. 2001, p. 142.

16. Breanden Delap, *Mad Dog Coll: An Irish Gangster*, Mercier Press, 1999, p. 27.

17. See Eric Hobsbawm, *Bandits*, The New Press, 2000, for historic descriptions of bandits as primitive revolutionaries who may on occasion join peasant armies in "exalted hope." "When banditry thus merges into a large movement, it becomes part of a force which can and does change society," p. 33.

18. Rich Cohen, *Tough Jews: Fathers, Sons and Gangster Dreams*, Simon & Schuster, 1998, p. 155.

19. Ibid., p. 97.

20. Ibid., p. 90.

21. Henner Hess, *Mafia and Mafiosi: Origin, Power and Myth*, NYU Press, 1998, p. 72.

22. Cohen, p. 21.

23. *New York Times*, Dec. 20, 2002.

24. Kerby Miller, *Emigrants and Exiles*, Oxford, 1985, p. 499.

25. Thrasher, p. 290.

26. Ibid.; see also Herbert Asbury, *The Gangs of New York*, Thunder's Mouth Press, 1998 edition of the 1927 version by Knopf, pp. xiii, xiv.

27. Cohen, p. 241.

28. John Hagedorn, "The Gangs of . . . ," *Chicago Tribune*, Jan. 19, 2003.

29. Frank Main, "Crime, Inc.," *Chicago Sun Times*, Dec. 22, 2002, p. 11.

30. Karl Evanzz, *The Messenger: The Rise and Fall of Elijah Muhammad*, Pantheon, 1999, p. 46.

31. From hearings of the Chicago Commission on Race Relations, cited in Thrasher, p. 327.

32. Thrasher, p. 335.

33. *New York Times*, July 22, 2002. A new Italian CD in that year, entitled *Il Canto di Malavita*, lamented the loss of the original codes. "Today everything happens because of money," one anonymous old-timer complained.

34. See T.J. English, *The Westies*, St. Martin's, 1990, for the history of New York's West Side Irish; Dick Lehr and Gerard O'Neill, *Black Mass: The Irish Mob, the FBI, and a Devil's Deal*, Perseus/Public Affairs, 2000, for the contemporary Boston Irish mob; Dan Moldea, *Dark Victory: Ronald Reagan, MCA and the Mob*, Penguin, 1986, for an account of the Jewish mob in Hollwood; and Sally Denton and Roger Morris, *The Money and the Power: The Making of Las Vegas and Its Hold on America, 1947–2000*, Knopf, 2001, for a narrative of the mob in Las Vegas.

35. Cohen, pp. 134, 136. See also Richard Gid Powers, *Secrecy and Power: The Life of J. Edgar Hoover*, Free Press, 1987, pp. 332–33. In 1959, Hoover had 400 agents in the New York office investigating Communism, and just four assigned to organized crime, p. 335. Hoover was a racist who told an audience of editors as late as 1965 that

"the colored people are quite ignorant, mostly uneducated, and I doubt if they would seek an education if they had an opportunity"; he complained that courts required police officers to use courteous language instead of the customary "boy, come here," p. 411.

36. James B. Jacobs, with Friel and Radick, *Gotham Unbound: How New York Was Liberated from the Grip of Organized Crime*, NYU Press, 1999.

37. Deborah Lamm Weisel, "The Evolution of Street Gangs: An Examination of Form and Variation," in U.S. Dept. of Justice, *Responding to Gangs, Evaluation and Research*, July 2002, pp. 33, 35.

38. Ibid., p. 52.

39. Thrasher, p. 264.

40. Ibid., p. 32

41. Ibid., p. 268.

42. Ibid.

43. Ibid., p. 33.

44. Ibid., p. 230.

45. Ibid., p. 339.

46. Ibid., p. 343.

47. Ibid., p. 350.

48. Ibid., p. 231.

49. Ibid., p. 355.

50. Ibid., p. 360.

51. Ibid., p. 350.

52. Ibid., p. 124, reference to Franklin Chase Hoyt, *Quicksands of Youth*.

53. Ibid., p. 356.

54. Ibid., p. 366.

55. Ibid., p. 353.

56. See Powers, p. 364.

57. Sudhir Alladi Venkatesh, *American Project: The Rise and Fall of a Modern Ghetto*, Harvard, 2000, pp. 139, 254.

58. Ibid., p. 152.

59. These were the exact words of Los Angeles mayor James Hahn in a public debate when he was city attorney in the late nineties.

60. This account is from an interview with Harvard political scientist Michael Dawson, author of *Black Visions: The Roots of Contemporary African American Political Ideologies*, University of Chicago, 2001. The late congressman Dawson was Michael Dawson's great uncle.

61. Ibid., pp. 26–27, who cites V.P. Franklin, *Living Our Stories, Telling Our Truths: Autobiography and the Making of the African American Intellectual Tradition*, Scribner, 1995, p. 150.

62. Dawson, interview with author, 2003.

63. Ibid.

64. According to Elijah Muhammad, the sign of the real Muhammad was a "little black stone" in Mecca, a "stone for building the kingdom of heaven on earth." Evanzz, pp. 159–60.

65. John Fry, *Locked Out Americans*, Harper & Row, 1973, is both lyrical and empirical, and should be required reading for any student of the times. Unfortunately, the book is out of print.

66. Ibid., preface.

67. Ibid., p. 108.

68. Ibid., p. 109.

69. Ibid., p. 63.

70. Ibid., p. 65.

71. Ibid., p. 162.

72. Interview in 2003 with a source aware of the internal analysis of the city's gang-intelligence unit at the time.

73. Ibid.

74. Mike Royko, *Boss*, E. P. Dutton, 1972, pp. 206–7, cited in Fry, pp. 61–62.

75. Fry, pp. 167–74.

76. Evanzz, pp. 371–72.

77. Communication from source through John Hagedorn.

78. *The Economist*, June 15, 2002.

79. Klein, p. 167.

80. Spergel cites a *Chicago Sun Times* article of Jan. 10, 1992. See Irving Spergel, *The Youth Gangs Problem: A Community Approach*, Oxford, 1995, p. 194.

81. Klein, p. 167.

82. *Christian Science Monitor*, July 15, 1996.

83. Larry Hoover's letters are quoted in George W. Knox, director of National Gang Crime Research Center, Chicago, "The Impact of the Federal Prosecution of the Gangster Disciples," vol. 7, no. 2, winter 2000 publication.

84. Knox, p. 11 of 49, citing Sept. 27, 1982, Hoover memo.

85. *Newsweek*, "Winning a Gang War," "the inside story," Nov. 1, 1999.

86. Knox, p. 37 of 49.

87. Ibid.

88. Larry Hoover letter, March 15, 1995, in Knox, p. 38. http://www.ngcrc.com/ngcrc/page14.htm.

89. *Chicago Sun Times*, April 11, 1995.

90. Knox, p. 43 of 49.

91. Ibid., p. 40 of 49.

92. *American Prospect*, Oct. 19, 2002.

93. Knox, p. 40 of 49.

94. *Chicago Sun Times*, April 7, 2002. During the time of the federal prosecutions, the Gangster Disciples were described as making $100 million annually in drug profits. In 2002, the low estimate was $500 million for gangs like the GDs, Vice Lords, and Latin Kings; a federal drug enforcement coordinator claimed the annual profits were closer to $1 billion.

95. Ibid. Figure for 1995 from Richard Block, based on Chicago Police Department annual reports.

96. Ibid.; *Christian Science Monitor*, July 15, 1996.

97. *Chicago Sun-Times*, April 7, 2002.

98. Ibid.

99. Ibid.

100. For example, Knox writes that "the best estimate is that one out of three gang members in America would rat on their homies in a New York minute, if they had the proper motivation to do so, i.e., un-indicted co-conspirator, charges dropped, plea agreement, etc." Knox, p. 42 of 49.

101. Interview with Willis, *Sojourners*, Aug. 1993.

102. *New York Times*, April 26, 2002.

103. Royko, p. 206.

104. Thrasher, p. 133.

105. *Chicago Tribune*, Jan. 19, 2003.

106. George Knox of the "Gang Crime Research Center," in "Crime, Inc." by *Chicago Sun-Times* reporters Frank Main and Carlos Sadovi, Dec. 2002, www.suntimes.com/special sections/crime/est-nws-ganghist22.html.

107. Ibid.

108. Thrasher, p. 133.

109. Hagedorn, "The Gangs of . . ."

110. Gus Russo, *The Outfit: The Role of Chicago's Underworld in the Shaping of Modern America*, Bloomsbury, 2001, pp. 304–5.

111. Ibid.

112. Ibid.

113. Ibid.

114. Hagedorn, "The Gangs of . . ."

115. *Scientific American*, May–June 2002.

116. As noted, three Stones were indicted for *conspiracy* to defraud.

117. Luis Rodriguez, *Hearts and Hands: Creating Community in Violent Times*, Seven Stories Press, 2001, p. 44.

118. *Time*, Aug. 5, 2002.

119. John Hagedorn, "Building a Way to Stop Murder," *Chicago Tribune* online, June 1, 2003.

120. In January 2002, Dolores Mission representatives traveled to Chicago with officials from the mayor's office, city council, and Hollenbeck Division of the LAPD. The purpose was to study Chicago's alternative policing strategies (CAPS).

121. Irving Spergel et al., *Draft Evaluation of the Gang Violence Reduction Project in Little Village*, University of Chicago, May 2002.

122. Ibid., p. 50.

123. Eric Schneider, *Vampires, Dragons and Egyptian Kings: Youth Gangs in Postwar New York*, Princeton, 1999, p. 194.

124. Ibid., p. 199.

125. Ibid., p. 204.

126. In addition to its roots in the Chicago school, the theory drew heavily on the work of Richard Cloward and Ohlin and others at Columbia University who viewed the gang phenomenon as a rational response to pursue illegitimate opportunity structures since conventional ones were closed.

127. Schneider, p. 212.

128. Ibid., p. 214.

129. Ibid., p. 215.

130. Ibid.

131. Gerald Horne, *Fire This Time: The Watts Uprising and the 1960s*, University Press of Virginia, 1995, p. 183.

132. Kerner Commission report, p. 29.

133. Ibid., p. 561.

134. Ibid.

135. The cost of 1 million public sector jobs is in Lynn A. Curtis and William E. Spriggs, "Leave No One Behind," in Robert Borosage and Roger Hickey, *The Next Agenda*, Perseus/Westview, 2001, p, 232. The estimate of $30 billion in annual tax cheating is from the Internal Revenue Agency, Paul Krugman, *New York Times*, Oct. 22, 2002.

136. Kerner Commission report, p. 16.

137. Ibid., p. 290.

138. Ibid.

139. Ibid., p. 297.

140. In his introduction to the *New York Times* edition of the Kerner report, Tom Wicker noted that critics demanded to know "where were Stokely Carmichael, Floyd McKissick, Martin Luther King, such white radicals as Tom Hayden or such fiery evangelists as James Baldwin?", p. v.

141. J. Edgar Hoover memo, Special Report, Interagency Committee on Intelligence, cited in affidavit of attorney Sheldon Otis in *People v. Newton*, Nos. 64624A and 65919, Alameda Municipal Court. In Newton, p. 94.

142. *New York Times*, Sept. 8, 1968, cited in Book III, *Final Report* of the Select Committee to Study Government Operations with Respect to Intelligence Activities, 94th Congress,

2d Session, 1976, p. 188, and Sanford J. Ungar, *FBI*, Little, Brown, 1976, p. 12, in Newton, p. 93.

143. Ibid., p. 54.

144. The information on FBI penetration of the Panthers is from Ward Churchill, citing staff reports in U.S. Senate hearings and documents from the litigation of *Hampton v. Hanrahan*, p. 12. Ward Churchill, " 'To Disrupt, Discredit and Destroy': The FBI's Secret War Against the Black Panther Party," in Kathleen Cleaver and George Katsiaficas, eds., *Liberation, Imagination and the Black Panther Party*, Routledge, 2001, pp. 78–117.

145. Churchill, p. 111.

146. Ibid., p. 87. FBI agents visited markets and businesses in Oakland urging merchants not to contribute to the programs.

147. Ibid., p. 105.

148. See Arthur Jefferson, staff counsel to the Senate Select Committee on Intelligence Activities and the Rights of Americans, editor of the FBI's Covert Action Program to Destroy the Black Panther Party.

149. Ward Churchill, Jim Vander Wall, *Agents of Repression*, South End Press, 1990, pp. 65–66.

150. In Newton, pp. 76–77.

151. According to Huey Newton, there were 233 documented counterintelligence actions by the FBI against the Panthers. In Newton, p. 53.

152. Louis Yablonsky, *Gangsters: Fifty Years of Madness, Drugs and Death on the Streets of America*, NYU Press, 1997, p. 29.

153. James Diego Vigil, *A Rainbow of Gangs: Street Cultures in the Mega-City*, University of Texas, 2002, p. 75.

154. Rodriguez, p. 34.

155. Street Gangs Telecourse, Part III, African-Americans, by Commission on Peace Officer Standards and Training (POST Commission), State of California, Mar. 24, 1994, p. 3.

156. Interview with author, Aug. 5, 1997.

157. Rodriguez, p. 26.

Chapter 9: Education, Politics, and the Future

1. See James Diego Vigil, *A Rainbow of Gangs: Street Cultures in the Mega-City*, University of Texas, 2002. The *New York Times* education writer Richard Rothstein estimated that 26 percent of American kids failed to graduate high school in 1990, jumping to 30 percent in 2000 (*New York Times*, Oct. 9, 2002). State figures for California showed a 30.3 percent failure-to-finish rate in 2000 and 30.4 percent in 2002 (*Los Angeles Times*, April 24, 2003). Education officials have never agreed on a definition for dropouts, arguing, for example, that many students leave school to take up education in other places. Califor-

nia leads the nation in numbers of children living in households headed by a high school dropout (*Los Angeles Times*, March 8, 2002).

2. *Los Angeles Times*, July 14, 2002.

3. Jeannie Oakes, UCLA School of Education, Center X, interview with author. Also see "Facing the Poverty Factor," *Los Angeles Times*, Nov. 1, 1998, which concludes, "Poverty exerts a powerful impact on student achievement. Studies have consistently shown that wealth is the strongest influence on test scores. As the percentage of poor students increases, scores decline."

4. Pew Hispanic Center study, *Los Angles Times*, June 13, 2003.

5. *Los Angeles Times*, July 14, 2002.

6. *New York Times*, July 11, 2003. The $1 billion "best urban school" prize awarded to Houston was from the Broad Foundation, sponsored by billionaire Eli Broad, a close ally of former mayor Richard Riordan, who is investing a fortune in grants and political contributions to transform school districts into corporate-style entities. The Texas model was cited by George Bush in his successful campaign for the presidency in 2000, and became the national model for tougher standards. Bush's education secretary, Rod Paige, was previously the superintendant of the same Houston district.

7. *New York Times*, July 11, 2003.

8. *New York Times*, Aug. 21, 2003.

9. *Los Angeles Times*, March 8, 2002.

10. *New York Times*, Aug. 5, 2002. In North Carolina, for example, the number of immigrant limited-English students increased fivefold from 8,900 to 52,500 between 1993 and 2002. About 290,000 additional bilingual teachers are needed in addition to the current 50,000, according to Harvard professor Marcelo Suarez-Orozco.

11. Vigil, p. 40.

12. From 1980 to 2000, poor families were forced to use a "steadily larger portion of their income to attend the nation's public universities." (*New York Times*, May 2, 2002).

13. According to the Civil Rights Project at Harvard University, "Black and Latino students are now more isolated from their white counterparts than they were three decades ago, before many of the overhauls from the civil rights movement had even begun to take hold." Black students typically are a majority in the schools they attend, even though they are 17 percent of the total school population. Latinos are in the same condition with 16 percent of the total. Native Americans, representing only 1 percent of public school children, are typically one-third of the enrollment of the schools they attend. *New York Times*, Jan. 21, 2003.

14. Jonathan Kozol, *The Nation*, June 10, 2002.

15. Vigil, p. 168.

16. *New York Times*, June 30, 2002, p. 19.

17. Bob Herbert, "The Iota Standard," *New York Times,* July 1, 2002.

18. *New York Times,* June 25, 2003.

19. *Los Angeles Times,* May 19, 1998.

20. For a complete discussion of the controversy, see Russell Jacoby and Naomi Glauber-man, *The Bell Curve Debate,* Times Books, 1995, p. x.

21. *Williams et al. v. State of California,* April 11, 2000.

22. *Los Angeles Times,* Aug. 30, 2002.

23. Lou Harris survey, April 30, 2002; http://www.publicadvocates.org/presswilliams.html.

24. From Jane Fell Greene and Judy Fell Woods, *Language Readers,* Level 1, Book A, Units 1–6. Quote from Dr. Jeff Duncan-Andrade, Director of Urban Teacher Development, Oct. 30, 2002.

25. Marc Cooper, *L.A. Weekly,* June 28–July 4, 2002.

26. Matute-Bianchi, "Ethnic Identities and Patterns of School Success," referenced in Alejandro Portes and Ruben Rumbaut, *Legacies: The Story of the Immigrant Second Generation,* University of California Press, 2001, p. 60.

27. Marcelo Suarez-Orozco and Carola Suarez-Orozco, "The Cultural Patterning of Achievement Motivation: A Comparative study of Mexican, Mexican Immigrant, and Non-Latino White American Youth in Schools," in Rumbaut and Wayne Cornelius, eds., *California's Immigrant Children: Theory, Research, and Implications for Educational Policy,* University of California—San Diego, 1995, referenced in Portes and Rumbaut, p. 60.

28. In Malcom W. Klein, *The American Street Gang: Its Nature, Prevalence, and Control,* Oxford University Press, 1995, p. 186, and Joan W. Moore and James Diego Vigil, "Chicano Gangs: Group Norms and Individual Factors Related to Adult Criminality," in *Aztlan* 18 (1989): 31.

29. Vigil, p. 156.

30. James Q. Wilson, *The Moral Sense,* The Free Press, 1993, p. 249.

31. Ann Arnett Ferguson, *Bad Boys: Public Schools in the Making of Black Masculinity,* University of Michigan Press, 2001, p. 22.

32. Ibid., p. 87.

33. Herbert Kohl, *I Won't Learn from You: The Role of Assent in Learning,* Milkweed, 1991, pp. 16–17; Ferguson, p. 99.

34. L. Jannelle Dance, *Tough Fronts: The Impact of Street Culture on Schooling,* Routledge, 2002, p. 6. See also Peter Pericles Trifonas, ed., *Pedagogies of Difference: Rethinking Education for Social Change,* RoutledgeFalmer, 2003.

35. Ferguson, p. 232.

36. *New York Times,* Dec. 15, 2002.

37. For a discussion of ODD, see Ferguson, p. 195, or the American Psychiatric Association, *Diagnostic and Statistical Manual of Mental Disorders,* 4th ed. Washington D.C., 1994, pp. 91–92. ODD is officially a pattern of "negativistic, defiant, disobedient, and hostile behavior towards authority figures" that must last for six months. Four of eight

symptoms must be recurrent: (1) losing temper, (2) arguing with adults, (3) actively de-
fying or refusing to comply with the requests of rules of adults, (4) "deliberately doing
things that will annoy other people," (5) blaming others for his or her own mistakes, (6)
being "touchy" or "easily annoyed," (7) being angry and resentful, (8) being spiteful or
vindictive. "Deliberate or persistent testing of limits" is added as a general sign. That is,
the diagnosis could be triggered if a student lost their temper in an argument with a
teacher, became annoyed by the teacher's response, deliberately annoyed the teacher
back, and blamed the school for inferior learning conditions. In an unconsciously racist
society, the possibilities for discriminatory use of the diagnosis are manifold. Ominously, the APA manual stresses that students who blame the system are not to be
taken seriously; in fact, their resistance is seen as a symptom of being ODD. As the
manual declares, "usually individuals with this disorder do not regard themselves as
opposition[al] or defiant, but justify their behavior as a response to unreasonable demands or circumstances."

38. *Mental Health: A Report of the Surgeon General*, 2002, www.surgeongeneral.gov/library/
mentalhealth/chapter3/sec6.html, p. 5.

39. Paulo Friere, *Pedagogy of the Oppressed*, Continuum, 1973, 1990.

40. bell hooks, *Teaching to Transgress: Education as the Practice of Freedom*, Routledge, 1994.

41. Oakes and Lipton, *Teaching to Change the World*, McGraw-Hill College, 1999, pp. 260–61.
See also Michael W. Apple, *Educating the "Right" Way: Markets, Standards, God and Inequality*, Routledge, 2001, an attack on conservatives by an experienced practicioner.

42. See Shauna Clark, "Impact Evaluation of Drug Abuse Resistance Education (DARE),"
Journal of Drug Education, Vol. 22 (4), 1992, pp. 285–93.

43. For an evaluation of GREAT, see Esbensen, Freng, Taylor, Peterson, and Osgood, "National Evaluation of the Gang Resistance Education and Training (G.R.E.A.T.) Program," in U.S. Dept. of Justice, *Responding to Gangs*, 2002, pp. 141–67. The authors ask,
"How effective can individual-based prevention programs be?"

44. *New York Times*, July 3, 2003.

45. Dance, p. 144.

46. Ibid., p. 146.

47. Ibid.

48. The Inglewood and Lennox schools are known as Animo (for "vigor" or "spirit")
Leadership Charter high schools, initiated by Steve Barr, who previously led the fight
for the "motor voter" bill during the Clinton years. One is named for Oscar de la Torre,
who contributed $1 million to the project. The Pico-Union Leadership Academy was
started by Roger Lowenstein, an attorney and screenwriter.

49. *Los Angeles Times*, Feb. 19, 2002.

50. *Los Angeles Times*, April 6, 2000.

51. Another program behind the walls is Unusual Suspects, created by actress Laura Leigh
Hughes, which recruits entertainment industry talent to work with incarcerated

homies to develop their own ideas, scripts, acting techniques, and productions before live audiences, who have a unique experience of observing creativity in chains.

52. Interview with author, July 2003.

53. *Los Angeles Times*, May 10, 2003. The program at Ironwood state prison in Blythe, California, includes 280 inmates seeking a two-year degree, with 800 more inmates on a waiting list. The guards' union successfully pressured to shut down a similar program at another state prison.

54. Notes provided by David Brotherton, 2001.

55. David Brotherton, "Education in the Reform of Street Organizations in New York City," in Louis Kontos, Brotherton, and Luis Barrios, *Gangs and Society, Alternative Perspectives*, Columbia University, 2003, pp. 137–55.

56. As Frederic M. Thrasher concluded in his 1926 gang studies, "The gang boys' interviews in the great majority of cases gave the impression of normal, and often superior, intelligence and a normal development of emotional responses and sentiments." Thrasher, *The Gang, A Study of 1,313 Gangs in Chicago*, University of Chicago, 1927, 1963, p. 277.

57. *Los Angeles Times*, June 27, 2002.

58. An example of the cover-up of cover-ups, I investigated the internal reviews of guard violence at Corcoran State Prison in 1997. On April 7, 1997, there appeared a document titled "Cover Up of Excessive Force," by the prison system's assistant director for investigations, which stated that Corcoran authorities "engaged in the selective cover up of excessive force." On Nov. 14, 1997, a few months later, an identical document was produced omitting the substantiation of management cover-up in the April version. The redacted document also erased previous references to questionable integrity as well as earlier charges of violations of prison policy in firing 37 millimeter gas guns against inmates. Hayden Senate hearing files, Aug. 13, 1998.

59. *Los Angeles Times*, June 27, 2002.

60. *Los Angeles Times*, editiorial, Jan. 7, 2004.

61. Interview with Shauna Clark, 2003.

62. Klein, p. 233. He cites a 1992 study tracing decline of federal social programs during the Reagan years: job training, from $23 billion to $8 billion; general revenue sharing, from $6 billion to zero; Community Development Block Grants, from $21 billion to under $14 billion; and cuts of 890 percent in federal support for housing programs. According to Occidental College professor Peter Dreier, federal urban assistance declined from 15 percent of city budgets in 1997 to just 5 percent in 1997 (Peter Dreier, "America's Urban Crisis a Decade After the Los Angeles Riots," *National Civic Review* 92, no. 1, Spring 2003).

63. Demietrios Kyriacou, "The Relationship Between Economic Factors and Gang Violence in Los Angeles: Policy Considerations," Oct. 28, 1997, University of California Wellness lecture series.

64. *Los Angeles Times*, June 11 2002.

65. *New York Times*, June 12, 2002.
66. *New York Times*, Sept. 28, 2003. According to the Congressional General Accounting Office (GAO), many of the convictions dealt with "common crimes like document forgery."
67. For this analysis I am indebted to Eve Rosenhaft, "Organizing the Lumpenproletariat: Cliques and Communists in Berlin During the Weimar Republic," in Richard J. Evans, ed., *The German Working Class*, Barnes & Noble, 1982, online at www.geocities.com/capitolhill/lobby/2379/evansl.htm.
68. Billboard's Top 10 songs in October 2003 were hip-hop by black artists, the first time in the fifty-year history of the Billboard charts that black musicians have so completely dominated. *Boston Globe*, Oct. 4, 2003.
69. *New York Times*, Mar. 24, 2002. The United Nations goal for cutting poverty in half by 2015 requires that rich nations contribute 0.70 percent of their gross economic product to a fund for food, literacy, and shelter. The U.S. contribution to such programs during the JFK presidency was 1 percent of the nation's gross economic resources. In 2002, it was 0.10 percent, a 90 percent decline since the Kennedy era. In 2003, President Bush pledged to raise the amount to 0.13 percent, with strings attached.
70. See John Balzar, "The Incredible Shrinking Middle Class," *Los Angeles Times*, May 19, 2002. The top 1 percent, according to Balzar's sources, amassed 38 percent of America's wealth. The "bottom" four-fifths shared in only 17 percent. It was the most uneven income distribution since 1941. According to Michael Hout and Samuel R. Lucas at the University of California—Berkeley, the gap between rich and poor in America is wider than at any point during the past seventy-five years. "Narrowing the Income Gap Between Rich and Poor," *The Chronicle of Higher Education*, Aug. 16, 1996.
71. Jacob Riis, 1890, from Frederic Thrasher, *The Gang: A Study of 1,313 Gangs in Chicago*, University of Chicago, 1927, 1963, p. 2.

Afterword: Looking for Miracles

1. John Buntin, "Murder Mystery," *Governing*, June 2002.
2. Jenny Berrien and Christopher Winship, "Should We Have Faith in the Churches? The Ten Point Coalition's Effect on Boston's Youth Violence," in Bernard Harcourt, *Guns, Crime and Punishment in America*, NYU Press, 2003, p. 225.
3. See Sean Flynn, *Boston DA: The Battle to Transform the American Justice System*, TV Books, 2000.
4. Buntin, "Murder Mystery."
5. *Boston Globe*, Nov. 29, 2003.
6. Berrian and Winship, p. 241.
7. Ibid., p. 243.
8. Confidential interview, 2003.
9. *Lynn Daily Item*, Aug. 13, 2003.

10. Phillip Kassel, "The Gang Crackdown in Massachusetts' Prisons: Arbitrary and Harsh Punishment Can Only Make Matters Worse," *New England Journal on Criminal and Civil Confinement,* Boston, Winter 1998, pp. 37–63.

11. *Boston Globe,* Nov. 25, 2003.

12. Kassel, p. 46.

13. Communication from Christopher Winship, Harvard sociology department, Dec. 19, 2003.

14. James Gilligan, comments from his presentation to the seminar on mass violence, Harvard University, winter 2003.

15. E-mail, Nov. 24, 2003.

16. Interview with Allen Callahan, formerly of Harvard Divinity School, author of a manuscript on the Bible and African Americans, and who has written on Tupac Shakur, 2003. Tupac's reference to "all the people you threw away" is from the documentary film *Tupac: Resurrection* (2003).

Index